GARDENING

'ROUND ATLANTA

GARDENING

'ROUND ATLANTA

the best plants for Atlanta ...and more

by Avis Aronovitz
and Brencie Werner

with Barbara Allen, Nancy Beckemeyer, Eve Davis,
Tara Dillard, Cathy Farmer, Jean Johnson Givens,
Raymond Goza, Jim Harrington, Jackie Heyda, Dottie Myers,
Mildred Pinnell, Jeff Potter, Paula Refi, Sandra Sandefur,
Allen Sistrunk, Lewis Shortt, Lloyd Snyder,
Gary Spikula and Sue Vrooman

Eldorado Publishers
Atlanta, Georgia

NOTE: Reference works about plants do not always agree with regard to botanical nomenclature, and the nomenclature is constantly evolving. Gardeners, growers, plant societies, and writers don't always agree on which sources should be referenced. For the sake of consistency, we have chosen *Hortus Third, A Concise Dictionary of Plants Cultivated in the United States and Canada* (MacMillan - 1976) as the main source for plant names for this book. Individual contributors have sometimes referenced other or additional sources.

Edited and produced by Phyllis Mueller
Designed by Couch Communications, Inc.
Typesetting by Nancy Kahnt, Bill Moe
Printing by Daly Graphics
Cover photographs by Richard Clapp
Authors' photo by George Eckard
Illustration on page 6 created from a drawing by Barbara Allen
Illustration on page 121 created from a drawing by Lewis Shortt

Published and distributed by Eldorado Publishers
2143 Eldorado Drive, N.E.
Atlanta, Georgia 30345

First Printing February 1997

ISBN 0-9656345-0-7
Printed in the United States of America

5 4 3 2 1

Contents

To Our Readers

Welcome! You are part of Atlanta's continuing gardening renaissance. You realize there is more to gardens and gardening than dogwoods, azaleas, and daffodils in spring, and your enthusiasm is tied to an emerging, distinctly American style of gardening geared to contemporary American lifestyles. You want to add beauty, order, and tranquillity to your hectic, fast-paced, high tech life, and you want to learn to do it within the framework of your limited leisure time. You also want to leave your challenges for the Peachtree Road Race.

If you are new to the Atlanta garden scene, you are likely a new homeowner, too. You may or may not have gardened before, but you've noticed the plants here look unfamiliar and the red clay soil is nearly impenetrable. Statistics indicate that you may be a professional who works long hours and often travels during the week, and you don't want to spend your weekends doing yard work. Or you may be a working mother, a single parent, or parents of young children who would like to avoid time-consuming gardening chores that compete with carpools to soccer games and ballet lessons.

You are probably, also, dissatisfied in some way with the appearance of the outside areas of your home, and you don't know quite what to do about it. You could be watching the rains wash your front yard down the street and feel the urgency to do something quickly. Or you may have a creative bent to add some color and interest to a monotonous green—or worse yet brown—landscape. You want to know about shrubs and flowers that grow well in Atlanta, because failure is depressing and expensive.

This book will help you garden easily and successfully anywhere in Atlanta and its immediate suburbs and point the direction to a quick fix by organizing the efficient development of a low maintenance landscape and garden. This means learning how to avoid the folly of the wrong plant in the wrong place, so we've made extensive lists of plants that have proven successful in our gardens. And if you do wish to try the unusual, tricky options and challenging plants are listed also.

P.S. If you are a more traditional gardener who enjoys gardening and loves flowers, this book is intended for you, too. No matter how long you have gardened in Atlanta, there is always a new plant to try and a new method to test.

Dedication

To my darling husband Gerson, who supported me in my dream to put into book form the specific information that Atlanta gardeners need and who, in the end, made it all possible.

Acknowledgements

If we could choose just one friend, every one of us would choose Brencie Werner. Sharing my dream, she did a yeoman's job bringing this book to print—writing two chapters and working tirelessly compiling the pages of the original manuscript in the computer, proofreading the final draft, and preparing the book's indexes of plants.

Further testing the limits of friendship, I also asked Paula Refi, Tom Purdom, and Mildred Pinnell to proofread sections of the manuscript. Their comments were appreciated and incorporated into the book.

I sincerely thank the 19 contributing authors who agreed to give their time, knowledge, and efforts gratis and share their particular expertise with Atlanta gardeners: Barbara Allen, Nancy Beckemeyer, Eve Davis, Tara Dillard, Cathy Farmer, Jean Johnson Givens, Raymond Goza, Jim Harrington, Jackie Heyda, Dottie Myers, Mildred Pinnell, Jeff Potter, Paula Refi, Sandra Sandefur, Lewis Shortt, Allen Sistrunk, Lloyd Snyder, Gary Spikula, and Sue Vrooman. They hold with Brencie and me these premises: that this book is important and needed, and that all proceeds from its sale should benefit the Atlanta Botanical Garden.

I extend a special note of appreciation to Linda Fraser, who stepped in late in the project to contribute the artwork that enhances "My Atlanta Garden." Thank you for sharing your exceptional talent with us. Your illustrations demonstrate that you share the love I have for my garden.

I'm grateful to my dear friend, award-winning photographer Dick Clapp, whose beautiful photographs of flowers and plants continue to delight gardeners and grace the cover of this book.

Avis Aronovitz
December 1996
Atlanta, Georgia

Part One

Getting
Started

Chapter One

Getting Your Garden Started

by

Avis Aronovitz

Getting Your Garden Started

Scene One: The Garden Center

Stop! Put down that plant! An inexperienced gardener at a garden center is like a kid in a candy store. Each plant is more beautiful, more colorful, than the next. It is difficult to resist the impulse to buy them all to plant in your own yard.

Atlanta garden centers offer a wide assortment of eye-catching plants. Some are local favorites; some are a bit unusual. Some will grow in your garden, and some are doomed from the start. Decisions about which plants to offer for sale are often made by a nursery staff unfamiliar with your yard, where it is located, or what your gardening ability is. However, they do not want you back with a dead plant.

Scene One should not take place at the garden center. You need to do some homework first.

The First Steps

Raise Your Visual Awareness

Do some sleuthing. Look carefully at the landscaping surrounding area homes and large apartment complexes. Post Properties, the trendsetter, demonstrated to other local commercial and residential developers that innovative, well-designed, well-maintained landscaping sells. Study their work. Ask yourself these questions: Why is the landscaping so effective? What foundation plants, shrubs, and ground covers are used together? Are these plantings in sun or shade? What are the design patterns? How are shades and textures of foliage combined to create harmony? Which flowers, annuals, and perennials have been selected for display? What colors are used together?

Seek Out Your Personal Style

Observe the landscaping of homes in Atlanta neighborhoods. Look particularly at houses similar in architectural style to your home. Decide which landscaping schemes and plants appeal to **your** aesthetic sense.

Do Some Research

Visit the Atlanta Botanical Garden and observe the plants growing there. From their labels, find the names of those shrubs, plants, and flowers you like and identify other plants that thrive in our area. Sign up for classes that will help answer your questions and solve your gardening and landscaping problems. Go to the Southeastern Flower Show. Participate in the ABG Connoisseurs' Tour and symposia. (See Appendix C for more information.)

Stop by the Atlanta History Center and tour the gardens there. Attend their gardening seminars. Go on garden tours sponsored by plant societies and neighborhood groups. Take in the shows and exhibits staged by organizations whose members have become specialists in certain plants.

Select books with photos and instructions on garden planting, landscaping, perennials, and annuals from the Atlanta Botanical Garden Museum Shop and area bookstores or use ABG's botanical library for research. One of the best is a hardcover book, *Creative Home Landscaping*. If you modify the information in this book for Atlanta's growing conditions, you can learn a great deal about all aspects of landscape design, drainage, lighting, and choosing landscaping material and plants. The text, with good photos and instructions, guides the design process through installation. For photo-identification and information on perennials and annuals, seek out paperbacks published by HP and Ortho. Be sure to check the Recommended Reading and References lists at the back of this book. They're arranged according to chapter topics and are a compilation of books our contributors have found useful and informative.

Assess Your Outdoor Living Space

Inventory the trees, shrubs, and plants already growing on your lot. Do you need to fix an established landscape or develop an entirely new one? Are you starting with the barest landscape, little more than a contractor's unimaginative, possibly inappropriate, foundation plants, shrubs, and grass?

You may find unexpected treasures—native plants that can be encouraged and integrated into the home landscape—even within the city limits. For more information, see Chapter 24 "Native Plants" and

Chapter 25 "Atlanta's Native Plant Treasures" and request the booklet, *Native Plants for Georgia Gardens,* from the Cooperative Extension Service.

During the evaluation process, before you begin your plan and certainly before you reach for the shovel, take out your compass. It is important to consider the direction your front, back, and side yards face. Exposure affects the amount of sunlight the plants receive, the temperature extremes endured, and the potential moisture available. Are there sun and shade areas on your property? A wooded area could be the site of a future shade garden.

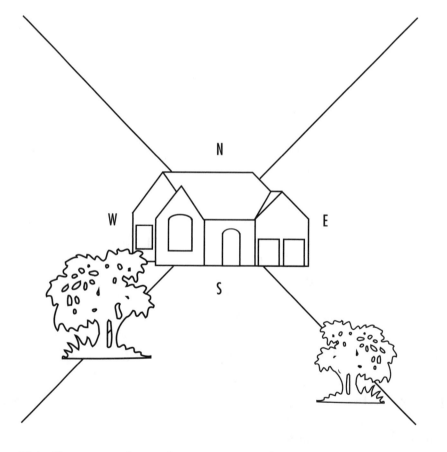

This illustration shows the orientation of a residence with respect to the compass. Sun-loving plants would grow best on the southern side (the front yard). Shade lovers and more cold-tolerant plants would be suitable for the northern side (the back yard).

Seasonal winds and the sun's path cause different conditions on each side of your home and create microclimates that can be important when selecting plants. East-fronting areas will receive several hours of pleasant morning sun, sufficient for most shrubs and flowers.

Plants are labeled according to the amount of sunlight they need for optimal growth. Knowing how much light a plant requires can help you choose the right plant for the right place. Use these definitions as guidelines:

Full sun: A minimum of six hours direct sunlight per day. (Caution! Atlanta's western afternoon sun is too intense for some plants labeled "full sun.")

Full shade: Mostly shaded site with two hours or less of direct sun. (No green plant blooms profusely in full shade.)

Part shade: Periods of direct sun, but protection from midday and western sun in late afternoon. No more than three to four hours of sun; afternoon shade is preferable.

Part sun: Just a little more sun than part shade.

Dappled shade: The amount of sunlight that shines through deciduous trees.

Develop a Landscape Plan

If there were only one bit of advice to give to those building a new home or renovating one, it would be develop a landscape plan along with the house plan. Ideally, a landscape architect should work alongside your architect or builder and designate certain areas of the grounds for lawn, gardens, play, shrub border, etc. Remember summer heat and humidity keep Atlantans in the air-conditioned indoors, and bone-chilling Atlanta winter days force even ardent gardeners to remain housebound. Therefore, create views for the windows, especially for glass areas in dining spaces. Finally, determine all trees eventually necessary to remove. It is much less expensive to cut them down while heavy equipment is still at the site.

Whether you choose to draw your own or seek professional help, it is useful to have a landscape plan for your property, even if it's only a sketch on paper. Indiscriminate planting can be regretted quickly, particularly if the site has been inadequately evaluated and prepared.

Unless you have artistic or engineering skills, you may be more comfortable seeking out a landscape architect or designer. In the long run, you will probably save money and time using the services of a professional.

Professionals prefer customers who have done their homework, even if the ideas you bring have to be modified to work successfully for your property. Besides checking out other area home landscapes for details you like or would prefer to avoid, refer to available books featuring landscape plans. An inexpensive paperback, *The Home Landscaper*, provides 55 professional landscapes, one of which may be ideal for your home. The designers match the landscapes with 40 architectural styles, but prudently do not specify plant lists that would restrict the landscape design to a particular section of the country. Notations like "deciduous shade tree," "low flowering evergreen," and "flowering evergreen groundcover" allow you or your landscaper to choose the proper plant material for the Atlanta area and your special site. The plans can be easily altered for any terrain.

Find the Right Professional Help

If you want professional help, begin by finding a local landscape you admire, and ask that homeowner lots of questions. Who did the work? Did the landscaper listen to the homeowner's ideas and desires? Did the cost of the work stay within the estimated budget? Was the work completed on time? Is the homeowner satisfied?

If you choose a landscape professional on the basis of an advertisement rather than a personal recommendation, ask the landscaper for a client list. Check out the jobs and question the clients.

You may find that the finished landscape was the coordinated effort of a landscape architect, a landscape designer, and an installer or contractor or that it was the work of one firm. Titles can be confusing. Distinctions among landscape service providers are blurred. If you browse through the Yellow Pages, it's easy to become thoroughly bewildered.

The landscape architect is university trained to handle drainage problems, re-grade your plot, design features like lighting, decks, steps, swimming pools, and provide a professional finished look to a landscape. Landscape architects usually know their foundation plants, but many are not as knowledgeable about shrubs and flowers.

The landscape designer often works with a landscape architect, but a designer can also work alone. Atlanta has some wonderful designers who have put their marks on the front yards and gardens of our city, using innovative designs and newly introduced horticultural material. You see their work often on the covers and in the pages of local and national magazines.

The designer, like the architect, often employs a landscape installer to do the actual planting. Installers and contractors who work on their own, promising to design gardens and choose plants, should be scrutinized closely. It is important to know how long the company has been in business and if there is a trained horticulturist or professional designer on staff. Be wary if the contractor requires more than 25% of the cost of the project in advance.

Landscapers will do a job of any size, but they often encourage homeowners to do small landscaping projects themselves because it's more cost efficient. Obtain cost estimates for the work you need. Remember, however, that the lowest figure may not guarantee the imagination, experience, and reliability you are seeking. Ask about warranties on plants. Many landscape companies guarantee their plants will live for a specified period of time.

Some landscapers have computer software that can show you how the proposed landscaping will look when it's newly installed around your home and how the mature specimens will look a few years from now. Inquire about the availability of this high tech help when selecting your landscaper. Software is also available that allows the homeowner to design flower beds on a home computer.

The Landscape Plan

A landscape plan, which includes trees, shrubs, and perennial and annual beds, should achieve these five goals:

Pleasing Appearance. The landscape should first of all enhance the home, increasing its resale value. It should appear pleasing to the homeowner and passersby. An observer of Atlanta neighborhoods will notice that some homeowners are more easily pleased than others.

Minimal Maintenance. Everyone's busy, and good yard maintenance people can be expensive and difficult to find, so low-upkeep landscaping is a priority. However, there is no such thing as a "no maintenance" landscape. Plants are alive. They grow; sometimes they die. Strive for wise planning and planting—less grass to mow, fewer shrubs to prune, and fewer plants to water—to keep yard work at a minimum.

Permanence. Once paid for and planted, a landscape (with the exception of annual beds) should be permanent. Landscaping is rarely inexpensive, so the plants selected must be hardy in our climate and be chosen to thrive where planted. Remember, also, that survival of the landscape material depends on good drainage, proper soil preparation, adequate watering, and meeting all cultural requirements.

Seasonal Interest. A good landscape plan should also offer continuous color or interest during all the year. This is a tall order, but possible to achieve in Atlanta by a skillful professional or a committed home gardener. Perennials and annuals can be selected to give continuous bloom throughout the growing season. And don't forget a landscape without one blooming flower can be made interesting by mixing and matching shades and textures of foliage.

Xeriscaping Considerations. Xeriscaping is water sensitive landscape design—it does not mean planting desert plants like cactus here in Atlanta. You can adhere to the seven xeriscaping principles (good design, limited turf areas, soil improvement, properly chosen plants, efficient irrigation, use of mulch, and attentive maintenance the first few years) and grow any plants you want—but group them according to water use. Use water-loving plants sparingly and locate them close to the house. Your landscape plan should allow for water conservation and the possibility of watering restrictions during drought conditions.

For further information on garden design see Chapter 2, "An Atlanta Landscape."

Soil Preparation

With landscape plan in hand, plants selected, and installation poised to begin, be sure to check soil preparation and drainage. Only when the soil preparation is complete should planting begin.

Atlanta's soil is usually described as 6" of sandy loam over red clay. The clay holds moisture well, but it drains poorly and compacts when wet, leading to plant rot—our biggest problem. The best soil contains

4-5% organic matter and is well watered and aerated to promote the microbial life that constantly converts the organic matter into humus.

Following house construction, little topsoil may remain to support plant life. If you are starting with a clean slate, where it is not necessary to undo your own or someone else's mistakes, consider this advice from experienced gardeners. From the advantage of hindsight, we would urge you to cover all areas eventually slated to be planted with grass, trees, shrubs, and garden with 6" of river bottom topsoil, available by the truckload from advertisements in local papers.

To improve your soil, incorporate additives (called "amendments") like dried chicken manure, mini pine bark nuggets, and sand to keep the mixture loose and well-drained. Amendments help create pockets for air and improve water circulation. Amending the soil is not an expensive undertaking, and the results justify the expense.

On already developed land, where it is impossible to add truckloads of topsoil, prepare beds, borders, and individual plantings by working in bags of Nature's Helper soil conditioner and inexpensive planting soil. Popular now, also, are additives like mushroom compost, granite sand, Mr. Natural mixes, and gypsum. Be aware that amendments such as Nature's Helper and Earth's Helper are not composted, only aged, and will compete with plants for nitrogen. Compensate by using extra fertilizer, at least for the first few months. Mr. Natural mixes are composted, so extra fertlizer isn't necessary. You can purchase these materials at garden centers.

Homemade compost is an excellent amendment that you can make yourself from leaves, grass clippings, and vegetable and fruit parings and scraps. Home Depot sells a 3' x 9' recycled plastic grid that snaps together to form a 3' x 3' compost bin. Buy several to facilitate turning. You need to turn the pile to allow the heating process to affect all the material, so weed seeds will be killed and you will not reintroduce them in your garden when you use the compost.

Experienced Atlanta gardener Shirley Kennedy says the secret to making good compost is to alternate thin (no more than 4") layers of green and brown materials, to use 1 cup of ammonium nitrate over each layer, and to water each layer. If you are short on fallen leaves for brown material, shred newspapers and cardboard. If you lack green material, ask your neighbors for their lawn clippings. If all materials are shredded, the pile will heat up overnight and raw materials will be reduced by half in three days. Kennedy keeps seven 3' diameter bins composting. She says if she turns the contents every three days, she can have compost ready in three weeks.

Atlanta gardener Jackie Heyda's compost pile began with a gift pitchfork. She adds vegetable matter, fruit, paper towels, and shredded cardboard to her pile. Pine straw can be added to the compost pile, but it takes longer to break down than leaves. It also makes the compost acidic, which is fine for azaleas and other acid lovers.

A caution: Compost can attract raccoons. Raccoons in some parts of the metro area may be rabid.

Two items that probably don't belong on an Atlanta gardener's shopping list are bone meal and peat moss. Bone meal is rather ineffective, and peat moss clumps together in our clay.

Follow package instructions when adding amendments, so drainage is good and the consistency is such that you can plant a bush or perennial just by parting and moving the soil with your hands. Incorporating amendments is fast and less backbreaking and achieves results about as good as double-digging. (You can find a description of laborious double-digging in other gardening books.) If the clay in your yard resists your shovel and pick, consider raised beds. Fill the raised bed with the ideal soil mixture required by the intended plantings.

Shrubs and trees need no soil amendments to thrive. Amended soil actually wicks water out of surrounding clay, creating an over-watered situation that causes roots to rot. When planting shrubs and trees, prepare by breaking up the soil in an area as wide and as deep as two to three times the root ball's width.

Soil in this area is usually strongly acid, with a pH of 5.5 to 4.5. (Neutral pH is 7; numbers greater than 7 indicate increasing alkalinity.) You can have your soil tested for pH by the County Extension Service or with a home test kit. Local soil is adequate for most acid-loving plants. For those which require alkaline soil, add dolomitic lime.

Buying Plants

The chapters in Part Two of this book have detailed charts and lists of plants that will grow in Atlanta. Use them as guides for selecting plants for your garden.

Resist buying plants in bloom or even bud—the plant with neither will have a greater chance for success because its total energy will go toward re-establishing itself in your bed or container. Of course, this guideline must be weighed against the desire to see the flower quality of the plant and the desire to know the plant is genetically floriferous. If you do buy a plant with open flowers, ruthlessly pinch them off. You can leave the buds.

Unless you are buying a plant that is supposed to have purple, blue, rose, yellow, or gray foliage, avoid buying plants that do. This is a sign of stress. Brown or damaged leaves should also be avoided, as should any signs of spider webs or small insects. Also check undersides of leaves.

Generally, it's better to choose plants that are grown on their own roots, rather than being grafted. Pruning suckers from the root graft is time consuming, and the plant will come back true to type if cold weather kills the top growth.

If you stop for other errands on your way home and have to leave plants in your car, leave the windows open slightly.

Planting and Transplanting

The labels on plants you purchase have guidelines for planting, and the chapters in Part Two of this book contain a great deal of planting advice.

The best time to transplant plants is morning. The hotter the expected temperature, the earlier you should begin the job. Plants are full of moisture in the morning and are more likely to survive. Plants are weakest in the evening hours, having lost moisture during the day. In the evening, their transplant survival rate is less.

Transplanting Tips

Use an an open brown bag to shade a newly planted perennial or small shrub or vine from frost or sun for 24 to 36 hours to reduce transplant stress.

If you have to plant a shrub in summer in a hot, sunny area, insert four stakes in the ground around the plant and drape a layer of cheesecloth over the stakes. After a month of sufficient watering, the plant will be established enough to remove the protection.

A temporary drip irrigation system can be fashioned by inserting a plastic bag into the new plant's empty container and fastening it around the rim. Puncture a few tiny holes in the bag's bottom. Stabilize the container with a rock, fill it with water, and place it beside the plant. Water will slowly drip around the new planting.

To control the spread of an invasive plant, cut the bottom out of a old one gallon nursery container (plastic pot). Dig a hole and insert it in the soil with the lip about 1" above ground. Place the plant in the pot in good soil, and its roots will stay inside the container. Mulch around the plant to hide the pot.

Labeling

To label plants with permanent markers, order from the least expensive source we have found, Paw Paw Everlast Label Company, P.O. Box 93-C, Paw Paw, MI 49079. Avis Aronovitz prefers their cap style marker "C" for its unobtrusive visibility. Brencie Werner prefers their rose style marker "E" because there's enough space on the marker to include botanical and common names as well as family. Used with plastic adhesive-backed labels printed out on the Brother P-Touch, this label withstands most Atlanta weather and the mischief of birds and other overzealous guests in your garden. If you don't like the aluminum color, paint with a dark-colored exterior paint and use white instead of black lettering on clear labels.

Mulch

The purpose of mulch is to conserve moisture, eliminate weeding, moderate soil temperature, and give a professional finished look to the planting. After plants are in the ground, 2-4" of pine bark mulch or pine straw can be added to top off garden areas. A deeper mulch will result in poor aeration and soggy soil.

You can gather pine straw fallen from your own trees or ask your neighbors to let you rake their yards. Pine straw lasts a long time, stays in place, and allows water to run through it. When you rake pine straw and aren't planning to use it right away, cover it before it becomes littered with leaves or polluted with lawn chemicals.

When mulching a bed on a slope, avoid using bark chips. They will float away in a downpour. Instead, use pine straw or coarsely shredded bark that can knit together and stay put.

Watering

"How often should I water?" is the first question a new gardener asks about a plant selection. The answer is always "more often for the newly planted plant, less often for an established plant." At planting, thoroughly water in all new additions to the garden.

Keep in mind that although more plants are lost from over-watering than from lack of water, a new annual, perennial, or even a shrub may need water daily during a dry period. Watch for signs of stress, such as wilting and loss of foliage, and act quickly. Once a plant is established, a good soaking (1" of water measured in a calibrated cylinder) once a week is better than brief daily applications. Remember to mulch your plants.

Dragging hoses is a miserable chore. During summers with record rainfalls and moderate temperatures, watering is not a problem. But other Atlanta summers can mean record-breaking temperatures accompanied by severe drought, and supplying lawn and garden areas with the required 1" of water per week to keep them in optimal condition can be difficult. For this situation, permanent watering systems should be considered when designing or updating a landscape plan.

Explore the innovative irrigation equipment for delivering water to the garden and lawn now on the market. New hose material allows such a system to be buried, hidden by plants, or covered by mulch. Using an impulse sprinkler is simple—alone or attached in series to hoses, it can be left in place for the season. The arc of the mechanism can be adjusted to water lawns and annual beds. Other systems offer spring-driven (by water pressure) pop-up heads that spray water on designated terrain. These, too, can be installed by the homeowner.

Soaker hoses that apply water to the ground evenly can be easily attached to existing hoses to irrigate perennial borders or fruit gardens.

The newest drip irrigation systems can be easily added to hoses to release water to roots of specific plants in a shrub border or individual containers and are effective and efficient. With both soaker hoses and drip systems, remember to only turn the faucet one-eighth of the way to limit the force of the water.

When to Water

The ideal time to water is 10 a.m. Wet foilage increases the potential for disease. It's best to avoid watering early in the morning and in the evening, when applied water adds to normal dew and lengthens the total time the plant is wet. Because overhead watering can help spread disease, use soaker hoses or aim hoses at roots. It is more efficient to water on cloudy days so the sun does not too quickly evaporate the added moisture.

Tools for Gardening

Every gardener must start with certain basic tools appropriate to the task. Choose your tools carefully. The ones that feel comfortable to you will minimize the aches sometimes associated with gardening. Well-made garden tools are a good investment, even if they are more expensive. Experienced gardeners will tell you not to buy cheap plants or cheap garden tools, because both will have to be replaced quickly.

A beginner's list would include these basic tools:

For digging - a shovel, a pick ax, a digging fork, and a garden rake; for planting - trowels in two sizes (one narrower than the other), a hose, and a watering can; for pruning - pruners, loppers, and telescoping tree pruners. You'll also need a leaf rake and a wheelbarrow or garden cart.

Personal preference also plays an important role in the selection of gardening aids. I use a lightweight pick quite often, but never a pitch-fork. I wear a garden apron that holds my small tools so I can carry them with me as I work. I also find knee pads, attached securely with elastic webbing or Velcro, are great for kneeling on hard, wet ground. Good waterproof garden gloves are another necessity. A short handled spade with a smaller pointed blade, sometimes called a fox-hole shovel, is the best tool I have found for planting perennials. I have learned that wheelbarrows and garden carts with bigger wheels are more maneuverable. In a small garden, use a hoe to weed. The hoe not only controls weeds and grass, but it also breaks up crusty soil and aerates the soil.

Disposable latex medical/dental gloves are wonderful for tasks that require a sensitive touch and save your fingernails. (Of course, your hands will sweat in summer heat.) Wear latex gloves under your regular garden gloves when working in wet, cold earth. If you run your fingernails over a bar of soap before working in the garden, the soap will keep soil from remaining under your nails when you wash your hands.

Homeowners need hoses long enough to deliver water to the far corners of their cultivated property. Since hoses can be unsightly and are easy to trip over, you may want to consider manual or automatic-rewind reels for your hoses.

Power Tools

If you don't contract for maintenance, you will need power tools— a lawn mower, string trimmer, leaf vacuum/mulcher, and perhaps hedge clippers. (Insurance regulations require that landscape maintenance people use their own tools.) Gasoline-powered tools perform heavy duty tasks better and are not burdened by electrical extension cords that can be easily severed. However, gasoline-powered tools require strength to be used correctly and safely and are expensive to buy and maintain. They also emit fumes and higher noise levels than electric tools.

The style and type of lawn mower (reel or rotary, riding or push, manual or power) you need is determined by the kind of grass you grow and the size of the turf area. (See Chapter 19, "Lawn Grasses," for more information.) Edging your lawn with an edger or string trimmer gives a finished, professional appearance to your landscape and may allow you to go a little longer between mowings, if necessary.

Remember to wear devices that protect your sight and hearing when operating power garden tools. In development now are earplugs that will filter out hearing-damaging noise but still allow the wearer to hear normal sounds and conversation.

Chapter Two

An Atlanta Landscape

by

Paula Refi

Designing Your Atlanta Landscape

Landscapes, like architecture, display pronounced regional characteristics. Just as Atlanta residences reflect local building styles and materials, venerable Atlanta gardens display familiar plants in different combinations.

Certain gardening styles predominate in particular neighborhoods. Massed foundation shrubs and expanses of turf or English ivy often typify stately formal homes on the city's north side, while personal flair is likely to be found in Atlanta's intown communities. New suburban subdivisions sometimes impose landscape design guidelines that necessarily confer a degree of conformity.

Whatever the location, a home and its landscape together create a setting for a family's personal lifestyle. Atlanta offers a wide array of choices to satisfy its diverse population.

For years, our southern plant list was not only regional, it was parochial. Recently, however, a more mobile population of gardeners has brought to the city many new garden-worthy plants. The guiding influence of the Atlanta Botanical Garden and high visibility commercial landscapes (exemplified by Post Properties) have enhanced public awareness of the power of plants. An increasing number of local specialty growers continually select and evaluate the best new species for Atlanta's gardens, while the proliferation of horticultural publications and mail-order nurseries has further expanded our catalog of available landscape plants.

Enthusiastic gardeners are acquisitive by nature and, without a well-conceived plan, the resultant landscape might easily become a collection of botanical species. When plant lovers make selections within the guidelines of a master plan, they choose only those plants that are consistent with the overall concept for the garden. No longer do they wander, befuddled, with their latest horticultural acquisition in one hand and a shovel in the other, searching for an appropriate location. Just as an interior designer guides the homeowner in the selection of color schemes and furniture to create a functional and beautiful home, an experienced garden designer guides the confused gardener in the selection and placement of "furnishings" for the landscape.

Landscape Design Principles

The principles governing design apply regardless of the garden's regional setting. Some principles, as presented in this book's introduction, are plainly practical; others are aesthetic. A successful landscape design begins with general considerations, reflecting the functional requirements of the family as well as personal taste. The selection of individual plants is the last item in the sequence of design tasks.

Conventional design wisdom dictates that a home's public areas be presentable in all seasons, and in traditional Atlanta landscapes this is accomplished with areas of lawn, evergreen foundation plantings, and large trees framing the house. The color splendor of Atlanta's springs can be rivaled by carefully selecting shrubs and small trees that are noted for their fall foliage color.

Recently, innovative designers have been more liberal in placing color and deciduous material in the public view. Homeowners are becoming more inclined to express individuality in their streetside plantings. As long as this is done with a view to the overall landscape concept, the result will be pleasing.

Practical Considerations

Begin by sketching a base map of the property, noting its orientation with respect to the compass. Measure and draw to scale all the property's structures and major landscape features. Be sure to include trees, shrub masses, and areas of lawn or groundcover. Once a base map is drafted, it becomes a simple matter to overlay tracing paper and quickly sketch ideas for additions or alterations.

Designate areas for public, private, and service use. Define entries and plan for appropriate access to all areas of the landscape. Incorporate into the circulation plan any service areas, such as storage sheds or compost piles. Assess topographical problems, especially slopes that will govern drainage problems. Determine if shade is needed, an important consideration in the sunny South.

Assess the soil for drainage qualities, pH, tilth, and fertility. It is easier in the long run to work with the characteristics of the site. Observe the path of the sun as it moves over the property. Try to anticipate seasonal changes in the pattern of shadows.

Consider how much time will be spent maintaining the landscape. Many homeowners prefer a "mow and blow" landscape, while dedicated plant lovers rarely utter the word "maintenance."

Aesthetic Considerations

Identify unsightly views that require screening, such as a neighbor's deck or utility equipment. Remember vantage points from within the house should influence the placement of plant groupings. "Borrow" pleasing vistas nearby. Consider ways to soften noise from nearby expressways or airports that intrudes on a landscape.

Determine whether the garden's style is to be formal or naturalistic. Should plant masses be linear and symmetrical or curved and free-flowing? The architecture of the residence factors into this decision, as well as the character of the neighborhood. Sometimes it makes sense to repeat a trim or brick color in the plant material, thereby relating the house to the landscape.

Landscape design principles are similar to those followed in other artistic realms. Balance and scale are crucial. Plant masses have both visual and physical "weight," and their combined effect should create a sense of equilibrium. Similarly, the scale of plant masses should be proportional to the other masses within view, including the structures. Texture can also affect balance, since several finely textured plants will be needed to balance a coarse specimen.

Successful landscapes convey a feeling of unity. In traditional Atlanta landscapes, a generous and well-defined lawn effectively integrates diverse planting areas. Unity can also be achieved by repeating plants or colors. A contrasting plant creates emphasis, an "exclamation point," and ought to be used carefully. A small structure (a bench, arbor, or ornament) can serve the same purpose. Fragrance, though more subtle, can be used to advantage in more refined gardens.

Color is the most compelling source of emphasis in the landscape. Its effect is almost irresistible, and it is usually best to limit its use to high-impact areas that require accentuation. See Chapter 3 for Barbara Allen's detailed discussion of color in the garden.

Discriminating gardeners often respond to more subjective characteristics of the site. How does the site "speak" to you? It may generate recollections of trips taken or childhood memories, prompting the inclusion of specific plants or artifacts in the garden. These less tangible but nonetheless important aspects of site assessment reveal themselves with time. Observations made over the course of an entire growing season yield the most information.

Beds and Borders

Ornamental plants, whether chosen for their bloom or foliage (or both), display themselves best when combined with appropriate companion plants. Just as we select and arrange furnishings within a room to complement one another, so should we thoughtfully locate plants within beds or borders.

A **border** surrounds a central open area and is viewed from one side. A hedge, wall, or fence functions as background. Plants are arranged in layers from back to front, the lowest ones are near the viewer. Occasional violations of this principle, however, add the element of surprise.

A **bed** is sited within an open area, usually a lawn, and is seen from several vantage points. Its configuration, whether formal or naturalistic, should relate to the rest of the landscape. Its size and placement should conform to the principles of scale and balance. Within the bed, the tallest plants are placed toward the center, surrounded by layers of plants descending to the margin.

Carefully controlled color is a critical factor in creating a successful planting bed. Exercising personal preference, the gardener ought to choose a color scheme and adhere to it. Options vary from strongly contrasting tones (such as blue or violet with yellow) to those incorporating related colors (perhaps pinks, mauves, and blues). Color schemes can be used effectively at different seasons; *e.g.*, a plan utilizing blue and white will "cool" a bed in the heat of an Atlanta summer. Some may prefer monochromatic themes.

Arranging Plants

Think of groups of flowering plants as companions that show each to best advantage. Successful plant combinations have blooms that differ in shape and color. An example might combine three plants that do well in Atlanta: purple Siberian iris, pinkish-purple foxglove spikes, and white ox eye daisy. Don't overlook the effect of the plant form—is it upright, mounded, or spreading?

Most gardeners plan for a sequence of bloom to carry through the entire growing season. If the landscape is large enough, there can be several garden areas that peak at different times, with changing points of emphasis. Swimming pools demand summer enhancement, while woodland sites necessarily bloom in the spring.

Atlanta gardeners are fortunate in their ability to grow a number of winter bloomers, as well. Plants selected for their winter traits (including foliage, bark, and fruit) provide another gardening dimension.

Drifts of plants are more pleasing than linear arrangements (except in formal gardens), and it is best to plant in odd-numbered groupings. When deciding how many of each plant will be needed, take into consideration the color of the bloom. If it is pale, more plants will be required to make an impact; conversely, a single dose of a very strong color may be sufficient. Position drifts of color to emphasize curves or corners. Repeating the same plant or the same color unifies the planting. Include white and gray plants to blend groupings.

Tips from the Experts

When deciding how much growing room to allow new shrub plantings, space them based on their expected size in five years.

Gardens with sizable herbaceous plantings can be made to look more presentable in winter by meticulous maintenance; *i.e.*, freshly applied mulch and neat edging treatments.

Dark, coarse foliage (like that of holly and wax myrtle) recedes in a landscape and is most effectively used as a background or in the distance. Light, fine foliage advances and is best in the foreground.

New landscapes need re-evaluating after eight or 10 years, when plants have grown in size and beds will need enlarging.

Don't be afraid to use new, untried plants in a landscape, but use them in limited quantities so that, should they fail, replacing them will not be a hardship.

The Atlanta metropolitan area is full of microclimates and extremely unique sites, so never assume you can't grow something everyone and every book has told you "can't be done." Experiment, be adventurous, and learn. Mike Dirr put it best, "Plants can't read books!"

Fine textured plants such as weeping willow, cotoneaster, and spirea are more appropriate in small spaces or to accompany architectural structures with smooth surfaces and fine details. Medium textured plants such as dogwood, azalea, camellia, and cleyra provide contrast. Usually coarse-textured plants such as magnolia, oak, and loquat are more in harmony with large spaces and coarse building materials.

If you have plants that hang over too far on a walkway close to your house, try one of these: dwarf nandina, dwarf acuba, crimson pigmy barberry, dwarf sansanqua, curly leaf ligustrum, low growing azaleas.

Variegated liriope and mondo grass are good fillers for difficult spots.

Try espaliering dwarf *Magnolia grandiflora* 'Little Gem.' It is a more vigorous grower than other evergreens that are usually used, and it is easier to control than a vine. The plant's glossy foliage and prolific, large creamy white blossoms are spectacular when tied to a wall. Espalier sansanqua camellias on walls not exposed to afternoon sun.

Sarcococca (sweet box) is one of the few shrubs that will grow under an evergreen magnolia.

Sugar Maples are great shade trees here, and their fall yellow or fire-colored foliage is magnificent.

Yuletide camellia (*Camellia sasanqua* 'Yuletide') always blooms for Christmas in Atlanta. Add small white twinkling lights to this shrub with large, flat red blooms. Planted near your entryway in a large container or as a foundation plant, it enlivens holiday spirits.

Plant genera holding much promise for use in Atlanta gardens, according to Vines Botanical Gardens Executive Director Allen Sistrunk, include pulmonaria, hydrangea, aster, and ferns.

Chapter Three

Color in the Garden

by

Barbara Allen

Color in the Garden

Color in the garden is important to some gardeners and entirely ignored by others. The person with some knowledge of color use will go to great lengths to find a flower with just the perfect shade, while another will be happy with hues others see as conflicting or offensive.

Color is the first thing that catches the eye. Learning to use color correctly can help you create the peaceful, spacious atmosphere that is admired in a garden.

Using Color

By using an artist's color wheel, you can learn how colors relate to each other and how they influence the viewer. A simple color wheel consists of six colors, the primaries (red, blue, and yellow) and the secondaries (green, violet and orange). The colors are always arranged the same, with complementary colors opposite each other. Learning these six colors and how they influence emotions will give you a good base for designing.

Primary Colors. Red is warm, even hot. It is enthusiasm, an exclamation point in the garden. Red shouts, "Look at me!" Use red only where attention is wanted (never around the garbage can or cable box). Its complementary color is green. Red can stand alone in a green garden.

Blue is cool. Blue tends to recede into the distance. It is also a good color to use for blending other colors together. There is a fine line between violet and blue in flowers. If there is not too much red in the violet, blue and violet can be used interchangeably. Blue is the complement of orange.

Yellow is a cheerful color. Yellow gets along with most garden flowers. It brightens up a dark spot, is great in a shady garden, and is sorely missed when it is absent. Its complementary color is violet. Most blues are also acceptable complements of yellow.

Secondary Colors. The secondary colors are combinations of the primary colors. Green is a combination of yellow and blue. It is peaceful, cool, and refreshing. It is the perfect background color, blending with everything. Green is neutral in the garden, lending perfect balance. It is important to learn to recognize the many shades of green. The complementary color of green is the primary color red.

Violet is a combination of red and blue; it shows up least in the garden. It almost demands the companionship of yellow. Violet always needs white behind it to make it show.

Orange, a combination of two hot colors, red and yellow, rivets the eye. It can be outstanding alone with green. It works best in a monochromatic scheme, with softer shades of apricot or salmon, or in an analogous scheme with red-orange or yellow-orange. Blue is its complementary color.

Color Schemes

A **monochromatic** or one-color scheme is the easiest to plan. All one has to do is find flowers in tints and shades of one color. This can be serene and attractive to one gardener and totally boring to another. An example is the all white garden at Sissinghurst in England.

A **complementary** scheme combines colors opposite each other on the color wheel—for example, violet and yellow. This color scheme is one of the most pleasing, and its combinations are the easiest.

An **analogous or harmonious** scheme uses any three adjoining colors on a more advanced color wheel—for example, yellow, yellow-orange, and orange. Because a combination of analogous colors varies and builds up a common color, the impact is strong.

Using Neutrals and Backgrounds

Gray is an important blending color. The mother of perennial gardening, Gertrude Jekyll, always started her garden with gray foliage plants. These pale colored plants can light a garden path at night or can be used to separate one color scheme from another in the same garden. Brown is a neutral, almost unnoticed color in the garden.

Flowers look best with the good background Mother Nature provides. However, many backgrounds are houses. A gray house is the easiest to color coordinate since most colors look good with neutral gray. White flowers need the background of dark green foundation plantings to show up in front of a white house. Brick homes give the biggest challenge since brick can be brown, red pink, or orange. The color of the brick must be the first consideration when planning a flower garden for a brick home.

Many books have been written on the subject of color coordinating a garden. Rules are made to be broken. No sooner are rules formulated than someone breaks them beautifully. The greatest offender, of course, is Mother Nature herself.

Chapter Four

Climate and Hardiness

by

Jim Harrington

Gardening in Atlanta's Climate

Gardening in Atlanta's erratic climate is both a blessing and a curse. Just when we get used to mild winters, a sub-zero freeze comes along and devastates all but the most hardy plants. Another year, a late April frost will ravage all the early buds and spring flowers. Unlike gardening further north or south, luck as well as skill determines gardening success in Atlanta. But with a little luck and a thorough knowledge of Atlanta's weather patterns, we can pick fresh flowers all year. This is the blessing of gardening in Atlanta—Atlanta's climate gives us the opportunity to grow great gardens.

Hardiness

The plant hardiness system is based on a plant's ability to survive at certain cold temperatures. Each plant is classified by zones, ranging from 1 to 11, drawn on the United States Department of Agriculture Plant Hardiness Zone Map of North America. Each zone division is based on a 10-degree variation in average low temperatures. Zones are further divided into sub-zones, such as 7A and 7B, each with a five-degree variation. Plants for sale are labeled with the zone numbers for which they are best suited.

According to the USDA Hardiness Zone Map, Atlanta is located in a transition area between Zone 7A and Zone 7B. This location gives us a large number of plant species to grow but makes the more tender plants vulnerable to cold damage. I see this as advantageous, because if a somewhat tender plant can survive just for a few years, it is worth growing. A good example of this is the Mexican bush sage, *Salvia leucantha*. Most years it will survive through the winter, but will need replacing eventually.

Rainfall

Atlanta's annual average rainfall is just under 50", usually evenly dispersed throughout the year. However, even uniform dispersion can lead to wet, cold soils in the winter that can cause perennials to rot. Uniform rainfall dispersion also promotes taller, less compact growth. This can make it easier to mix flowers in a garden design; plants grow well together and share their strength for support. With the large dwarf plant selection available now, we can also design gardens with more conventional delineation between plants.

Averages can be misleading. I often find myself wishing for a little more or a little less rain. Because of rainfall fluctuations, I have found that the best answer for Atlanta is a garden that includes drip irrigation. Due to our high summer humidity, drip irrigation has another benefit. Often, we awaken to 80% humidity, followed by 60% during the day. This leads to mildew, fungus, and rot. Drip irrigation helps reduce these problems, because water goes directly to the soil without wetting the foliage.

Temperature

Along with high summer humidity, we have high summer temperatures. July's average day temperature is 77 degrees (often much hotter) and the average night temperature is 69 degrees. The small variation in day and night temperatures limits our plant selection. Plants that require cooler night temperatures and grow well further north deteriorate here. Their growth is inhibited, and buds abort or don't form in hot spells.

The temperature in January, our coldest month, averages a low of 32 degrees and a high of 51 degrees. Averages can be misleading, as we witnessed in winter of 1985, when the low was -8 degrees. Even during unusually cold years snow cover is rare, making our plants vulnerable to damage considered unusual further north where snow cover insulates plants from freezing temperatures.

Another problem is the spring-like temperatures that can occur in February. The warm days can cause perennials to emerge, only to be killed or damaged by a late cold snap. Most gardens will sustain some frost damage each year due to the false springs of February. Our average last frost is April 15.

Microclimates

The best way to work with Atlanta's inconsistent weather patterns is to find your garden's microclimates. Microclimates are spots in each garden where temperatures vary a few degrees from the rest of the garden.

Many microclimates are easy to determine and can be used to advantage. For example, the north side of your house will be a few degrees cooler than the south side. A plant that likes mild winters should be placed in a southern exposure; one that resents our hot summers should be given a home with a northern exposure. Using microclimates is an excellent way to successfully grow more marginally hardy plants in your garden.

Chapter Five

Pests and Diseases

by

Jim Harrington

Pest and Disease Management in Atlanta Gardens

If you plant your plants properly and keep them in good health with adequate watering and correct feeding, they will better withstand the pests and diseases that threaten them. Good cultural care will not, however, prevent all problems, so it's important to learn to identify and treat problems as they arise.

Insect Control

The extremely variable climatic conditions we have in Atlanta give a number of good and bad insects the opportunity to invade our gardens. This insect mix is part of nature's process of checks and balances, and our goal in a garden is certainly not to eliminate all insects. The goal is, rather, to control harmful insects to reduce unsightly plant damage.

We all have been bothered by a honey bee determined to investigate our lunch, and we have sat in wonderment, watching a honey bee work the first spring flowers. Like the honey bee that pollinates the flowers, all insects have a purpose. The termite helps decompose trees and branches that fall in the forest, and the yellow-jacket feeds on the aphids infesting our crape myrtle.

Insect control is a maintenance task, and the goal of keeping insects in a manageable balance will vary a little in each garden. To me, it means growing plant varieties that require minimal insect control. Any plant that must be sprayed weekly to live in my garden must be so special that it stops passing cars. Otherwise, given the hundreds of choices, it seems foolish not to substitute a more carefree alternative. Therefore, insects in my garden generally are not much of a problem and can easily be chemically controlled when they cause more damage than I choose to tolerate.

It is worth your time to learn about insects and which plants they are likely to infest. Certain insects tend to gravitate to particular plants. This knowledge is more useful and effective than a shed full of chemicals. As I learn which plants attract which insects, I can treat the plants in late March or early April while the harmful insect population is small. Often timely control prevents more serious problems later in the season.

When you do use chemicals, proper timing and thorough applications save you labor and money. I use the least toxic chemical at the right time to break the cycle of infection, usually getting satisfactory results.

Dealing with Specific Pests

Aphids are a major insect problem because they multiply quickly. They feed on tender new growth and deform flowers and leaves. A secondary problem with aphids is that they secrete "honey-dew." Honey-dew is a food for sooty mold, a black fungus which covers leaves and slows photosynthesis. My greatest dilemma with aphids is their tendency to become a problem when other insects are inactive. They are easily controlled with a 10% solution of mild soapy water, but often must be treated every 10 days—more often if they are infesting trees in the vicinity of your perennial garden. Aphid infestations are inhibited only if it is very hot or very cold and, therefore, sometimes are active all year in Atlanta.

Beetles will be found in any Atlanta perennial garden. Some are harmless; others cause great damage. Flea beetles are very small, but chew holes in the foliage of a variety of plants. I have not found them to be a real problem except in the more neglected gardens. Japanese beetles are a problem in late spring and quickly devour many perennials. They are difficult to control because of their mobility. To prevent serious damage, thoroughly cover your plants with a residual insecticide. When it rains, re-apply the chemical. Presently I use liquid Sevin or Diazinon. Traps are also available, but traps will attract beetles from great distances which could very well create a bigger problem in your garden. The most effective control that I have used in my own garden is to pick them off plants early in the morning when they are sluggish and destroy them by dropping them into soapy water.

Cucumber beetles, blister beetles, and other beetles should be treated with the same insecticides only if they are causing obvious damage.

Caterpillars are the larval stage of moths, butterflies, and beetles. Most are easy to control when young, but as they age they are less susceptible to insecticides. Some, like the sawfly larva, seem to appear overnight and quickly defoliate plants. Treatment of caterpillars must be done quickly. If you are using a biological stomach poison, such as *Bacillus thuringiensis* (which must be ingested to be effective), apply it before plant damage occurs. I also have had success with Orthene as a contact insecticide.

Snails and slugs are a year round problem except perhaps in the very coldest months. They feed at night and so are rarely seen. It is easy to identify their damage by the slime trail left behind as they move across a plant. Damage from their feeding can vary from holes in leaves to completely shredded foliage. In Atlanta, I have found their favorite plants to be hostas, pansies, and just about any tender seedling. I treat these pests with slug and snail bait in all the gardens I maintain before damage is seen.

Lace bugs are a pest for Atlanta's favorite plant, the evergreen azalea. These little fly-like bugs hide under the leaves and feed on the leaf cells. A whitish speckling forms on the leaf top. When the leaf is flipped over, black fecal specks can be seen. Most pesticides control these insects, but only if all leaf surfaces are covered. Miss a few leaves, and your problem will return. I find certain azalea varieties, such as 'Fashion,' have more problems with lace bugs when planted in sunnier locations.

Spider mites are a devastating problem in Atlanta because, left unchecked, these pests are capable of killing most plants. Since they are a mite, insecticides will not work. Infected plants must be treated with a miticide. I have many clients who sprayed weekly with insecticides, only to watch a lovely butterfly bush slowly die.

A large number of perennials are attacked by spider mites, so most gardens will have at least one plant with this problem. I have found that vulnerable plants must be treated in early spring before damage is seen. If you want success, complete coverage of the plant is essential. Because they harbor spider mites, plants such as foxgloves should be treated as annuals. Once flowering is complete, remove them from the garden. The most common miticides are Pentac and Kelthane, both of which give good control. A variety of other products, probably equally effective, are available.

Thrips are miniature, long, narrow insects that damage flowers in bud and bloom. They are a sporadic problem in the Atlanta area. During the spring and summer of 1994, thrips did serious damage to many white blooms in local flower beds—perhaps due to an insect population explosion. (Apparently white flowers top this insect's list of delicacies.) Atlanta gardeners unfamiliar with this insect were mystified. White flowers on roses, gardenias, and other plants either opened imperfectly or appeared to fade quickly. Sometimes foliage was also deformed. Plants without white blooms also were seriously affected. Thrips can be controlled by applying any of the common insecticides. First remove infested flowers, then follow with thorough insecticide coverage to ensure best results.

The hardest insect to control in Atlanta is the **white fly**, which multiplies quickly and shows some resistance to insecticides. They are easy to identify—little white flies swarm, forming a small white cloud above an infected plant when it is disturbed. I recommend removing badly infected plants. White flies can be managed if a strict schedule of continuous insecticide application is used. If you are not consistent in your spraying, they will return quickly. It is also important to alternate insecticides. An example is applying Diazinon one week and Orthenex III the next. However, the white fly usually wins in the end. Never purchase or plant an infected perennial—it's never worth the potential and probable problems. Complete control of this destructive pest has eluded me in my garden so far.

Plant Diseases in Atlanta Gardens

The seriousness of plant diseases in the Atlanta area fluctuates with the seasonal weather patterns. Wet years are plagued with problems; dry years give relief. In the summer of 1993, most diseases were not a problem due to late summer drought. During wet years, they can be almost uncontrollable. Most plant diseases in Atlanta are caused by fungi, for which there are controls. Viruses cause wilts, and there is no control. There are also bacterial diseases, but by the time they are identified, little can be done.

Controlling Diseases

Diseases caused by fungi will always be present in Atlanta gardens. Some easily infected plants will prove to be too much of a problem and should be ruthlessly removed. You may, however, elect to grow a susceptible plant. Likes and dislikes are personal choices that give each garden individuality.

The following paragraphs review plant diseases that occur every year, along with the problems most common during wet spells. Every gardener in Atlanta eventually will be exposed to most of these.

Crown rot affects some plants during the growing season and some during wet, cool winters. Even during the dry summer of 1993, I had dianthus with crown rot. By treating early with Daconil, an all-purpose fungicide, I was able to reduce the spread of the crown rot. Controlling winter crown rot depends on good soil preparation and proper mulching. Never mulch the crowns of perennials any time of year. Our soils are just too wet during the winter. In the summer, I find great results are achieved with mulch between plants rather than on top of them.

Powdery mildew occurs even in dry years. It looks like white flour covering the foliage. It is common to phlox and will eliminate flowering if left untreated. The key to control is constant fungicide applications. I spray on a weekly basis with Orthenex III, a miticide/insecticide/fungicide mixture. The end result is worth the bother. Powdery mildew is common on a host of plants, usually in the spring and fall. Phlox, roses, crape myrtles, euonymus, and verbena can quickly become completely infected. These perennials give early warning signs of an increasing problem.

A secondary fungus problem I find is **sooty mold**. This black mold grows on honey-dew (see "Aphids" in the "Insect Control" section). The best treatment is to control the aphids. If a bad infestation occurs and sooty mold is prolific, some improvement can be achieved by spraying with a 10% solution of soapy water. The soap breaks down the honey-dew and the sooty mold flakes off the leaves. White fly and scale insects can also cause sooty mold.

Black spot or **anthracnose** needs a fairly specific sequence of environmental conditions to multiply, so some years it is prevalent and in others nonexistent. Black spot causes symptoms that range from a few unsightly spots to complete defoliation of perennials. Most black spots are specific to a plant species and can be controlled with an all-purpose fungicide like Daconil. New growth needs to be treated because it is the most susceptible. The key is to control at the first sign of damage. Spots cannot be removed, so it is important to stop the spread quickly.

Rust is a disease with a specialized life cycle. During the year, it grows on two different host plants, usually different species. Good rust control is easily accomplished by removing one host plant. I find fungicide applications are less helpful. The most common plants that are attacked by rust include aster, goldenrod, tricyrtis, juniper, and crabapple.

A common disease affecting flowers is **botrytis**. This disease causes flowers to appear water soaked, and they seem to melt. The flowers also show some brown color. Botrytis is very common in fall on chrysanthemums if it rains when the plant is in full flower. Chrysanthemums planted when in full flower seem particularly susceptible. Botrytis occurs more often on flowers that are double or peony-like. It can be reasonably controlled by applying a fungicide just as the flowers begin to open. Removal of infected flowers is also advised. Fortunately, botrytis is not much of a problem in Atlanta.

Treating Ongoing Problems

Ongoing problems should be treated on a preventive basis, not after total infection has occurred. If an infected plant is dropping leaves, remove all of the fallen leaves as well as any visibly marked leaves. Often this simple action is effective protection for new growth. The plant may even flower later in the season. If it's already too late in the season, pruning to promote a fall flush of growth might be a better option. One July, I cut back a very sick miniature rose bush severely. Ten weeks later, following weekly fungicide applications, I was rewarded with a bush covered with many perfect flowers and no signs of disease.

Getting Help

For a pest problem or disease that defies treatment, try asking long-time successful gardeners what they do. You might find local gardeners have already given up on that particular plant. Then again, they might suggest an improved method or give the name of a recently developed product that offers better control. Two other sources of assistance are your County Extension Agent and plant pathologists at the University of Georgia. Remember all gardeners have spectacular failures, but trying again the next year is what makes gardening so enjoyable.

Maintenance Gems from Sandra Sandefur

Landscape designer Sandra Sandefur offers these tips for pest and disease control:

Use the mildest pesticide form which gives results on a targeted pest problem.

Do major spraying in March or early April to kill pests' first generation and hold population explosions in check. By spraying early, you also will miss the beneficial insects that emerge later, hungry for pests.

Do not prepare more insecticide or fungicide than you will need. Having too much can lead to shotgun application—spraying everywhere and killing beneficial insects as well.

Spray *Ilex* 'Nellie R. Stevens' and *I. fosteri* in winter with dormant spray Volck Oil to smother adult tea scale from the previous summer. Mid-March or early April, use systemic Orthene to catch newly emerging crawlers before they create the hard armor which makes controlling them difficult. During the growing season, superfine SunSpray Oil can be used. For increased effect, add Orthene at one-fourth the recommended rate. Oil smothers on contact; insecticide gets good contact on the waxy leaf surface. This treatment keeps insect numbers at a level plants can tolerate and beneficial insects can control.

Dormant crape myrtles should receive a dose of Orthene in March or April to control aphid infestation. Apply as an insecticide band around each trunk. The width of the band should equal the trunk's diameter.

Shotgun holes in 'Otto Luyken' laurels (a fungal infection spread on damp leaves) can be treated in early March or April with systemic Daconil 2787 which remains within the plant to fight off the disease.

Hot, dry spells mean spider mites on junipers. Wet foliage down to change from their ideal environment. As a last resort use a miticide, not an insecticide. For bad needle dropping and browning, use Isotox (which contains Vendex). Do not use oil; oil can remove the waxy coat (blue color) of some junipers.

Spray only soap solutions in a perennial garden. Sandefur doesn't like the scent of Safer Soap, so she mixes 1 tablespoon Murphy's Oil Soap in a gallon of water and sprays the mixture on soft-bodied pests.

Flea beetles on black-eyed Susan can be better controlled if sprayed on the full moon (when local longtime expert gardener Jimmy Stewart says they hatch).

To capture white flies, make sticky traps by smearing petroleum jelly on yellow butter tub tops placed close to the infestation. (White flies are attracted to the color yellow.)

If you spray often, rotate your chemicals so insect/disease targets do not become immune to one chemical.

More Tips from Expert Gardeners

A solution of 1% Clorox bleach is an environmentally safe contact spray that kills some types of scale. A 1-1/2% solution is effective on black molds caused by white fly and other insects. The mold will wash off 30 minutes after initial application.

Disease can decimate perennial foliage, but that does not always translate into the demise of the plant. *Phlox divaricata, Astilbe spp.,* and *Coreopsis verticillata* are examples of plants that will usually survive defoliation. Wait until the following spring. If no growth is evident, discard the plants then.

If you have a problem with carpenter bees drilling holes in exterior wood surfaces, spray those places with Dursban when the bees appear in the spring. Repeat the spraying several times during the season. Read directions carefully. Wear rubber gloves, goggles, and protective clothing when spraying. Use a pressurized tank sprayer to reach under eaves and high-up areas on outside walls.

Chapter Six

The Fertilizer Mystery

by

Avis Aronovitz

Solving the Fertilizer Mystery

Nothing can be more confusing to a new gardener than the mysterious names and numbers on fertilizer package labels, but the language of fertilizers is easy to understand once you learn the code.

Printed in the largest letters, the brand name is important if you are looking for a recommended product. What is more important are the numbers like 12-6-6 or 12-55-6 that usually come next. These numbers tell you the amounts of the three primary nutrients in the fertilizer. The first number is the percentage of nitrogen (N). The second is the percentage of phosphorus (P) or (P_2O_5), and the third is potassium (K) or (K_2O), also referred to as potash.

What do these nutrients do for plants? **Nitrogen** stimulates foliage formation, increases vegetative growth, and gives leaves their healthy glow. So for lawns, choose a fertilizer with a nitrogen ratio that is higher than the phosphorus or potassium, such as 12-4-8.

Phosphorus encourages strong root formation and good flowering. To produce flowers and fall berries, use a type of product with a higher phosphorus ratio like 5-10-5 or 5-55-8. These fertilizers will change the ratio of phosphorus to nitrogen in the soil, accomplishing your goal. Be cautious, though. Too much phosphorus in the soil can restrict plant growth, mainly by interfering with uptake and availability of other nutrients.

Potassium or potash promotes hardiness, disease resistance, and plant strength.

Major Nutrient Deficiencies

Plants show their hunger for nutrients with definite symptoms. Signs of insufficient nitrogen include stunted growth and pale leaves. The oldest leaves are affected first, turning pale green, then yellow, beginning at the leaf tip. There are no signs of wilting.

Indications of an insufficiency of phosphorus are reddish/purplish leaves. Again, the oldest leaves change first. Another symptom of phosphorus deficiency is reduced or nonexistent blossoming. Water and weather also influence plant nutrition. In cool, early spring, transplants may exhibit phosphorus deficiency until soils warm. This is because phosphorus is bound tightly by the soil until temperatures rise, so roots cannot absorb it.

Potassium's deficiency indicators are reduced vigor and leaf-tip scorch. In older leaves, death begins at the tips and proceeds (in contrast to lack of a nitrogen) only along the leaf margins.

Choosing a Nitrogen Source

Nitrogen is the most important element because it is required in large quantities for plant growth. It is usually the most expensive ingredient, too. The source of the nitrogen can be important because various types break down at different rates. (Here it gets a little bit complicated, so read the label carefully.) Nitrate nitrogen is the only form of nitrogen that plants can readily absorb. It gives plants a quick boost, but is not held in the soil well and leaches out quickly. Ammoniacal nitrogen is retained very well in cool soils, but when soil temperatures go above 50 degrees (as can happen early in the season in Atlanta), ammoniacal nitrogen converts to the nitrate form and is used up readily.

Urea is a concentrated nitrogen source that can break down quickly, but it can be artificially coated to slow its release. If you need to have your fertilizer last more than three weeks, choose one that has a relatively high percentage of slow-release nitrogen like coated urea. Sometimes the term "water-insoluble nitrogen" is used. This nitrogen releases slowly, so it's available for months. Higher quality fertilizers tend to have more of this form of nitrogen.

What's the Best Buy?

A large array of fertilizers, in all sorts of mixes and formulations, are for sale. Nitrogen, phosphorus and potassium are in a ratio in every fertilizer mix. When you look closely, you will find that many are very similar. Your plants will not likely know the difference, either.

The cheapest fertilizer is not always the most economical. Discount stores do not, as a rule, sell slow-release fertilizers which are more expensive. Compare. If the sources of the nitrogen are about the same in two fertilizers, check carefully to see which really is the better buy. Here's an example: A 50-pound bag of 8-8-8 costs $4. A similar bag of 13-13-13 costs $5. The 8-8-8 has 4 pounds of nitrogen (8% of 50 pounds), so the cost is $1 a pound. The 13-13-13 has 6.5 pounds of nitrogen (13% of 50 pounds) or 77 cents per pound of nitrogen. If all you are interested in is the nitrogen, the more expensive bag is the better buy.

Other Nutrients

As many as 16 other nutrients are needed for healthy plants. When present in fertilizer they, too, are noted on the label. The secondary elements—calcium, magnesium, and sulfur—are found in most soils. Micronutrients, including boron, chlorine, copper, iron, manganese, and zinc, are vital to plant vigor and are needed in tiny amounts. Some fertilizers are jazzed up with particular micronutrients, such as extra iron in azalea/camellia food. Splotchy pale green to yellow areas between the leaf veins (called "chlorosis") in these plants sometimes can be corrected this way. Other times calcium, in the safe form of gypsum, is needed.

Unless your soil is deficient in secondary or micronutrients, there is usually no reason to pay extra money for them. However, it won't hurt to include the extra nutrients in a regular feeding program to keep plants healthy.

Secondary and Micronutrient Deficiencies

How do you know if your soil really is low in vital secondary nutrients or micronutrients? Plants can tell you this, too. Magnesium is mobile in plants, so older leaves are affected first, turning yellow between the veins.

If the tips of growing shoots and young leaf margins die, often after first cupping or curling, the plant lacks sufficient calcium. Calcium is immobilized in plants, so when they have too little, new growth suffers. Iron is immobile, too, so the interveinal yellowing that is a sign of iron deficiency occurs first on younger leaves.

Soil pH and Nutrient Absorption

Before dashing outdoors to drench the soil beneath a hungry plant with fertilizer, consider that the necessary elements may be present in the soil, but the plant itself, for some reason, is not absorbing them. The pH (acidity) of the soil must be in the correct range for some plants to take up a vital element.

Azaleas, rhododendrons, and blueberries must grow in a soil with a pH of 4 to 5 to use available iron. Most other garden plants absorb nutrients best in slightly acid soils with pH of about 6.5. Some perennials, such as campanulas, lisianthus, lilacs, peonies, and scabiosas, are better able to pull out needed nutrients in soil with a neutral or slightly basic pH.

There is nothing magic about pH, but its impact is most obvious in the common summer *Hydrangea macrophylla* where the bluest blooms occur in the most acid soils when aluminum is more available to the plant. To change the flowers of hydrangeas from pink to blue, add 1/4 cup wettable sulfur per 3' plant. To make the flowers a more vivid blue, dissolve 1 teaspoon alum in a gallon of water and drench the soil around the plant. To change color from blue to pink, apply 1/4 cup hydrated lime to a 3' plant. Dolomitic lime can be used, but the results will not be as immediate or dramatic.

If you have any questions about the pH or nutrient content of your soil, have it tested by your County Extension Service.

Choosing Fertilizers

Is it better to apply a liquid fertilizer or one in granular form? There are advantages to each. Choose liquids for quick absorption and quick results. Liquids can be applied with a watering can or hose-end sprayer to roots or foliage, but because the nutrients are at low concentrations, liquid fertilizers must be applied consistently and often. They are best used, in my opinion, as a supplement to granular feeding.

Although I get a slower response from granules, I know they will be more effective for a longer time. Teamed together, the plant is assured of receiving high quality, constant nutrition.

There are two basic categories of fertilizers—organic and inorganic or chemical. Organic fertilizers are made from materials that are or were alive, such as compost, dried cow or chicken manure, guano, or fish meal. The percentages of the major nutrients in organic products do tend to be lower than their chemical counterparts, and the nutrients may be released more slowly, so they may not provide the quick fix you need for an ailing plant. However, organic fertilizers improve the soil's structure and aeration, increasing its ability to hold moisture and creating an environment conducive to the growth of microorganisms which aid in the absorption of nutrients. The labels of organic fertilizers, like chemical fertilizers, are required by law to list nutrient composition.

Two granular chemical fertilizers popular with Atlanta gardeners are Nursery Special and Osmocote. Nursery Special, 12-6-6, used in small amounts is a good fertilizer that adds needed nitrogen to plants for growth, not flowering. Osmocote, 14-14-14, is a time-release fertilizer that lasts for about three months. It's great on pansies and other annuals and just about everything else. It is less expensive than bulb food and probably works about as well on bulbs, too. Many of us use a liquid fertilizer with a higher middle number in combination with Osmocote to spike heavier flowering on annuals and perennials.

Use a plant starter, 3-10-3, to help plants adjust to transplanting by encouraging the development of healthy roots. Long-acting or slow-release fertilizers added to annuals and perennials at planting will keep them growing well, particularly if you don't have time for monthly fertilizing or should happen to neglect this task a month or two. Slow-release fertilizers work for three to six months.

Fertilizing Bulbs

To produce good flowers from bulbs, use either a balanced fertilizer like 8-8-8 or 10-l0-10 or bulb booster food, 9-9-6, twice a year. Bulb booster food is a slow-release or time-release fertilizer that is particularly good to use when planting bulbs. A balanced fertilizer used at planting may be washed away by rain before the bulb roots begin to grow and can reach it. Time-release fertilizers work well, but since bulb roots are short and may miss the fertilizer, I apply bulb booster immediately after blooming and again when foliage reappears, usually in spring. Sometimes I even apply a light feeding in fall when foliage of spring bloomers has already emerged.

This heavy feeding schedule has produced better flowering and reflowering of my bulbs, except in the case of *Iris reticula*, where heavy feeding can produce too much foliage which completely overwhelms the blooms. Caution: Never allow the bulb fertilizer to come in direct contact with the bulbs. When planting, mix the bulb food thoroughly with the soil.

The fertilizer mystery is solved!

Chapter Seven

A Seasonal Schedule

by

Avis Aronovitz

A Seasonal Work Schedule

Certain gardening tasks, such as planting, fertilizing, watering, weeding, and pruning, are best performed according to a schedule. But if your work or family responsibilities keep you from gardening during the optimal week or month designated for a particular chore by a garden expert in a book or on a local radio show, don't despair. All is not lost; your garden is not doomed.

Plants are resilient, and they can adapt to your schedule. You may not win blue ribbons at the flower show or your neighborhood's "yard of the month" award, but you can still have a pleasing landscape and garden.

In general, avoid working in your garden when foliage is wet to avoid spreading disease from one plant to the next. Don't plant or work in wet soil either. It compacts the soil.

Planting

Soil preparation before planting is so important that if you cannot take the time to prepare the soil properly, skip this season and wait for the next planting opportunity. (See Chapter 1, "Getting Your Garden Started" for information on soil preparation.) While you're waiting, do your homework. Study this book and those publications listed in the Recommended Reading section (Appendix B) so you can choose appropriate plants and learn what they need. If you do, you won't enrich the soil—expending time, money, and effort—only to discover that the rose campion or nasturtium you planted prefers a lean environment and will produce foliage but few flowers.

Planting Times

There are conflicting opinions regarding the best planting time in Atlanta. Those who favor fall planting will tell you that planting in late September, October, or early November allows the plant to get a head start on forming roots, which eventually will support a better plant.

Proponents of fall planting also say that winter rains make watering less necessary, but winter rains and cold temperatures may cause rotting even when good drainage is thought to be present. The alternating cold and warm temperatures in winter months can be equally destructive to plants, and extreme cold can cause the plant to be heaved out of the ground.

Spring planting may be done in February, March, or April—even into May if the weather doesn't warm up too fast. Planting in spring means that you have to babysit the new plants, making certain that they are watered to their individual needs—unless, of course, it is a rainy spring. Unfortunately, new plants can get zapped easily by a sudden spring freeze because their roots have not yet adjusted to their new home.

Vines Botanical Gardens Executive Director Allen Sistrunk says that 20 years of gardening in Atlanta has taught him that any shrub, perennial, or tree planted between November and March requires up to 70% less establishment maintenance than those planted any other time of the year.

Most Atlanta gardeners plant in both spring and fall. Sometimes plant availability determines planting time, and since you should never plant when the soil is wet enough to form clumps, weather conditions are a major influence on planting time. Some plants can only be planted in a particular season and, because of their unique growing cycle, resent being disturbed at any other time.

Logic also governs planting times. Fall blooming bulbs, like colchicums, autumn crocus, and sternbergia must be put into the ground in late August or early September to bloom in September and October. Spring blooming bulbs should be planted as soon as they arrive, which is usually October or November. (See Chapter 17, "Bulbs.") Madonna lilies (Lilium candidum) must be planted in fall.

Many mail-order catalogs specify certain perennials for fall planting only, and the catalog purveyors give you the opportunity to specify, within the constraints of a few months, when you want your order shipped. This allows you to select a time when there might be a break in your own schedule.

Remember to schedule certain cool-growing annuals for planting in the fall or very early spring (See Chapter 16, "Annuals"). Plants of questionable hardiness (those that might not survive a late spring freeze) must be planted after the final spring frost. Summer blooming bulbs go into the ground then. February is a good time to plant some cool-growing annuals, such as flax, poppies, or stock. Late March is a good time to plant any perennials that are at the garden centers. Some-times annuals such as geraniums, petunias, and marigolds will appear at the garden centers before the possibility of final frost passes. A word of caution: Even though the weather seems warm and spring-like, do not succumb to the urge to buy and plant these annuals. They could be heavily damaged or killed by a sudden cold snap.

Plant dogwoods in March for best growth response. Do not plant dogwoods too deeply, and mulch them to conserve moisture during dry periods.

Dead of winter and hottest summer days are not good times to plant anything, even if we're enjoying a stretch of mild weather. If you plant in summer, you'll have to construct a shade structure and water three times a day. If you plant in winter, you have to face the possibility of having to dispose of lots of dead, frozen plants.

Transplanting Established Plants

Major garden renovation is best done in late September or early October. The ideal time to transplant trees and shrubs is before they leaf out, giving roots time to adjust before leaves start demanding food and water. Complete transplanting of trees and overgrown shrubs by March. Removing one-fourth of the top growth at transplanting time helps shrubs cope with transplant shock.

Divide spring-blooming perennials, pulmonaria, dicentra, lamiastrum, astilbe, and phlox in the fall. Divide hostas just as their leaves begin to fade; early spring division is also acceptable. Divide fall-blooming chry-santhemum, aster, solidago, and eupatorium in mid-March or early April. Daylilies can be divided any time, even in the heat of summer, but don't over-water them after transplanting. Divide bearded iris in July and August.

Maintenance

If liriope has cold damage or appears scruffy, cut it back in early spring with a lawn mower or string trimmer or, for a neater appearance, use hand shears. Cut back winter damaged foliage of helleborus in early spring to encourage larger clumps. Garden phlox can be cut back in late spring to prevent it from growing too tall.

Deadhead black-eyed Susan, shasta daisy, coreopsis, and purple coneflower to extend bloom time into fall. Veronica, penstemon, and spigelia will bloom a second time with deadheading. Garden phlox should also should be deadheaded in late summer to remove spent blooms and to encourage secondary flowering. Pinch mums continually until July 4 for many-branched, compact plants with more flowers later in the season, when they will last longer.

Crape myrtles can be made to bloom longer by cutting off spent flowers before seeds are formed. A second flowering should occur that season.

Verbenas grown as annuals bloom on new growth (the ends of stems) throughout the season. Cutting them back by half in late June or early July rejuvenates fall flower production **and** helps control spider mites without spraying.

Do not cut back bulb-type perennials like *Liatris* 'Kobold' early in the season. If you do, you'll have no flowers that year.

Watering

If plants undergo too much stress because of lack of water at any time during the year, including winter, you will lose them. However, over-watering and poor drainage will do as much damage as under-watering. (See Chapter 1, "Getting Your Garden Started.")

You can help evergreens through a severe winter by keeping them well watered. When a hard freeze is predicted, cover questionably hardy evergreens with bushel baskets, or use a deep mulch to create dead air space around the plant.

Weeding

Weeding is a task that can be scheduled for your convenience, but don't put it off until weeds overwhelm you, the plants in your garden, and your neighbor's patience. Plants can't thrive when they're competing with other plants or weeds. Sometimes a low-growing weed serves as a mulch to cool the roots of a special perennial (you can try to convince yourself this is true).

Learn to recognize common weeds so that you don't accidentally remove young seedling perennials or annuals that have reseeded. Manual removal of weeds is best. If you do use chemical weed killers, read the directions thoroughly and apply them carefully. Remember weed killers can kill good plants and lawn grass as well as the weeds.

Pest Control

Spray when an insect or disease problem is obvious. Preventive care is important too. (See Chapter 5, "Pests and Diseases.") April and May are the time to apply insecticides to prevent white flies and spider mites. In October or when temperatures are in the appropriate range, apply Volck Oil to prevent scale on camellias and sasanquas.

Fertilizing

What fertilizers are best for Atlanta gardens and what is a good feeding schedule? Every longtime Atlanta gardener has a different answer, but each will tell you that fertilizers won't help much if the soil has not been properly prepared.

It is better to err on the side of underfeeding rather than overfeeding your plants. Plants, like people, need a well-balanced diet but not too much food. Too much fertilizer can damage the root system, severely injuring or killing your plant. For information on understanding fertilizer labels, types of fertilizers, and identifying nutrient deficiencies, see Chapter 6, "The Fertilizer Mystery."

Seasonal Feeding

Local landscape architect Nancy Beckemeyer insists that by applying a high phosphorus (4-16-16) fertilizer to rhododendrons on about March 15, she ensures heavy budding the following year.

A good fertilizing schedule for summer, beginning in April and continuing through August, would be an application of Osmocote at planting or in the spring and an application of liquid fertilizer with a high phosphorus content every four to six weeks to encourage abundant flowering in annuals or perennials.

By summer's end, insects, disease, and hot sun have taken their toll on plants, so other problems can often be mistaken for nutrient deficiencies. However, if you are convinced the plant's sickly color is due to an inadequate nutrient supply, a quick-fix fertilizer may be the solution.

Cut back annuals in August and fertilize for an outstanding autumn display with a readily soluble chemical fertilizer mixed with water. In late August, I often use a 12-55-6 fertilizer to deliver phosphorous quickly to tender *Evolvulus* 'Blue Daze,' datura, ageratum, Swan River daisy, and any other annuals slowing down flower production. Most perennials are best left alone until early spring.

Bulbs like muscari (grape hyacinth), ipheion (starflower), scilla, and *Arum italicum*, where foliage appears in late summer, do well with bulb food in fall. Fall fertilizing appears to increase flowering of helleborus.

Use Nursery Special in January on rhododendrons and other spring blooming evergreen shrubs. I also use Nursery Special on crape myrtles in late February or early March after pruning. Another application in April or June is helpful, too. Other woody plants can get some Nursery Special as early as January if the weather is agreeable.

Additionally, I use Nursery Special on azaleas, sasanquas, and camellias immediately following blooming. Azalea/camellia food has a similar formulation, 11-5-5, so the two can be used almost interchangeably.

Pansies planted with long-acting Osmocote in late October or November need some high phosphorus fertilizer, like Super Bloom, every six to eight weeks and probably could use more Osmocote by February, too. When your pansies' flowering slows down in early spring, add more high-phosphorus fertilizer.

Pruning

Prune plants that bloom on old wood after flowering. Spring-flowering plants such as evergreen azalea, all rhododendrons, spirea, weigelia, forsythia, viburnum, quince, 'Lady Banksia' rose, *Akebia quinata*, and *Gelsemium sempervirens* bloom on old wood. They should be pruned immediately following flowering and before July 15. If you prune these spring-flowering plants in early spring, you will not hurt the plant, but it won't flower that season. If you prune in summer after July 15, the plants will have developed next year's flower buds and, again, you will reduce next spring's flowering. Some plants, such as *Abeliophyllum distichum* (white forsythia), need hard pruning as soon as they have bloomed in order to produce flowers next spring.

Winter bloomers, such as dawn viburnum, hamamelis, and *Camellia japonica*, are pruned in early spring soon after flowering. Some clematis, like *C.* 'Candida' need pruning of dead wood down to healthy buds in March. A few clematis that bloom in summer and fall, like the sweet autumn clematis and *C.* 'Comtesse de Bouchard,' should be pruned yearly in the spring to 12" from the ground for best performance.

Prune plants that bloom on new growth in early spring. Summer and fall bloomers, including crape myrtles, spirea bumaldas and japonicas, butterfly bush (*Buddleia davidii*), caryopteris, and rose-of-Sharon should be pruned in late winter or very early spring prior to leaf break. *Callicarpa dichotoma,* a shrub with Chinese eggplant-shaped fruit in autumn and winter, performs best if cut back to 6" in late winter or early spring. The woody vine *Campsis radicans,* which blooms on new wood, should receive severe pruning in late winter during dormancy to insure heavy blooming from late June through September. Do the same for *Aster carolinianus.*

Since the fall/winter bright coral red of the *Acer palmatum* 'Sango Kaku' (coral bark maple) is only present in young stems, this tree benefits from heavy late winter or early spring pruning to promote new growth. *Cornus serica* 'Silver and Gold' with its variegated leaves in summer and yellow stems in winter also should be cut back in late winter because the best color is produced on young stems.

Prune hybrid roses in late February. The Greater Atlanta Rose Society conducts a class each year on the last Sunday in February at the Atlanta Botanical Garden. Plan to attend if you want to learn to prune roses properly.

Hydrangeas planted in the right place require no pruning. Prune new wood bloomers like *H. paniculata* 'Tardiva' and 'Grandiflora' (often called PeeGee hydrangea) prior to leafing out in the spring. For old wood bloomers, thin out old canes to ground level prior to leaf break.

Certain fall-blooming perennials, such as *Helianthus angustifolius* and boltonia, need to be pruned back by 1/3 to 1/2 at mid-season to make them sturdier and shorter.

Plants not grown for flowers and shade trees with diseased or broken limbs are best pruned when dormant. Do not prune any plant in late summer or fall, except lightly for the sake of grooming and appearance. Heavy pruning brings on tender new growth that will be killed when frigid weather strikes.

For general information about pruning, see Chapter 8.

Chapter Eight

Pruning

by

Avis Aronovitz

The Kindest Cut of All

Pruning is an opportunity to improve the performance of your shrubs and plants, and proper pruning is the kindest cut of all.

There are several reasons to prune:

1. To remove unwanted growth, such as dead, broken, or undisciplined branches and base suckers.

2. To stimulate growth or flowering.

3. To restrain size.

4. To rejuvenate an overgrown, ignored plant.

5. To constrain a plant to a specific shape.

6. To groom, to remove spent flowers and seeds, and prevent disease spread.

When pruning, try to preserve the plant's natural height and form. This saves work and makes the plant's appearance more aesthetically pleasing.

How to Prune

Which tool? Use hand pruners for branches 1/2" or less in diameter and loppers for branches 1/2" to 2" thick. Anything larger requires a pruning saw. Use a telescoping pole saw for trimming or removing dead branches in trees. If you have a formal hedge or tall screen, you will need to invest in hedge trimmers.

How much? Be careful to cut back to 1/4" above any growth bud. If you leave more stem, it can rot; if you prune more closely, you can cause bud damage. Slightly angle the cut to prevent rain water from collecting on the cut. Always prune back to an outward-facing bud so the new growth points away from the plant's center. This will open up the plant and prevent rubbing or crossing of branches. When pruning a hedge, shear the hedge so that it is slightly wider at the base than at the top so sunlight can reach the lower branches. Parts of the hedge that don't receive sunlight can thin and even die, leaving the hedge leggy and bare.

Never prune more than one third of a plant at one time. Some plants, like azaleas, resent severe pruning. Evergreen shrubs like hollies can be kept compact or returned to a compact size with heavy pruning—one third each year. (If your evergreen shrub looks dreadful after pruning, you have probably done it correctly.)

Deciduous shrubs, such as forsythia, spirea, weigelia, and mock orange and cane-type evergreens such as abelia, eleagnus, nandina, and mahonia can be renewed by cutting one-third of the plant's oldest canes to the ground for a period of three years. New growth will appear soon after each pruning, and the plant won't look ugly. A skillfully pruned, continuously well-maintained shrub may appear only slightly smaller or less dense after pruning, so it may be difficult to detect that it has been worked on at all.

To confine pines and hemlocks to screening size desired, use hand pruners or hedge trimmers to shorten new growth in the spring when it is soft. Never cut back farther than the innermost needles.

When to Prune

For information on when to prune, see Chapter 7, "A Seasonal Schedule."

To Avoid Pruning

To avoid pruning, select plants according to their ultimate size. For example, choose the *dwarf* variety, not the standard form, of Burford holly if you want a hedge 6-8' tall. In the same situation, Leyland cypress would be a poor choice because it would require continuous pruning. Check the ultimate height and width of plants before you plant. Height and size information can be found on the plant's label or tag and in many of the charts in this book.

Part Two

Choosing Plants

Chapter Nine

Foundation Plants

by
Nancy Beckemeyer
and Dottie Myers

Best Foundation Plants for Atlanta

Billowing boxwoods that hid dogs sleeping under the verandahs were the traditional foundation plantings of southern plantations. A century later, our desire to manipulate our environment resulted in sculpted, aerospace-inspired shapes around the foundations of our homes. A drive through any neighborhood reveals the outdated "rockets" standing at attention on the corners of houses and rounded "planet" balls orbiting the house. Come down to earth! Nobody has time to sculpt shrubs, and the damage done by shearing can be fatal to them. Proclaim your freedom! Throw away your electric hedge clippers.

Foundation plants should accent the architecture of your home, not dominate it. Plan your foundation plantings carefully. They are the backdrop and the beginning of your entire landscape. You probably will live with them a long time. Consider particularly the design principles of texture and contrast. For example, combine the bold leaf of a *Rhododendron maximum* with the needle-like foliage of *Cephalotaxus harringtonia,* or the shiny green leaf of *Prunus laurocerasus* 'Otto Luyken' with the rounded matte finish of an *Ilex crenata* 'Helleri.' Be sensitive to plants' foliage and flower colors. Know the environmental factors that will impact their growth—sun, shade, moisture tolerance, and soil conditions—as well as their mature heights. Select foundation plants so the mature shrubs do not cover windows or become out of scale with the house. Perhaps one of the many dwarf and compact varieties now available would be a good choice.

Usually, evergreen plants are used in foundation plantings to give year-round effect; however, deciduous shrubs with evergreens used as a backdrop or groundcover can also make an effective design. Possible deciduous selections are the low Japanese barberry 'Crimson Pygmy' for red foliage color, the spirea 'Goldmound' for wonderful, yellow color; the hydrangea 'Annabelle' for dried flower color in winter; and the fothergilla 'Mount Airy' for spectacular fall color.

Remember the principles of architect Mies van de Rohe, "Less is more" and "Elegance via simplicity." To avoid detracting from the design of your home, limit the number of shrub varieties used. A simple boxwood at each corner and an evergreen groundcover in between can provide a clean, well-maintained, elegant foundation planting.

If your home is surrounded by an overgrown tangle of shrubs, be daring and rip them out. You will feel better, your house will look better, and your neighbors will have something to talk about. Visit your local nursery and discover new shrub varieties. If a salesperson tries to tell you to put something tall on each corner and round "planet" balls in between, smile knowingly and walk away. You have met a space alien trying to recreate the "rocket" landscapes of the 60s and 70s. It's your house; express yourself. Think and plan before you plant, and have fun with your foundation plants.

The following charts will help you select foundation shrubs that will be the appropriate size in five to 10 years. There are listings for shrubs under 3', from 3-6', and over 6' in height.

FOUNDATION PLANTS
Shrubs under 3' in height

Botanical Name	Common Name	Exposure	5th-Year Ht.	Comments
Abelia x grandiflora 'Sherwood' A. 'Edward Goucher'	Dwarf Abelia 'Sherwood' and 'Edward Goucher'	Full sun	3' 3-4'	Blooms May-June till frost; do not shear; 'Sherwood' has white flowers; 'Edward Goucher' has pink flowers; fine texture
Aucuba japonica 'Nana'	Dwarf Aucuba	Shade	3-4'	Showy fruit in winter; coarse texture
Azaleas: Girard Group	Silver Sword Azalea	Sun/shade	18"	Variegated foliage; dark pink blossom; Post Properties landscaping favorite
North Tisbury 'Pink Pancake' 'Red Fountain'		Semi-shade	Low, prostrate	More beautiful with age; extends bloom season to June; good under basement window, in contemporary landscape
Robin Hill 'Hilda Niblett' 'White Moon'		Sun/part shade	low growing varieties only	Perfect mounds; large blooms; good color selection; withstands western afternoon sun; 'Hilda Niblett' is pink/rose; 'White Moon' is ruffled
Satsuki	Gumpo	Part shade	Low, dwarf	Protect from afternoon sun
Cephalotaxus harringtonia var. drupacea or prostrata	Dwarf Japanese Plum Yew	Part sun/shade	2-3'	Needs good drainage; nice fine needle foliage
Chamaecyparis obtusa 'Nana Gracilis'	Dwarf Hinoki Cypress	Sun/part shade	18"	Handsome conifer for foliage effect
Cotoneaster dammeri 'Coral Beauty'	Bearberry Cotoneaster	Sun	1-2'	Covers large area in short time; free-fruiting; coral red fruit

FOUNDATION PLANTS
Shrubs under 3' in height

Botanical Name	Common Name	Exposure	5th-Year Ht.	Comments
Erica carnea x 'Springwood Pink'	Heath	Sun/part shade	2'	Blooms in winter
Ilex cornuta 'Carissa'	Carissa Holly	Sun/part shade	3'	Lustrous, waxy deep green leaves with white margin
Ilex crenata 'Helleri'	Helleri Holly	Sun	2-3'	Needs good drainage; not drought tolerant
Ilex vomitoria 'Schillings'	Schillings Holly	Sun	3-4'	Tolerates moist soil
Juniperus horizontalis 'Blue Rug'	Blue Rug Juniper	Sun	6"-1'	Hot, dry conditions; must have 3'+ spacing
J. h. 'Bar Harbor'	Bar Harbor Juniper	Sun	6"-1'	Hot, dry conditions; must have 3'+ spacing
J. h. 'Prince of Wales'	Prince of Wales Juniper	Sun	6"	Blue-green foliage with purple cast in winter
Kalmia latifolia 'Elf'	Mountain Laurel 'Elf'	Part sun/shade	2-3'	Compact; nice foliage; needs good drainage
Nandina domestica 'Firepower'	Dwarf Nandina 'Firepower'	Sun	1-2'	Brilliant red winter color
N. d. 'Gulf Stream'	Compact N. 'Gulf Stream'	Sun	2-3'	Red winter color
N. d. 'Harbour Dwarf'	Harbour Dwarf Nandina	Sun	18"-3'	Red winter color; red berries and white flowers

FOUNDATION PLANTS—cont'd
Shrubs under 3' in height

Botanical Name	Common Name	Exposure	5th-Year Ht.	Comments
Prunus laurocerasus 'Otto Luyken'	Otto Luyken Laurel	Sun or shade	3-4'	Shiny green foliage; upright habit; good drainage
Rhododendron dwarf hybrids	Rhodo-dendrons	Part sun/shade	3'	See Chapter 14 for specific varieties
Yucca filamentosa 'Gold Sword'	Variegated Adam's Needle	Sun	3'	Bold accent shrub

Botanical Name	Common Name	Exposure	5th-Year Ht.	Comments
Aucuba japonica	Aucuba	Shade	5'	Green and variegated forms
Elaeagnus pungens 'Simonii'	Simonii Elaeagnus	Sun/shade	3-4'	Compact form; thornless, silver-backed foliage
Ilex cornuta 'Burfordii Nana'	Dwarf Burford Holly	Sun/part shade	4' pruned	In full sun can become quite tall if not kept pruned; good berries
Ilex cornuta 'Needlepoint'	Needlepoint Holly	Sun/part shade	3-4'	More delicate look than Burford Holly
Ilex crenata 'Compacta'	Compacta Holly	Sun	3-5'	Ordinary, dependable, tough, inexpensive shrub
Ilex glabra 'Shamrock'	Shamrock Holly	Sun/shade	3-4'	Good for wet areas; spineless holly
Ilex vomitoria 'Nana'	Dwarf Yaupon Holly	Sun/part shade	3-5'	Fruit hidden in foliage; adaptable, tough shrub
Illicium floridanum	Florida Anise Tree	Shade	5-6'	Choose shrub with green apple leaf aroma
Illicium parviflorum	Small Anise Tree	Sun/shade	5-6'	One of the best screening evergreens for shade
Juniperus chinensis 'Sea Green'	Sea Green Juniper	Sun	3-5'	Good dark green foliage; spreading, but dense
Kalmia latifolia 'Olympic Fire,' 'Snowdrift,' 'Nipmuck,' 'Carousel'	Mountain Laurel	Part shade	4-5'	Needs excellent drainage; plant following instructions for rhododendrons; see Chapter 14

FOUNDATION PLANTS—cont'd
Shrubs 3' to 6' in height

Botanical Name	Common Name	Exposure	5th-Year Ht.	Comments
Loropetalum chinense	Loropetalum	Sun/part shade	4-6'	Fragrant, feathery blooms in early spring
Mahonia bealei	Leatherleaf Mahonia	Shade	3-4'	Coarse holly-like foliage; bright yellow blooms in winter followed by light blue fruit
Mahonia aquifolium	Oregon Grape Holly	Shade	3-4'	Softer look than *M. bealei*
Nandina domestica	Heavenly Bamboo	Sun	3-5'	Brilliant red fruit; red winter foliage if in sun
Osmanthus heterophyllus 'Rotundifolius'	Roundleaf Holly Osmanthus	Sun/part shade	3-4'	Attractive green foliage with wavy margins; fragrant flowers
Pieris japonica 'Valley Valentine', 'Mountain Fire'	Pieris	Part shade	3-4'	Needs good drainage; beautiful bell-shaped flowers in clusters
Prunus laurocerasus 'Schipkaensis'	Schip Laurel	Sun/part shade	4-5'	Wide vase shape
Prunus laurocerasus 'Zabeliana'	Zabel Laurel	Part shade/sun	4-5'	Wide arching habit; needs good drainage
Rhododendron maximum	Rosebay Rhododendron	Part shade	4-6'	Native to Georgia; slow grower; requires excellent drainage

FOUNDATION PLANTS
Shrubs 3' to 6' in height

Botanical Name	Common Name	Exposure	5th-Year Ht.	Comments
Rhododendron minus	Piedmont Rhododendron	Part shade	3-5'	Compact
Rhododendron Hybrids See Chapter 14				
Ternstroemia gymnanthera (Cleyera japonica)	Cleyera	Sun/shade	4-5'	Shiny green foliage; reddish new foliage; may be killed in severe frost
Viburnum tinus 'Spring Bouquet'	Laurustinus	Sun/part shade	4'	Evergreen; late winter bloom

FOUNDATION PLANTS

Evergreen shrubs over 6' in height for use on windowless walls or for screening

Botanical Name	Common Name	Exposure	5th-Year Ht.	Comments
Agarista populifolia	Florida Leucothoe	Shade	8-10'	Arching, irregular habit
Camellia japonica	Japanese Camellia	Part shade	8-15'	'Debutante' popular. See Chapter 11, "Camellias"
Cedrus deodara	Deodar Cedar	Sun	40-70'	Graceful conifer
Cryptomeria japonica 'Yoshino'	Japanese Cedar	Sun/part shade	30-50'	Minimal foliage die back; retains green foliage; conifer
x Cupressocyparis leylandii	Leyland Cypress	Sun	40-50'	Needs good airflow; not stress tolerant; rapid grower; easily kept at lower heights
Ilex 'Nellie R. Stevens'	Nellie R. Stevens Holly	Sun	10-20'	Pyramidal habit; prolific red berries; fast-growing holly
Ilex x attenuata 'Fosteri'	Foster's Holly	Sun	15-25'	Needs selective pruning to give fullness; upright conical habit
Ilex x attenuata 'Savannah'	Savannah Holly	Sun	30-40'	Needs selective pruning; upright loose habit
Ilex latifolia	Lusterleaf Holly	Sun/part shade	15-25'	Large holly leaf 4-8" long; lots of red berries
Magnolia grandiflora 'Bracken's Brown Beauty'	Bracken's Brown Beauty Magnolia	Sun	30-40' 15-25' wide	Brown back leaf

FOUNDATION PLANTS
Evergreen shrubs over 6' in height for use on windowless walls or for screening

Botanical Name	Common Name	Exposure	5th-Year Ht.	Comments
Magnolia grandiflora 'Claudia Wannamaker'	Claudia Wannamaker Magnolia	Sun	30-40' 15-25' wide	Brown back leaf; blooms as a young tree
Magnolia grandiflora 'Little Gem'	Little Gem Magnolia	Sun	15-20' 10-15' wide	Bushy, rounded shape; free blooms all summer into fall; smaller leaves; nice espaliered to a wall
Myrica cerifera	Southern Waxmyrtle	Sun/part shade	8-10'	Nice as multi-stem tree form; aromatic foliage; tolerates moist soils
Osmanthus x fortunei	Fortune's Osmanthus	Sun/part shade	10-15'	Slow grower; white fragrant flower; hardier than *Osmanthus fragrans*
Pinus thunbergiana	Japanese Black Pine	Sun	20-40'	Irregular; pyramidal
Pinus virginiana	Virginia Pine	Sun	15-40'	Inexpensive screen; retains lower branches; tolerates poor soil
Prunus caroliniana	Carolina Cherry Laurel	Sun/part shade	15-20'	Retains lower limbs as it matures
Tsuga canadensis	Canadian Hemlock	Sun/shade	30-50'	Needs good drainage; not drought tolerant; not pollution tolerant
Viburnum x pragense	Prague Viburnum	Sun/part shade	8-10'	One of the few evergreen viburnums; responds well to selective pruning to keep dense

Chapter Ten

Flowering Shrubs

by

Mildred Pinnell

Best Flowering Shrubs for Atlanta

Shrubs form the backbone of the garden, whether used as a foundation planting for a house, as the backbone to a perennial border, or in a mass by themselves. One of the best things about our climate is the large number of flowering shrubs that are available for use in Atlanta gardens. Whether evergreen or deciduous, it is possible to have a shrub in flower in your garden each month of the year.

Once established in the landscape, shrubs require little maintenance except fertilization and occasional pruning. Shrubs are best planted in the fall, when they have time to establish good, healthy root systems for the coming year's growing season. Fertilize with a granular, all-purpose garden fertilizer (8-8-8 or 10-10-10) in mid-spring. This can be supplemented by top-dressing with manure (1-2") during the winter season.

It is best to consult a reference book, such as Dr. Michael Dirr's *Manual of Woody Landscape Plants,* to determine the proper time for pruning a shrub. In general, prune early to mid-season flowering shrubs after they flower. Summer flowering shrubs often bloom on new growth and can be pruned in late winter. See also Chapter 7, "A Seasonal Schedule."

Choosing Flowering Shrubs

The key to the successful use of shrubs in the landscape is to carefully consider the site and the ultimate size of the shrub. The following charts are divided into sun-loving and shade-tolerant shrubs for use in the Atlanta area.

Many excellent local nurseries and garden centers offer a wide selection of shrubs for use in the home landscape. These include Pikes, Hastings Nature and Garden Center, Buck Jones, Goza Nursery, Greenhouse Nursery (Japanese maples a specialty), Homeplace Garden, Piccadilly Farms, Wild Wood Farms, Land Arts, and Wilkerson Mill Gardens. (For addresses, see Appendix A.)

But don't be afraid to order shrubs from a mail-order nursery. While the plants may be small (1 gal. or less), many treasures can be found. See Appendix A.

BEST-SUN-LOVING-FLOWERING SHRUBS

Common Name	Botanical	Height	Flower	Bloom Time	Comments
Butterfly Bush	Buddleia davidii	5'	cultivars range from white to pink to dark purple	Late May through frost	Deciduous
Winterhazel	Corylopsis spicata	8'	yellow, fragrant	Late March to April	Deciduous; good yellow fall color
Virginia Sweetspire	Itea virginica 'Henry's Garnet'	6'	Arching branches terminate in 8" white flower spikes	May	Outstanding claret-red fall color
Natchez Mockorange	Philadelphus x 'Natchez'	12'	fragrant 3" white	May	Remove old canes from center to keep in shape
Mohawk Viburnum	Viburnum x 'Mohawk'	6'	pink in bud, opening to white, fragrant	April	Glossy dark green foliage; National Arboretum introduction
Blueberry	Vaccinium corymbosum	6'	white	Early spring	Produces edible fruit; brilliant orange fall color
Wintersweet	Chimonanthus praecox	15'	yellow, fragrant	January	Good yellow fall color; benefits from part shade

BEST SUN-LOVING FLOWERING SHRUBS cont'd

Common Name	Botanical	Height	Flower	Bloom Time	Comments
Rose of Sharon	*Hibiscus syriacus* 'Diana'	6'	white, 3"	June-August	Dark green glossy foliage; National Arboretum introduction
Chinese Abelia	*Abelia chinensis*	6'	large fragrant white flower clusters	July-September	Semi-evergreen; attracts butterflies
Inkberry	*Ilex glabra*	8'	insignificant	n.a.	Loose, evergreen, suckering; prune to keep in shape; tolerates wet soil

Common Name	Botanical	Height	Flower	Bloom Time	Comments
Summersweet Clethra	*Clethra alnifolia*	8'	fragrant white spikes	July-August	Deciduous; tolerant of moist soil
	C. alnifolia 'Rosea'	8'	pink spikes		
	C. a. 'Humming-bird'	3'	white spikes		
Mt. Airy Fothergilla	*Fothergilla gardenii* 'Mt. Airy'	5'	white, bottle-brush shaped	Early spring	Deciduous; outstanding fall color (orange, yellow and red) persisting late in season
Oakleaf Hydrangea	*Hydrangea quercifolia*	8'	large terminal clusters, white fading to lavender	June- July	Deciduous, good fall color (red, purple, orange); cinnamon colored exfoliating bark
Florida Leucothoe	*Leucothoe (Agarista) populifolia*	12'	white	Mid-spring	Evergreen, arching shrub resembles shiny green bamboo
Witchhazel	*Hamamelis mollis* 'Pallida'	10'	fragrant pale yellow	Late February-March	Deciduous; good fall color
Winter Daphne	*Daphne odora* 'Aureo-marginata'	3'	fragrant pink	February	Evergreen; worth the effort of finding perfect, protected location with moist, well-drained, rich soil

BEST SHADE-TOLERANT FLOWERING SHRUBS cont'd

Common Name	Botanical	Height	Flower	Bloom Time	Comments
Henry's Illicium	*Illicium henryi*	12'	small, pink	Mid-spring	Excellent upright evergreen for shade
Bottlebrush Buckeye	*Aesculus parviflora*	8'	white spikes (to 15")	June	Deciduous; excellent yellow fall color
Dwarf Himalayan Sweet Box	*Sarcococca hookerana humilis*	8"	fragrant - a real treat	January-February	Tough, evergreen groundcover for dry shade, even under *Magnolia grandiflora*
Pink Loropetalum	*Loropetalum chinense var. rubrum*	12'	hot pink	Early spring, reblooms sporadically	Semi-evergreen; dark purple foliage is nice contrast to flowers

G.'R.A. Additional Recommendations

Acer palmatum (Japanese Maple)

Aesculus pavia (Red Buckeye)

Calycanthus floridus 'Athens' (Yellow-flowered Sweet Shrub)

Caryopteris x clandonensis (Blue Mist Shrub)

Chaenomeles speciosa (Flowering Quince)

Clerodendron trichotomum (Harlequin Glory Bower) Be aware—it quickly forms satellite trees. Use only in uncultivated areas.

Cotinus coggyria 'Royal Purple' (Smokebush)

Deutzia gracilis (Deutzia) Also dwarf variety *D. g.* 'Nikko'

Forsythia x intermedia cultivars (Forsythia)

Hamamelis x intermedia 'Arnold Promise' (Witchhazel)

Hydrangea spp. and hybrids Try all available. They all do well here. Recently, hydrangeas have become very popular in our area. Check with Wilkerson Mill Gardens for more information.

Lagerstroemia indica hybrids (Common Crape Myrtle) Select mildew-resistant varieties. Wide color and size choice

Kalmia latifolia 'Carousel' and *K. l.* 'Ostbo Red' (Mountain Laurel) Use same planting procedure as hybrid rhododendrons.

Syringa laciniata (Cutleaf Lilac) This and the following lilac do very well here. Fragrance is almost as delicious as the French or Persian varieties.

Syringa meyeri 'Palibin' (Meyer Lilac)

Viburnum x juddii (Judd Viburnum) *V. carlesii, V. x carlcephalum, V. x burkwoodii,* and *V. fragrans* are other good choices.

Vitex angus-castus (Chastetree) Summer-blooming shrub (July/August) 8-10' tall. Tolerates wet areas.

Weigelia florida (Weigelia)

Caution: *Pyrus calleryana* 'Bradford' (Bradford Pear) may have severe splitting from crotch in older trees. The tree may literally fall apart. Not recommended.

Sources for Flowering Shrubs

Sources in Georgia

Buck Jones

Goza Nursery

Greenhouse Nursery

Habersham Gardens

Land Arts, Inc.

Melton's Nursery

Wilkerson Mill Gardens

Mail Order Sources

Camellia Forest Nursery

Greer Gardens

Gossler Farms Nursery

Forest Farm

Piccadilly Farm

Wild Wood Farms

Woodlanders, Inc

Chapter Eleven

Camellias

by
Gary W. Spikula

Camellias in the Atlanta Area

One of the chief glories of a southern winter is the blooming of the camellia. No winter-blooming plant of the temperate zone is more spectacular, and no garden in Atlanta should be without this rose of winter, this queen of the winter garden.

We can grow beautiful camellias in Atlanta, but our cold weather sometimes is very near the limit many camellias can withstand. Most of the cultivated camellia varieties are rated hardy through USDA hardiness Zone 7 (Atlanta is in Zone 7), with an average minimum temperature of 0 to 10 degrees F. When temperatures dip to near zero, it's really tough on camellias, especially when the lows follow weeks of unseasonably mild weather. Because of the weather and our red clay soils, careful planting, culture, and variety selection are required to obtain optimal results.

Providing the Proper Microclimate

First in importance is providing the proper microclimate for your camellias. Microclimate applies to the climatic factors of a small area, such as that found on a certain exposure of a building or hedge, near a body of water, or even that found next to a rock in your rock garden. Various factors, including wind diversion and heat absorption and release, play into the survival of plants in the near vicinity.

Protect from Wind

The main microclimate condition for camellia prosperity, and even survival, is protection from the extremely cold northwesterly winter winds. These winds can be slowed down (decreasing the wind chill factor on your plants) by planting on the leeward side of buildings or hedges, or even by planting in woodland, where surrounding trees and other vegetation help block the wind.

Avoid Morning Sun

Another microclimate factor is the avoidance of morning sun. On cold, frosty mornings, early sun thaws the frozen blooms and leaves too quickly, resulting in far more browning of blooms and leaf burn than would occur otherwise. Camellias are really happiest as understory plants (under taller shrubs or trees that give protection), and dappled winter shade is ideal. Some people advise planting on a north wall, but this total lack of direct sun seems to cause delayed flowering—maybe not such a bad plan if one wants to extend the bloom season of a variety by planting in multiple exposures. My favorite place to plant camellias is in pine woodland, since the shade and wind protection are generally very good and because of the benefit of a beautiful and free pine straw mulch.

Mulch

Mulching increases moisture retention and eventual plant nutrition, and it also helps prevent winter damage by insulating tender root tissues from extreme cold. This insulation from mulching also helps provide more water (in a non-frozen form) that can be taken up by roots in times of cold, drying winds. One reason the winter of 1985 was so devastating to camellias and other broadleaf evergreens was that little rain had fallen that winter, and soil moisture was very low. When this was coupled with drying, subzero winds, our camellias were freeze-dried alive!

Water

Adequate water should be provided *year round*. Yes, we have droughts in winter too, and if conditions merit, pull the hoses back out.

Promoting Healthy Growth

General good health increases any plant's chances of survival. Good health can be maintained by providing proper soil conditions, fertilization, and pest control.

Camellias love acidic soil loaded with humus, as do azaleas and rhododendrons. Fortunately, our soils are usually of a suitable acidity, but we need to add lots of humus to the clay. Finely ground pine bark is long-lasting and excellent for this purpose. Be careful when planting a camellia to set it at the same depth it was growing in the pot or perhaps slightly higher. Planting too deeply will cause root rot to develop, either killing or stunting your plant.

Regular fertilization, especially in spring when new growth is just beginning, is also vital for the continued good health of your plants. Usually, a good slow-release food for acid-loving plants will do, like that used for azaleas or rhododendrons. (Scotts makes a good one.) But if your soil is already sufficiently acidic, you may want to try a more general, slow-release, shrub-type formula. (Sta-Green's Nursery Special is a good one.) Organic foods also are slow-release fertilizers. Try cottonseed meal, any compost, blood meal, fish emulsion, and well-rotted (broken down so it doesn't burn) manures. (Well-rotted manures make an excellent spring mulch, also.)

Pests and Problems

Probably the worst pest I have witnessed in Atlanta is tea scale. It is a tiny insect, usually found on the underside of the leaves, that yellows and mottles the foliage horribly and can even be fatal in cases of very heavy infestation. Various insecticides are available for controlling this pest, such as Volck Oil or Malathion. A home remedy recommended by local camellia expert Tom Troutman is to wash the leaves with Octagon soap.

Another serious problem for camellias is flower blight, caused by a fungus. Petals on fresh blossoms develop ugly brown patches, usually appearing near the center of the bloom and moving outward. There is also a darkening of the tiny veins in the flower from the infection. This is in contrast to the browning caused by cold or wind damage which usually forms on the outer edges of the blooms. A good preventive measure here is to remove the diseased blossoms, both from the bush and from the ground beneath, and either burn or deeply bury them (a foot or more deep). The fungus continues its life cycle on these dead blooms, and the spores that develop on the ground from the fallen blooms can continue to re-infect other plants even five years later.

Dieback, a fungal disease that attacks and kills twigs and branches, is another serious problem. The fungus usually gains access through any injuries to the branches via contact with splattering rain (or irrigation water) that contains the spores. The period of leaf fall in late spring is a very susceptible period, since the leaf scars from the fallen leaves allow ready access. There is a wide variation in the susceptibility to dieback among the various species and varieties of camellias. The sasanqua and reticulata species seem especially susceptible, as are particular japonica varieties. Selecting dieback-resistant varieties and minimizing the surface area of damaged wood on your plants can help prevent dieback.

These problems, along with all the other critters and diseases of camellias, can usually be controlled by the vast arsenal at your local nursery. Consult your favorite nursery or extension service office for help with diagnoses and recommendations on what to do for a particular problem. There are also many good books available on insect and disease control.

Personally, I never spray unless it is a life or death situation for a very special plant. (It is definitely survival of the fittest in my garden.) I don't want to breathe the chemicals. Also, remember that these plagues often come in cycles, and Mother Nature usually provides a way of balancing things out.

Selecting Camellias

Try to get camellias growing on their own roots, not grafted, if you possibly can. The vast root systems of many camellias will survive even abnormally cold temperatures and can sprout gorgeous plants again if the top growth has been killed. But if your plant has been grafted, all you will have is whatever that root stock happened to be—not the prized variety you planted.

Select as healthy a plant as you can find. And also, for a faster effect in the garden, it is wise to get as large a specimen as you can afford. Many camellia varieties are very slow growing (a benefit for pot culture) and take several years to make the impact desired. Of course, if you're like me and thrive on a vast diversity, you might only be able to afford the smaller ones.

The hardiest of the most frequently grown species are *Camellia japonica* and *Camellia sasanqua*. The blooming season for *Camellia japonica* can be a very long one when selected varieties are grown. One form or another can be found in bloom any time from September to April. *Camellia sasanqua* is primarily a fall bloomer, from September to December. Variations in cold hardiness among these are quite noticeable, so it pays to know which ones can weather the cold here best. Generally, the single and semi-double blooms are better at handling the cold. Lighter colored and white camellias tend to show frost injury more readily than darker colors; for example, blooms of 'Debutante' and 'Snow-on-the-Mountain' blemish quickly.

Not only is the cold-hardiness of the bloom a factor, but even more important is the hardiness of the plant itself. I have included a list of some very cold-hardy varieties for Atlanta, but there are many more that will do well here. The camellia collection at the Atlanta Botanical Garden, a wonderful donation made by the family of Tom Troutman, is also a way to discover the best varieties for Atlanta.

A great way to learn more about camellias is by joining the various camellia societies. The North Georgia Camellia Society puts on a wonderful show early each spring and is filled with knowledgeable and helpful members. We are also very lucky here in Atlanta to be located so close to the national headquarters of the American Camellia Society in Fort Valley, Georgia, just a short distance from Interstate 75 south of Macon. The gardens are a piece of heaven and provide an excellent opportunity to see hundreds of different varieties. A membership in the American Camellia Society provides four beautiful quarterlies and a yearbook, all loaded with helpful information. Their address is: American Camellia Society, One Massee Lane, Fort Valley, GA 31030.

Camellia Varieties for the Atlanta Area

The following lists are a small sampling of some of the most cold-tolerant camellia varieties and include bloom times and flower types.

Camellia Japonicas

Governor Mouton - medium red, often variegated with white, mid-season bloomer, semi-double to peony

Dr. Tinsley - light pink semi-double, mid-season to late

Grace Albritton - white with pink shadings, formal double, mid-season to late

Chandleri elegans and others - a wonderful series of sports (branch mutations) with various colors and forms, mid-season to late

Kumasaka - rose-colored, semi-double, late

Leucantha - white, semi-double, mid-season to late

Kramer's Supreme - deep red, large peony-form, wonderful fragrance too!

Daikagura and others - very early, peony form, various color sports

Jarvis Red - deep red semi-double, late

Glen 40 - deep red formal double bloom (tightly doubled with no stamens visible), late

White Empress - white semi-double, early

Berenice Body - soft pink semi-double, early

Camellia Sasanquas (fall-flowering)

Maiden's Blush - softest blush-pink single flowers and lovely oriental fragrance (as with most sasanquas)

Showano Sakae - light pink double flowers; quite early

Day Dream - single white flowers with pink markings; very upright grower

Yuletide - single flowers that are almost a scarlet red; usually blooms a little later than most sasanquas; not one of the hardiest to cold, but valuable for its unusual color for a sasanqua

Shi Shi Gashira - deep rose semi-double, dwarf growth, blooms later than most sasanqua types

Jean May - soft pink double, exquisite!

Camellia Hybrids

Several wonderful hybrids between *Camellia oleifera* (probably the most cold-hardy of all camellia species) and various sasanqua-type varieties have been produced by Bill Ackerman of the National Arboretum. Many of these can handle temperatures in the range of 10-12 degrees F. below zero, so even colder and more exposed areas can include this fall spectacle! They are all fall-blooming. Some of them are:

Winter's Hope - white, semi-double

Winter's Charm - lavender pink, peony form

Snow Flurry - white, anemone form

Winter's Rose - shell pink, formal double

Sources for Camellias

Camellia plants, both japonica and sasanqua, are readily obtainable at local Atlanta nurseries, such as Pike's and Hastings. For an even larger assortment of varieties, the following specialty camellia nurseries may be contacted. See Appendix A for addresses and telephone numbers.

Camellia Forest Nursery

Dean's Nursery
(does not ship)

Gerbing's Camellia Growers
(does not ship)

Nuccio's Nursery

Roslyn Nursery

Tammia Nursery

Chapter Twelve

Evergreen Azaleas

by

Avis Aronovitz

Growing Evergreen Azaleas Successfully in Atlanta

As the signature of an Atlanta spring, nothing quite equals in beauty the vivid colors and pastel shades of evergreen azaleas beneath clouds of dogwood blossoms. It is possible to achieve this scenic panorama around your own home by selecting the right azaleas and planting them in the right spot with a little bit of care. Most evergreen azaleas seem comfortable with our local climate and terrain. This is not surprising since the ancestors of these evergreen azaleas grew in Japan in a climate very similar to ours. They suffer only when a sudden spring cold snap kills or damages flower buds. Occasionally, freezing temperatures will kill exposed, less hardy plants.

There are more colors and color patterns of evergreen azaleas than there are varieties. These azaleas can be solidly colored in all subtleties of whites, pinks (pale pastel to peachy salmon pink to deep rich pink with blue undertones), purples (pale mauve to rich magenta to deep dark purple) and reds (salmon to orange red to crimson). Pigments can occur in a uniformly variegated form on all flowers of a variety like James Harris 'Frosted Orange.' 'Frosted Orange' always has an orange/red margin ringing each of its white flowers. Other varieties have random, even astonishing patterns that are different on nearly every bloom on the plant. Glenn Dale 'Festive' and all Satsukis are like this. The flower patterns may be multi-colored, also. Color patterns can be in only one petal section or cover the entire bloom surface. Some azalea flowers will have patterns of color specks. Other azalea varieties have blooms with a pattern of specks in their throats. This is called a *blotch*; and the orchid lavender flowers with a magenta blotch of Southern Indica 'George Tabor' represents this variegation pattern.

F l o w e r   F o r m s

Colors and color patterns seem endless in evergreen azleas, but these azaleas do have four distinct flower forms. Azalea varieties with **single** blooms demonstrate the classic perfect flower. They are usually larger than other azalea flower forms, providing the plants with a generous splash of color that is unmistakable in a 'Hino Crimson' display. 'Coral Bells' is an example of a **hose-in-hose** azalea form. The sepals (outer green bud covering) form "petals" that take on the flower's actual petal color and pattern. These blooms appear to have two sets of petals (one set inserted on top of the other). In an azalea like 'Elsie Lee,' some male reproductive filaments or stamens have become petal-like, although somewhat smaller, in form and color to create a fuller flower center. This is called a **semi-double** bloom. These flowers have a carnation-like appearance. If all the stamens become normal petals, as in Kehr's 'White Rosebud' and the bloom has extraordinary center fullness and a rosebud appearance, the flower is said to be **double**.

Planting and Care

An expert local commercial azalea grower, Ray Goza, urges that evergreen azaleas be planted in a well-drained, shady area with good air circulation. Planting under pine trees is ideal, but a high canopy of hardwood trees will do. He cautions that although adequate sunlight is necessary for good flower production, too much hot sun fades blossom color and shortens the blooming period. An overabundance of sunlight compounds drought conditions and increases heat stress on the azalea, too.

Evergreen azaleas prefer a 6" deep, light, porous, acidic soil. Most Atlanta soil is acidic; to improve its character, add 50% Nature's Helper or composted ground pine bark and 25% sandy topsoil to the existing soil. (If available, rich woodland soil is ideal.) Dr. Joe Coleman, who's recognized for his own superior, well-grown azaleas, agrees, "If you want your plants to flourish, spend money on their holes. All azalea roots are within the top 6-8", so the medium is important."

Evergreen azaleas should be planted in a slightly raised bed or a broad shallow hole 18" across and 6" deep. Fill the hole with 3" of soil mix and position the azalea in the hole with bottom roots flared and the top of the root ball about 3" above the hole. **It is best not to cover the azalea root ball with soil.** Firm up soil around the plant and mulch with about 3" of pine straw. Water in. **Do not fertilize when planting.** Fertilize immediately following blooming with an azalea/rhododendron/ camellia food or Nursery Special, following product directions.

Evergreen azaleas like moist roots but not wet feet. One inch of water weekly, applied in the early morning, is required by any azalea during warm weather if there is no rain. Some azaleas seem to attract insects. Control them with Orthene and/or Dursban. Spray following label directions at about three-week intervals during warm weather months.

Ten Best Evergreen Azalea Groups for Atlanta

Longtime members of the Azalea Chapter, American Rhododendron Society have selected the ten best azalea groups for Atlanta. The discussions of each group give information about how the plants were developed and their growing habits. The charts that follow the text list specific varieties and their characteristics.

1. Kurume

Kurume varieties like 'Coral Bells,' 'Hino Crimson,' and 'Snow' are the most popular azaleas or blooming plants seen around Atlanta. The Kurume azaleas were introduced in the U.S. in 1918 by E. H. Wilson of Boston, Mass., but it was not until after World War II that they were made popular in Atlanta by plantsman Frank Smith. He encouraged their use as foundation plantings and in large island beds surrounding retained native pine trees in neighborhood front lawns, changing the look of Atlanta's residential areas forever. Kurumes are hardy. Most varieties are early or early mid-season bloomers, offering a wide color range in single or hose-in-hose flowers 1/2-1 1/2" wide. When pruned after flowering, these bushes can be kept low-growing and dense. Unpruned, some can reach 6-12' in height within 10 years.

2. Glenn Dale/Back Acre

Glenn Dale azaleas were first developed at the U.S. Department of Agriculture at Glenn Dale, Md. by Ben Y. Morrison from 1947 to 1949. These azaleas are cold hardy, have flowers almost as large and magnificent as the Southern Indicas, and fill the gap between early-blooming Kurumes and the late-blooming Satsukis. (This allows us a three-month blooming period for azaleas.) These plants vary in height, determined by the trait in their parents.

Back Acre azaleas were created by Ben Morrison in retirement on his small farm in Mississippi about 1964. He succeeded in these later attempts to capture some astounding color combinations. He also worked to produce superior late-blooming varieties, with heavy foliage that would flourish both in hot southern climates as well as cold northern ones. Back Acre azaleas have superior double and bicolor blooms with white or light centers and a broad range of bright colored borders. Flowers of Back Acre azaleas are not as cold resistant as some Glenn Dales.

3. Robin Hill

This group, developed by Robert Gantrell in New Jersey between the late 1930s and the mid 1960s, features large flowers with the best qualities of Satsukis, but even more winter hardiness. Some possess unusually soft pastel tones and are mid-season or late bloomers. Robin Hills do better than Satsukis in sunny areas, such as a southwest facing foundation planting. Robin Hills are said to be the finest group of azaleas ever developed. We have listed three choices; try other varieties too, you'll like them.

4. Harris Hybrids or James Harris Azaleas

Produced by James Harris of Lawrenceville, Ga. since 1970, these plants have been well-received all over the South. However, even with national recognition, not enough local gardeners are aware of these outstanding azaleas. This azalea group has light centers on unusually large blooms. Bloom time is usually late mid-season. Harris azaleas have greater heat tolerance, making them suitable for southern climates. Pendulant types have a cascading growth habit and are as limber as ivy. They can be used in hanging baskets (as long as they are protected in winter) or as a groundcover.

5. August Kehr Azaleas

These outstanding hybrids were developed by Dr. August Kehr, a plant geneticist at the U.S. Department of Agriculture in Washington, D.C., now retired to Hendersonville, N.C. He is working to produce medium tall varieties of evergreen azaleas with improved double blooms. Adhering to extraordinary high standards, Kehr limits his introductions. To date, four new varieties have been released.

6. Satsuki (Gumpo)

These late-blooming, low-growing May azaleas arrived in the U.S. from Japan after the Kurumes. Some are singles; others are hose-in-hose or doubles. Flower size ranges from less than an inch to 5". The range of flower color and variegated patterns, form, leaf shape and color, and growth habit is greater than any other azalea group. Expect the unusual from these azaleas. They are a good accent in the late spring border. They may not be as cold hardy as some other azaleas and resent Atlanta's hot western sun. Provide shade from afternoon sun. All names are Japanese; choose the ones you like from the selection in bloom at the garden center. Joe Coleman picked two, Wakaebisu and Shinkigen.

7. Joseph Gable Azaleas

This group was bred by Joseph Gable, a farmer-nurseryman in Stewartstown, Pa., for beauty and extreme cold hardiness. This makes them the most dependable and floriferous of azaleas. Plants are of medium height, 4-6'.

8. North Tisbury

These groundcover azaleas were developed in Japan over two decades ago and introduced by Polly Hill of Martha's Vineyard to the U.S. in 1975. Their name is derived from a town on the island. These cushiony, low growing azaleas make a serviceable, fine-textured, and unique groundcover. Plant them to trail down a bank or wall or in a rock garden.

9. Shammerello Hybrids

Introduced from Ohio, these azaleas are noted for exceptionally beautiful, large blooms. They are sturdy, cold hardy, and compact plants.

10. Ralph Pennington Azaleas

These azaleas blend the best features of Glenn Dale and Satsuki azaleas to improve flowers and plant habit. They were developed in the 1960s and 70s by Ralph Pennington, a Covington, Ga. native. His commercial Covington Nursery Company offered one of the largest azalea collections in the southeast. All are moderately sized, 3' x 6'.

Challenging Azaleas to Grow

SOUTHERN INDICAS—During the first half of the 19th century, Belgian Indicas were imported from Europe, but they proved too tender to survive in northern regions of our country and most died. Some were tried in public gardens like Magnolia Gardens outside Charleston, S.C. Those that did well were given the name Southern Indicas. Southern Indicas have huge flowers on 8-10' fast growing bushes and are very popular in Atlanta, even if they are risky business. The blooms can easily be destroyed by cold temperatures if the azalea is not planted in a sheltered area. There can be no guarantee of flowers every year on this group of azaleas in Atlanta.

Other challenging azaleas are also listed in the charts that follow.

Sources for Evergreen Azaleas

See listing at end of Chapter 13, "Native Azaleas," for sources.

K·U·R·U·M·E A·Z·A·L·E·A·S

Name	Bloom Color	Bloom Type	Bloom Size	Bloom Time	Comments
Appleblossom	white-tinged strong pink	single	1 1/4"	mid-April	Classic; Wilson introduction; long blooming time
Bridesmaid	dark salmon pink		1 1/2"	usually early April	Rich, lush color
Cattleya	white, flushed lilac mallow	semi-double	1 3/8"	mid-April	Beautiful blush lilac; dependable bloomer
Coral Bells	bright deep pink	hose-in-hose	1 1/2"	early April	Overused; doesn't drop spent blossoms
Hino Crimson	brilliant red	single	1"	early April	Compact; brilliant color; balance with pastels
Orange Cup	strong orange	hose-in-hose	1 3/4"	early April	Very striking
Old Ivory	yellowish white	hose-in-hose	1"	mid-April	Naturally low; unique color
Ruth Mae	moderate pink, white stripes, lighter margin	single	1 1/2"	mid-April	Relatively hardy; moderate grower
Salmon Bells	yellowish pink	hose-in-hose	1 1/4"	mid-April	Counterpart to coral bells; rich color; long blooming
Koromo Shikibu	light purplish pink	spider-like petals	2"	mid-April	Fuzzy foliage
Hahn's Red	vivid red	round petals, single	2"	mid-April	Larger size plant; absolutely scarlet

GLENN DALE AZALEAS

Name	Bloom Color	Bloom Type	Bloom Size	Bloom Time	Comments
Allure	light purplish pink	single	2 3/4"	early	Spreading; 5'; true to its name
Boldface	white center, red blotch, deep purplish margin	single	3"	mid-season	Broad, spreading; 4', remove branch sports; striking when planted near solid purples
Cream Cup	white to yellowish green, a few red flakes	single	2"	mid-season	Compact, dense; 5'; glows with color; should be in every garden
Fashion	deep yellowish pink, purple-red blotch	hose-in-hose	2"	early	Erect to arching habit; 6'; very dependable
Festive	white, no blotch, dusted and striped purplish red	single	2 1/2"	early, great show	Grow under pine tree cover to protect flower from frost damage; no two flowers are the same; quite striking
Scout	light purplish pink	single	2"	early	Broader than tall; 5'; unusual color

GLENN DALE AZALEAS—cont'd

Name	Bloom Color	Bloom Type	Bloom Size	Bloom Time	Comments
Treasure	white with pale pink blush margin and blotch, buds pale pink	single	3 1/2-4 1/2"	early	Vigorous, broad spreading; 5'; luminous
Glacier	white	single	2 1/2"	mid-season	Dependable; foliage rounded; great just for foliage
Dayspring	white center shading to light purplish pink margin	single	2"	early	Flowers look variegated; Joe Coleman says, "This one starts the spring, and what a great way to start!"

BACK ACRE AZALEAS

Name	Bloom Color	Bloom Type	Bloom Size	Bloom Time	Comments
Ivan Anderson	white center, vivid purplish red border	double, 10-15 petals	2 1/2-2 3/4"	late mid-season	2 1/2' tall (7 years); in time can get huge; give it some sun for best bloom
Margaret Douglas	large light pink center, deep yellowish pink edge	single	2 3/4-3"	late April	4' tall; true bi-color; striking plant in full bloom
Marion Lee	strong red border, white center with purple tint	single	3"	late April	Beautiful flower; combines well with 'Margaret Douglas' and rich apricot colors
Red Slippers	strong scarlet red with some faux petals	single, rounded petals	3"	late April	Challenging since it is tender until firmly established; redder than red

R-O-B-I-N—H-I-L-L A-Z-A-L-E-A-S

Name	Bloom Color	Bloom Type	Bloom Size	Bloom Time	Comments
Conversation Piece	variable: white, moderate purplish pink with dots, blotches, flakes of pink or red, or all red	single, wavy	3 1/2"	late	Mounding habit; 2' by 2'; must see it to appreciate the name; very striking
Maria Derby	brilliant scarlet red, slightly orange tinged	hose-in-hose	3"	mid	Can take sun
White Moon	white with occasional pink specks	flat	3 1/2"	late	Low, mounded; 18" by 29"; huge bloom; Satsuki bred

JAMES HARRIS AZALEAS

Name	Bloom Color	Bloom Type	Bloom Size	Bloom Time	Comments
Frosted Orange	white with orange-red border	single	3 1/2"	very late	30" x 36"; good container plant
Miss Susie	strong red	hose-in-hose	1 1/2"	early to mid-season	Compact, dark green plant; 24" x 36"; brilliant color
Rivermist	light reddish purple	cluster-like	1 1/2"	early	Blooms long lasting; plant 42" high; delicate color
Vibrant	white with pink border	single, flat	4"	early late season	24" x 36"; true to its name
Midnight Flair	black or brick-red	single	2 1/2"	late	One of Harris's newest and best
Pink Cascade	deep yellowish pink	single; trumpet shaped	2"	late	Cascading basket plant or groundcover; impetus for Harris's azalea hybridizing career

AUGUST KEHR AZALEAS

Name	Bloom Color	Bloom Type	Bloom Size	Bloom Time	Comments
Anna Kehr	purplish pink	fully double, resembles a camellia	2 1/2"	mid late	Hardy, but best to protect young plant from wind; 2 1/2' x 2'
White Rosebud	white with green throat	resembles a rose	1 1/2"	mid late	Striking specimen plant; flowers are back to back on stems
Great Expectations	bright orange-red	double	2"	late	Slow growing; 5'; requires some care as a young plant
Mary Lou Kehr	pink	double, camellia type	2"	late mid-season	Fragrant; slow to flower

SATSUKI (GUMPO) AZALEAS

Name	Bloom Color	Bloom Type	Bloom Size	Bloom Time	Comments
Wakaebisu	deep yellowish pink to hot coral	hose-in-hose	2 1/2"	very late	Should be in every garden
Shinkigen	white with varied white, pink, or red stripes and solids	single	3-4"; huge	very late	Up to five different colors

JOSEPH GABLE AZALEAS

Name	Bloom Color	Bloom Type	Bloom Size	Bloom Time	Comments
Corsage	cattleya orchid lavender	single	2 1/2"	early	fragrant flower
Purple Splendor	rich dark purple	hose-in-hose	2"	mid-season	Nice contrast with 'Corsage'

NORTH TISBURY AZALEAS

Name	Bloom Color	Bloom Type	Bloom Size	Bloom Time	Comments
Mt. Seven Star	bright vivid red	single, lobes wavy	2"	late	Very low growing; dense; 4" x 24"
Pink Pancake	strong pink with purplish red spotting	single, wavy	2 1/2"	late	Low; creeping; 10" x 36"

SHAMMERELLO HYBRIDS

Name	Bloom Color	Bloom Type	Bloom Size	Bloom Time	Comments
Elsie Lee	bluish lavender	semi-double	2"	mid-season	Long lasting blooming season; semi-dwarf; 3' x 3',very hardy
Helen Curtis	white ruffled	semi-double	2 1/2"	mid-season	Superior bloom; a must have; wonderful balance to strong color combinations

RALPH PENNINGTON HYBRIDS

Name	Bloom Color	Bloom Type	Bloom Size	Bloom Time	Comments
Beth Bullard	yellowish pink	single	4"	late	Low, compact plant

SOUTHERN INDICA AZALEAS

Name	Bloom Color	Bloom Type	Bloom Size	Bloom Time	Comments
George Lindsay Tabor	white flushed purplish pink, deeper blotch	single	3 1/2"	mid-season	Most dependable of the group
Mrs. G. G. Gerbing	white	single	3 1/2"	mid-season	Sparkling white; hardier than thought; give it room!
President Clay	strong red, darker blotch	single	2 1/4"	early mid-season	Tall, upright; does better in southern areas of Atlanta
Formosa	deep purplish red, darker blotch	single	3"	mid-season	Tall, upright
Southern Belle	strong purplish pink, darker blotch	hose-in-hose	2 1/2"	early April	Leaves variegated with fine white margin; does better in southern areas of Atlanta

OTHER CHALLENGING AZALEAS

Name	Bloom Color	Bloom Type	Bloom Size	Bloom Time	Comments
Girard's 'Hot Shot'	hot orange	single	2 1/2"	mid-season	Very intense; a real eye-catcher; must use carefully to blend in landscape
Linwood 'Hardy Gardenia'	white	hose-in-hose/ double	2 3/4"	mid-late season	Should do well here, but not popular yet
Pericats 'Hampton Beauty'	dark salmon	hose-in-hose	2 1/2"	mid-season	Excel in clarity and attractiveness of color, but are only moderately cold hardy; 'Hampton Beauty' can get big
'Hiawatha'	scarlet	single	2"	mid-season	
'Sweetheart Supreme'	light pink	single	2"		
Vuyk 'Palestrina'	white	single	2"	mid-season	Hardy; should be more popular

Chapter Thirteen

Native Azaleas

by

Avis Aronovitz

Best Native Azaleas for Atlanta

Long before Atlanta was developed, many native azaleas grew right here. To this day some can still be discovered in open woods, flowering in yet undisturbed places. Since they are endemic to our area and completely acclimated, native azaleas withstand unexpected cold temperatures as well as hot summers without showing any stress. They are also eager participants in our annual spring azalea display.

Native azaleas can be easily integrated into home gardens, in a pine island or at the edge of wooded or shady areas. In the wild, half the natives never bloom, or bloom sparingly, because of inadequate sunlight. You can select a site under deciduous trees where these azaleas receive enough sunlight to form sturdy plants that set multiple buds.

All American native azaleas are deciduous, but not all deciduous azaleas are native. Some have have been crossed either in nature or by people to create hybrids. Blooms on natives often resemble honeysuckle blossoms. Usually they are very different looking from cultivated evergreen azalea flowers.

Planting and Care

Plant native or any deciduous azaleas level with the ground or in raised beds, using a mixture of one-half pine bark and one-half rich woodland or commercial planting soil. Natives enjoy an abundance of water, but once established are remarkably drought tolerant. Fertilize with 1/3 cup Osmocote 14-14-14 once a month during the growing season, spring and fall. Fertilizing lightly and often is the secret. Grow under deciduous trees so they'll have full sun in the spring and shade during the summer. Native azaleas are remarkably tough, but they are also, as the late nurseryman George Beasley said, "opportunists that luxuriate under good care."

Companion Plants

Suggested companion plants for a rhododendron or azalea garden include hostas, ferns, wildflowers, *Helleborus orientalis* (lenten rose) and other helleborus, tricyrtis (toad lilies), *Fothergilla gardenii* (witch alder), *Hamamelis* 'Arnold Promise,' *Acer palmatum* (Japanese maple), rainbow leucothoe (fetterbush or dog-hobble), edgeworthia (paperbush—blooms in heavy shade), *Viburnum x carlcephalum* and

V. x burkwoodii, heuchera, *Kalmia latifolia* (mountain laurels 'Elf,' 'Ostbo Red,' 'Sarah,' 'Carousel,' and 'Nipmuck') and *Gordonia lasianthus* (loblolly bay—remains small evergreen tree here with white blossoms from late May until frost).

Top Native Azalea Choices

These native azaleas are listed in order of number of recommendations received from members of the local American Rhododendron Society, Azalea Chapter who are longtime growers of these plants. Descriptions are from George Beasley, who knew these native azaleas intimately. Additional descriptive material is from Fred Galle's definitive book on the subject, *Azaleas*. All azaleas are rhododendrons (genus). R. stands for *Rhododendron* in the name and appears along with the species designation.

1. Piedmont or Florida Pinxter Azalea

(R. *canescens*) Blooms in late March on naked branches to break the grip of winter. Blooms are white to pink and fragrance is fair to fabulous. Height 5-15'. This is the most common azalea seen in bare woods in early spring.

2. Oconee Azalea

(R. *flammeum* or R. *speciosum*, older name) Clear yellow through orange to blood red flowers, 1/2-2" across. Can set as many as 12 buds in a cluster, resulting in a perfect baseball shape. Natural hybrids with R. *canescens* will range in color from pale apricot to red with yellow blotches and fragrance. A collection of flammeum hybrids runs the gamut of peach, pink, yellow, orange, and red shades. Height can be 2-6'. Early to mid-April flowering, following the Piedmont azalea and before the Swamp and the Alabama azalea. However, some years all these azaleas bloom simultaneously. This accounts for unusual and variable natural hybrids.

3. Plumleaf Azalea

(R. *prunifolium*) Blooms after leaves are fully developed during late July and through August in beautiful shades of orange and red. Blooms are large and showy. Easy to grow. Height is 5-15'. Native to areas in southwest Georgia near Callaway Gardens. No fragrance. Must be planted in shady areas, the same as other late-flowering azaleas, avoiding hot sun. Local azalea hobbyist Chris Early has developed a breeding program to extend the blooming period of the Plumleaf azalea into late August, making this native even more desirable for Atlanta gardens.

4. Florida Azalea

(*R. austrinum*) One of the first to show color in late March/early April. Flowers are pale cream to deep orange, borne before the leaves or as they are developing. There is a form that is pure gold with no red in the tube of the flower that is outstanding. Flowers are small and numerous, the fragrance intoxicating. Grows 5-15'.

5. Sweet Azalea

(*R. arborescens*) Magnificent large white flowers, blooming usually about late June/early July here, although the typical bloom period is late May/early June. Some forms, probably hybrids, have a showy yellow blotch. At high altitudes can be only 3' tall, but is usually 8-16'. This azalea is by far the best mid-season white. Its perfume is similar to heliotrope.

6. Alabama Azalea

(*R. alabamense*) A rare plant—white with yellow blotch flowers. Typical plant is low, 3-6', and stoloniferous. Flowers mid to late April with an appealing lemony scent. Hybrids with the Piedmont azalea produce attractive flowers and are included with *R. alabamense*.

7. Coastal Azalea

(*R. atlanticum*) Low growing and strongly stoloniferous with pure white blooms or white flushed with red, some with a distinct yellow blotch. Fragrance is pleasing. It is said to be extremely hardy and should be used more here.

8. Pinkshell Azalea

(*R. vaseyii*) Tall, upright plant with delicate white to pink freckled with bright orange flowers quite unlike other azaleas. Blooms, which appear in mid-April before foliage, are more bell-shaped and seem to have separate petals. Grows 5-10' and has colorful fall foliage.

9. Cumberland Azalea

(*R. bakeri*) Found first in North Georgia and named for Dr. W. B. Baker of Emory University. The beautiful foliage and flowers have a peculiar porcelain-like sheen that is most attractive. The flowers come in shades of yellow through orange to blood red. It blooms about the same time as *R. arborescens*, late June and early July. It is low-growing, flat topped, and non-fragrant. Wild "dwarf" forms grow rapidly to 5' when given adequate soil, moisture, and fertilizer.

10. Flame Azalea

(*R. calendulaceum*) Large 3" flowers are in all shades of yellow, orange, and red. Oddly, the ones that bloom dark orange-red are usually from higher altitudes. No fragrance, but superior form and color. They are 6-12' tall. This is the native that John Bartram discovered and described as, "The most gay and brilliant flowered shrub yet known." (He had not seen the other native azaleas!) It was used as one of the parents of the Ghent hybrids after being brought to England in the early 19th century. Some bloom as early as April 15, others mid to late June, determined by altitude of origin.

10. Pinxterbloom Azalea

(*R. periclymenoides*, formerly *R. nudiflorum*) This one ties for tenth place with the Flame azalea among locals as best native azalea in their gardens. Flowers are near purple to light pink, fragrant, and open mid-April on 5-8' bushes. Also used for breeding English deciduous large-flowered cultivars.

Other Native Azaleas

A few Atlantans grow Swamp azalea (*R. viscosum*) White blooms sometimes have a strong, spicy aroma. Usually blooms about two weeks after *R. arborescens* and comes in a poor second in all other categories. However it does enjoy a number of loyal fans. Bill Johnson, who lives in northwest Atlanta, reports that he is able to grow 14 different natives, including the true challenges such as the Texas azalea (*R. oblongifolium*), which is similar to our Swamp azalea. The Hammock-sweet azalea (*R. serrulatum*), a small flowered white with clove scent that extends the azalea bloom season well into August, even September, can also be found in his garden. Many Atlantans also grow the Choptank River hybrids, derived from Polly Hill's find by that New Jersey river, a natural offspring of *R. atlanticum* and *R. periclymenoides*. These are low, 2-4', and bloom white to pink with a strong, clove-like perfume which permeates the entire garden.

Two native azalea hybrids are very popular because they grow well here: 'Hazel Hamilton' and 'My Mary.' There is only one large-flowered deciduous azalea that is completely reliable here, the Exbury azalea 'Gibraltar'. There are species rhododendrons (natives) that do well here also. One is *R. maximum* with white or pink flowers on a 7' plant. Another is small-leaved *R. minus* 'Chattahoochee Dawn' with soft pink delicate flowers and *R. minus* 'Chattahoochee Twilight' with peach pink small blooms. Both were found by Lewis Shortt on that river's bank south of Atlanta. *R. chapmanii* and its hybrids also do well here.

Purchasing Azaleas

Native azaleas and native rhododendrons are best purchased at sources listed below. These establishments sell only nursery propagated plants. Other advertised natives may have been dug from the wild, depleting our natural resource. Even if a plant has been rescued from destruction, it will be difficult to reestablish in your garden.

Sources for Evergreen and Native Azaleas

See Appendix A for addresses and phone numbers.

Recommended Local Sources

Goza Nursery

Hastings Nature and Garden Center

Home Depot

Homeplace Garden

Pike Family Nurseries

Transplant Nurseries

Recommended Catalog Sources

Greer Gardens

Additional Recommended Sources

From Dr. Joe Coleman, who has an outstanding collection of superb azaleas:

Farmers and Consumers Market Bulletin

Ed Stephens in Cobb, Ga. near Cordele (thousands of natives azaleas, annuals, and perennials)

Varnadoe Nursery (numerous natives and standard evergreens, too)

Woodlanders (nice mail-order selection, native azaleas, own crosses, shrubs, and native companions; catalog $2)

Goodness Grows (on site only, fine selection of 3 gallon natives)

Nuccio's (known for quality camellias, extensive Kurume selection, own Kurume hybrids which do well here, Belgian hybrids (Caprice, Gay Paree, Easter Parade—they are tricky and can take three years to establish), also Southern Indicas and Satsukis) "Perhaps the best listing I have seen, and these plants can go right into the ground," says Joe Coleman.

The Cummins Garden (natives by mail with a particularly good group of Clarence Towe natives)

Schild Azalea Gardens and Nursery (complete selection of southern natives, Cliff Gunn hybrids, and hardy evergreen azaleas)

Hills Nursery (nice listing of Back Acre, Southern Indica, Kurume, Robin Hill, Satsuki, Linwood, Pericat, others)

Reids Azaleas (evergreen azaleas, common to unusual choices, including own introductions)

Stubbs Shrubs (evergreen azaleas such as Satsuki, Glenn Dale, Eden, Kehr, Kurume, Harris, Robin Hill, Linwood, Girard, Back Acre, North Tisbury, Greenwood; for the collector, the entire collection of new Kurume releases from the National Arboretum)

From Callaway Gardens:

Lazy K Nursery (natives, particularly *R. prunifolium*)

James Harris (evergreen azaleas)

Azaleas-To-Go (evergreen azaleas)

Melton's Nursery (specializes in native and evergreen azaleas, some rhododendrons)

Chapter Fourteen

Hybrid Rhododendrons

by

Avis Aronovitz

with

Raymond Goza and Lewis Shortt

Hybrid Rhododendrons - A Mystery Solved

Today Atlanta gardeners grow rhododendrons easily and successfully. However, a few years back, most area gardeners thought rhododendrons almost impossible to grow. Observation demonstrated that the ones which lived and flourished were planted on slopes, accidentally providing the necessary good drainage. Plantsmen like the late Frank Smith recognized that rhododendrons planted in our red clay were being sentenced to die by drowning or root rot. Smith introduced an easy, above ground planting method, refined by current rhododendron specialists, that works.

Planted correctly for Atlanta conditions, rhododendrons rarely need further care, except watering at appropriate times. Most rhododendrons grow and bloom in filtered sun. Some tolerate sunny situations. In dense shade, rhododendrons rarely bloom.

Ray Goza's Guidelines for Successful Rhododendron Growing in Atlanta

BUYING. Attempt to purchase plants that have been grown in hot, humid areas for at least one summer. Plants shipped into Atlanta from mountainous or cool areas may develop root rot. It's preferable to select plants growing in pine bark, not heavy west coast soils. An alternative is to hose off *all* soil from the roots before planting. Choose plants with sufficient roots to nourish and support plant's top growth. Buy recommended named plants.

SELECTING A SITE. Select a planting site with filtered sun or high shade, adequate light (neither all day full sun nor dense shade), north or east exposure, good drainage, and good air flow (the plant should not be crowded by other shrubs or structures).

PLANTING. Plant rhododendrons only in the spring, fall, or winter, but avoid times of extreme temperatures. Plant very shallow. Dig a hole 4" deep and 3' in diameter. Discard the soil. Place mini pine bark nuggets about 1" deep over entire bottom of hole.

Remove plant from container and loosen root ball. If possible, spread roots. Place plant in center of hole, mounding pine bark around root system border out to perimeter of hole. **Do not place pine bark on top of root system.** With your hands, firm up bark around roots. This helps hold the plant upright and secure. Usually it will take 9 cu. ft. of bark per plant. Place a mulch of 4-5" of pine straw over root system and all exposed pine bark. Do not allow pine straw to touch stem. Water well during the next week.

Lewis Shortt's Typical Planting Schematic

To ensure root-rot free years to come, Lewis Shortt prefers a slightly deeper hole filled with a 50/50 mixture of coarse sand and uncomposted pine bark for 6" below the root ball.

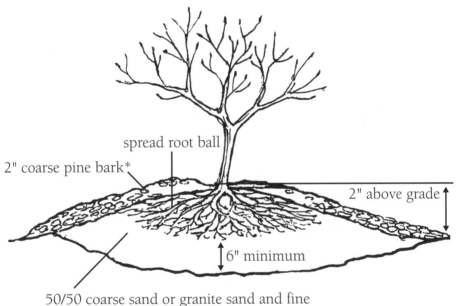

spread root ball

2" coarse pine bark*

2" above grade

6" minimum

50/50 coarse sand or granite sand and fine pine bark (not composted) or Nature's Helper

*Top pine bark mulch with 8" pine straw for late spring and summer.

Add to planting mix (for a 3 gallon plant):

Ferrous sulfate - 1/2 cup

Calcium sulfate (Gypsum) - 1 cup

Magnesium sulfate (Epsom salts) - 1/2 cup

0-14-14 fertilizer - 1/2 cup

Rhododendron Care

Fertilizing at Planting

Local commercial grower Ray Goza recommends no fertilizer at planting. Lewis Shortt adds 1/2 cup of 0-14-14 per three-gallon plant. Shortt also adds a generous cup of gypsum, 1/2 cup ferrous sulfate, and 1/2 cup Epsom salts at planting. He says these additives release necessary elements for the rhododendron.

Watering

Give root system a deep soaking for a short period of time. According to weather conditions, a rhododendron may need water every other day the first summer and fall. With normal rainfall, an established plant requires little watering in summer and fall and none in winter. During periods of severe drought any season of the year, water rhododendrons. To prevent disease, Ray Goza applies water in the daytime so foliage can dry off before nightfall.

Fertilizing

Ray Goza fertilizes in January at the rate of 2 tablespoons of Nursery Special or azalea/rhododendron fertilizer per 2' rhododendron height sprinkled on top of pine straw mulch. Lewis Shortt prefers to fertilize immediately following blooming, but only if the plant appears distressed or its foliage has poor color. Both growers get excellent results.

Insect and Disease Control

These are minor problems in rhododendrons. Chewing insects can be controlled by spraying the ground and plant with Orthene tree and ornamental chemical. Leaf spot and fungus require spraying with the systemic Daconil, sometimes as often as every two weeks.

Tips from the Experts

Lewis Shortt suggests buying the largest rhododendrons you can afford. In his experience, they adjust better to transplanting than small ones, and prove hardier to temperature extremes.

Remove dead or spent flowers from rhododendrons.

Remember that rhododendrons, unlike most other shrubs or perennials, do not always form bloom buds every year.

For information on the local Azalea Chapter of the American Rhododendron Society, contact the Atlanta Botanical Garden.

Choosing Hybrid Rhododendrons

The following chart lists the Ten Best Rhododendrons for Atlanta. Their selection was based on a poll of local longtime rhododendron growers, members of the Azalea Chapter, American Rhododendron Society.

On the second chart, More Rhododendrons for Atlanta, the list becomes more specific to the gardener and the garden. Notes Avis Aronovitz, "The impact of micro-climates is ever present. Varieties that do well on the north side of a hill in a wooded area of my garden in northeast Atlanta may differ from those that do well in a garden in East Point." Most rhododendrons on this chart are Dexters. Dexters are a group of rhododendrons that were developed by a New England industrialist. (Number 3 on the Ten Best chart, Scintillation, is also a Dexter.) Dexters do particularly well in all areas of Atlanta.

Other charts list Rhododendron Options (those that are more difficult, but usually successful in Atlanta), True Rhododendron Challenges, and Rhododendrons Destined for Stardom (those whose diminutive size allows them to be easily grown in a perennial bed or shrub border).

Recommended Local Sources

Goza Nursery
Homeplace Garden
Transplant Nursery
Pike Family Nurseries
Hastings
Home Depot

Recommended Catalog Sources

Cardinal Nursery
Greer Gardens (Remember to hose off heavy west coast soil from plant roots.)

See Appendix A for addresses and telephone numbers.

TEN BEST RHODODENDRONS FOR ATLANTA

Name	Color	Ultimate Ht.	Bloom Time	Comments
1. Roseum Elegans	Rosy lilac	6'	Early May	Dependable; fast growing; 150 years old; small flower clusters by today's standards
2. English Roseum	Rosy lavender	6'+	Early May	Following Spring '84 cold snap, only #1 and #2 bloomed in a Roswell garden
3. Scintillation	Pastel pink, bronze throat	5'	Early May	Tolerates sun; large flowers with good substance; striking foliage
4. Cynthia	Rosy crimson	6'+	Mid-April	Sun and heat tolerant; vigorous; open habit; showy; large spectacular flower clusters
5. Trude Webster *	Clear china pink	5'	Late April	Large flowers in huge flower clusters; deep green foliage; award winning
6. Anna Rose Whitney	Rosy pink dark, bright	6'	Late April	Vigorous; upright, dense foliage; well-shaped plant; funnel-form flowers
7. Caroline *	Orchid pink	8'	Very late April/Early May	Fragrant, large flowers; compact to ground; heavy flowering; artfully twisted leaves
8. A. Bedford	Pale mauve, black blotch	6'	Late April/Early May	Dark, glossy leaves; compact, dome-shaped flower clusters; open, ragged form; best as background landscape plant; tolerates sun
9. County of York	White	6'	Late April	Apple-green foliage; blooms in deep shade
10. Blue Ensign	Lilac blue, purple blotch	4'	Late April	Compact plant; sun tolerant; very hardy

* Avis Aronovitz's favorites for Atlanta gardens

MORE RHODODENDRONS FOR ATLANTA

Name	Color	Ultimate Ht.	Bloom Time	Comments
Parker's Pink *	Dark pink, center fading to white	5'	Late April-Early May	Scented flowers; large leaves; sets buds easily; really great rhododendron!
Dexter's Giant Red	Striking red, dark blotches	5'	May	Upright, broad plant
Dexter's Purple	Dark lavender with gold blotch	5'	Mid-April	Frilly, beautiful flowers; tight spherical clusters; sun and wind tolerant
Dexter's Cream *	White, pink shading	4'	Late April	Fragrant; heavy bloomer
Janet Blair	Lavender pink, greenish throat	6'	Early May	Blooms easily; good-looking plant; best foliage
Wheatley *	Soft pink streaked with silver	6'	Early/Mid-April	Round flower clusters; blooms heavily

* Avis Aronovitz's favorites for Atlanta gardens

RHODODENDRON OPTIONS

Name	Color	Ultimate Ht.	Bloom Time	Comments
Gigi	Rose red	5'	May	Heavy bloomer; very slow to flower
Todmorden	Striking bicolor (rose-red/light pink)	6'	Late April	Outstanding selection, also slow to bloom
Vulcan	Bright red	5'	May	Dark green leaves
Mary Fleming *	Bisque yellow with streaks of salmon pink	3'	2nd week March (Blooms froze in '96)	Long, blooming period; small leaves and flower clusters; winter bronze
Nestucca *	White with greenish brown throat	3'	Mid-April	Rounded, compact bush; glossy foliage; heavy bloomer; easy to flower
Catawbiense Album	White, greenish-yellow spots	6'	Early May	Easy to grow; dark green leaves
Pseudochrysanthum * spp. tall/dwarf forms	Pink buds, white flowers	4'	Late March/Early April	Silvery surface on new growth for weeks; perfect for a small garden
Platinum Pearl	Pearlescent pink with deep rose blotch	6'	Late April	Withstands heat/cold; large, leek green leaves; sturdy stems; huge flower clusters; light shade best

* Avis Aronovitz's favorites for Atlanta gardens

RHODODENDRON OPTIONS cont'd

Name	Color	Ultimate Ht.	Bloom Time	Comments
Wild Affair *	Bright red, yellow blotch	6'	Early May	Exciting to the eye; easy to grow
Olga Mezitt *	Pink	3'	Late March through Early April	Green summer foliage; mahogany in winter; small leaves; easy to grow
Manitau *	Light pink	3'	Late March through Early-Mid April	Compact; small leaves; luscious flowers; easy to grow
Nova Zembla	Deep rosy-red	5'	Early May	Compact plant; good foliage; hardy; extremely showy
Anah Kruschke	Reddish purple	6'	Very Early May	Sunny, hot location; easy to grow; medium-size tight flower clusters; lush foliage
Mrs. Tom H. Lowinsky	White and orange with brown blotch	5'	Second week of May	Dark green, lustrous leaves; slow to bloom
Purple Lace	Lacy purple	5'	May	A favorite
Madrid *	Dark pink	5"	Late April-Early May	Dependable bloomer; heavy bloomer; a personal favorite
Marketa's Prize *	Brilliant Red	5'	Mid-Late April	Heavy bloomer; easy; deep fir-green foliage
Vivacious *	Strong red	4'	Early May	Extra heavy bloomer; long slender foliage; superb

* Avis Aronovitz's favorites for Atlanta gardens

RHODODENDRON OPTIONS

Name	Color	Ultimate Ht.	Bloom Time	Comments
Dora Amateis*	Pure white	3'	Early April	Sweetly scented, loose clusters on deep green foliage
Yaku Angel	Pink buds, snow white flowers	3'	Late March/ Early April	Brown velvety undersides of long narrow leaves; buds young; mixed border; best Yak for Atlanta

* Avis Aronovitz's favorites for Atlanta gardens

TRUE RHODODENDRON CHALLENGES

Name	Color	Ultimate Ht.	Bloom Time	Comments
Baden-Baden	Deep red	2'	Early May	Bell-shaped blooms; use in flower border; buds blast from cold
Mahmoud	Lavender pink with large yellow eye	4'	May	Different; eye appeal
Grace Seabrook	Currant red	5'	April	Early display
Colonel Coen	Purple	4'	Late April	Hardy; buds young
Van Nes Sensation	Light orchid pink	5'	Early-Mid April/Late April peak bloom	Fragrant; strong; beautiful; difficult to flower well
Olin O. Dobbs	Wine red	4'	April	Waxy flowers
Mrs. A. T. de la Mare	White with green spots	6'	May	Large flower cluster; takes exposure well
Cadis	Light pink	5'	May	Fragrant; enjoys sun
Azor	Salmon	6'	May	Best in woodland
Ruby F. Bowman	Rose pink, ruby throat	4'	Early May	Sun tolerant
Faggetter's Favorite	Blended white, pink and cream	6'	May	Fragrant; good plant and flowers
PJM	Bright lavender	4'	April	Small leaves; mahogany foliage in winter; difficult
Good News	Bright red	4'	Late May	Valuable for its late flowers

RHODODENDRONS DESTINED FOR STARDOM

Name	Color	Ultimate Ht.	Bloom Time	Comments
Percy Wiseman	Apricot yellow fading to ivory	3'	Late April/Early May	Floriferous and vigorous; dark green foliage; great low foundation plant
Bashful	Pink and white	3'	Mid April	Large flower clusters; use in mixed borders or low foundation plantings
Mardi Gras	Soft pink	3'	May	Excellent foliage plant
Normandy	Bright Pink, darker edge, tangerine spotting	3'	Very Late April	Blanket of pink, broad rounded plant; withstands adverse conditions
Golden Torch	Soft yellow	3-4'	Late April	Compact
Temple Belle	Rose pink	3'	Late April/May	Oval, matte-green leaves; bell-shaped flowers in loose tumbling clusters; very attractive plant
Shrimp Girl	Salmon pink	2.5'	Mid April	Difficult color in the garden

Chapter Fifteen

Perennials

by

Avis Aronovitz

Growing Perennials Successfully in Atlanta

The year-round beauty of perennials is uplifting and inviting. The landscape may be enviable, the bulb display enticing, the small tree or shrub in flower or fall color exciting—but in the perennial beds or border the gardener really has opportunity for self-expression.

When gardeners refer to "perennials," they are using shorthand for "herbaceous perennial plants." These are plants with non-woody stems whose top growth dies back, but whose crown remains alive to send up new growth the next blooming season. That's the best thing about perennials: They don't have to be replanted each year. Some need dividing every three or four years to continue flowering well. Others perform for years with minimal attention.

Not so long ago, people believed that it was too hot in Atlanta to grow perennials. They enjoyed the dogwood and azaleas in the spring, and the gardening season ended there. Today the beautiful perennial beds and borders in our neighborhoods through most of the year prove this was not true. Our long growing season lends itself to success with many popular perennials, if you choose varieties that withstand our heat, humidity, and absence of a drop in night temperatures through the growing season. If, on the other hand, you model your garden after an English or even a northern one, you are going to have a rough time.

Our long growing season is a gift and a challenge because it requires that you accept the responsibility to maintain adequate moisture and nutrients for your plants through months of active growth. In the Atlanta area plants often flower earlier, are taller, and have weaker stems. Heat speeds up the growing process, and for certain perennials, heat can retard flowering, too.

Summer daytime temperatures of 80-90 degrees with little relief after sundown can produce overgrown plants. To compensate, choose dwarf or lower growing varieties, or pinch back tall, late-blooming types in early summer to keep plant height in check. High night temperatures combined with over-watering also invite root rot and fungus. This means a disciplined program of disease control, also. See Chapter 5, "Pests and Diseases."

Planting Perennials

Since perennials are permanent residents in the garden, much care must be taken in soil preparation at planting. Most perennials will rot, starve, or at the very least languish if they are not provided with a generous-size hole, good drainage, and food.

The recipe for the additives that will do the job varies from gardener to gardener and from year to year. Most agree that the ideal soil will come as close as possible to duplicating a sandy topsoil, made richer or leaner with compost according to the dietary preferences of the perennial to be planted there. The soil pH or acidity can be important, too, Sometimes an incorrect pH can prevent the plant from absorbing needed nutrients from the soil mixture. See Chapter 6, "The Fertilizer Mystery."

Choosing Perennials

The charts that follow list the best perennials to grow in Atlanta. The selections were compiled from survey responses of 24 members of the Georgia Perennial Plant Association and members of local garden clubs. The charts are divided for sun or shade. With a perennial shade garden, you can preserve your trees and grow flowers beneath them. Also see Chapter 26, "Shade Gardens."

Before you select your first perennial, buy and read Allan Armitage's *Herbaceous Perennial Plants.* His writing style is delightful, and Professor Armitage has never met a perennial whose most minute quirks he doesn't know. He writes about perennials from his current viewpoint, Georgia, as well as the Yankee perspective we find in most books on the subject. For a cursory look at perennials, along with some excellent color photos, *Armitage on Perennials* is a worthwhile possession. See the Recommended Reading and References section for this chapter for a list of other books about perennials.

TEN BEST SUN PERENNIALS

Common Name	Botanical Name	Height	Color	Bloom Time	Comments
1. Daylily	*Hemerocallis*	15-36"	shades of yellow, orange, pink, red	May 15-June 15, late ones July	Some varieties re-bloom sporadically in summer. This is the "almost impossible to fail" plant in Atlanta. See Part Four.
	H. 'Stella d' Oro'	12-15"	gold	May 15-frost	Blooms heavily, almost continuously
	H. 'Ida Miles'	3-4'	pale yellow	June-July, occasionally August	Tolerates part shade; open nights; fragrant
	H. flava	4'	lemon chrome	Very early	Favorite for 350 years
	H. fulva	3'	brownish orange	Late	Used to prevent erosion
	H. Decatur series	18-30"	various	June-July	Fine series developed for area gardens
	H. Atlanta series	21-30"	pale pink, yellow, red	June-July	Costly tetraploids; large flowers
	H. Chicago series	24-36"	red, pink, lavender, purple	Mid June	True, clear colors

TEN BEST SUN PERENNIALS cont'd

Common Name	Botanical Name	Height	Color	Bloom Time	Comments
	H. 'Golden Prize'	26"	gold	Late	Classic tetraploid
	H. 'Joan Senior'	25"	near white, lime green throat	Early-mid season	Evergreen; 6" ruffled flower; incredible vigor
	H. 'Moon Traveler'	dwarf	true yellow	All summer	Saul Nursery introduction
	H. 'Happy Returns'	15-18"	lemon yellow	All summer	Wayside introduction; 3 1/2" bloom; ruffled crepe
2. Clove or Cheddar Pinks	Dianthus 'Bath's Pink'	6-8"	soft pink	Late April-May	Evergreen, gray-green spreading foliage; flower delicate, single (1"), clove-scented; floriferous; needs full sun and excellent drainage
Maiden Pinks	D. deltoides 'albus'	1/4-1/2"	pure white	8-10 weeks in early summer	Low evergreen mat; prefers well-drained, slightly alkaline soils
Sweet William	D. barbatus 'Indian Carpet'	10"	various	Late spring/summer	Add lime to soil; flowers in flat clusters
Cottage Pinks	D. plumaris 'Sonata'	8-12"	pink	May	Flowers in pairs
	D. p. 'ItSaul White'	8-12"	white	May	

TEN BEST SUN PERENNIALS

Common Name	Botanical Name	Height	Color	Bloom Time	Comments
3. Garden Phlox	*Phlox paniculata*	24-30" or taller	white, pink, purple, rose red	Late June-October	Dominates garden mid to late summer; spray prevents powdery mildew; afternoon shade best!
	P. 'Mount Fuji'	36"	best white	July	Fragrant, long-blooming; rain-resistant; 'David' has best mildew resistance of white phlox; cut flowers
	P. 'David'	3-4'	glistening white	July	
	P. 'Bright Eyes'	24-30"	soft pink with red eye	July	
	P. 'Sandra'	18-24"	rose red	August	
	P. 'Orange Perfection'	24"	orange red	August	
Thrift	*Phlox subulata*	6-12"	pink, blue, lavender	March-April	Full sun, well-drained soil for best performance
Wedding Phlox	*Phlox carolina* 'Miss Lingard'	30-36"	pure white	May-August	After flowers fade, cut back 1/3, feed, water; sturdy stems; somewhat mildew resistant
4. Sedum	*Sedum spectabile* 'Autumn Joy'	18-24"	coral pink to deep rusty red with age	August-September	Only tall sedum that is not floppy
	Sedum 'Brilliant'	15-22"	hot pink	September-October	Very relaxed appearance

Common Name	Botanical Name	Height	Color	Bloom Time	Comments
5. Black-eyed Susan	*Rudbeckia fulgida* 'Goldsturm'	24-36"	gold rays with large black center	July-September	Good sized flower; prefers moist, rich soils
Three-lobed Coneflower	*R. triloba*	48-60"	yellow rays with brown-purple center	July-September	Biennial; reseeds well; many flower heads on branched stems; great fence plant
Cut-leaf Coneflower	*R. lanciniata*	48-60"	greenish center, drooping yellow ray flowers	July-October	Full sun to part shade; best in moist soils
Shining Coneflower	*R. nitida* 'Herbstonne' or 'Autumn Sun'	4-5'	long drooping sulfur yellow petals	Late August-late September	One of the finest coneflowers for the garden
6. Purple Coneflower	*Echinacea purpurea* 'Bright Star'	36-42"	rose	May-September	Tolerates part shade, but taller and weaker in shade
	E. purpurea 'Alba'	36-42"	cream white rays, greenish disc	May-September	In wet summers grows very tall with huge flowers

T E N B E S T S U N P E R E N N I A L S

Common Name	Botanical Name	Height	Color	Bloom Time	Comments
7. Common Yarrow	*Achillea millefolium* 'Oertel Rose'	12-18"	rose pink fading to white	May-November	Tolerates part shade; sturdy stems; large flower "plates"
Sneezewort	*A. ptarmica* 'The Pearl'	24"	white	Early summer	Profusion of double button flowers on sprawling stems
8. Siberian Iris	*Iris siberica*	24-30"	two to five blue, purple, lavender or white flowers per stem	April-May	Best in moist, fertile soil; resents being disturbed; less disease-prone than tall bearded iris; lance-like foliage
	I. siberica 'White Swirl'	24"	clear white with a hint of yellow	Mid April-early May	Lights up a spring flower bed
9. Lamb's Ears	*Stachys byzantina*	6-18"	gray woolly foliage; tiny hot-pink flowers	May-June	Forms nice clumps; spreads well; prefers a poor, well-drained soil; after bloom remove lower melted foliage

TEN BEST SUN PERENNIALS cont'd

Common Name	Botanical Name	Height	Color	Bloom Time	Comments
10. Speedwell	*Veronica spp.*	varies	blue spikes	May to frost	Full sun; well drained soil; easy
	V. pinnata x 'Sunny Border Blue'	18-24"	violet blue	Mid May to fall	Holds up in wet summers
	V. pinnata 'Blue Charm'	15-18"	lavender blue	Early May through summer	Stout stems; abundant dense flower heads
	V. alpina 'Goodness Grows'	10-12"	long blue violet spikes	Mid April-fall	Low-growing
	V. longifolia 'Icicle'	18-24"	white	June-September	Finest white

S U N P E R E N N I A L S : T H E R U N N E R S - U P
Tricky or just lacking a good press agent

Common Name	Botanical Name	Height	Color	Bloom Time	Comments
1. Coreopsis	*Coreopsis spp.*				All need good air circulation
Thread Leaf Coreopsis	*C. verticellata* 'Moonbeam'	18-24"	soft muted yellow	June-October	Long flowering time; bright colors; fine cut foliage; drought tolerant; long-lived; flower buds can blacken and rot
	C. v. 'Golden Showers'	18-24"	bright yellow	Summer	
	C. v. 'Zagreb'	12-18"	deep yellow	Summer	Compact, bushy plants
Mouse Ear Coreopsis	*C. auriculata* 'Nana'	12-24"	bright yellow	April	Needs water; floriferous
Tickseed Coreopsis (Better as annual)	*C. grandiflora*	24-30"	orange-yellow	Summer	Dead-head for continuous bloom; divide after 2nd year
	C. g. 'Sunray'	24"	yellow (double)	Most of Summer	
2. Orphanage Plant	*Astermoea mongolica*	24"+	double, white rays yellow stamen	May-frost	Likes afternoon shade; spider mites mid-summer; cut back for rebloom; group for stronger show
3. Chrysanthemum	*Chrysanthemum spp.*				All grow best in poor soil; seeds heavily
Ox-Eye Daisy	*C. leucanthemum*	24-30"	single white daisy, yellow center	April-May	Short lived, but reseeds well; tolerates part shade

SUN PERENNIALS: THE RUNNERS-UP cont'd
Tricky or just lacking a good press agent

Common Name	Botanical Name	Height	Color	Bloom Time	Comments
Garden Mum	C. x morifolium 'Ryan's Pink'	24-30"	dusty lavender-pink, slight white halo around yellow center	September-October	Allow plants to relax forward; cut back in mid-summer.
Garden Mum	C. spp. 'Pink Daisy Mum'	24-36"	true pink, yellow center	October/November	Smaller than 'Ryan's Pink,' long lasting, no care plant; pinch back in early summer for shorter compact plant
Shasta Daisy	C. x superbum 'Ryan's Daisy' or 'Becky'	36-42"	white daisy	June-August	Strong stems; lush foliage; huge clumps
4. Peony	Paeonia	varies	white, pink, red	April-May	Loves cold winters; early blooming, single, or Japanese types do better
	P. 'Festiva Maxima' See Part Four	34"	white double crimson flecks	Early April	Sturdy stems; fragrant; full sun means better foliage

SUN PERENNIALS: THE RUNNERS-UP
Tricky or just lacking a good press agent

Common Name	Botanical Name	Height	Color	Bloom Time	Comments
Tree peony	P. suffruticosa x P. lutea	Consult the American Peony Society, 250 Interlachen Road, Hopkins, MN 55343		Seem to do better in our northern suburbs	Woody stems remain in winter; requires slightly basic soil; good drainage; part shade; very difficult here
5. Stokes' Aster	Stokesia laevis 'Blue Danube'	12-24"	lavender blue; also white form (less vigor)	Late May-July	2-3" flowers open one at a time on single stalk; intolerant of wet feet in winter
6. Purple Loosestrife	Lythrum salicaria	48-72"	rosy purple; invasive in north, not here	June-August	Happier in the north, but tolerates southern gardens with adequate moisture; attracts Japanese beetles
	L. virgatum 'Morden's Pink'	36"	bright pink	June-September	More compact plant; misguided Georgia Legislature attempted ban
7. Red Hot Poker or Torchlily	Kniphofia or Tritoma uvaria	24-36"	two-toned shades of red, orange and yellow	June-July	Likes poor, well drained dry soil; hot sun; no winter wet feet; eyesore after flowering; protect from freezing; good foliage
	K. u. 'Primrose Beauty'	24-30"	primrose yellow	July	Smaller; tubular drooping spikes
8. Candytuft	Iberis sempervirens	6-12" 18" wide	white	March-May, some re-bloom	Evergreen edging, border, ground-cover; good drainage

Tricky or just lacking a good press agent

Common Name	Botanical Name	Height	Color	Bloom Time	Comments
9. Swamp Sunflower	*Helianthus angustifolius*	5-7' unpinched	bright yellow	September-October	Fertilize; sun; lots of water; in shade, pinch back early summer; aggressive!
Many-flowered sunflower	*H. x multiflorous*	3-5'	yellow	June-fall; July-August best	Sun or shade; needs water and fertilizer
Tall narrow-leaved sunflower	*H. simulans*	>8'	3" bright yellow	September-November	Persists after frost; super backdrop; seen for miles.
10. Balloon Flower	*Platycodon mariessii* 'Blue'	12-24"	blue	June-July, can re-bloom	Low maintenance; emerges late; yellow fall foliage. Super!
	P. plenus	24"	blue, double	Later June-July	Less freeze tolerant
11. Blue Star Flower	*Amsonia*	36"	pale blue	Mid-April	Starry flowers persist 3-4 weeks; attractive foliage especially in fall; afternoon shade best; in part shade, prune
12. Blazing Star or Gayfeather	*Liatris spicata* *L. spicata*, dwarf form	18-24" 12"	purple purple, blue, mauve	June-July June-October	Blooms from top down; good vertical accent; short lived in Atlanta gardens
13. Bee-Balm Wild Bergamot	*Monarda didyma* (Try 'Jacob Cline,' a better red) *M. fistulosa*	36"	red lavender	June-July, late summer	Attracts hummingbirds; invasive; powdery mildew; best in moist, uncultivated area; *M. fistulosa* is better—less floppy, mildew, weedy.

SUN PERENNIALS: THE RUNNERS-UP
Tricky or just lacking a good press agent

Common Name	Botanical Name	Height	Color	Bloom Time	Comments
14. Artemisia	*A. absinthium* 'Powis Castle'	36"	silver foliage, no flowers	n.a.	Fine texture; pleasant aroma; shrubby; prune
15. Mrs. Huff's Lantana	*Lantana camera* 'Mrs. Huff'	48-60"	simultaneous yellow or pink	May to frost (froze '96 winter)	Attracts butterflies; shrub
16. Gooseneck Loosestrife	*Lysimachia clethroides*	24-36"	white	July-August	Arching spikes; full sun or shade; moist soil; invasive
17. Butterfly Weed	*Asclepias tuberosa*	12-18"	bright orange; less vigor pink, white, yellow	May-June with re-blooming	Attracts butterflies; likes hot, sunny spot with poor soil; superb plant here
18. Hardy Ice Plant	*Delosperma cooperi*	1/4" 24" wide	hot pink	Summer through fall	Succulent; cylindrical, evergreen foliage; likes hot, dry areas

More Recommended Sun Perennials

Asters New England Asters *A. novae-angliae* 'Harrington's Pink' A reliable pink display by mid-July to fall. Other varieties bloom August or September. *A.* x 'Hella Lacy' offers purple show September-frost. *A. tataricus* becomes pale blue clouds in late September. Asters vary in height from low bedding plants to over 6'. *A. carolinianus* is the final aster to bloom (in late November) with *Camellia sasanqua* 'Cotton Candy.'

White Wild Indigo *Baptisia pendula* White 2-3' Full sun/part shade. Many spikes of pea-like, long-lasting flowers under wet or drought conditions. Takes three years to reach top form. Resents competition. Plant expert George Sanko ranks it #1!

Sweet Rocket *Hesperis matronalis* purple or white (alba form) 3-3 1/2' Full sun/part shade April-June (purple form lasts longer). Phlox-like flowers on tall stems. Heavy feeder. Prefers moist, well-drained soil. Short lived perennial. Easy from seed. Sweet frangrance noticeable at night.

Pincushion Flower *Scabiosa* 'Butterfly Blue' and 'Pink Mist' 12" Full sun. Pink can tolerate light shade. Spring-Fall. Prefers cooler temperatures. 2" bloom. Gets rangy! Try a bit of lime.

Knautia *Knautia macedonica* deep crimson 18-24" Summer. 1-2" scabiosa-like double flowers. Silvery stamens resemble pins in a pin cushion. Easy to grow if you add a little lime to well-drained soil.

French Hollyhock *Alcea zebrinus* 30". Blue-purple and white striped flower. Blooms summer to hard frost (through December in '94) Prune often during growing season. Stake! Great with fall colchicum; then with *Callicarpa dichotoma's* Chinese eggplant-colored winter fruit. Better as an annual.

Gaura, Variegated *Gaura lindheimeri* 'Variegata' 15-24" Pink/white butterflies on wiry stems. April-October. Variegated foliage outstanding. Slightly sandy, well-drained soil required. Cut stems back to encourage flowering. Not as strong a perennial as green foliage form. Group for stronger show.

Hardy Hibiscus *Hibiscus spp.* Following mild winters, do well in sun in Atlanta gardens. (Tender Florida hibiscus cannot be left outdoors in freezing weather.) Swamp Hibiscus (*H. coccineus*) is 5-6' tall with 6-8" rose red blooms June-August; returns from seed. *H. moscheutos* has 9-10" clear pink blooms on 4' plant. *H. m.* 'Disco Belle' series have pink, red, or white blooms with red centers; 2' tall; bloom June-September; 9" flowers. *H. m.* 'Southern Belle' has 8" flowers in pink, red, or white with deep red eye; 4-5' tall; blooms June-September. Confederate Rose (*H. mutabilis*), an old-fashioned cottage plant, has large flowers that open white and fade to pink. *H. lasiocarpus* is 3-7' tall with 8" pale yellow flowers with maroon center; blooms June-August.

Bottle or Closed Gentian *Gentiana andrewsii* Several dark blue or sometimes white flask-shaped 1 1/2" flowers (which never open) on ends of unbranched stems. Easy in wettish area. Plant in part sun or shade.

Rabbit's Ear Lavender *Lavandula stoechas* 'Pedunculata' French lavender blooms in late May/early June. Purple flowers are crowned with two short bracts that resemble a rabbit's ears.

'Martha Roderick' Common Lavender *Lavandula angustifolia* 'M.R.' Rather ordinary-colored dwarf. Unusually attractive. Bloom time follows the rabbit's ear. These two lavenders in a somewhat protected, part shade area with great drainage are guaranteed to do well here.

Bog Salvia *Salvia uliginosa* 3-4' true blue May-November. Outstanding, truly hardy salvia. Combines well with 'Heavenly Blue' morning glory and *Rudbeckia lanciniata*. Late in the season, excellent with 'Pink Daisy Mum.'

Verbenas *V. tenuisecta, V. canadensis, V. bonariensis, V. x hybrida* 'Abbeville,' and *V. x hybrida* 'Homestead Purple' do well here in all but cool, wet summers.

Serbian Bellflower *Campanula poscharskyana* Rapidly spreading low plant with lovely blue-lilac star-shaped flowers May into early June. Plant in part shade.

Dalmatian Bellflower *Campanula portenschlagiana* 'Resholt' Part sun. Charming bell-shaped lavender blooms on low spreading plant. Blooms slightly later than Serbian variety. These two are the only campanulas that will return year after year here.

Summer Iris *Cypella plumbea* 3'. (See description in Chapter 17, "Bulbs.")

TEN BEST SHADE PERENNIALS

Common Name	Botanical Name	Height	Color	Bloom Time	Comments
1. Hosta, Plantain Lily, Funkia	Hosta spp. and cultivars	6-36"	white or lavender	Spring, summer, some in fall	Foliage all shades of green, blue and patterns of green and white

This is an old-time plant fallen into disregard, but now revived by interest in incredible, new varieties. Though hostas are tough, slugs and snails can devour emerging foliage. Use slug bait frequently for control. June weevil can be controlled with Sevin dust.

	H. 'Royal Standard'	24"	glossy green foliage, white flowers	Late summer	Sweet scented blooms
	H. undulata	18"	pale purple blooms	Early summer	Shade to half sun; rounded mound
	H. 'Sum and Substance'	30"	light green foliage, lavender flowers	Late summer	Superior substance; pest resistant; half to full sun
	H. 'Golden Tiara'	12"	light green, yellow-margined foliage, purple bloom	Midsummer	Mounded; rapid grower; neat looking
	H. sieboldiana 'Elegans'	8-12"	lavender flowers	Summer	Immense blue gray, puckered foliage

TEN BEST SHADE PERENNIALS

Common Name	Botanical Name	Height	Color	Bloom Time	Comments
2. Astilbe	*Astilbe spp.* and cultivars	6-30"	pink, white, red, peach	May-June; late varieties in July	Long-lasting in shady, moist sites; dryness causes brown foliage margin, then withering death
	A. 'Bridal Veil'	18-30"	white	June	
	A. 'Peach Blossom'	18"	fragrant, pale peach arching sprays; foliage bronze tinted	May-June	
	A. 'Fanal'	18-24"	dark red, long lasting	May-June	Requires more water and mulch in hot, dry weather
	A. 'Avalanche'	30"	pure white plumes; deep green ferny foliage	May-June	Great arching plumes; popular, attractive plant
Fall astilbe	A. *taquetii* 'Superba'	36-42"	raspberry pink	Late July	Strong, erect spikes if kept particularly moist
Dwarf Chinese astilbe	A. *chinensis* 'Pumila'	12-24"	mauve-pink spikes	June-July	Low, fern-like foliage; most drought tolerant of the group
3. Lenten Rose	*Helleborus orientalis* (Most hellebores are great!)	12-18"	white, cream, or pink to purple	February-April	Nodding, rose-like flowers; coarse, palmate evergreen leaves; spreads easily from seed
4. Ferns	See Chapter 23, "Ferns."				

TEN BEST SHADE PERENNIALS cont'd

Common Name	Botanical Name	Height	Color	Bloom Time	Comments
5. Bleeding Heart	*Dicentra spectabilis*	18-24"	rose-pink	March-May	Dormant in summer; white form blooms April-June
Fringed Bleeding Heart	*D. eximia*	9-18"	light pink	May-August and into fall	Stemless; foliage and flower come directly from root
	D. x 'Luxuriant'	15"	cherry red	Summer	Blue green foliage; difficult to bring through summer
6. Columbine	*Aquilegia*	18-36"	blue, white, yellow, red	Spring	Erect clump; slender branching stems
Native Columbine	*A. canadensis*	18-24"	yellow petals, deep red sepals, short backward pointing spurs	April-May	Foliage somewhat evergreen; colonizes freely in lean, well-drained soil; hybrids feature larger flowers; some color choice, but plants are short-lived
7. Hardy Begonia	*Begonia grandis*	18-24"	pink, angel-wing shape; white flowers rare and less vigorous	Late July	Heart shaped leaf with burgundy underside; spreads so easily no one sells it; obtain bulblets from fellow gardeners
8. Foamflower	*Tiarella cordifolia*	6-12"	white or pinkish	April-May	Tufted evergreen foliage turns bronzy in winter; likes moist woodland
	T. cordifolia 'Oakleaf'	12-15"	white	April-May	Beautiful! Aptly named

TEN BEST SHADE PERENNIALS

Common Name	Botanical Name	Height	Color	Bloom Time	Comments
9. Blue Phlox	*Phlox divaricata*	12-15"	soft blue	April-May	Good for woodland garden
10. Toad Lily	*Tricyrtis hirta*	24-36"	white or lavender covered with dark purple spots	September-October	Dominates the fall shade garden; try all tricyrtis available, all excellent here
	T. formosana var. *amethystina*	24-30"	bluish purple; white throat spotted red	May-October	A jewel in the shade garden; must be kept dry in winter

MORE SHADE PERENNIALS

Runners up: not necessarily challenging, just not as well known

Common Name	Botanical Name	Height	Color	Bloom Time	Comments
1. Anemone, Japanese Anemone	*Anemone japonica*	30-42"	white, pink, or rose red	September-November	Slow to establish, but can be free-flowering after second year
	A. 'September Charm'	24-30"	clear pink	September-October	Try 'Honorine Jobert,' 'Whirlwind,' and 'Bressingham Glow,' and 'Marguerite'; all prefer a wet summer
Grape Leaf Anemone	A. *vitifolia*	18-36"	white single	August-September	Spreads by underground roots, so weed out in spring, leaving a few good clumps; intolerant of heat and drought
2. Foxglove, Common	*Digitalis purpurea*	36-48"	purple, white; purple and white spots	April-May	Biennial; rosette first year, flowers second year; demands lots of water; replace after flowering with annuals
	D. *purpurea* 'Foxy'	30"	large bell-shaped, purple	May-June	Flowers first year from seed
Strawberry Foxglove	D. *mertonensis*	36-42"	coppery rose	May-June	Fresh looking, velvety foliage
Straw Foxglove	D. *lutea*	36"	creamy yellow	May	Small nodding flowers on slender spikes
Yellow Foxglove	D. *grandiflora*	24-36"	yellow outside brown within	May-June	Short-lived; prefers part shade, other foxgloves tolerate part shade
3. Variegated Solomon's Seal	*Polygonatum odoratum* 'Variegatum'	24-36"	dainty white, bell-shaped	April-May	Best in cool, moist soil, undisturbed

MORE SHADE PERENNIALS
Runners up: not necessarily challenging, just not as well known

Common Name	Botanical Name	Height	Color	Bloom Time	Comments
4. Virginia Bluebells	*Mertensia virginica*	12-18"	pink buds, blue flowers	April-May	Prefers cool, moist area with enough sun to promote flowering; if undisturbed, easy; disappears by summer
5. Lungwort or Bethlehem Sage	*Pulmonaria officianalis* 'Sissinghurst White'	8-12"	large white flowers; silver-white spotted leaves	March-April	Blooms early and long; short sprays of flowers
	P. saccharata 'Roy Davidson'	12"	sky blue; leaves dark green mottled with silver	March-April	Selection made by an American plantsman; many are English plants
6. Coral Bells	*Heuchera*	varies	varies	Spring-summer	Best in rich, moist, well-drained soil
Alumroot	*Heuchera americana*	12-18"	pinkish green	July-August	Evergreen, heart shaped foliage
	H. micrantha 'Palace Purple' (Also try *H.* 'Bressingham Bronze')	12-24"	almost white	July-August	Glossy maple-shaped mahogany foliage fades to bronze green in summer; large mature plant better here

M O R E   S H A D E   P E R E N N I A L S   cont'd

Runners up: not necessarily challenging, just not as well known

Common Name	Botanical Name	Height	Color	Bloom Time	Comments
	H. sanguinea	9"	reddish white	Late spring	Poor in heavy, acid soil; add dolomitic lime
	H. Bressingham Hybrids	18"	salmon to scarlet	Late spring	Add coarse sand, manure, dolomitic lime to improve performance
7. Celandine Poppy or Wood Poppy	Stylophorum diphyllum	12-18"	bright yellow	April-June	Likes moist shade; cheery; colonizes easily
8. Wild Ginger	Asarum arifolium	3-5"	brown, jug-shaped	May-June	Needs good woodland soil
European Wild Ginger	A. europaeum	6-8"	dull brown, urn-shaped	Spring	Leathery, glossy, evergreen leaves; needs cool, moist site; intolerant of heat
Canadian Wild Ginger	A. canadense	6- 12"	dull brown, urn-shaped	Spring	Glossy deciduous leaves; more heat tolerant than A. europaeum
9. Japanese Roof Iris	Iris tectorum alba	12-18"	white, delicate	May	Part shade best; more vigorous than blue variety which also does well in shade
10. Green and Gold or Goldenstar	Chrysogonum virginianum 'Piccadilly'	6-10"	bright yellow daisy with slightly notched petals	May-June and sporadically through fall	Low, spreading plant; good ground-cover

MORE SHADE PERENNIALS
Runners up: not necessarily challenging, just not as well known

Common Name	Botanical Name	Height	Color	Bloom Time	Comments
11. Italian Arum	Arum italicum				See Chapter 17, "Bulbs"
Cyclamen	Cyclamen hederifolium				
Iris	Iris cristata Iris unguicularis				
Trillium	Trillium spp.				
12. Cast Iron Plant	Aspidistra elatior	18-24"	n/a	n/a	Evergreen; dark green; excellent foliage plant for shade
13. Spiderwort	Tradescantia virginiana x andersoniana	12-24"	Blue-purple, pink, white flowers on dull green grass-like foliage	May-October	Each flower lasts one day, plant flowers for eight weeks; fewer flowers in shade; foliage flops, plant declines after flowering
14. Lily-of-the-Valley	Convallaria majalis	12"	white, fragrant bells	Spring	Sentimental favorite
15. Corydalis	Corydalis ochraleuca	18"	creamy-yellow green spot	All year except coldest winters	Part sun; most reliable corydalis here; order from NW U.S. mail order catalogs

CHALLENGING SHADE PERENNIALS

Common Name	Botanical Name	Height	Color	Bloom Time	Comments
1. Yellow Corydalis	*Corydalis lutea*	9-15"	golden yellow, spurred flowers	Spring	Likes shady, moist rock gardens; prefers English climate; try all newly available blue corydalis
2. Heartleaf Brunnera	*Brunnera macrophylla*	12-18"	azure blue with yellow center	Spring	Requires heavy shade, consistent moisture

Local Sources for Perennial Plants

Arthur A. "Buck" Jones & Assoc.*

Autumn Hill Nursery*

Carter's Nursery*

Chattahoochee Home and Garden*

Farmers and Consumers Market Bulletin

Flora Farm*

Forget-Me-Not Flowers*

Forrester's Flowers*

Garden Party*

GardenSmith Greenhouse & Nursery #

GardenSouth (Gold Kist Inc.)

Goodness Grows #

Habersham Garden*

Hall's Flower Shops

Hastings Nature and Garden Center*

Heistaway Gardens

Highland Hardware*

Hosta for Sale (Only hostas, hardy fern, and rare black elephant ear, by appointment)

Intown Hardware*

Ladyslipper (Native perennials)

Land Arts, Inc.*# (Also shrubs, trees, annuals, and native plants)

Living Colors Unlimited, Inc.

Lost Mountain Nursery*

Lush Life*

McGinnis Farm* (Also roses, native wildflowers, and shrubs)

Melton's Nursery*

Morrison Farms

Mountain View Gardens*# (Formerly Funkhausers)

Outdoor Environments, Inc.*

Piccadilly Farm # (Also hostas, ferns, hellebores, and woody plants)

Pike Family Nurseries

Planters*

Potted Plant*

Providence Garden Mart*

Randy's Nursery and Greenhouses

Robert Harris (Hostas only)

Rolling Oaks Farm (Hanson Farms)

Smith Ace Hardware

Walker Nursery*

Ward's Nursery, Inc.*

Wilson Brothers Nursery (Also shrubs, trees, annuals, and native plants)

*Saul Nurseries is a local grower that has introduced new plants to our area and supplied these * nurseries with all types of excellent perennials well-suited to Atlanta area gardens.

These are outside metro area, but certainly worth the journey.

Mail Order Sources
for Perennial Plants

Arrowhead Alpines (Good choice for unusual NW plants)

Andre Viette Farm-Nursery (Good plants)

Collector's Nursery (For the true collector, catalog $2)

Heronswood Nursery, Ltd. (Great selection—choice plants)

Klehm Nursery (Peonies and hostas)

Niche Gardens (Good selection of natives; care requirements indicated; some difficulty in re-establishing plants)

Park Seed Company (A lot like Wayside)

Plant Delights Nursery, Inc. (2200 varieties of perennials!)

Reflective Gardens Nursery (Good selection NW plants)

Siskiyou Rare Plant Nursery (Woodland and rock garden plants for the connoisseur; many difficult or impossible to grow here)

Sunlight Gardens (Good selection of perennials and wildflowers)

Van Bourgondien Brothers (Plants not of consistent quality)

Wayside Gardens (Expensive, healthy, well-grown plants; honors its guarantees)

We-Du Nurseries (Nursery propagated SE natives; unusual woodland perennials)

White Flower Farm (Superb plants. Re-establish with care)

The Wildwood Flower (Excellent selection of unusual Lobelia)

Winterthur

Yucca Do Nursery

Chapter Sixteen

Annuals

by
Avis Aronovitz
with
Eve Davis and Jeff Potter

Best Annuals for Atlanta

Annuals are plants that complete their entire life cycle in one growing season or less, so they must put on a show of bright colors or decorative foliage for as long as possible to attract pollinators. This makes them ideal in beds around commercial developments or residences either in mass plantings or combined with other plants.

Annuals can also be used in perennial beds to fill empty niches created when those herbaceous plants complete their bloom periods. Annuals can cover unsightly remnants of bulbs' yellowing foliage, too. Used well, annuals can bring together an entire garden to fashion a lovely landscape. Annuals in the garden are a constant source of cut flowers for the home.

In recent years, with the development of heat and humidity resistant varieties that perform better here, bedding plants and annual displays have reappeared in Atlanta landscapes. Post Properties horticulturists and landscapers showed us that beautiful scenes can be created from imaginative combinations of colors and textures that are available only in annual plants. They also rediscovered the pansy and the petunia for Atlantans. People like gardener Sara Groves at Georgia Tech and Eve Davis (then-proprietor of Eve's Garden nursery) were also prophets in this movement to awaken Atlantans to the value of annuals, not just as bedding plants in displays but as the core of a home garden. They also helped to acquaint local gardeners with the great variety of annuals available from seeds that do well here.

Choosing Annuals

Some annuals, such as Swan River daisy, candytuft, marigold, and nasturtium, require planting in a dry area or the plant will rot. Rotting can affect either the foliage, the flower, or the roots—any part of the plant or all of the plant. Select a site the rain doesn't reach or where the drainage is so good that any water drains away immediately. Usually a dry area is in sun, but it is possible to have areas of dry soil in shade, also. Most annuals recommended for shade usually do not tolerate dry soil. The few exceptions include a scarlet sage, *Salvia splendens*. Annuals such as forget-me-not, primrose, cleome, vinca, and viola perform best in moist soils. That does not mean standing water.

Most annuals need full sun to bloom their best. In times of drought, these bedding plants can require daily watering. When planted in less sun, plants produce less flowers, but do not wilt as quickly. Impatiens, monkey flower, and black-eyed Susan vine are content with shade and bloom well. Annuals for specific sites must be chosen carefully, after study of the available moisture and exposure. Areas near driveways and sidewalks may reflect amounts of light and heat difficult to calculate. Be prepared to pull out and replace annuals that may receive more or less sun, heat, or even wind than you anticipated.

Best Annuals for Dry Areas

Candytuft
Cornflower
Dahlberg Daisy
Dianthus
Dusty Miller
Four O'clock
Gaillardia
Gazania
Globe Amaranth
Gloriosa Daisy
Grasses, Ornamental
Gypsophila

Joseph's Coat (Amaranthus)
Marigold
Mexican Sunflower (Tithonia)
Nasturtium
Petunia
Phlox
Portulaca
Salvia
Sanvitalia
Swan River Daisy (Brachycome)
Verbena
Vinca
Zinnia

Best Annuals for Wet Areas

Forget-Me-Not
Monkey Flower
Nasturtium
Primrose
Spider Plant (Cleome)
Vinca
Viola

Growing Annuals

Since annuals usually have less than a year in our care, it is very important that they are given optimal growing and flowering conditions. Local gardeners use various soil amendments, but all agree soil preparation strongly influences the results that you will have with your annuals. Therefore, learn their appetites. Most require a rich, loose, well-drained soil (which means adding compost and the commercial product, Nature's Helper). Others, such as nasturtium, form excessive foliage and few flowers in overly rich soil.

Some gardeners choose to start seeds inside; others sow them directly into the ground. Always read directions on the packet carefully. Others prefer to buy the annuals as small plants or even already blooming.

Fertilize annuals with Osmocote and 5-10-5 (for immediate availability) at planting time and apply Super Bloom or any fertilizer with a high phosphorus (center) number if flowering seems to be declining. Water at the first signs of wilt. Be wary of snails, slugs, thrips, and aphids. Act quickly with appropriate home remedies or commercial preparations from the garden center if any of these villains attack.

Advice from Eve Davis

Before Eve Davis relocated to North Carolina for the greater gardening opportunities of the open spaces and unpolluted air, she shared her feelings about annuals: "I love annuals because I grew up with them gardening as a child in Charleston. They have become a bit of a crusade for me these last few years when so many gardeners became obsessed with perennials. Annuals were being banished from the flower garden. The truth is that, particularly in the South, annuals are the lifesaver of the flower garden because so many of them reseed, coming back more reliably than some perennials. Also, they can take the heat and humidity of summer with nonstop blooming.

"I always tell people that if they want a garden in full bloom from March through November in Atlanta, they would be hard-pressed to do that without annuals, especially during the summer. Another advantage to annuals is that they are further encouraged to bloom even more prolifically and longer if they are picked regularly. Annuals have a primary goal to produce seed for the next year. Therefore, if they are picked, they just keep on trying, blooming on and on.

"One of the problems that people have with growing annuals is timing! Seed needs to be planted at the appropriate time of year. This is especially true for cool weather annuals. Many of these beauties should be sown outside in the fall or indoors in the late winter. Our spring is so short that they often cannot establish themselves well before hot weather comes. The old-fashioned classics, such as larkspur, poppy, bachelor's button, nasturtium and sweet pea are best planted in fall, as well as are a number of more unusual or rarely seen flowers. Because most seed packets and books are geared to northern or English gardens, if you follow the printed instructions to plant in April or May, you will be discouraged by the resulting failure. Keep trying, but plant earlier. You may even consider a cold frame for starting these seeds. One major cause of poor germination is planting seed too deeply. The appropriate planting depth is generally two times the diameter of the seed."

Eve's favorite annuals from seed for Atlanta gardens appear on the following chart. After that, you will find charts of annuals that can be purchased as plants, usually budded or blooming, in local nurseries and garden centers at various times of the year. State of Georgia Horticulturist Jeff Potter contributed his choices for Best Foliage Annuals, too. Look for seeds and plants at local garden centers.

EVE DAVIS'S FAVORITE ANNUALS FROM SEED

Common Name	Botanical Name	Height	Color	Seeding Time	Bloom Time	Comments
Baby Blue Eyes	Nemophila	6"	sky blue white eye	Fall/early spring	Spring	Takes part shade; sow in ground; reseeds
Baby's Breath	Gypsophila elegans	12-18"	white, rose	Fall	Spring	Cut flowers; nice in containers
Bachelor's Buttons or Cornflower	Centaurea cyanus	12-24"	blue, pink purple	Fall	Spring	Reseeds; cut flowers
Calliopsis	Coreopsis tinctoria	24-48"	yellow, brown, purple-red	Spring	Spring to summer	Reseeds; needs sun; cut flowers
Candytuft, annual	Iberis umbellata	12-18"	white, pink, purple	Late winter	Spring	Cut flowers
Cockscomb	Celosia cristata	12-36"	white, yellow, purple, red	Spring	Summer	Slight reseeding; dries well; cut flowers
Cosmos	Cosmos bipinnatus	3-4'	white, pink, crimson	Spring	Summer/spring	Reseeds; sun; cut flowers
Cosmos	Cosmos sulphureus	18-48"	gold, yellow, red	Spring	Summer	Reseeds
Cupflower	Nierembergia hippomanica	6-12"	purple, white	Late winter	Summer	Reseeds; in part shade may overwinter
Dahlia	Dahlia hybrida	varies	mixed	Spring	Summer/fall	Sun; cut flowers
Daisy, Dahlberg	Dyssodia tenuiloba	4-6"	yellow	Spring	Summer/fall	Sun

Common Name	Botanical Name	Height	Color	Seeding Time	Bloom Time	Comments
English Daisy	Bellis perennis	6"	white/pink	Fall/winter	Winter	Reseeds
False Queen Anne's Lace	Ammi majus	3-4'	white	Fall/winter/spring	Spring/summer	Reseeds; cut flowers
Flax	Linum spp.	12-18"	blue/white/red	Winter	Spring	
Floss Flower	Ageratum houstoniantum	6-18"	blue, lilac, lavender, white	Spring	Spring to frost	Tolerates light shade
Flowering Kale	Brassica oleraceae	6-12"	white/lavender	Late summer	Winter	Containers
Flowering Tobacco	Nicotiana	12-18"	white to scarlet	Late winter	Summer	Part shade or sun; fragrant
Forget-Me-Not, Chinese	Cynoglossum amabile	8-14"	aqua blue	Spring/fall	Spring	Reseeds; cut flowers
Forget-Me-Not, Summer	Anchusa capensis	10-18"	blue	Winter	Spring	Reseeds
Forget-Me-Not, true	Myosotis sylvatica	10-12"	blue	Winter	Spring	Reseeds
Foxglove	Digitalis purpurea	24-48"	purple, pink, white	Fall	Spring cut flower	Biennial, but treat like annual; shade
Globe Amaranth	Gomphrena globosa	6-18"	purple, red, rose, orange	Spring	Summer/fall	Slight reseeding; dries; cut flowers

EVE DAVIS'S FAVORITE ANNUALS FROM SEED

Common Name	Botanical Name	Height	Color	Seeding Time	Bloom Time	Comments
Gloriosa Daisy	*Rudbeckia hirta* 'Gloriosa Daisy'	18-36"	orange-yellow with brown center	Spring	Summer/fall	Part shade or sun; reseeds
Hollyhock	*Malvus* 'Pinafore Mixed'	3-4'	mixed	Spring	Spring/fall	Biennial, but treat like annual
Johnny Jump-Up	*Viola tricolor*	6-12"	yellow to purple, blue, or white	Fall	Spring	Part shade, reseeds
Larkspur	*Consolida ambigua*	3-4'	white, pink, purple	Fall	Spring	Reseeds; sun; dries; cut flowers
Lobelia	*Lobelia erinus*	4-6"	blue	Winter	Spring	Part shade or sun
Love-Lies-A-Bleeding	*Amaranthus*	3'	pink, mauve	Late spring	Summer/fall	Reseeds; dries; cut flowers
Mexican Sunflower	*Tithonia rotundifolia*	4-8'	orange or gold	Spring	Summer/fall	Reseeds
Moonvine	*Ipomoea alba*	vine	white	Spring	Summer/fall	Part shade or sun
Moss Verbena	*Verbena tenuisecta*	6"	white/purple	Late winter	Summer/fall	Reseeds
Nasturtium	*Tropaeolum majus*	6-12"	cream to red	Early spring	Spring/early summer	Edible; some reseeding; 3-4 hours shade prolongs bloom
Pansy	*Viola x wittrockianna*	6-12"	mixed	Late summer in cool place or winter	Winter/spring	Keep picked; seeds often

Common Name	Botanical Name	Height	Color	Seeding Time	Bloom Time	Comments
Petunia	*Petunia x hybrida*	8-12"	mixed	Winter	Spring/summer	Keep picked; old-fashioned flowers; reseeds
Phlox, Annual	*Phlox drummondii*	12-18"	mixed	Late winter/spring	Spring	Reseeds; sun; cut flowers
Pincushion Flower	*Scabiosa*	2-3'	mixed	Late winter	Summer	Great cut flowers
Poppy, Iceland	*Papaver nudicale*	12-24"	mixed	Winter	Spring	Takes part shade; cut flowers
Poppy, Opium	*Papaver somniferum*	3-4'	mixed	Fall	Spring	Sun
Poppy, Shirley	*Papaver rhoeas*	36"	white to red	Fall	Spring	Reseeds; don't cover seed
Pot Marigold	*Calendula officinalis*	1-2'	yellow, orange, apricot	Early fall	Spring	Set plants out in fall or late winter
Sage, Blue	*Salvia pitcheri*	2 1/2'	blue	Winter	Summer/fall	Part shade; cut flowers
Sage, Mealy Cup	*Salvia farinacea*	1-2'	blue, white	Winter	Summer/fall	Dries well; cut flowers
Sage, Mexican	*Salvia leucantha*	5'	lavender	Fall	Fall	Treat like annual; pinch back in July
Sage, Scarlet	*Salvia coccinea*	3'	red, white, peach	Spring	Summer/fall	Reseeds!
Snapdragon	*Antirrhinum majus*	1-3'	mixed	Winter	Spring	Cut flowers

EVE DAVIS'S FAVORITE ANNUALS FROM SEED

Common Name	Botanical Name	Height	Color	Seeding Time	Bloom Time	Comments
Spider Flower	*Cleome hasslerana*	4'	white, pink, lavender	Spring	Summer/fall	Part shade or sun; keep picked
Stone Mountain Daisy	*Helianthus porteri*	2-3'	yellow	Spring	Late summer	Reseeds
Sweet Alyssum	*Lobularia maritima*	3-6"	white, pink, purple	Fall/spring	Spring/fall	Part shade
Sweet Peas	*Lathyrus odoratus*	6'	mixed	February	Spring/early summer	Climbs; likes rich soil; plant deep
Tassel Flower	*Emilia javanica*	12"	orange	Spring	Summer/fall	Reseeds
Toadflax	*Linaria maroccana*	18"	mixed	February/March/April	Spring	Reseeds some
Wishbone Flower	*Torenia fournieri*	6-12"	violet, yellow, white	Early spring	Summer/fall	Takes part shade; keep picked
Zinnia	*Zinnia* 'Ruffles Hybrid'	3'	mixed	Spring to August	Summer/fall	Sun; dries well; cut flowers; mildew resistant
Zinnia, Creeping	*Sanvitalia procumbens*	6"	yellow	Spring	Summer/fall	Good over walls and in baskets; 6-8" spread
Zinnia, Creeping White	*Zinnia linearis* 'Alba'	12"	white	Spring	Summer/fall	Sun
Zinnia, Narrow Leaf	*Zinnia angustifolia*	12"	bright orange	Spring	Summer/fall	Sun

Best annuals for sun

Common Name	Botanical Name	Height	Bloom Color	Bloom Time	Comments
Abelmoschus	*Abelmoschus moschatus* 'Mischief'	14-18"	cherry red with white center	July to frost	Numerous 2 1/2-4" hibiscus-like flowers; prefers hot summers, warm nights; perfect for Atlanta
Angel's Trumpet	*Brugmansia*	6-7'	white to apricot, pink, yellow	Mid-summer to late fall	Poisonous; will over-winter in ground if cut back severely and heavily mulched; 20" funnels; fragrant
Angel's Trumpet	*Datura meteloides*	2'+	white edged in pale violet, purple outside	Mid-summer to frost	Poisonous
Balsam	*Impatiens balsamina*	12-18"	various	Summer to frost	Plant after frost; sun or part shade; heavy reseeder
Blanket flower	*Gaillardia*	12-18"	gold with red center	Spring to frost	Better in our northern suburbs; plant in early spring
Blue Daze	*Evolvulus nuttalianus*	8"	blue	Summer	Needs some shade or lots of water in hot weather; winter in greenhouse
China Aster	*Callistephus chinensis*	12"	red, blue, pink, white	September to frost	Buy plant in September; tolerates light shade; plant in different soil each year to prevent disease spread
Delphinium	*Delphinium* 'Belladonna'	3'	deep blue	April-June	Plant in fall or early spring

MORE ANNUALS FOR ATLANTA
Best annuals for sun

Common Name	Botanical Name	Height	Bloom Color	Bloom Time	Comments
Egyptian Starflower	*Pentas lanceolata*	dwarf 8" regular 2'	pink or red shades	Summer to fall	Vivid accent; almost continuous blooming
Flowering Maple	*Abutilon*	Varies	orange, yellow, crimson	All summer to frost	1 1/2" pendant bell-shaped flowers
Four O'clocks	*Mirabilis incana*	2'	yellow, red	Spring to frost	Reseeds reliably
Transvaal Daisy	*Gerbera jamesonii*	15-24"	wide color range, yellow, orange, pink, red, white	Summer, but more in spring and fall	Cool nights required for flowering; will return for many years in right spot
Glory Bush	*Tibouchina urvilleana*	4' bush	iridescent purple	Summer	Over-winter in house or greenhouse
Hawk's Beard	*Crepis rubra*	2'	pink, white	April-May	Plant in fall; full sun; cold kills.
Hollyhocks	*Alcea rosea*	dwarf 2 1/2'	mixed	Mid-summer	Biennial; reseeds; spray for diseases
Jacobinia or Brazilian Plume	*Jacobinia carnea*	2 1/2'	hot pink, white	July to frost	Will return every July if not removed
Lantana	*Lantana montevidensis* 'Alba'	18" +	white	Summer to fall	Beware of white flies
Marigold, Dwarf	*Tagetes spp.*	6" to 3'	yellow gold, orange	Summer	Avoid varieties that cease blooming in heat

Common Name	Botanical Name	Height	Bloom Color	Bloom Time	Comments
Melampodium	*Melampodium paludosum* 'Showstar'	18-24"	yellow-gold	Summer	Mounding plant; long blooming star-shaped flowers; best with heat and full sun; reseeds well
Mexican heather	*Cuphea hyssopifolius*	2'	purple, pink, or white	Summer to fall	Shrub can be over-wintered in greenhouse
Money or Silver Dollar Plant	*Lunaria annua*	2-3'	purple or white	April-May	Biennial; full sun to part shade; self-sows freely
New Guinea impatiens	*Impatiens*	15"	red, pink, white, fuchsia	Summer until frost	Protect from hot, dry afternoon sun
Periwinkle, Madagascar	*Vinca catharanthes rosea*	4-10"	white, pink, purple	Early summer to frost	Takes heat and humidity
Petunia	*Petunia integrifolia* 'Pearl' Series, 'Madness' Series, 'Purple Wave' or 'Pink Wave', *P.* 'Surfinia'	All cascade	magenta, azure blue, deep blue rose, light pink, royal blue, arctic white, etched pink or blue	Summer/fall	Only petunias that tolerate our heat and humidity; all relatively small flowers
California bluebell	*Phaecelia campanulata*	12"	blue	Summer	Tolerates heat; blooms sun and shade

MORE ANNUALS FOR ATLANTA
Best annuals for sun

Common Name	Botanical Name	Height	Bloom Color	Bloom Time	Comments
Poppies, Iceland	*Papaver nudicaule* 'Champagne Bubbles'	2' or less in brief spring	white, yellow, orange	Spring until hot/humid	Plant fall or early spring in sun
Portulaca/Moss Rose	*Portulaca grandiflora*	4-6"	all colors but blue	Spring to frost	Plant spring/summer; reseeds somewhat; enjoys drought and sandy soil
Queen Anne's Lace	*Daucus carota*	4-5'	white	May to September	Biennial
Red Mustard, Giant	*Brassica juncea* 'Giant Red'	2'	fuchsia	Late fall plumes	Likes cool fall weather; may not survive severe freeze; mixes well with pansies/flowering cabbages
Salvia, Annual	*Salvia*	12-15"	red, blue	Summer	Needs pinching to promote blooms; bedding or accent plant; these five salvias are brilliant beacons as weather cools; tender perennials that occasionally survive local winters
	S. coccinea	3'	red	Prime-fall	
	S. c. 'Alba'		white		
	S. guarantica	4'	dark blue	Prime-fall	
	S. 'Indigo Spires'	4'	blue	Prime-fall	
	S. leucantha	3'	purple/white velvet	Prime-fall	
	S. 'Van Houtii'	3 1/2'	maroon-red	Prime-fall	
Shoo-fly Plant	*Nicandra physalodes*	3-4'	blue flowers with white base	Summer to fall	Cup-shaped, tiny morning glory; repels insects, whiteflies; opens p.m; one day only; reseeds reliably

MORE ANNUALS FOR ATLANTA cont'd

Best annuals for sun

Common Name	Botanical Name	Height	Bloom Color	Bloom Time	Comments
Scaevola	Scaevola aemula 'Blue Wonder' and a new selection with smaller, more numerous flowers	Sprawling to 7"	blue	Summer	Fan-shaped flowers; prefers hot, humid weather; repeat bloomer
Skyflower	Duranta repens	to 3'	lavender	Summer	Attractive fleshy golden seeds
Southern Star	Oxypetalum caerulea	18"	powder blue	Early summer	Plant seedling in spring
Stock	Matthiola	15-30"	varied colors	Spring	Fall/spring planting
Sunflowers	Helianthus annus	3-7'	yellow, gold, white, red	Summer to fall	Seed in spring
Swan River Daisy	Brachycome iberidifolia	6"	two varieties in two shades of blue with yellow centers	Summer to fall to frost	Ground hugging mound of daisies, lighter shade is hardier; compact; spreading
Sweet William	Dianthus barbatus	4-12"	white, pink, purple, crimson	Mid-spring/ early summer	Plant in fall in part shade; reseeds; can be short-lived perennial; weak in center; continue by covering stems with soil to root

MORE ANNUALS FOR ATLANTA
Best annuals for sun

Common Name	Botanical Name	Height	Bloom Color	Bloom Time	Comments
Treasure Flower	*Gazania*	6-15"	cream, yellow, golden orange, bronze, pink, red in combinations	Late spring to frost	Tight mat of foliage; 3-5" flowers; open morning, close at night; full sun and excellent drainage required
Verbena	*Verbena x hybrida*	6-12"	red, white, pink, blue	Summer	Takes heat, drought, nutrient-starved soil
Wallflower	*Cheiranthus allionii*	2'	orange, yellow	Winter/spring	Plant in fall, takes part shade

MORE ANNUALS FOR ATLANTA
Best annuals for shade

Common Name	Botan. Name	Height	Bloom Color	Bloom Time	Comments
Begonia (Wax or Fibrous Rooted)	*Begonia semperflorens*	6-12" Three sizes	rose, pink, white, bicolors	Spring through fall	Takes shade or sun; long-blooming; foliage bronze or green
Browallia or Amethyst Flower	*Browallia speciosa*	12-18"	blue or white	All summer until frost	Part shade; has some difficulty here
Cineraria	*Senecio x hybridus*	12"	blue, red, pink, white	Brief spring	Cool conditions necessary
Heronsbill	*Erodium*	5" flower stem	pink-white, veined darker	Summer	Part shade; hardiness unknown
Persian/German Violet	*Exacum affine*	7"	lavender blue; yellow short, thick stamens	June-September	Part shade; average soil; plant crown at soil level
Primrose	*Primula obconica*	12"	blue or pink (at Pike's in February)	Spring through summer into October	Part shade; blooms through wet, warm summer; mulch in winter or over-winter indoors
Primrose, Cowslip	*Primula veris*	2-6"	soft yellow with orange or gold center	February/March	All primroses can be purchased at Pike's for containers or in-ground planting

M O R E   A N N U A L S   F O R   A T L A N T A
Best annuals for shade

Common Name	Botan. Name	Height	Bloom Color	Bloom Time	Comments
Monkey Flower	*Mimulus x hybridus*	4-24"	scarlet, orange, yellow with contrasting blotches	Spring or early summer	Velvety, freckled, funnel-shaped flowers; prefers cool weather
Sultana, Impatiens, Busy Lizzie	*Impatiens wallerana or cultorum*	12-24"	various	Summer to fall	Reseeds heavily, particularly in wet areas

JEFF POTTER'S BEST FOLIAGE ANNUALS

Common Name	Botanical Name	Description
Flowering Maple	*Abutilon hybridum* 'Souvenir de Bonn'	Creamy white-margined maple-shaped leaves; hanging salmon bell-shaped flowers
Flowering Maple	*Abutilon pictum* 'Thompsonii'	Mottled yellow and green maple-shaped leaves; hanging orange bell-shaped flowers
Lance Copperleaf	*Acalypha wilkesiana godseffiana* 'Heterophylla'	Long finely cut leaves edged in rich cream and copper on delicate weeping stems
	A. w. 'Java White'	Broad leaves splashed creamy yellow and pink, giving good contrast
	A. w. 'Louisiana Red'	Large broad leaves of deep red and bronze
Alternanthera	*Alternanthera*	Chartreuse
Asparagus Fern (Sprenger Asparagus)	*Asparagus sprengeri*	Fine, ferny foliage; keep moist, likes cramped roots, regular doses of liquid fertilizer
Coleus	*Coleus* 'Trailing Red'	Burgundy/blue
	Coleus 'Variegata'	Green/cream
Curry Plant	*Helichrysum minus*	Systemic rose insecticide necessary at planting to prevent demise
Licorice Plant	*Helichrysum petiolaris*	Round, silver-gray, soft velveteen leaves; trailing
Limelight Licorice	*H. p.* 'Limelight'	Same as above with lime-sherbet-colored leaves
Pink Polka Dot Plant	*Hypoestes* 'Pink Splash'	Oval leaves liberally spotted with pink dots
Parrot's Beak	*Lotus berthelotii*	Lacy, needle-like, silver, trailing foliage
Dusty Miller	*Senecio cineraria*	Rain resistant; can be used in winter as well as rest of year; silver

JEFF POTTER'S BEST FOLIAGE ANNUALS

Common Name	Botanical Name	Description
Pepper, Ornamental	*Capsicum annum*	Tolerates part shade
Ochre Flame Trailing Coleus	*Plectranthus amboinicus* 'Ochre Flame'	Fuzzy succulent paired leaves; avocado green edge with lime and mint green center; trailing
Giant Candle	*Plectranthus fosteri marginatus*	Erect square stem with fuzzy scalloped green leaves, edged with white margins
Giant Candle	*P. f.* 'Green on Green'	Same as *P.f. marginatus* except leaves have light lime green to gold margin
Purple Heart	*Setcreasea pallida*	Succulent, long purple leaves; semi-trailing habit; pink flowers

Chapter
Seventeen

Bulbs

by
Avis Aronovitz
with
Gary Spikula and Sue Vrooman

Growing Bulbs Successfully in Atlanta

Bulbs are easy to grow if you treat them with a little tender loving care. Most bulbs require a sunny, well-drained spot; bulb failure is usually caused by rotting due to poor drainage. Soil preparation, correct planting depth, adequate and proper watering, and sufficient nutrition will mean the difference between success and failure for your bulbs.

Growing Bulbs

Since most bulbs are heavy feeders, mix bulb food with the soil beneath the bulb at planting time. Top dress when the foliage appears each year. Many recommend another feeding in the fall, too. This will increase flowering and the life of your bulb. Remember bulbs make flowers, but bulb food makes bulbs.

Fortunately, bulbs are rarely bothered by diseases or insects, so spraying is rarely necessary. However watering is most important, particularly as the plant begins to grow and bloom. Keep soil evenly moist until the leaves yellow.

Plant spring-flowering bulbs when the ground is cool, but not yet frozen—late September through (if you haven't found time) early December. October is probably best since essential root growth occurs in autumn and early winter. Plant daffodil bulbs about 6" deep and smaller bulbs at lesser depths. A too-shallow planting will require more frequent lifting and division as the bulbs will split up more quickly. This is good for propagating, but not flowering.

Plant summer flowering bulbs after the last frost is over in spring. Plant fall blooming bulbs in early fall. (By late August is even better.) Most fall blooming bulbs such as fall crocus, sternbergia, and colchicum will bloom the same autumn that they are planted; others the following autumn. Others will perform as an annual and not return the next fall. Sometimes fall bloomers will skip flowering a year or two if the summer weather is not to their liking. Summer bloomers such as ginger lily, nerine, allium, and autumn snowdrop may be planted in spring, along with the summer flowering bulbs. Always follow the planting instructions that accompany the bulbs.

Although it is easy to be successful with bulbs, it is certainly necessary to learn the specific needs of any bulb you plant. Read and follow carefully the directions that come with the bulbs you purchase.

Hyacinths

Although hyacinths are said to be short-lived, some purple ones situated on an incline in my garden for 30 years, blooming by March first, are just beginning to decline. Thirty-year-old yellows in the same area bloom in late February. Flower clusters loosen, but remain attractive. Hyacinths need good drainage and can become so heavy in flower that they need staking.

Tulips

Allan Armitage states in *Herbaceous Perennial Plants* that in the South, tulips are short-lived perennials at best. Others say that tulips should be treated as annuals. Most tulips here do not return the second year. **An exception:** five perennial tulip varieties from White Flower Farm. Following their directions, I have tulips returning for seven or eight years without declining, actually increasing in number. The secret of success with these tulips is planting 8" deep and feeding.

Crinums

Crinum lilies are rare, expensive bulbs, with lush tropical foliage and sometimes large flowers from June through fall. They bloom in late afternoon or night and the flowers of some varieties droop by noon the following day. Their fragrance has no equal. Crinums are best left undisturbed for heavier blooming, but they benefit from mulching, fertilizing, and watering.

Daffodils

Daffodils are probably the most common bulb grown here. They will bloom in wooded areas, but perform better on open, sunny land. They bloom dependably year after year, multiplying and vigorously increasing flower yield. Daffodils are not as demanding of perfect drainage as tulips and some other bulbs, but they will not tolerate standing water. Daffodil bulbs contain a poisonous fluid that acts as a strong repellant to most pests. Select firm bulbs, preferably "double nosed" ones (a mother bulb with one or more noses or offsets that are small bulbs attached to it like a Siamese twin). These bulbs promise at least two flower stalks with flowers the following spring. Generally speaking, bulbs of large cup daffodils should be 2-3" in diameter .

Be aware that recent spring freezes proved double daffodils like 'Golden Ducat' and 'Obdam' are poor choices here.

Summer Bulb Challenges

Gladioli sometimes are seen growing successfully in Atlanta, but they are not highly regarded except as cut flowers because of their stiff appearance, dead flowers on stalk, and floppiness.

Dwarf dahlias usually do not bloom well in our hot summers. Buds and blooms turn black. Cool weather in fall brings better blooms for surviving plants.

Dutch Iris *Iris* 'Oriental Beauty' and *I.* 'Romano' grow 16-18" in blues, whites, purple, and yellow bronze combinations. Plant in sandy soil. They require dry summer soil; tolerate water-logged spring soils. Bulbs are not long lasting.

Tips from Experts

From Beverly Barbour, Lawrenceville's expert daffodil grower: "To improve drainage, I work in pine bark mulch, sharp granite sand, and a complete fertilizer such as 10-10-10 (one cup per square foot). Fertilizer should never come in direct contact with any bulb. I add bone meal or a commercial bulb food in spring when the foliage appears, again immediately following blooming, and once more in the fall."

From local members of the Georgia Daffodil Society: Following flowering, leaves should **never** be cut from a plant or even braided since they are essential in the rebuilding of the bulb after flowering. A dry spring requires watering to keep foliage green as long as possible. When the foliage has dried, remove it and cultivate the ground to prevent insects from having a direct path to the bulb. Divide clumps when flowers become smaller and fewer, usually every four to five years. Dig as foliage turns yellow, and store until fall in a cool, airy place. Do not forcibly break off small offsets from bulbs. Use a sharp knife to separate.

They also remind us that newly purchased, good bulbs already have flower buds within them and should produce a flower the following season that is true to name and description. If not, let the seller know and request a replacement. Remember some flowers take several days to acquire "catalog color" (the enticing flower color of the catalog illustration). Pinks are at their best in a cool, moist season. Bulbs can fail to flower or give smaller blooms the second season as they adapt to your soil, your climate, and your care. The third season will bring a generous supply of blooms if conditions are right and sunlight adequate. For information about joining the Georgia Daffodil Society, contact the Atlanta Botanical Garden.

Choosing Bulbs

There are many good bulbs for all seasons that perform well in local gardens, listed in the following charts. Unfortunately, many are much under-utilized. With each type, special cultural information is given. Bloom dates can differ from year to year as much as a month. The length of time a bulb is in bloom can vary, depending on climatic conditions.

Caution: Buy only nursery-propagated bulbs. In all catalogs from which you order, look for a disclaimer stating that all bulbs sold are from commercial sources. Bulbs collected in the wild can be identified by several cues. If the price appears "too good to be true," if the nursery uses off-beat or improper botanical names, or if the pictures are highly colored and unnatural, be wary.

Sources for Bulbs

See Appendix A for addresses and telephone numbers.

Local Sources

Atlanta Botanical Garden Plant Sale (choices often already proven successful at ABG)

Eco Gardens (natives, hardy exotics)

Farmers and Consumers Market Bulletin (good source for Southeast natives, particularly crinums suitable for blooming in Atlanta, at very reasonable prices)

Hall's Greenhouses

Hastings

Home Depot

Pike Family Nurseries (select early, shop sales)

Mail Order Sources

Daffodil Mart (good selection, particularly reliable)

Dutch Gardens (best prices, popular selection, good bulbs)

Franz Roozen (bulbs direct from Holland)

Novelty Daffodils (recommended by local expert daffodil growers)

Greer Gardens (excellent cyclamen, trillium, schizostylis)

Jacques Armand (unusual bulbs, English-based company, pricey, large choice *Arisaemas*)

McClure and Zimmerman Quality Flower Bulb Brokers (excellent, large selection of hardy bulbs)

Park Seed Company (expensive, usually excellent bulbs and service)

Plant Delights (callas and *Zephranthes*)

Plumeria People (tropical gingers, subtropicals)

Siskiyou Rare Plant Nursery (sternbergia, trillium)

Van Bourgondien (good prices and selection, quality not consistent)

Wayside Gardens (expensive, usually excellent bulbs and service)

We-Du Nurseries (unusual bulbs)

White Flower Farm (perennial tulips and more)

Woodlander's Nursery (*Habranthus, Zephranthes*, ginger lily)

Common Name	Botanical Name	Height	Color	Bloom Time	Comments
1. Crocus	Crocus species, cultivars and hybrids	2-4"	various	December-March	Blooms well under deciduous trees; plant all 4" deep, 3-6" apart
Scotch Crocus	C. biflorus	4"	white with purple striping	Mid February-mid March	Tolerates semi-shade; long-blooming; raised area; fast drainage; returns well
Snow Crocus	C. chrysanthus	3-4"	variable	Late January-early March	Golden yellow throat; rounded flowers distinguish it from the Scotch crocus; long lasting; floriferous; charming
	C. c. 'Blue Bird'	3"	violet-blue exterior, cream inside	1/29-3/1	
	C. c. 'E. A. Bowles,' 'E.P. Bowles'	3"	lemon yellow, purple veining	1/19-2/24	'E. A. Bowles' has larger flowers than 'E. P. Bowles'
	C. c. 'Gypsy Girl'	4"	yellow, flamed bronze	1/21-2/24	
	C. c. 'Snowbunting'	3"	white with gray feathering	2/15-2/26	
	C. sieberi	2 1/2"	pale to deep lilac, yellow throat	Late December-early January	Orange stigma protrudes like a tongue from the unopened bud

TEN BEST SPRING-FLOWERING BULBS AND THEIR KIN

Common Name	Botanical Name	Height	Color	Bloom Time	Comments
	C. s. 'Bowles White'		white with orange throat	Late December-January; others in February	
	C. s. 'Violet Queen'		amethyst violet		
	C. s. 'Firefly'		rich lilac on yellow base	2/8 in '94	
Cloth of Gold	C. susianus	2 1/2"	golden, brown-feathered	2/9 in '94	Thick flower clusters
Gold Bunch	C. ancyrensis	3"	golden, brown-feathered	early February	Thick clusters; probably the easiest, most reliable crocus here
	C. fleischeri	3"	pure white feathered scarlet orange stigmas (Looks like coral.)	Before mid-March	Star-shaped 3" bloom; sun-loving; narrow foliage appears before flower
Hungarian Crocus	C. tomasinianus species/cultivars 'Whitewell Purple'	3"	reddish-violet; silver-grey in bud Amethyst/bluish	Mid-January-early March 2/14-3/10	Naturalizes well; superior crocus for this area
	C. vernus 'Pickwick'	3"	white petals/striped lilac	Late March	Short, rounded, large flowers

TEN BEST SPRING-FLOWERING BULBS AND THEIR KIN cont'd

Common Name	Botanical Name	Height	Color	Bloom Time	Comments
2. Daffodil	Narcissus spp. and hybrids; 11 divisions	12-18"	yellow, white, pink shades or mixed	February to March	Good under deciduous trees; rodent proof; part shade tolerant; plant 6" deep in early fall
	N. 'Barrett Browning'	14-16"	white with orange red	3/8 in '94	Small cupped
	N. 'Carlton'	18-20"	two-toned yellow	2/20-3/13	Vanilla fragrance; naturalizes; often mistakenly sold as 'King Alfred'
	N. 'Ice Follies'	14"	creamy white, light yellow	2/20-3/20	Multiplies well; large flowers, flat cup; withstands wind, rain
	N. 'Mt. Hood'	15-17"	white	3/9-late March	Dependable white
	N. 'Silver Chimes'	12-15"	pale yellow	Late mid season	Best multi-flowered on one stem; fragrant as hyacinths
Tazetta	N. 'Geranium'	14-17"	orange	Late mid season	Multi-flowered stem; fragrant
Cyclamineus	N. 'February Gold'	14"	bright gold	2/4-3/5 (varies)	Early bloomer
	N. 'Jetfire'	12-14"	deep yellow red/orange, cupped		By early mid season; display spectacular
Triandrus Daffodils Orchid Narcissus	N. 'Thalia'	16"	pure white	3/7-4/20	One of the loveliest of all daffodils; 2-3" pendulous, fragrant blossoms

TEN BEST SPRING-FLOWERING BULBS AND THEIR KIN

Common Name	Botanical Name	Height	Color	Bloom Time	Comments
Split-Corona Daffodil	N. 'Mondragon'	14"	golden yellow petals; deep orange collar	3/15 mid-season	Apple scent; orchid-flowering; superior return here; increases number quickly
Intermediate Daffodil	N. 'Susie' (Jonquilla)	15-17"	sunproof orange yellow	late March	Multi-flowered stem; long-lasting; fragrant; 'Peeping Tom' is like 'February Gold', but has smaller blooms
	N. 'Peeping Tom'	14-16"		February	
Species and Wild	N. bulbocodium conspicuous 'Hoop Petticoat'	4-6"	yellow	2/27-4/6 (mid season)	Megaphone-shaped cups with reed-like petals; reseeds; tricky, but pure charm
	N. odorus-campernellii	5"	bright yellow	2/28-3/15	Fragrant
Miniature Daffodil	N. spp.	6-10"			Plant early fall, 4" deep; 2-4" apart
	N. 'Minnow'	6-8"	white-bright yellow center	late March	Fragrant; multi-flowering
	N. 'Hawera'	6-8"	lemon yellow	3/11-4/12	Dainty, pendant flowers
	N. 'Jumblie'	5-6"	yellow petals; reflexed thin, yellow/orange cup	3/20-4/11	Long-lasting flowers; great in containers and small places

Common Name	Botanical Name	Height	Color	Bloom Time	Comments
	N. 'Sun Disc'	8-12"	pale primrose petals, butter yellow cup	After mid-April	Dainty 1-1 1/4" flat frilled cup outlined in pale primrose
	N. 'Tête-à-tête'	6-8"	buttercup yellow petals, yellow-orange cup	February/March	2-3 flowers per stem; holds up to wind and rain; best in semi-shade; a rock garden cutie
	N. juncifolius	5"	deep yellow	Early March	Does well in part shade; 1" flower
3. Glory-of-the-Snow	Chionodoxa luciliae (Probably C. sieheri)	4-6"	blue with white eye	3/22-4/16	Same color clumps best; 6-12 flowers per stem; plant Chionodoxa 2-3" deep
	C. l. 'Pink Giant'	6-8"	blush pink/white eye	3/7, 3/13, 4/16	Very sturdy; 8-10 flowers per stem
	C. gigantea alba	4-6"	white	3/27	Woodland shade or sun; up to 10 starry flowers stem
4. Hyacinth, Dutch	Hyacinthus orientalis	8-10"	white, pink, blue, purple, yellow, red	March	Very fragrant; plant 4-6" deep; avoid top-sized bulbs whose flower stalks require staking, 1st/2nd size adequate
	H. o. 'Anna-Marie'	8-10"	pastel pink	Early to late March	About first established hyacinth bloom
	H. o. 'Pink Perfection'	6-8"	hot pink	Late March	Strong fragrance; often double-stalked

TEN BEST SPRING-FLOWERING BULBS AND THEIR KIN

Common Name	Botanical Name	Height	Color	Bloom Time	Comments
Hyacinth, Dutch (cont'd)	H. o. 'Carnegie'	8"	white	3/20	Outstanding; blooms for more than 2 1/2 weeks; densely flowered spike
	H. o. 'Delft Blue'	8"	soft lilac blue	3/15-3/30; Established 3/1	Naturalizes here
	H. o. 'Blue Jacket'	8"	dark blue	Mid-March	Extremely large flowers
	H. o. 'Violet Pearl'	4-6"	mallow-purple	3/15-3/20	Boasts lovely fragrance
	H. o. 'City of Harlem'	6-8"	pastel yellow	3/15	Best yellow ever developed
	H. o. 'Hollyhock'	4-6"	rosy-red double	3/20	Dense spikes (double florets) long lasting; fragrant
Roman Hyacinth	H. o. var. albulus 'Roman Hyacinth'	8"	white (blue or pink-later and rare)	Very early	7-12 flowers on 3 or 4 spikes per bulb; more graceful; tolerates heavier soils
5. Hyacinth, Grape	Muscari neglectum	8"	blues or white	2/20-4/6	Fragrant; resemble clusters of grapes; foliage appears in late summer; multiplies; plant 2-3" deep
	M. armeniacum 'Early Giant'	6"	white spikes rimmed in cobalt blue	3/15	Less vigorous, less invasive

Common Name	Botanical Name	Height	Color	Bloom Time	Comments
Italian Grape Hyacinth	M. botryoides	6"	sky blue rimmed in white	3/15	The original grape hyacinth; fragrance of plums; two spikes per bulb
Feather Hyacinth	M. lactifolium	10-12"	medium blue over deep violet	3/15-3/20	Intensely fragrant; extraordinary flowers; one or two broad leaves
Feather Hyacinth	M. plumosum	6"	feathery purple mass	3/15	Sterile branching thread-like petals
6. Snowdrops, Common	Galanthus nivalis	5"	white with single green spot	1/28-2/6 (can be as late as 2/20)	Solitary, delicate nodding flower on leafless stem; don't allow bulbs to dry out in summer or before planting; likes rich, woodsy soil; shade; plant 2" deep
7. Snowflake	Leucojum	varies	white tipped with green	varies	Heirloom bulb; plant 3" deep
Spring Snowflake	L. vernum	9"	white tipped with green	Immediately following Snowdrops	Bulbs dry out easily; order, plant early; bell-shaped blooms with a subtle, sweet fragrance
Summer Snowflake	L. aestivum	12-18"	3-5 green-tipped bell-like white flowers on arching stems	About same time	Almost foolproof; likes moist site; larger and more floriferous than spring snowflake
Summer Snowflake	L. aestivum 'Gravetye Giant'	20"	same	Late March (3/13 in '94)	Larger and more robust than summer snowflake; 7 flowers per stem

TEN BEST SPRING-FLOWERING BULBS AND THEIR KIN

Common Name	Botanical Name	Height	Color	Bloom Time	Comments
8. Squills	*Scilla*	varies	blue or pink	Varies	Tolerates shady areas; plant 2-3" deep; petals separate at base
Meadow Squill	*S. amethystina* or *S. pratensis*	5-10"	veronica violet bunch of 12-30 flowers	April	Mildly fragrant
Twin-leaf Squill	*S. bifolia*	3-4"	gentian blue, dangles in loose bunches	February	Flowers rotate stem; upward facing star-like flowers
Bright Pink Squill	*S. bifolia* 'Rosea'	4-6"	rosy pink in bud; dirty, off-white in flower	Early February	Attractive color apparent in bud only
Bluebell, Spanish or Wood Hyacinth	*Hyacinthoides hispanicus*	9-17"	blue, pink, or white	4/17-5/6	Drooping bells on upright, tall stems; can become invasive through seedlings; not fragrant; needs spring moisture
Bluebell, English	*Hyacinthoides non-scriptus*	12"	blue		Less robust; sweetly scented; flower stalk tip nods gracefully; best used in woodland gardens; prefers cooler, damper conditions; difficult here
Squill, Siberian	*S. siberica* *S. s. alba* (less vigor)	4"	deep blue white	3/20 in '94 3/5 in '95	Most beautiful blue in the spring garden; naturalizes; plant 2" deep; 3-4 drooping, bell-like flowers to a stem

TEN BEST SPRING-FLOWERING BULBS AND THEIR KIN cont'd

Common Name	Botanical Name	Height	Color	Bloom Time	Comments
	S. s. 'Spring Beauty'	6-8"	bluest blue	2/4, 3/27 4/16	Sterile, won't reseed
Squill, Lebanon or Striped	Puschkinia scilloides or libanotica	6"	white, striped/pale blue	Pre mid-March	Full sun or part shade; petals fused at base
	S. tubergeniana (S. mischt-schenkoana)	3"	white with blue midrib, bright yellow stamens	Late January-late February (2/20/95)	Flowers as it emerges from the ground; long-blooming, growing more beautiful
9. Starflower, Spring	Ipheion uniflorum or Triteleia	9-10"	bluish white	3/17-4/1 Best 3/10/-3/20/95	Fragrant blooms; bruised leaves have onion smell; can reseed in lawn or garden
	I. uniflorum 'Wisley Blue' or 'Rolf Fiedler'	9-10"	deeper blue	Slightly later than above	Not as vigorous as common form
10. Tulip	Tulipa				
Perennial tulip		28"; 24"; 24"; 32-36"; 24"	opens yellow, becomes ivory white; red, two-toned scarlet, pink, yellow with black base	3/30 3/30 April 6 Mid-March March-April	Store in refrigerator until planting; Milorganite should be mixed with soil in bottom of hole; feed heavily spring, fall, and after blooming; cut foliage back as soon as it begins turning yellow to prevent formation of bulblets; full sun; sturdy stems; huge blooms

TEN BEST SPRING-FLOWERING BULBS AND THEIR KIN

Common Name	Botanical Name	Height	Color	Bloom Time	Comments
Darwin Hybrid Tulip	*T.* x 'Appledorn'	24"	cherry red, base black	Mid spring	Brilliant color
Single Late Garden Tulip	*T.* 'Dreamland'	26-28"	blush pink, flamed white	Early April	
Triumph Tulip	*T.* 'Negrita'	18"	pinkish opening to purplish black	3/30	Excellent cut flower; huge bloom; received raves at ABG 1992 spring
Lily Flowering Tulip	*T.* 'White Triumphter'	26"	pure white	Early April	Giant, superb blooming
Peony Tulip	*T.* 'Angelique'	18-20"	soft pink	April	Flowers resemble peonies; long lasting
Single Early Tulip	*T.* 'Belladonna' *	15"	golden yellow	April	Heavenly scent
Fringed Tulip	*T.* 'Burgundy Lace' *	28"	wine red	Early April	Looks like a fine goblet
Darwin Hybrid Tulip	*T.* 'Golden Oxford' *	18"	pure bright yellow	April	
	T. 'Golden Parade' *	18"	buttercup yellow, fine red edge	April	One of the best tulips
	T. 'Gudoshmik' *	18"	yellow, red streaks	April	

Common Name	Botanical Name	Height	Color	Bloom Time	Comments
	T. 'Orange Bouquet'*	18"	reddish orange	April	
	T. 'Oxford' *	18"	vivid red-orange, yellow center	April	Very strong
	T. 'Parade'	18"	bright signal-red	April	One of the best; very large; strong
Multi-flowering Tulip	T. 'Toronto'	18-24"	salmon red flowers, purple mottled foliage	Late March	3-5 blooms per stem
	T. 'White Emperor'	12-18"	white	Early	Blooms with daffodils
Species Tulips	T. chrysantha	6-8"	yellow-red, dramatic	Early mid season	Since 1607
Lady Tulip	T. clusiana	8-12"	red/white candy striped	3/31	Full sun to part shade
	T. eichleri	8"	scarlet red	Very early	
	T. hageri	5"	Dull red, tinged olive-brown	Mid late season	Wee species; several coppery bells

TEN BEST SPRING-FLOWERING BULBS AND THEIR KIN

Common Name	Botanical Name	Height	Color	Bloom Time	Comments
	T. praestans 'Zwanenburg'	7"	red	Early	Flowers resemble poinsettia flower; big; spectacular
Kaufmannia Tulip	*T. kaufmannia* 'Waterlily'	6-8"	vivid yellow	3/20	Looks like its name and is great in containers; low growing

*Tulips that stand up to summer heat recommended by Professor Paul Nelson at North Carolina State University, supplied by *Southern Living* magazine.

MORE GOOD CHOICES FOR SPRING-FLOWERING BULBS

Common Name	Botanical Name	Height	Color	Bloom Time	Comments
1. Aconites, Winter	*Eranthis hyemalis*	3-4"	yellow/green thin foliage	Mid January, as late as 2/5 (2-week bloom period)	Flourishes in shade/sun; soak before planting; best results from fresh bulbs; naturalizes best in alkaline soil, so add a little lime; plant 2-3" deep
2. Anemone, Poppy Florist's Anemone	*Anemone coronaria* 'Hollandia' or 'His Excellency'	15"	deep vivid red, white base, black center	Mid February-April (3/20/95)	May not persist, but worth frequent replanting; coronaria has the largest and most flowers; plant 2-3" deep
	A. c. 'The Bride'	10-18"	white, single	3/12	
Peony flowered Anemone	*A. c.* 'St. Brigid'	12-14"	bright colors	before 3/15	Large double/semi-double flowers of every color; feathery, fern-like foliage
Grecian Wind Flower	*A. blanda*	4-6"	blue, pink, white	2/27-4/10; 3/20 peak	Flowers for about a month; spreads petals wide; needs cool root run
	A. b. 'White Splendor'	3-6"	white petals, golden center	March/April	Blooms abundantly; spreads
European Wood	*A. nemorosa*	6-10"	light blue	March 27	Lasts many years; simply beautiful
3. Arum	*Arum italicum*	12" or more			Arrow-shaped foliage appears in fall; persists through winter to spring, disappearing in summer; Jack-in-the-pulpit type flower in April, followed by orange-red berries on spikes in late summer; sun/shade; foliage good for winter flower arrangements; plant 3-4" deep

MORE GOOD CHOICES FOR SPRING-FLOWERING BULBS

Common Name	Botanical Name	Height	Color	Bloom Time	Comments
4. Cyclamen, Hardy	*Cyclamen coum*	4-6"	white, pink, magenta	2/6-3/6 (in shade)	Needs excellent summer drainage; plant in wire basket among tree roots on sloping land; mulch; through winter, exquisitely patterned foliage
5. Iris, Juno	*Iris bucharica*	12"	yellow-cream	Late March-early April (3/24/95)	Try dry, sunny area; superb drainage; difficult; 5-7 flowers per stem; plant 2-4" deep
Iris species	*I. reticulata*	6"	purple, blue	Early March	Flowers sometimes overwhelmed by foliage; don't fertilize; plant 2" deep
	I. r. 'Cantab'	4-6"	flax blue, pale yellow blotch	2/13-2/24	
	I. cristata	3"	blue or white	Mid-March-mid-April	Not a true bulb; native; temperamental bloomer; feed heavily; blooms full week
	I. danfordiae	5"	yellow, little brown spots	Mid-January at ABG; My garden early February-mid-March	Flower standards reduced to bristles between showy falls; treat as annual since bulbs split into tiny non-blooming bulblets; great in containers
	I. 'Katherine Hodgkin'	5"	pale blue/yellow	2/13	Unusual; dwarf; treat as annual

MORE GOOD CHOICES FOR SPRING-FLOWERING BULBS cont'd

Common Name	Botanical Name	Height	Color	Bloom Time	Comments
6. Lily, Trout/ Dog's Tooth Violet	*Erythronium*	6-10"	yellow, pink purple, white	March-April (3/21/95)	Graceful nodding heads; striped/ mottled leaves; plant in masses in partial shade in very light soil, 3" deep, 3-6" apart
	E. 'Pagoda'	7-8"	yellow with brown ring	3/13-4/11	Takes a year to settle in; must be planted on arrival in rich, moist soil
7. Onion, Flowering	*Allium*	varies	blue, pink, white, yellow	Spring, summer or autumn	Flowers tight or loose umbels; plant 3" deep (smaller bulbs 2" deep); full sun/light shade
	A. triquetrum	14-18"	white bells	Early April	Needs shade and moisture
	A. unifolium	12-18"	pink, rose	All May	Native; long blooming period
Star of Persia Onion	*A. albopilosum/ christophii*	18-30"	amethyst	4/12-5/21	Allium with largest flower
Naples Onion	*A. neapolitanum* 'Grandiflorum'	15"	white with rosy stamens	4/12-5/20	Mild, sweet scent; loose 3" "shuttlecock" umbels; happy in soggy soil in spring
	A. schubertii	12-24"	200 pink florets	Late spring into summer	Sensitive to frost; cover with mulch to protect; volleyball size (15") umbels; mix of 8" male and 1 1/2" female flowers
	A. giganteum	36-48"	deep purple	5/15-6/15	Tallest allium; dense 5" umbels; persists!
	A. 'Globemaster'	42"	violet	before 5/15-6/1	Giant flowers; fantastic

MORE GOOD CHOICES FOR SPRING-FLOWERING BULBS

Common Name	Botanical Name	Height	Color	Bloom Time	Comments
8. Snake's Head Iris Widow Iris	*Hermodactylus tuberosus/ I. tuberosa*	12"	lime green velvety brown falls	2/6-3/6	Sweet, peppery scent; plant in evenly moist soil; exotic late winter beauty
9. Star of Bethlehem	*Ornithogalum umbellatum*	10"	white with green mid-rib	4/11-4/29	Easy, but difficult to control because invasive; closes at night
Chincherinchee/African Wonder Flower	*O. thyrsoides*	18"	cream or white	Mid-May	Much better behaved; popular for flower arrangements; far less hardy.
10. Wake Robin	*Trillium*	See Ch. 24, "Native Plants." Now propagated by tissue culture. **Don't buy collected bulbs.**			
Catesby's Trillium or Rose Trillium	*T. catesbaei/ T. stylosum*	8-10"	pink	Early April for one month	Flowers held beneath foliage; sides of leaves turn upward; common native
Toad Trillium	*T. sessile/ T. cuneatum*	6-12"	maroon	4/11	Fragrance like Sweet Shrub; most common southeast sessile trillium; flowers (never open wide) held directly on mottled foliage
	T. luteum	8-10"	yellow/green	March/April	Sessile
	T. grandiflorum	10-15"	white aging pink	3/20-4/11	Large flower, opening wide on short stem above foliage
11. Atamasco Lily	*Zephyranthes atamasco*	8-10"	white or pale pink	4/12-4/24	Common rain lily from southeast swampy areas; sweet fragrance; trumpet-shaped, short-lived flowers; dormant after blooming; do not allow to dry out entirely; use 5-10 bulbs for good show under deciduous trees

Common Name	Botanical Name	Height	Color	Bloom Time	Comments
12. Garlic, False/ Crow Poison	*Nothoscordum bivalve*	8-10"	cream with yellow center	Spring to fall	Southeast native; full sun; loose umbels; no onion smell; sweet, spicy carnation-like perfume
13. Hardy/ Chinese Ground Orchid	*Bletilla striata* B. s. 'Alba'	12" 12"	pink/purple white	4/1 4/1-5/15	Rich, even moist soil; part shade; mulch in winter; miniature orchid; frost and drought kill flowers

REAL CHALLENGES IN SPRING BULBS

Common Name	Botanical Name	Height	Color	Bloom Time	Planting Tips	Comments
1. Byzantine Gladiolus (Corn Flags)	*Gladiolus byzantinus*	24"	purple-red (magenta)	Spring	Plant 5" deep, 4" apart; full sun, well-drained loam	Tolerates heavy soils; lift when overgrown; no crowding; freeze can kill
2. Camassia	*Camassia leichtlinii* 'Blue Danube'	30-36"	tall spikes, dark blue star-like flowers	Mid-late April	Tolerates dampness, heavy soils	Alba form less vigorous; Native American bulb
3. Crown Imperial	*Fritillaria imperialis*	30"	orange or yellow bell-like flowers	Late March	6' deep, 8" apart	Almost impossible here; requires perfect drainage, lime; best not disturbed; emits odor that repels rodents and humans
Checkered Lily or Guinea Hen	*F. meleagris*	12"	bronze, gray, purple, white checkered	Spring	2", no deeper; for shade garden	Both have pendant bell-like flowers; easier than *F. imperialis*
	F. 'Aphrodite'	12"	pure white			Hybrids easier than wild forms
4. Ixiolirion	*Ixiolirion*	15"	sky blue	June (in woods)	3" deep, 4" apart	Difficult to obtain bulbs; doesn't return well

REAL CHALLENGES IN SPRING BULBS cont'd

Common Name	Botanical Name	Height	Color	Bloom Time	Planting Tips	Comments
5. Wood Sorrel or Lady Sorrel (Shamrock)	Oxalis O. crassipes (O. rubra)	6-8"	pink, red, or white	Almost all year; spring/summer to frost	1-2" deep; keep dry in winter; cut back to stimulate new growth	Small funnel-shaped flowers usually close at night, open the next morning; short stems, low-growing clover-like foliage; see "Wood Sorrels" in The Little Bulbs by Elizabeth Lawrence; visit Eco-Gardens
	O. c. 'Alba'	8"	pink-wine colored markings; white-gray markings			
	O. regnelli O. r. 'Trian-gularis'	8"	white pale pink/bright reddish purple leaves	Almost all year	Full sun/ partial shade	Flowers show well against triangular green leaflets (purple beneath); enjoys damp ground
6. Snake Palm	Amorphophallus rivieri	3'	blackish red	Spring	Exotic in sheltered area of shade garden; flowering requires drying in winter; lift	Enormous goblet flower arises from bare ground and emits foul odor; in summer has one leaf resembling a palm tree; stem is mottled
7. Monarch of the East (Voodoo Lily)	Sauromatum guttatum	3' leaf stalk	green outside; yellow/reddish purple interior; bracts round black-purple central spike	Spring	Moist, shady conditions	Exotically lush leaves on stalks marked with dark purple spots; lift tuber in fall to give required dry rest period; will flower unplanted; foul smelling; 12-20 4" flowers

REAL CHALLENGES IN SPRING BULBS

Common Name	Botanical Name	Height	Color	Bloom Time	Planting Tips	Comments
8. **Garden Dragon** Green Dragon	*Arisaema* *A. dracontium*	12-18"	pale green "Dragon-Tongue" is 5-6" long	May-June (foliage precedes flower)	Damp woods, bright shade, spring water essential; tolerant of summer drought	Temperate zone relatives of the sauromatum; retains horseshoe leaf pattern of tropical relative; more modest foliage suggesting hellebore
9. **Jack-in-the-Pulpit**	*A. triphyllum*	varies	purple/green	Spring	Occurs naturally in rich, damp woods.	Three-parted leaves; plant in cool shady area; never allow roots to dry out
	A. quinatum	varies	greenish/white	Spring	See above	Five-part foliage
10. **Asiatic Arisaema**	*A. candidissimum*	2 1/2-3'	hooded white spathe, inside delicately striped pink, pale green markings on exterior	Late spring	Flower appears before 3-part leaf expands	Asiatic varieties of arisaemas just becoming popular here; look for more testing of these

TEN BEST SUMMER-FLOWERING BULBS

Common Name	Botanical Name	Height	Color	Bloom Time	Comments
1. Calla Lily (Pig Lily)	*Zantedeschia*	15-20" varies	pink, yellow, white, or red	Early June-July	Large cup-shaped waxen flowers (spathes); needs moisture/compost; survives moderate winters; good in containers; sun/part shade
2. Canna, Hybrid	*Canna*	18"; 2-1/2 to 3'; 3-4'; 5-6'	reds or yellows, variations/ combinations	May-September	Spreads, give plenty of room; tender types need heavy mulch in winter
3. Lily	*Lilium*				Lilies, except the Madonna Lily, are usually planted in spring
Asiatic Hybrid	*Lilium*	3-3 1/2'	yellow, orange	May 15 to early June	Most feature upward facing flowers; prefer sun; tolerate shade; pest and disease resistant
Oriental Lilies	*L.* 'Casa Blanca'	4-5'	pure white	July 20 (7/12/96)	Does not return reliably, but worth planting each year; soil preparation critical, add humus and sand; be wary of virus infection; up to 8 richly fragrant 10" flowers per stem
	L. auratum 'Platyphyllum'	5-6'	golden rays waxy white/ crimson dots	2nd week in June	Many sensational 10" bowl-shaped flowers
	L. 'Stargazer'	18"	vivid red/white margin	Varies	Good in containers; flower has particularly strong substance; vigorous; one of best!

TEN BEST SUMMER-FLOWERING BULBS

Common Name	Botanical Name	Height	Color	Bloom Time	Comments
Trumpet Lilies	*L. longiflorum* 'Golden Splendor'	6'	gold, trumpet-like flowers	Early June	Long lasting bulb and flowers; striking in landscape
	L. speciosum 'Uchida'	4-6'	waxy crimson	July	Disease resistant; fragrant; hardy for many years; lost all of mine spring '96
	L. s. 'Rubrum'	3'	carmine flowers, stems purple/brown	August	Well-drained soil; partial shade
Turk's Cap	*L. superbum*	4-7'	green base shades tawny, tip scarlet	Early June	Bulbs rot easily; rodents seem to enjoy also
	L. henryi	8'	light orange green throat, brown spots	Mid July	Good, permanent lily; enjoys a little lime and heavy soil; sun or shade; requires staking
Madonna Lily	*L. candidum*	6'	clear, waxy white	Early May; spring-early summer	Plant only 1" deep in fall (only lily that must be planted in fall)
Philippine Lily	*L. philippinense*	6-8'	white tinged with green	Mid August	Flower substance poor and short blooming in extreme heat and drought; fragrant
4. **Milk and Wine Lily**	*Crinum latifolium* var. *zeylanicum*	3'	white with red or pink streak, evergreen foliage	June and August	Dependable but short-lived blooms; plant November-April with neck above ground; single digit temperatures may destroy potential blooms

TEN BEST SUMMER-FLOWERING BULBS cont'd

Common Name	Botanical Name	Height	Color	Bloom Time	Comments
Southern Swamp Lily/ Florida Crinum	Crinum americanum	3'	white	Spring and summer	Takes some shade; enjoys very wet soil; showy; fragrant; stemless
	C. 'Catherine'	2'	pure white wide petals	Mid-summer and fall	Good in small garden
	C. 'Cecil Houdyshel'	3-4'	rose-pink	All summer (8/5 in '93)	Tulip-shaped blooms
	C. 'Ellen Bosanquet'		deep rosy pink	7/14	Fragrant, wide flowers; Sue Vrooman says it's "rock dependable"
	C. powellii album	3'	white	June	Trumpet-shaped blooms; only dependable crinum in my garden
5. Onion	Allium				
Italian	A. narcissiflorum	12-14"	rose	July-fall	Rarely offered; nodding in bud, erect in flower
	A. senescens	8"	rose-whitish	Late Spring-July	Attractive
Chinese or Garlic Chive	A. tuberosum	10"	white	August into September	Aromatic, strap-like foliage; star-shaped flowers
Lavender Globe Lily	A. tanguticum	18-24"	opalescent red-violet	Late summer	Tall stems, fluffy heads
6. Pineapple Lily	Eucomis	20"	green flowers on "corn cobs"	July	Flower resembles a pineapple; hardy if mulched well

TEN BEST SUMMER-FLOWERING BULBS

Common Name	Botanical Name	Height	Color	Bloom Time	Comments
7. Rain Lily, Fairy Lily, Zephyr Lily	*Habranthus* and *Zephranthes* (two related genera)	4-10"	White, yellow, shades of pink	Summer/Fall	Bloom heavily after a rain storm (special type nitrogen from lightning triggers flowering); doesn't perform as well as in home territories (Florida, Texas, Mexico, or South America)
	Z. candida	4-6'	white, crocus-like	Late summer (7/9)	Long-lasting bloom; tolerates semi-shade; seen at Callaway Gardens and under conifer near walk from ABG car park
	H. robustus	1'	lavender with greenish throat	July (intervals through summer)	Blooms nod and face outward from the stem; plant shallowly; requires a winter mulch
	H. brachyandrus		orchid pink above shading to burgundy	Summer/autumn	Medium-size blooms
	Z. grandiflora	8-10"	bright pink, large	7/18	Flowers intermittently, often a few days after a rainstorm
8. Society Garlic	*Tulbaghia violacea*	12-20"	bright lilac	Early June, intermittently in summer	Clusters of 12-30 flowers; probably an annual here, but worth replanting every year; try mulching in winter; plant in sandy soil just below surface; *T. v.* 'Variegated' has beautiful foliage but less vigor

Common Name	Botanical Name	Height	Color	Bloom Time	Comments
9. Star of Good Hope or Ivory Coast Lily	*Ornithogalum saundersiae*	3'	creamy white with dark green pin-cushion eye	Late August-early October	No flowers following period of single digit temperatures previous winter
10. Blackberry Lily	*Belamcanda chinensis*	30-36"	orange with red spots	July	Likes sun and poor, dry soil; glossy seeds resemble blackberries; foliage iris-like
	B. flabellata 'Hello Yellow'	shorter 18-24"	lemon yellow	Slightly later	Performs well in part shade; interesting flower; heavy substance and eye-catching color
Candy Lily	*x Pardancandra norrisii* 'Lollipop'	18-24"	deep purple or mahogany red, pink, lavender	July-August	Easy, but probably short-lived; all blackberry lilies' flowers last little more than a day on plant, but others immediately open

MORE GOOD SUMMER-BLOOMING BULBS

Common Name	Botanical Name	Height	Color	Bloom Time	Comments
1. Brodiaea	*Brodiaea laxa* 'Queen Fabiola' a.k.a. *Triteleia laxa*	12"	deep blue or violet	Most of June	Long-lasting star-like flowers on strong stalks; dry soil in summer; sun or part shade
2. Crocosmia	*Crocosmia x* 'Lucifer'	3-3 1/2'	flame red arching wand	6/11-7/7	Possibly weakened by viral infection, can be infested with spider mites; full sun; Sue Vrooman finds it blooms "brilliantly and constantly"; multiplies well; summer foliage poor
	C. 'Jenny Bloom'	2'	yellow	Late July-early August	Multiplies vigorously; extreme cold spell/hot, dry summer can kill plants or prevent buds from opening; sun
3. Lily-of-the-Nile, Blue or African Lily	*Agapanthus africanus* 'Head-borne Hybrids'	2-2 1/2'	medium blue	May-July	Hardier variety; no bloom '94-96 summers after freezes; prefers cool spot; morning sun; best as annual or in pot
4. Parrot, Chilean, or Inca Lily	*Alstroemeria psittacina*	2-3'	red and green	6/10; intermittently in summer	Long-lasting blooms; used commercially as cut flowers; can reseed, but doesn't wander far; plant 4-6" deep; sun or part shade
5. Resurrection Lily or Naked Lady	*Lycoris squamigera*	2-3'	lavender pink	Late July/early August	Bloom appears before strap-like leaves; very fragrant; tolerates shade
6. Spider Lily	*Hymenocallis caroliniana*	2'	pure white, spidery like	July	Native to southeast; rare plant; highly fragrant; sun

Common Name	Botanical Name	Height	Color	Bloom Time	Comments
7. Peruvian Daffodil	H. 'Sulphur Queen'	3'	yellow/green star in throat	Late June (can vary)	Seems reliable except following spring single-digit temperatures; sun
	Ismene calathina/H. narcissiflora	2'	white/green along stamen ribs	July	Produces 5 petaled, fringed funnel-shaped flowers after mild winter; sun
	H. x festalis	2'	white	July	Resembles H. n.; orchid-like petal curling; sun; questionable hardiness
8. Amarcrinum	Amarcrinum howardii	2-3'	clear rose, white throat	Late August-September	Sends up multi-stems; vanilla scent; better in heat/strong sun than crinum
9. Tuberose	Polianthes tuberosa 'Mexican Single'	15"	white	June	Annual; clusters of waxy flowers; single more reliable and fragrant than double; plant 2" deep; sun or part shade
	'The Pearl'	15"	waxy white, double	August-September	Full sun; mulch in winter with dead tuberose foliage; planting in June delays blooming until cool weather
10. Peacock Orchid or Abyssinian Gladiolus	Acidanthera bicolor/A. murielae/ Glad callianthus	3'	3" creamy with purple throat	Mid-summer (established plants up to frost)	Annual use; dig, store in winter; sun; prefers damp borders; fragrant; cut flowers long-lived with preservative

MORE GOOD SUMMER-BLOOMING BULBS

Common Name	Botanical Name	Height	Color	Bloom Time	Comments
11. Scilla	*Scilla autumnalis*	6-8"	blue	third week July	Rock or shade garden; tolerates shade well
	Scilla scilloides	20"	blue	very late June-early July	Rock or shade garden; tolerates shade well
12. Shell/Tiger Flower	*Tigridia pavonia*	15"	striking color	July	Well-drained, sunny area; annual use
13. Aztec lily	*Sprekelia formosissima*	10-12"	deep crimson	Spring/fall, early July	Pot culture; eye-catching bloom initiated by rain
14. Summer Iris	*Cypella plumbea*	3'	blue with yellow base	July-October	Fine addition to a summer garden; popularity growing; fleeting 3" flowers; sun or part shade

THE BEST FALL OR WINTER-FLOWERING BULBS AND THEIR KIN

Common Name	Botanical Name	Height	Color	Bloom Time	Comments
1. Crocus, Fall Showy Crocus	Crocus speciosus	12"	violet blue, or stamens	Late September-October 15	Large flower on weak stem; floppy; one of the easiest
Goulimy's Crocus	C. goulimyi	7"	intense blue blushed pink	2nd week October-November; peaks 10/15	Naturalizes; fragrant; sturdier stems; flourishes in open areas, sun or shade, well-drained soil; plant in cages if there is a rodent problem
2. Cyclamen	Cyclamen hederifolium/ C. neapolitanum	4-6"	reddish pink white form	Mid-August-mid-September	Easiest, most floriferous; enjoys good drainage between oak tree surface roots or shady wooded area; attractive marbled ivy-shaped leaves through winter and spring
	C. coum subsp. caucasicum or C. ibericum (Try other hardy ones)	3"	white to pink to deep magenta	December-March	Use cages to protect all cyclamen from rodents; long-lasting, more rounded leaves; purple undersides through winter; plant just beneath surface; use chopped oak leaf mulch
3. Ginger Lily or Butterfly Lily	Hedychium coronarium	over 4'	white	September-frost	Full sun or part shade; needs moisture; sweetly fragrant 2" flowers; mulch in winter; plant shallow; divide every 3-4 springs for good flowering
4. Winter Iris	Iris unguicularis	varies	lilac blue/ yellow at throat	October-March	Needs perfect drainage, sandy soil, sun; welcome blooms during winter; not usually reliable

THE BEST FALL OR WINTER-FLOWERING BULBS AND THEIR KIN

Common Name	Botanical Name	Height	Color	Bloom Time	Comments
5. Kaffir Lily	*Schizostylis* 'November Cheer'	24"	pink	October–November	Clump-forming perennial with 2" flowers on stalks above sword-like leaves; part shade; water heavily; lift before frost, pot and replant after danger of frost has passed
	S. 'Oregon Sunset'	24"	vivid red	October–frost	
	S. 'Sunrise'	32"	pink	Late August	
6. Lilies of the Field/ Yellow Autumn Crocus	*Sternbergia lutea*	10"	brilliant yellow	Established— September New—10/8-10/15	Not every bulb blooms yearly; requires well-drained area, summer sun baking; plant 3" deep; fragrant, funnel-shaped 2" wide flower
7. Meadow Saffron	*Colchicum agrippinum*	5-8"	lilac	Late August-late October	Very poisonous; rarely returns; needs some shade
	C. 'The Giant'	8"	violet/white base	9/17-10/15	Vase-shaped flowers
	C. byzantinum	6"	rosy lilac	September	4" across flowers; free-flowering
	C. cilicicum purpureum	5"	deep rosy-lilac	9/17	Very floriferous, 15 flowers per bulb; 2 1/2" long flowers
	C. speciosum 'Violet Queen'	7"	deep purple checks-pale background	September	6-8 chalice-type flowers
	C. 'Waterlily'	6"	rich lavender double	Late September-early November	Resembles real water lily; truly beautiful

THE BEST FALL OR WINTER-FLOWERING BULBS AND THEIR KIN

Common Name	Botanical Name	Height	Color	Bloom Time	Comments
8. Pink Agapanthus	*Nerine bowdenii*	18-24"	rose pink	Mid-November	Sun, well-drained soil; plant just below surface, ideally against south wall; bulb hardy; plant survives light frost; erratic bloom; good cut flower
9. Onion	*Allium thunbergii*	4-6"	rose-purple	November-January	Nice in rock garden or eye-level garden area
10. Oxblood Lily	*Hippeastrum advenum*	12"	sparkling red	August-September	Full sun or part shade; keep dry in winter
11. Snowdrop, Autumn	*Galanthus byzantinus*	8"	white/green blotch at base	Before Christmas	Sun or shade; difficult to obtain
12. Snowflake, Autumn	*Leucojum autumnale*	6"	white bells	Late summer-late September	Easy in sun
13. Spider Lily	*Lycoris radiata*	12-18"	crimson	Mid-September-October	Soil moisture influences flowering; evergreen foliage can be damaged in cold winter, prevents flowers the following fall
	L. albiflora	12"	ivory/hint of peach	Mid-September	Rare; blooms well after dry, hot summer; winter foliage damage prevents fall flowers
14. Dahlias	Tall, late dahlias require a regimented program of pruning, pinching, spraying, and other care. Contact ABG for information from the local Dahlia Society.				

215

Roses

by
Cathy Farmer

Growing the Queen of Flowers in Atlanta

Roses have a mysterious, almost magical hold on the imaginations of most people—especially gardeners. Despite a reputation to the contrary, roses are easy to grow in Atlanta. If you buy a quality bush and site and plant it carefully, you can expect lovely blooms from May to November, with only a small investment of time in regular care. So order those catalogs, make those lists, dig that clay, and enjoy the queen of flowers.

Buying Roses

I suggest buying No. 1 Grade, bare-root rose plants from a reputable mail-order nursery, especially if you're looking to buy a number of plants. Mail order nurseries offer a greater selection, and your order can be delivered in mid to late February, the best time to plant roses in Atlanta. If you need only a few plants and can find the varieties you want, buy from a local nursery that will guarantee them. Don't plant too many roses if you are just beginning. A bed of six hybrid teas, well-planted and cared for, will give you roses for arrangements all season.

Planting Roses

Roses love full sun—six hours minimum a day—and plenty of water and food. Select a well-drained, sunny site away from competing tree roots. Dig individual holes at least 18" deep and wide.

Discard most of the soil from the hole if it is clay and replace with a mixture of 1/3 top soil, 1/3 organic matter (ground pine bark or compost), and 1/3 coarse sand (sometimes called builder's sand). Rotted manure or mushroom compost are also good organic materials to add.

Mix the soil ingredients together. Place 1 cup dolomitic lime and 1 cup superphosphate in the bottom of the hole and add 2 to 3 shovels of the soil mixture. Combine this mixture well and form the soil into a cone shape in the bottom of the hole. Place the rose plant over the cone so the roots spread out naturally and the bud union (the swollen area just above the root system) rests flush with the top of the hole.

Fill hole with enough of the soil mixture to cover the roots and support the plant, pressing the soil firmly around the roots. Fill the hole with water and allow it to drain. Then fill with the remaining soil mixture, and water again. (This is a muddy process, so don't wear your hand-painted garden gloves!)

Mound extra soil mixture or ground pine bark around the base of the bush to a height of 6-8" to protect the canes from drying wind and sun until growth begins. Make certain the soil around newly planted bushes stays moist. Roses need at least 1" of water per week—more in hot weather.

Fertilizing

Roses are heavy feeders and respond well to a combination of organic-based and inorganic dry fertilizers, with liquid fertilizers as a supplement. Fertilize new roses after the first blooming period, giving each bush one cup of any good rose food or balanced fertilizer each month. Water well before and after feeding.

Begin feeding established roses in early April at about the same rate. Discontinue feeding after September. Remember a small, new rose bush needs less food than a large, established climber or shrub rose.

Caring for Roses

To keep your roses healthy and blooming, it is necessary to **prevent** the development of fungus diseases on the leaves, particularly the black spot fungus, by spraying weekly with a fungicide such as Funginex or Fungi-Gard. Many shrub roses, old garden roses, and climbers will tolerate some leaf loss from black spot and bounce back with growth and blooms. If you prefer not to spray, choose varieties from these categories.

Thrips (tiny sucking insects that cause petals to turn brown) are at their worst in May. Treat them by misting just the buds and blooms of your rose plants every four or five days with an insecticide, using a hand sprayer. (Orthene works well and is readily available.)

Pruning

Major pruning is done in late February, with the exception of spring-blooming climbers and shrubs, which should be trimmed after they bloom. To prune hybrid teas and grandifloras, cut out dead or damaged stems and any twiggy or congested growth and reduce the overall size of the bush by about half—more if the bush has gotten very tall. Floribundas need the same clean-up pruning, but leave as much good growth as possible, since more bush generally means more flowers, and floribundas are grown more for color in the garden than for cut flowers.

Deadheading—removing faded flowers to encourage repeat blooming—is recommended by expert growers because it really works. Cut the stem at a slant above a five-leaflet leaf.

If your roses have summer slump—leaf loss, poor growth, and small flowers—don't give up and let them go downhill. In mid-August, trim out all the dead and twiggy growth and shorten the bush by 1/3. Fertilize with a high nitrogen fertilizer and one cup of alfalfa pellets per bush. Water every other day for a week. Keep up your preventive spraying program and, by September, you'll have new growth and blooms.

Recommended Rose Varieties

There are roses for almost every garden situation—bushes, shrubs, miniatures, climbers—leaving you with the wonderful quandary of choosing which of the many fascinating, fragrant, and beautiful roses to grow. Here are some recommendations in several categories.

Best Hybrid Teas and Grandifloras

Hybrid Teas and **Grandifloras** are medium to tall upright bushes with beautifully formed flowers. They are wonderful for cutting.

Red Blooms:

'Mister Lincoln' - Tall bush with large, dark red, fragrant blooms of classic hybrid tea shape

'Olympiad' - Clear red blooms, excellent for cutting

'Chrysler Imperial' - An older variety, but still a dependable, highly fragrant red rose

Pink Blooms:

'Tiffany' - Medium pink, flushed yellow at the base, very fragrant one-to-a-stem rose

'Queen Elizabeth' - Very reliable, clear pink blooms in clusters on a tail bush

'Dainty Bess' - Beautiful light pink blooms with a single row of petals and maroon stamens, loved by all who grow it

'Touch of Class' - A coral-pink beauty with unbelievable form and long stems

'First Prize' - Very large, pink blend blooms with great form and staying power

Yellow Blooms:

'Peace' - Huge, pale yellow to ivory blooms blushed pink on the edges, shiny dark green foliage

'Gold Medal' - Yellow-gold petals, touched with soft red, tall and vigorous

'Elina' - A newer variety with primrose yellow petals and good form

White Blooms:

'Garden Party' - Ivory blooms edged with pink and a sweet scent

'Pristine' - White blooms of good form, faintly flushed with pink

Others:

'Double Delight' - White blooms heavily flushed with red and a strong, lemony fragrance

'Paradise' - Lavender blooms with rose-edged petals, unusual and beautiful

Best Floribundas

Floribundas are smaller-growing rose bushes with blooms in clusters. They are good for landscape color when planted in groups of three or more.

Red Blooms:

'Europeana' - Deep red roses in heavy clusters on a spreading bush

'Showbiz' - Bright red, showy flowers in large clusters, compact growth

Pink Blooms:

'Betty Prior' - Semi-double medium pink blooms in profusion

'First Edition' - Orange pink blooms, like small hybrid teas, in big clusters

Yellow Blooms:

'Sunflare' - Clear yellow roses in clusters on a disease-resistant plant with shiny foliage

'Sunsprite' - Fairly large, double, deep yellow flowers, very fragrant

White Blooms:

'Iceberg' - One of the best white roses of all, nice clusters of pure white blooms, excellent repeat bloom, vigorous and disease resistant

'French Lace' - Beautifully formed flowers of creamy white on an upright bush like a small hybrid tea

'Angel Face' - Mauve-pink blooms with ruffled edges and an intense old rose fragrance

Best Miniatures

Miniatures are perfect, tiny roses on small bushes. They are wonderful in containers, in arrangements, as edging for beds of larger roses, or grouped in perennial beds for season-long color. Care for them the same way as larger roses, using less fertilizer in proportion to their size.

Red Blooms:

'Beauty Secret' - Rose-red blooms in clusters, slight fragrance

'Red Beauty' - Deep red blooms like miniature hybrid teas

'Starina' - Orange-red, perfectly formed blooms

Pink Blooms:

'Minnie Pearl' - Beautiful pink-blend roses on a taller bush than most

'Cupcake' - Clear pink, well-formed flowers

'Pierrine' - Coral-pink, a newer variety

Yellow Blooms:

'Rise 'N Shine' - An older variety and one of the best, heavy blooming

White Blooms:

'Pacesetter' - Mostly one bloom per stem, pure white flowers

'Snow Bride' - A top exhibition miniature in the South and a good garden rose as well

'Linville' - A newer variety, white, tinged pink with larger flowers

Others:

'Magic Carrousel' - White with red edges and a profuse bloomer

'Jean Keneally' - Apricot-pink and perfect form

'Over The Rainbow' - Yellow and red blend, very colorful

Best Climbing Roses

Climbing roses must be trained or fastened to a support of some kind. They vary in size from pillar roses to tree-climbing ramblers. Most bloom very heavily in the spring with only scattered repeat bloom, and should be pruned only after the spring bloom cycle. They take several years to reach their full blooming potential and should be pruned little, if any, for the first few years.

Red Blooms:

'Don Juan' - Deep red fragrant blooms on a moderately sized plant with good repeat bloom

'Altissimo' - Rich red, single (one row of petals) flowers in clusters, very good repeat bloom

Pink Blooms:

'New Dawn' - Profuse, pale pink roses on a vigorous rambler with shiny, healthy foliage

'America' - Coral pink, mannerly climber with excellent repeat bloom and spicy fragrance

White Blooms:

'Sombreuil' - Climbing tea rose, creamy white with the old rose look and fragrance

Yellow Blooms:

'Golden Showers' - Semi-double, clear yellow, good repeat bloom

Others:

'Handel' - White, with soft pink on the edges of the petals, moderate size

Best Shrub Roses

The category of **shrub roses** encompasses both the "old garden" or "heritage" roses and the fast-growing modern shrub and landscape roses. As a group, they are very highly rated by the members of the American Rose Society.

Damask

'Rose de Rescht' - Repeat blooming, deep pink, compact

'Celsiana' - Pale pink, incredible fragrance, one of the best

'Madame Hardy' - Pure white, quartered blooms, amazingly beautiful

Gallica

'Apothecary's Rose' - Deep rose-red, low mounding shrub

'Charles de Mills' - Remarkable lavender-purple-pink blooms, very double

'Rosa Mundi' - Similar in growth to Apothecary's Rose, but the blooms are white with light and deep pink stripes and splashes, no two blooms alike

Albas

'Felicite Parmentier' - Palest pink, quartered blooms, sweet perfume

'Great Maiden's Blush' - Double blooms of a beautiful clear pink, fragrant

Bourbon

'Souvenir de la Malmaison' - Pale pink, fragrant blooms, excellent repeat bloom on a tidy shrub for any size garden

China

'Mutabilis' - Single blooms, opening primrose, then changing to pink and finishing red, quite a show on a wonderful garden shrub

Other Roses You May Want to Try

'Marchesa Boccella'

'Baronne Prevost'

'Nastarana'

'Bonica'

'Comte de Chambord'

'Lilian Austin'

'Ballerina'

'Heritage'

'Mary Rose'

'The Fairy'

'Frau Dagmar Hastrup'

'Rosa Rugosa Alba'

'Catherine Mermet'

'Maman Cochet'

'Old Blush'

For More Information

To learn more about roses, join the American Rose Society (P.O. Box 30000, Shreveport, LA 71130-0030) and the Greater Atlanta Rose Society, which meets the second Thursday of the month at the Atlanta Botanical Garden at 7:30 p.m. Visitors are welcome, and members are available to answer questions.

Sources for Roses

See Appendix A for addresses and telephone numbers.

Local Source

Antique Rose Emporium

Outstanding selection. If you want roses for your garden, shop here. The very interesting catalog ($5) features many unusual roses, including old tea and china roses, "mystery" roses, and early hybrid teas. At their garden in Dahlonega, Ga., a nice selection of perennials to grow with roses comes alive before your eyes. All roses are on their own roots.

Mail Order Sources

Large Roses

The following is a partial listing of commercial firms which will ship bare root roses for planting on the date you specify. All supply catalogs upon request. Bare root roses should be ordered in the fall and winter for early spring delivery.

Jackson-Perkins
One of the largest rose growers in the United States.

Pickering Nurseries
Long list of hybrid teas, grandifloras, and floribundas. Very long list of the old garden roses and the Austin English roses. Catalog $4.

Roses of Yesterday and Today
One of the few remaining firms specializing in old garden roses. A very beautiful catalog, $5.

Hortico Roses
Over 600 varieties or roses, including shrub and old garden roses. Catalog $3.

Wayside Gardens
A very nice (and expanding) list of roses of all kinds, and a beautifully illustrated catalog.

Heirloom Old Garden Roses
Extensive selection of unusual and heritage roses on their own roots. Catalog $5.

Roses Unlimited
Own-root roses selected for the South, in all categories. Send for free listing.

Edmunds' Roses
Good selection of roses. Beautiful catalog with an attempt made to give an honest appraisal of how each variety performs.

Miniature Roses

These firms supply miniature roses. The roses are shipped in small pots.

Bridges Roses

Mini Roses

Moore's Miniature Roses

Nor'East Miniature Roses

Tiny Petals Nursery

Oregon Miniature Roses

Chapter Nineteen

Lawn
Grasses

by

Brencie Werner

Best Lawn Grasses

The use of grasses as a groundcover began about the end of the last century as a result of pasture animals keeping meadows clipped with constant grazing. The advantage of using grasses for stabilizing soils from wind and water erosion along roadsides, disturbed sites, and new home sites was quickly realized, as were the grasses' effects of cooling and cleaning the air. Sports surfaces of turf quickly began to appear on soccer, golf, baseball, and football fields. Today the greatest advances in turf management come from golf course superintendents, since golf greens provide the greatest challenge in turf grass culture.

Atlanta is known for its abundance of trees and its beautiful expanses of lawns. Competition between these two plants, trees and turf, for light, nutrients, and water is the basis for most problems with having a beautiful lawn. Since nutrients and water can be applied, sunlight limits whether you can grow turf. Turf grasses grow rapidly and their energy requirements are high. Photosynthesis, which requires sunlight, is the only way grasses can obtain the energy they need to keep growing.

Trees create shade. To obtain enough sunlight to maintain a healthy lawn, trees limbs have to be cut off to 10' above the grass, and the crowns thinned with a telescoping tree pruner (if you do it yourself) or by professional tree pruners or an arborist. If you have dense, low-growing shrubs or trees such as an evergreen magnolia that should not be pruned, a groundcover rather than turf should be grown under the canopy. In general, if you have less than three hours of sunlight per day striking your lawn area, you should use a shade-tolerant groundcover. See Chapter 20, "Groundcovers."

How can you have a beautiful lawn that will enhance your neighborhood? The answer lies in three areas: correct choice of turf type, proper planting, and diligent maintenance.

Choice of Turf Type

If you have determined that you have enough sun for a lawn, you have a choice of turf grasses in the Atlanta area. Atlanta is in a transition zone. South of Atlanta, below the fall line which runs from Columbus through Macon to Augusta, a subtropical region exists, in which only warm season grasses are grown. These include Bermuda, centipede,

Saint Augustine, and zoysia. About 300 miles north of Atlanta, only cool season grasses, such as fescue and bentgrass, are grown. Atlanta is in a temperate zone, where the average temperature is at or above 50 degrees F. for at least seven months of the year.

The optimal growing conditions for warm season grasses are temperatures between 80 degrees F. and 95 degrees F. Warm season grasses are limited by the intensity and duration of cold temperatures during the winter, and are dormant (brown) when the temperature drops below 50 degrees F. The optimal growing temperatures for cool season grasses are between 60 degrees F. and 75 degrees F. Cool season grasses are green in the winter, but tend to suffer in the high heat and drought of summer; consequently, they grow and look best in the spring and fall. In general, warm season grasses tolerate closer mowing and are deeper rooted, so they are more heat, drought, and wear tolerant. Cool season grasses, on the other hand, are more cold and shade tolerant. With this as a general guideline, let's look at the specific advantages and disadvantages of each turf type.

Warm Season Grasses

Bermuda grasses (*Cynodon species*) are native to East Africa. They thrive in hot weather and are the worst choice for shade. Bermuda grasses are extremely vigorous and aggressive, spreading rapidly by above-ground runners (stolons) and underground runners (rhizomes). They are difficult to control around walks and flower beds.

Common Bermuda grass (*Cynodon dactylon*) is used primarily as a utility turf such as for athletic fields. It needs frequent fertilizer and frequent mowing. If allowed to produce seed, the seeds will germinate and cause weed problems in flower beds. It can be planted from seeds or sprigs.

Hybrid Bermuda grasses have been bred for finer texture, increased density, and better color. The seeds are not viable, so these hybrids must be planted using sprigs, plugs, or sod. They require even more intense maintenance than common Bermuda, with frequent fertilizing, close mowing, edging, and de-thatching.

Centipede grass (*Eremochloa ophiuroides*), a native of southeastern Asia, is at its northern limit in Atlanta. It is considered the lazy person's grass because it requires little mowing and fertilizing. Centipede produces only stolons, not rhizomes, and it is easily controlled around flower beds. It is slow growing, taking longer than Bermuda or St. Augustine to cover. It does not have the dark green color of other grasses.

St. Augustine grass *(Stenotaphrum secundatum)*, a native of the West Indies, is also at its northern limit in Atlanta, being very susceptible to winter injury. An aggressive grower, it spreads only by stolons, and so is easily controlled. St. Augustine is the most shade tolerant of the warm season grasses if it is receiving adequate moisture. However, frequent applications of insecticide are necessary to control chinch bug.

Zoysia grasses *(Zoysia species)*, natives of southeastern Asia, are the most cold tolerant of the warm season grasses and therefore are the most reliable for the Atlanta area. Of the two varieties, Meyerii and Emerald, Meyerii has a coarser texture and is somewhat more cold tolerant. If planted on well drained, fertile soil, zoysia is the most disease and insect resistant of all warm season grasses. It is also more tolerant of herbicides than other warm season grasses. If 3" plugs are planted on 6" centers, complete coverage will be achieved in one year. If planted on 12" centers, coverage takes two years.

Cool Season Grasses

Tall type fescue *(Festuca arundinacea)* varieties are the best of the cool season grasses for Atlanta. The species, native to Europe, is a bunch type grass, grown from seed, and best planted in the fall. The varieties have been developed for finer blades, denser growth habit, and more disease and drought resistance than the species. There are many of these varieties and blends of varieties on the market. Local county extension agents maintain a list of the 65 best varieties for this area, with Kentucky-31 being number 65. Irrigation is essential during the summer, but because of summer decline, these grasses need to be overseeded every fall. Fescue does not mat together well enough to be sold as sod.

Rye grasses, both perennial *(Lolium perenne)* **and annual** *(Lolium multiflorum)* are temporary turf grasses in Atlanta. They are used primarily for a winter cover on an area that has not yet been planted, and for overseeding to provide green color in the winter on dormant warm season grasses. The practice of overseeding can damage the warm season grass if the rye is not kept cut severely in the spring to prevent its robbing the established grass of moisture and nutrients.

Planting and Establishing a Lawn

When the decision of turf type has been made, the time of installation can be determined. Cool season grasses are planted in the fall to allow a long growing period for establishing good roots before the stressful summer season. For the same reason, warm season grasses are planted in the late spring and summer because this is their growing season, allowing them time to develop good roots before the dormant winter season. Establishing a lawn consists of three steps: soil preparation, planting, and care immediately after planting. Of these, the most important is the soil preparation.

Soil preparation begins with a soil sample. Collection bags and instructions are available from your county extension office and some garden centers. While waiting for the report, clean the area of rock, roots, and debris. If grading has to be done, save the topsoil and replace it after rough grading is completed. Grading should provide for a 1-2% slope away from buildings. For steeper slopes, use retaining walls or a low maintenance groundcover. If an irrigation system is to be installed, it is best to do it at this stage. If soil has become compacted, it must be broken up with a spring tooth harrow or a small rotovator.

Replace topsoil to a depth of 6-8". If there is insufficient topsoil, add organic matter in the form of leaf mold or compost at the rate of 1 to 3 cubic yards per 1000 square feet of lawn area. On clay soils, add granite sand at the rate of 8 to 10 cubic yards per 1000 square feet of lawn. Mix all materials to a depth of at least 6-8".

Add fertilizer and lime in the amounts indicated by the soil test. Mix into the top 3" of soil and water lightly. Do this immediately prior to planting so the soil does not become crusted.

Planting seed is best done with a mechanical seeder. For a home lawn, the broadcast seeder gives a uniform distribution if seed is divided in halves and sown in two directions at right angles. For fescues, 8 to 9 lbs. per 1000 square feet for a new lawn is sufficient, and for centipede, 1/4 to 1/2 lb. per 1000 square feet is all that is required. Applying seed above the recommended rate results in crowded plants which compete for moisture and nutrients. Drag the seed lightly into the soil with a rake to a depth of about 1/4". Firm with a manual roller, a cylindical weighted tool that presses the sod into contact with the soil beneath. (Some now question this procedure because it adversely may compact the soil.) Cover with straw or hay. Water lightly and keep watered.

Sodding, plugging, or sprigging is necessary for all grasses except fescues, common Bermudas, and centipede in the Atlanta area. Sodding is the most popular of these methods because it gives instant, complete coverage. Sod is laid solid over the prepared soil, rolled to make sure the roots are in contact with the soil, and watered in. Plugs are pieces of sod, cut 2-4" in diameter, and placed 6-12" on center. Sprigs are pieces of sod, entire plants, runners, rhizomes, or stolons that are placed in holes or furrows. With sprigs or plugs, the closer the pieces are planted to each other, the quicker complete coverage is achieved.

After planting care is critical. New grass plantings should never be allowed to dry out for the first two to three weeks. Unlike maintenance watering, establishment watering should be light and frequent, up to three times a day, if necessary, to keep new roots from drying. As the grass begins to take root and grow, watering can be decreased in frequency and increased in amount applied each time. Mow when the grass reaches 1 1/2 times its recommended mowing height.

Maintenance

Diligent maintenance is the key to an attractive lawn. It involves fertilizing, watering, mowing, cultivation, pest control, and occasional renovation.

Fertilizing need not be such a chore if soil pH is correct, allowing nutrients to be available to the plant. This can be checked periodically with a soil test. Use the recommended amounts of fertilizer, as shown in the chart in this chapter, to prevent injury to the turf. Always apply fertilizer when the grass is dry and water thoroughly. Rates can vary depending on whether grass clippings are being removed and how dark a green color is desired. When clippings are left on the lawn to decompose, about half as much fertilizer is required. Slow-release fertilizers require fewer applications and provide more constant feeding, but are more expensive.

Water is the most important requirement for turf grass survival. The water content of actively growing grasses is 90%. Water is necessary for photosynthesis and for transpiration (cooling) in the summer. But the healthiest lawns are ones that have been conditioned to get by on as little water as possible. Encourage deep rooted turf by watering infrequently, at the first sign of wilt, not before, and deeply enough to drench the soil to a depth of 5-7". This means leaving the sprinkler on for 2 to 3 hours. If run-off occurs, move the sprinkler to a new location until moisture is absorbed. Place several shallow cans (tuna or cat food cans work well) in the area to make sure you are getting a total of 1" of water. The best time of day to water is early morning. The worst time is late evening because grass that remains wet overnight is more susceptible to fungal diseases.

Mowing correctly can prevent other problems from occurring. Mowing is stressful to turf grasses. It reduces carbohydrate production and storage, causes temporary cessation of root growth, increases water loss due to the cut leaf surface, and creates a portal of entry for insects.

Correct mowing involves cutting at the proper height, mowing at the proper time, and using the right type mower. Recommended mowing heights are given in the chart that follows. The higher of the two numbers in the mowing height column is less stressful to the plants. The lower of the two numbers represents more intense culture and more expense since the plants will have more stress. To prevent interference with root growth, never remove more than 1/3 of the height of the grass at a time. Raise mowing heights on cool season turf grasses in the summer and on warm season turf grasses in the spring and fall and on all turf grasses in the shade. Scalping or lowering the cutting height and mowing the lawn in several directions just prior to spring green-up will help prevent thatch accumulation in zoysia and Bermuda lawns, according to Dr. Gilbert Landry, Jr., Extension Agronomist for Turf.

Reel mowers are recommended for hybrid Bermudas and zoysia. These mowers are used because of the low mowing heights and the density of the turf. The height of the turf to be cut should never be over 1/2 the cylinder height of the mower.

Rotary mowers are used with all other turf types with mowing heights equal to or over 1". The new mulching mowers are recommended for these turf types also. If the grass clippings are mulched as they are cut, returning them to the lawn can add organic matter to the soil and reduce fertilizer requirements.

Always mow grass when it is dry. The mowers work better, less time is required, the lawn looks better, and diseases are not spread as rapidly. Use a medium or slow speed setting of a self-propelled mower instead of the fastest speed to get a more even appearance.

Cultivation practices for lawn grasses include core aeration and vertical mowing (de-thatching). Core aeration increases air and water movement into the soil to relieve soil compaction. Power aerators with hollow tines can be rented from the hardware store. Use when soil is moist enough to allow the tines to penetrate deeply. The cores that are removed lie on the surface and are gradually absorbed back into the ground.

Vertical mowing is done to remove thatch accumulation. Thatch is a layer of non-decomposed dead plant material at the soil surface. It prevents water from penetrating into the soil, and it harbors pests and disease spores. It is mainly a problem with warm season turf grasses and can be prevented by using correct mowing techniques. If it has accumulated, it can be removed with a rented vertical mower in the early spring. Professional services are available in the Yellow Pages for both de-thatching and aeration.

Pest control includes control of diseases, insects, and weeds. Most turf **diseases** are due to fungi. Proper watering, fertilizing, and mowing will prevent disease so that fungicides will not be necessary. The five most common turf diseases in the Atlanta area are brown patch, dollar spot, helminthosporium, pythium blight, and spring dead spot. Brown patch *(Rhizoctonia solani)* can be recognized by light brown, straw colored roughly circular areas two to three feet in diameter. Dollar spot *(Sclerotina homeocarpa)* has bleached circular spots the size of a silver dollar, but the spots can join together. Helminthosporium is characterized by zebra stripes and brown lesions on the leaf blades. Pithium blight is sometimes called "grease spot." The disease makes the grass look mushy and spreads very rapidly. Spring dead spot normally occurs only on Bermuda between its third and sixth year of establishment. It produces a toxin in the soil which prevents grass from growing back in that spot in the spring. Both contact and systemic fungicides purchased at the garden center can be used to control these diseases. Susceptibility of a turf type to a particular disease is listed on the chart in this chapter. Easy identification of lawn grass diseases can be made by comparing to magazine and book photos of the blight.

Insects damage turf by chewing or sucking on leaves, stems, and roots. The four most common insects that damage turf in Atlanta are grub worms, billbugs, sod webworms, and armyworms. Grubs are white and eat roots of turf. Birds on the lawn are an indication of their presence. The billbug larvae eats turf roots, while the mature bug eats the stems and leaves. Sod webworms and armyworms, both caterpillars of moths, eat shoots and leaves of turf. Insecticides will control these if damage is evident. Other harmful insects are included in the chart in this chapter.

Weeds fall into three categories for control purposes: annual grasses, perennial grasses, and broadleaf weeds. One annual grass weed, *Poa annua*, a cool season annual, is controlled in cool season turf grasses by using a pre-emergence weed killer in September or October. Another is crab grass, a warm season annual, controlled in cool season turf with a pre-emergence weed killer applied February through April. Both annual grass weeds can be controlled in warm season turf with Round-Up applied in the winter.

Perennial grass weeds include common Bermuda, dollar grass, and nut sedge. Also included in this group for purposes of control are onions and garlic. They can be controlled in cool season turf by spotting with Round-Up in the fall before overseeding and in warm season turf with an organic arsenic such as Poast.

Broadleaf weeds are controlled on all turf grasses except centipede with 2,4D. On centipede, atrazine, as in Gallery, can be used.

Renovation becomes necessary when a lawn becomes thin and spotty or large dead areas appear. Causes may be wrong choice of turf, lack of soil preparation, improper maintenance, or insect or disease problems. If renovation is necessary, first remove weeds either chemically or mechanically. Remove thatch if necessary with a vertical mower. Cultivate the soil with a core aerator. Have the soil tested and correct pH and nutrients with lime and fertilizer. Overseed or plant sprigs, plugs, or sod, and keep watered until established. Mow when the grass reaches 1 1/2 times its desired height. Renovation (aeration and dethatching) of cool season turf lawns is done in the early fall. Warm season turf lawns are renovated in the early spring.

Tips from the Experts

English grass experts say to achieve the appearance and beauty of an English lawn, alternate the direction in which you mow your lawn. For warm season turf, particularly zoysia, scalping or lowering the lawn mower's cutting height and mowing the lawn in several directions just prior to spring green-up will help prevent thatch accumulation. This should be done every year in late February or early March. Aeration of warm season grasses should be done in early spring, also. Aeration is not usually needed every year.

The Future

Turf grass science is a relatively new science, in existence for only about 100 years. It is constantly changing and developing, but the most change is yet to come. By the year 2030, lawns, as we know them today, will not be a part of the average residential landscape. They are expensive, labor intensive, and require the use of many chemicals to keep them looking pristine. Environmental restrictions on chemicals alone will limit the planting of large turf areas to public parks and athletic fields. In California, where water restrictions have curtailed the watering of lawns, this is already taking place. Careful application of water and chemicals on the part of the homeowner will delay this from happening here as long as possible.

TURF TYPE	Saint Augustine	Bermuda Hybrids	Centipede	Zoysia	Tall Fescues
DESCRIPTION					
Texture	Very coarse	Fine	Coarse	Medium to fine	Coarse to medium
Cold tolerance	Extremely poor	Poor	Very poor	Fair	Excellent
Heat tolerance	Excellent	Excellent	Excellent	Excellent	Poor
Shade tolerance	Very good	Very poor	Fair	Fair	Good
Drought resistance	Fair	Excellent	Poor	Good	Good
Wear tolerance	Poor	Excellent	Poor	Average	Poor
PLANTING					
Method	Sprigs, plugs, or sod	Sprigs, plugs, or sod	Seed (1/4-1/2 lb. per 1000 sq. ft.), sprigs, plugs, or sod	Plugs or sod	Seed (5 to 8 lbs. per 1000 sq. ft.)
Time of year	May-June	May-July	May-June	May-July	Sept.-early Oct.
Preferred soil pH	6.0-6.5	6.0-6.5	4.5-5.5	6.0-6.5	5.5-6.5

COMPARISON OF ATLANTA'S BEST TURF GRASSES cont'd

TURF TYPE	Saint Augustine	Bermuda Hybrids	Centipede	Zoysia	Tall Fescues
CULTURE					
Fertilizer Rates	10 lbs. 12-4-8 per 1000 sq. ft.	10 lbs. 12-4-8 per 1000 sq. ft.	5 lbs. 12-4-8 per 1000 sq. ft.	10 lbs. 16-4-8 per 1000 sq. ft.	10 lbs. 16-4-8 per 1000 sq. ft.
Fertilizer times	Early spring Midsummer Early fall	Early spring Midsummer Early fall	Early spring Midsummer	Early spring Midsummer Early fall	April Early September November
Mower type	Rotary	Reel	Reel or rotary	Reel	Rotary
Mowing height	1.5-3"	0.5-1.0"	1-2"	0.5"-1.5"	1.5-2" Fall/Spring 2.5-3" Summer
Thatch removal	Yes	Yes	Yes	Yes	No
PESTS					
Diseases	Brown patch Dollar spot	Brown patch Dollar spot Spring dead spot Helminthosporium	Brown patch Dollar spot	Brown patch Dollar spot Rust Helminthosporium	Brown patch Pithium blight
Insects	Chinch bug	Armyworms Mole crickets Sod webworms	Ground pearls	Bill bugs Armyworms Mole crickets Sod webworms	Grub worms Armyworms Sod webworms

Chapter Twenty

Groundcovers

by

Jeff Potter

Best Groundcovers for Atlanta

Groundcovers add color, texture, and variety to the overall effect of a landscape. Many perennials, though not true groundcovers, are useful for their ability to cover the ground. Even vines make great groundcovers in certain conditions. Once established, groundcovers require much less maintenance than turf lawns and can solve a wide range of problems. You can underplant bulbs or cover exposed tree roots with them. They make superb underplantings for trees and shrubs, intensifying the color and texture of plants and acting as a living mulch to minimize weed growth and hold the soil in place.

There are hundreds of different groundcovers for the south. Many are native and should be purchased from nursery propagated stock, not collected from the wild.

How to Plant

There is no hard and fast rule regarding the spacing of groundcovers at planting time. The closer the spacing, the faster the bed will fill in, and also the greater the cost of installation. In general the spacing scheme is based upon the size of the plants, the gardener's personal preference, the location of the bed, and the budget. The spacing for an area in the rear of the property may be greater than an area near a walkway or a door. One should also keep in mind that the further the spacing, the longer it will take to fill in, and more maintenance (weeding and mulching) will be required. Plant groundcovers in a diamond grid pattern to avoid the look of straight rows.

To figure the number of plants required for a given area, multiply the number of square feet by the numbers of plants per square foot using the following table:

Spacing between plants:	Plants per square foot:
4"	9.10
6"	4.00
8"	2.25
9"	1.77
10"	1.44
12"	1.00
15"	.64
18"	.44
24"	.25

Example: If you have a bed that is 15' long and 5' wide (15 x 5 = 75 sq. ft.) and you want to plant on 8" centers, multiply 75 x 2.25 = 168.75 or about 169 plants.

Recommended Groundcovers

Best Groundcovers for Sunny Sites

Serbian Bellflower *Campanula poscharskyana* - 4-6" - Trailing plant; starry lavender-blue flowers.

Silver and Gold *Chrysanthemum pacificum* - 8-12" - Bushy mound of toothed green foliage with attractive silver backs. Yellow button flowers in late fall. Requires excellent drainage.

Bath's Pinks *Dianthus gratianopolitanus* 'Bath's Pink' - 6-8" - Introduced by Goodness Grows Nursery. Named for Jane Bath, a talented garden designer at Land Arts in Monroe, Ga. 'Bath's Pink' forms dense, matte-like, gray evergreen needle like foliage. Single pink, clove scented flower.

Pink Panda Strawberry *Fragaria x* 'Pink Panda' - 6" - Unique hybrid cross of *Fragaria* and *Potentilla*. Patented plant; proceeds benefit World Wildlife Fund. Nice strawberry groundcover plant which bears clear pink flower and small fruits. Starts blooming late winter.

Variegated Creeping Charlie *Glechoma hederacea* 'Variegata' - 4" - Rampant groundcover. Trailing stems of rounded scalloped leaves with creamy white edge. Roots as each leaf touches the ground.

Bitsy Daylily *Hemerocallis* 'Bitsy' - 14" - Lemon yellow flower with small crimped edge; blooms early.

Happy Returns Daylily *Hemerocallis* 'Happy Returns' - 18" - Good clear yellow. One of the most consistent re-bloomers, also a good landscape subject, like famous parent 'Stella de Oro'. Blooms mid-season.

Pardon Me Daylily *Hemerocallis* 'Pardon Me' - 18" - Cranberry red blossom with ruffled edge. Yellow throat with lime green base. Re-bloomer that blooms in mid-season.

Stella De Oro Daylily *Hemerocallis* 'Stella de Oro' - 18" - Famous rebloomer. Name refers to the golden light orange flower with ruffled edge. Consistent rebloomer, good landscape plant.

St. Johnswort *Hypericum calycinum* - 12-18" - Semi-evergreen, medium green leaf, spreading. Big rhizomes. Yellow flowers appear in late spring. Good plant for banks.

Blue Star Creeper *Laurentia fluviatilis* - 4" - Flat growing carpet of tiny, green leaves, light blue starry flowers. Ideal for planting between paving stones with light foot traffic.

Monkey Grass (Turf Lily) *Liriope muscari* - 12-15" - Grassy, evergreen leaves forms a dense clump/mat, short spikes of showy flowers in late summer. Evergreen, but benefits from a good trimming early spring for fresh new growth. *Liriope spicata* not recommended; has aggressive stolons/thin clumps.

John Burch Liriope *Liriope muscari* 'John Burch' - 12-15" - Wide, yellow-margined leaves with a slight twist. Dense lavender blooms.

Regal Purple Liriope *Liriope muscari* 'Royal Purple' - 12-15" - Wide green foliage, deep purple bloom.

Variegated Liriope *Liriope muscari* 'Variegata' - 12-15" - Green with white variegation on the outside of the leaf. Lavender flower spike.

Creeping Mazus *Mazus reptans* - 4" - Aggressive hugging groundcover forming green mats. Flowers lavender with yellow spots. Good for planting between paving stones.

Vera Jameson Sedum *Sedum x* 'Vera Jameson' - 9-12" - Mahogany-red foliage, arching stems of dusty pink flowers. Better habit than 'Ruby Glow.'

Best Groundcovers for Shady Sites

Bishop's Weed (Gout Weed) *Aegopodium podagraria* 'Variegatum' - 6" - White flowers with white margined leaves; a rapid, strong growing groundcover. If weedy, can be mowed close to the ground and fresh growth quickly returns.

Jungle Beauty Improved Ajuga *Ajuga* 'Jungle Beauty Improved' - 6" - Shiny, very large purple foliage, deep blue spike of flowers in spring. Performs better than *Ajuga repens*. The plant is about twice the size; leaves with good substance, less susceptible to spider mites.

Dwarf Goat's Beard *Aruncus aethusifolius* - 8-12" - Fine fern-like foliage with creamy white flower spikes.

Wild Ginger *Asarum canadense* - 6" - Green heart-shaped leaves, likes rich, moist soil, native, inconspicuous purplish-brown flowers. *Asarum europaeum* - 6" - Evergreen glossy, heart-shaped leaves, inconspicuous purplish-brown flowers. *Asarum arifolia (Hexastylis arifolia)* - 6" - Evergreen arrowhead shaped leaves, with considerable variation in their mottling patterns; inconspicuous purplish-brown flowers.

Dwarf False Spirea *Astilbe chinensis* 'Finale' - 8-12" - Fine fern-like foliage, late summer bloom, light lilac-rose flower, likes moist soil. *Astilbe chinensis* 'Pumila' - 8-12" - Fine fern-like foliage, late summer bloom, lilac-rose. *Astilbe crispa* 'Perkeo' - 8 to 12" - Crispy fern-like foliage, dark rose bloom late summer. *Astilbe simplicifolia* 'Sprite' - 8-12" - 1994 Perennial Plant of the Year. Dark bronze foliage with shell pink flowers, originating from Bressingham Gardens, England.

Lily of the Valley *Convallaria majalis* - 6" - A sturdy groundcover for difficult shady sites. Old-fashioned cut flower. Fragrant white bell-shaped flowers.

Wild Bleeding Heart *Dicentra eximia* - 12" - Blue-green fringed fern-like foliage. Pink heart-shaped flowers; heaviest bloom in spring, scattered blooms in summer. Needs moist, well-drained humus.

Bishop's Hat *Epimedium perralderanum* 'Frohnleiten' - 8-12" - Forms a compact mound of reddish heart-shaped foliage, with small yellowish flowers on wiry stems in spring. Tolerant of root competition and dry shade once established.

Ferns (Most ferns are good groundcovers, especially the ferns with long creeping rhizomes.) *Thelypteris hexagonoptera* (Broad Beech Fern) - Long creeping rhizome, fronds 15", deciduous, broad triangular fronds. *Thelypteris noveboracencis* (New York Fern) - Long creeping rhizomes, fronds 12", deciduous, delicate, yellow-green fronds. *Athyrium niponicum* 'Pictum' (Japanese Painted Fern) - Short creeping rhizome, fronds 12", deciduous, broad triangular fronds. *Polystichum acrostichoides* (Christmas Fern) - Rhizome with multiple fronds, 1', evergreen, arching.

Wintergreen (Checkerberry) *Gaultheria procubens* - 5-10" - Shiny evergreen foliage, pinkish white blooms in summer followed by bright red berries in fall. Likes acid soil. Native to Southeast U.S.

Lenten Rose *Helleborus orientalis* - 12-18" - Leathery, dark green palmate leaves with clusters of nodding cupped flowers from cream to deep purple, often with spots. Blooms in very early spring.

Palace Purple Coral Bells *Heuchera micrantha* 'Palace Purple' - 12-18" - 1991 Perennial Plant of the Year. Deep purple, ivy-shaped foliage, fading to bronze green under hot southern conditions. Seedling grown, so foliage color may vary. Has insignificant white flowers.

Hosta - 12-16" - Miniature to small hostas are best for groundcovers.

Hosta 'Allen P. McConnell' - 12" - Medium size variegated, green ovate leaves with white margin.

Hosta 'Blue Skies' - 10" - Medium size, extremely blue spring foliage turning blue-green by summer. Lilac flowers.

Hosta 'Golden Tiara' - 16" - Medium size, light green heart-shaped leaves with creamy yellow margins. Purple flowers.

Hosta 'Lemon Lime' - 10" - Medium size, chartreuse leaves hold until mid-summer then turn green. Purple flowers.

Hosta 'Sugar Plum Fairy' - 10" - Miniature, medium green lance-shaped leaves with wavy margin. Purple flowers.

Hosta 'Ground Master' - 12" - Medium variegated leaves, green base with undulating white margin. Lavender flowers.

Ivy *Hedera helix* - *Hedera helix* 'Hiberica' is the cultivar frequently sold as plain English Ivy, with large shiny leaves. In the last 30 years, many new ivies have been developed. These ivies are more compact, and show a wide range of size, shape, texture, and color, and are well behaved in the garden. *H. h.* 'Duckfoot' - Miniature, green, densely self-branching ivy-small three lobed leaves. *H. h.* 'Jubilee' - Dense growing, self-branching ivy variegated with shades of gray-green. *H. h.* 'Goldchild' - Leaves when young bright green and pale green in the center with a broad golden yellow margin becoming blue green and gray green edged in creamy yellow.

Creeping Jenny *Lysimachia nummularia* - 4" - Vigorous trailing stems form a bright green carpet. Golden yellow flowers appear occasionally from spring to fall. *Lysimachia nummularia* 'Aurea' - 4" - Bright golden leaves in good bright light. Contrasts well with black mondo grass, *Ophiopogon planiscapus* 'Ebony Night.'

Mondo Grass *Ophiopogon japonicus* - 6-8" - Thin grass-like leaves with insignificant white flowers in late summer. Spreads by short stolons. *Ophiopogon japonicus* 'Nana' - 6-8" - Dwarf mondo grass, small 2-3" dark green grass-like foliage. *Ophiopogon japonicus* 'Ebony Night' - 6-8" - Black mondo grass, unusual purple-black grass like leaves, slow to spread. Contrasts well with yellow or white foliage plants.

Spurge (Allegheny Spurge) *Pachysandra procumbens* - 6-8" - Native, foliage maturing to a marbled gray-green. Older foliage can be removed in spring for fresh new growth. Attractive white to creamy pink flower spike in spring. Likes moist humus. *Pachysandra terminalis* - 6-8" - Evergreen spreading by runners, prefers well amended soil, small white flowers in spring.

Woodland Phlox *Phlox stolonifera* - 6-12" - 1990 Perennial Plant of the Year. Semi-evergreen clumped foliage. *Phlox stolonifera* 'Bruce's White' - 6-12" - Pure white flowers with yellow eye spring. *Phlox stolonifera* 'Sherwood Purple' - 6-12" - Masses of purple flowers in spring. *Phlox divaricata* 'Fuller's White' - 6-12" - Strong stems of clear white flowers. *Phlox divaricata laphamii* - 6-12" - Dark blue flowers.

Creeping Raspberry *Rubus calycinoides* 'Emerald Carpet' - 6-8" - Fast growing, low spreading evergreen. Leaves are rough textured and scalloped. Small white spring flower followed by occasional small edible golden berries in fall.

Himalayan Sweet Box *Sarcococca hookerana humilis* - Dark evergreen foliage on short stems with small fragrant white flowers in spring.

Strawberry Begonia *Saxifraga stolonifera* - Rounded mottled leaves, tall white panicle flower spikes.

Foam Flower *Tiarella cordifolia* 'Oakleaf' - Foliage is lobed like an oak leaf, non-spreading clump form.

Variegated Big Leaf Periwinkle *Vinca major* 'Variegata' - Evergreen, dark green veining, oval-shaped leaves with white to cream margins, rapid growing.

Dwarf Periwinkle *Vinca minor* - Evergreen shiny green oval leaves. Trails or roots along the ground. Fast spreading once established. *Vinca minor* 'Bowles' - Lower growing than species, light blue flowers. *Vinca minor* 'Sterling Silver' - White and green variegated leaves, lavender flowers. *Vinca minor* 'Atropurpurea' - Flower burgundy wine color.

G.'R.A. *Additional Recommendations*

Candytuft, perennial *Iberis sempervirens* - White flowered evergreen, 9-12" tall. Begins blooming in March and persists for 10 weeks. Cut back after flowering. Some reblooming late summer, particularly 'Autumn Snow'. Likes full sun, well-drained soil. Use as edging groundcover for flower beds.

Goldenstar or **Green and Gold** *Chrysogonum virginianum* - Small, bright yellow, daisy-like flowers. 4-6" tall. Spring blooming, sporadically summer/fall. Likes moist, well-drained shade. Tolerates more sun in consistently wet soil.

Lamb's Ear *Stachys lanata* 'Helene Stein' - 6" velvety, woolly grey leaves; hot pink flowers on tall spikes late spring. Prefers hot dry areas. Looks best in spring. This newer variety holds up better in our hot, humid summers. Plant in well-drained soil in sun to partial shade.

Leadwort (Plumbago) *Ceratostigma plumbaginoides* - Deep gentian blue flowers in late summer into fall in sunny areas with some afternoon shade. 8-12". Leaves turn bronze-red in fall and then disappear. New foliage does not emerge until late spring. Use in combination with early spring groundcover like Virginia Bluebells.

Swan River Daisy *Brachycome iberidifolia* - Pretty blue 1" daisy-like flowers from early summer to freeze (December usually). 6-8" tall. Great summer edging groundcover. Not hardy.

Georgia Blue Veronica *Veronica peduncularis* 'Georgia Blue' - A gem from the former Soviet Georgia which blooms spring through June with bright blue flowers. Stretches to 12" high; more than 18" spread in some sun.

Dwarf Greek Oregano *Origanum vulgare* 'Compactum Nanum' - Lovely 3" tight groundcover with wonderful fragrant foliage.

Solving Problems with Groundcovers

Groundcovers are solutions for steep slopes, deep shade, or dry, moist, or rocky areas. Remember to use an interesting combination of plants.

For Sunny Wet Areas

Vinca minor or *major*

Lysimachia nummularia 'Aurea' (Gold Creeping Jenny)

Acorus gramineus variegata (Japanese Sweet Flag)

Iris ensata (Japanese Iris)

Iris fulva (Louisiana Iris)

For Sunny Dry Areas

Hedera helix (English Ivy)

Euonymus fortunei var. *coloratus* (Purple Wintercreeper)

Chrysanthemum pacificum

Phlox subulata (Thrift)

Sedum x 'Vera Jameson'

Thymus (Thyme)

For Shady Wet Areas

Aegopodium podagraria 'Variegatum' (Bishop's Weed)

Tiarella cordifolia (Foam Flower)

Thelypteris noveboracencis (New York Fern)

For Shady Dry Areas

Asarum (Ginger)

Epimedium

Mitchella repens (Partridge Berry)

Evergreen Groundcovers

For Sun

Juniperus spp.

Dianthus gratianopolitanus 'Bath's Pink' (Bath's Pink Dianthus)

Cotoneaster spp. (can take some shade)

For Shade

Pachysandra terminalis (Japanese Spurge)

Evergreen ferns

Ajuga

Ophiopogon spp. (Mondo Grass)

Liriope

Hedera helix (English Ivy)

Mitchella repens (Partridge Berry)

North Tisbury evergreen azaleas

Vinca minor (Periwinkle)

Chapter Twenty-One

Ornamental Grasses

by
Sue Vrooman

Ornamental Grasses for Atlanta

The city-weary eye takes pleasure in the wind dance of the grasses. Their movement makes August seem cooler, adds rustling sound to winter's scene, and prevents the garden from ever being static. Movement is only one of several qualities that make ornamental grasses welcome. Others include their texture, their subtle color (ranging from almost blue through green and yellow to shades of red), their ornamental flowers and seedheads, and their beauty in winter.

Grasses are among the most easily grown perennials. It is rarely necessary to spray for insects or disease. You can use them for mass plantings, as single specimens, in containers, mingled with meadow flowers, by pool or waterside, as a summer screen, in the perennial border, as an edging, or to conceal the bases of leggy shrubs. The seedheads can be dried and used in arrangements or left on the plant until the following spring for winter beauty and to attract birds. There are grass species and their look-alikes the sedges (*Carex*) and rushes (*Juncus*) for sun, shade, wet, dry, or average conditions. You can choose natives or exotics and sizes from midget to giant. For ideas on how best to use grasses, visit places like the Atlanta Botanical Garden or browse through some of the books recommended in the Recommended Reading and References section of this book.

Using Grasses in Your Garden

As a general rule, don't use a grass with foliage that is taller than three-quarters the width of your bed (the flowers can be taller). For example, if your bed is 8' wide, grasses 6' tall or less are your best bet. Do not, however, feel this rule is unbreakable. If you feel a specific spot calls for something taller, use it.

Consider using grasses when clashing flower colors need separating or when you need narrow leaves to contrast with a coarse-textured plant like *Sedum* 'Autumn Joy.' Use grasses as you would similar-size shrubs. The tall species are perfect screens for blocking ugly views. When using them as a screen, it is better to emphasize the grasses' natural grace and plant them in sweeps rather than in straight rows.

Grass seedheads and grasses with colored foliage are striking when sunlight shines through them from behind. You might wish to sight them with this in mind. Be sure to leave enough space for them to assume their natural shape—tufted, mounded, upright, or arching, depending on the kind chosen.

Plan groups of three to five small grasses or single clumps of larger grasses which have flowers or seedheads present at the time fall asters, black-eyed Susans, and chrysanthemums bloom. Leave seedheads and dried foliage of your grasses standing over winter to add interest when other flowers are dead or dormant. Grasses look particularly good at this time with evergreens as a background or against an unobstructed winter sky.

Ornamental grasses are the perfect answer for landscaping around a vacation home because of their low maintenance. Planted in masses and combined with hardy shrubs, they can replace a high-maintenance lawn, grace the edges of a lake site, or soften rock outcrops and steep slopes. Grasses look particularly nice in combination with junipers including our native red cedar (*Juniperus virginiana*).

It is now possible to purchase seed for some native grasses, which makes planting large areas economical.

When using grass as a specimen plant—one which gets the attention—it is better to use other plants like smaller perennials or shrubs to set off the grass, rather than placing the grass in the center of the lawn. You want it to fit into your landscape, not look like the ringmaster of a circus.

A planting of native grasses needs mowing once a year in late winter or early spring to control blackberries and seedling trees.

A word of caution: Overfertilizing can cause clump-forming grasses to sprawl outward and variegated varieties to lose some of their variegation.

Choosing Grasses

The following are selections of grasses and their kin which are easily grown in the Georgia Piedmont. Choose ones which best suit your site and give them a try.

Maiden Grass (*Miscanthus sinensis* 'Gracillimus') Sun, average to wet soils. Grows 6' tall with a slightly wider spread at midsummer. Fine textured foliage and graceful upright, arching fountain shape. Use at back of the perennial border, as a specimen plant, for massing, screening, cut flowers, winter interest, or around swimming pools. Also good in large containers. Easily maintained by cutting to ground in late February and dividing in spring after four years.

Morning Light Maiden Grass *(Miscanthus sinensis 'Morning Light')* Likes same exposure and growing conditions and has same shape as maiden grass, but it is slightly smaller in size. The margins of its narrow leaves are white, giving it a light green or silver green look. One of the most elegant grasses. Good in the same situation as maiden grass; requires the same maintenance.

Porcupine Grass *(Miscanthus sinensis 'Strictus')* Sun. Average to wet soils. Grows to 7'. Spreads less than 6' with flowers to 9'. Dense upright growth habit. Medium texture foliage is almost unique; horizontal yellow bands cross the green, giving an unusual checkered look. Since its leaves are held erect like porcupine quills the variegation is very effective. It is an excellent companion for yellow-flowered plants like coreopsis, yellow daylilies, or achilleas as well as blue-flowered salvias and bell flowers. Use as a specimen, in groups, for cut flowers, at water's edge, at rear of wide (10' or wider) perennial border for winter interest, or as a screen. Maintain by cutting to ground in late February before new growth starts and dividing in spring every five years. Do not over-fertilize.

Fountain Grass *(Pennisetum alopecuroides)* Sun. Average to moderately dry soil. Foliage 30" tall with similar spread. Flowers 4-4 1/2'. Mounded growth habit. Medium, fine-textured foliage. Flowering begins in midsummer with numerous flowers resembling large silvery-rose foxtails. Divide every five years or when center of plant starts to die out. Effective singly or in groups or masses. Wonderful in perennial borders. Can be used in containers near swimming pools. Niche Gardens recommends fountain grass as a background for dwarf conifers. There is a dwarf form, 'Hameln' or 'Hamelin,' which is a foot shorter than the type.

Switch Grass *(Panicum virgatum)* Native. Sun. Soils from wet to dry and from sandy to clay are accepted. 4-6' tall and half as wide. Medium textured foliage. Upright, narrow form. Valued for its sturdy upright form and diffuse fine-textured flower panicles which are effective from midsummer through winter, it's the perfect choice for naturalizing and to encourage wildlife in the garden. Best in large groups or sweeps. Green in summer, yellow in fall and light beige in winter. Flowers dark purple red fading to beige. Can establish using either plants or seeds. Cultivars include 'Heavy Metal' with a powdery blue summer color and the ability to withstand heavy rains and 'Hanse Herms' with a wine-red fall color and pinkish red flowers.

Indian Grass (*Sorghastrum nutans*) Native. Sun. Takes most soils and moisture levels. Drought tolerant. Foliage 32" tall, flowers 78" tall. Upright and clump-forming. Its attractive late-summer flowers, orange fall color, and good winter aspect make it effective as a specimen in groups or in meadows. Never needs staking.

River Oats (*Chasmanthium latifolium*) Native. Sun to light shade. Tolerates most soils but prefers fertile and well-drained. Medium texture. Foliage 3' tall, flowers 4' tall. Has upright, clump-forming shape. Seeds are oat-like and suspended at ends of gracefully arching branches. Very attractive from summer until the following spring. Pick seed stalks when they are green and dry for use in arrangements. Naturalizes by seeding in. Good naturalized in the middle of a wide perennial border or in the back of a narrower border, as a specimen, or near water. Fall foliage color in sun is brilliant gold. Also known as northern sea oats, wild oats, and spangle grass.

Compact Pampas Grass (*Cortaderia selloana* 'Pumila') Sun. Fertile, well-drained soils. Grows 6' with showy flowers above foliage. This plant will survive most Atlanta winters and should be easier to use in the landscape than its commonly seen 12'-tall big brother. Panicles make elegant cut flowers for fresh or dried arrangements. The large upright clumps are good as specimens or screens.

Striped Giant Reed (*Arundo donax* 'Variegata') Sun. Likes average soil and moisture but is drought tolerant. Foliage 8' tall, flowers a foot taller than foliage. Can be cut back in early summer to control height. Upright and clump-forming, it looks a bit like a coarse-textured corn plant with white stripes. Very striking. An old-fashioned plant for southern gardens, it makes an excellent specimen. Looks great near water. May revert partly to green in August. Becomes shabby in late fall and should be cut to the ground in late November.

Tender Purple Fountain Grass (*Pennisetum setaceum* 'Rubrum') Sun. Average to moderately dry soil. Foliage 50". Flower height 80". Upright, arching shape, fine texture. This clump-forming grass has burgundy-bronze leaves and long narrow plumes of an even darker purple. Very effective with silver-foliaged plants. **This grass is not hardy and dies in winter;** however, it is so striking you may want to use it.

Other Recommendations

Horticultural consultant Jim Harrington recommends Quaking Grass, *Briza maxima*, a full sun **annual** grass that performs well here in containers and as an accent in a small garden patch. A thin stalk, about 1' tall, sways with the slightest breeze and the cone-like flower clusters sound like rattles on a rattlesnake.

Wonderful Native Grasses Worth Growing

For those who want a truly Georgia look, here are wonderful native grasses:

Splitbeard Bluestem *(Andropogon ternarius)* Great on dry sunny slopes.

Broomsedge *(Andropogon virginicus)* Most conspicuous native grass of the Georgia Piedmont. Lends copper-orange glow to fall landscapes. Drought tolerant and sun-loving. Useful in groups or naturalized.

Little Bluestem *(Schizachyrium scoparium)* Loves sunny infertile land. Drought tolerant. Best naturalized. Beautiful in autumn and winter.

Purple-top *(Iridens flavus)* Grows anywhere in full sun. Its many purple panicles give a purple haze to meadows in fall.

Darrel Morrison of the University of Georgia's School of Environmental Design has these suggestions for growing native grasses: Buy or collect seed from roadsides and railroad right-of-ways in November or December. Store the seeds in paper bags in an unheated area until mid-April or the following fall and plant in a cleared area. Lightly cover with oat straw to prevent erosion. Water for the first month if it doesn't rain often; after that, watering should be unnecessary. Use 20 pounds of seed per acre; half a pound for 1,000 square feet. For a few plants, planting 10 seeds per pot lets you save only the strongest plant in each for the garden.

To see native grasses used in the landscape, visit the Atlanta History Center to view the plantings Morrison designed around the new museum building.

Grasses to Avoid

Two lovely grasses which are often offered can be very difficult to grow in Georgia. These are Japanese Blood Grass (*Imperata cylindrica* 'Red Baron') and Blue Fescue (*Festuca cinerea* and *Festuca ovina* var. *glauca*). Your money is better spent on other species.

A word of warning, too, about Ribbon Grass (*Phalaris arundinacea*). This grass, also known as 'Gardener's Garters,' does too well here and can be very invasive. It also becomes ratty looking as the season progresses. Plant at your own risk.

Sedges and Rushes

Sedges (*Carex spp.*) are a wonderful group of small grass-like plants which do beautifully in partly to lightly shaded areas, particularly if the areas are average to moist. Most are evergreen and many are variegated. Sedges are less likely to burn in winter than monkey grass (*Liriope*). They can be used as specimens, as groundcovers, or to contrast with the foliage of shade plants like hostas or ferns.

Rushes (*Juncus spp.*) will grow in the boggiest soil at water's edge and in the water itself. Their grass-like texture contrasts nicely with other bog plants. They do spread, however, so plan them carefully.

Purchasing Grasses

When purchasing ornamental grasses, check first with your local nursery. If they can't help you, try these sources. Addresses and telephone numbers are listed in Appendix A.

For Plants:

Kurt Bluemel, Inc. (Catalog $2; wholesale catalog available; probably the largest selection in the U.S.)

Wayside Gardens

Niche Gardens (Catalog $3)

Limerock Ornamental Grasses

For Seed:

Boothe Hill Company

Shooting Star Nursery

Loft Seeds, Inc.

Chapter
Twenty-Two

Vines

by
Allen Sistrunk

Vines in the Atlanta Landscape

Vines are an often overlooked plant form in the garden. There is no other class of plants which offers such a wide variety of uses and allows such an opportunity for anyone with original schemes. Vines literally go and grow where other plants will not. Vines can flower, shade, screen, add dimension, and direct the eye. They take up limited soil space, cover the soil, and hold the soil. Some vines, with their graceful character, can give that natural feeling to landscape and architecture by possessing an ability to successfully blend things together. In smaller gardens and balcony gardens, vines can be grown in containers and give enormous mass while being confined to restricted soil areas.

In planning the use of a vine in one's garden, the most important factor other than sun or shade is how the plant will make its ascent. Climbing plants make their way towards the sky by different methods. **Tendrils, aerial roots,** and **discs** are specialized plant appendages that actually grab, hold, and attach themselves to other surfaces, such as walls, fences, treebark, or shrubbery, allowing the plant to climb. **Twining** and **rambling** are stem responses that give the plant the ability to rise. Knowing the vine's ultimate size is also important. Providing the right support that will be able to take the weight of the climber (such as a sturdy pole, a trellis, or braided wire running horizontally and vertically) is critical to growing your rambling rose, clematis, honeysuckle and jasmine, or ivy successfully.

How to Plant and Grow Vines

Dig a hole at least three to four times the diameter of the vine's root mass at planting time and no deeper than the container in which it was grown. Make sure the soil is extremely friable, enriched with organic matter, and well drained in order to create a good environment for rapid, healthy root growth. Follow directions for the required cultural needs of each vine type. Besides the correct planting, the largest responsibility in gardening with vines is pruning and training. Consult the books listed in the Recommended Reading and References section for information.

Structures such as trellises, arbors, and gazebos beg the use of vines while walls, fences, and railings require more careful study to choose the appropriate vine. Take a look at how others have successfully incorporated climbing plants into the garden, and borrow or expand on already proven uses. Consider also some unlikely uses, such as letting a clematis or a rose intermingle with a shrub or tree, or planting a trumpet creeper or wisteria at the base of a dead or dying tree. There may be an element of your house that disturbs you. Remember what Frank Lloyd Wright said, "A physician can bury his mistakes, an architect can only plant a vine."

Vines and Vine-like Plants
Proven to Thrive in the Atlanta Area

Akebia quinata (Akebia) A fast-growing, woody, twining vine. Chocolate colored flowers in spring on year-old wood. Can be used as a groundcover if mowed back once a year in late winter. Attractive blue-green new foliage. Can escape cultivation to become a pest. Sun to medium shade. Semi-evergreen.

Campsis radicans (Trumpet Creeper) An aggressive, woody, aerial-root forming vine. Orange-red flowers spring through summer. Attracts hummingbirds. Foliage is a beautiful, lacy, medium green. Can reach very high places, 40' or more. With age, a beautiful trunk forms. Can tolerate containers well. Sun. Deciduous. Can tolerate wet soils. Prune heavily in late winter to promote flowering.

Clematis hybrida (Clematis) Semi-woody, tendril producing, rambling-twining, flowering vines. Although these plants may require a little extra effort, the reward is worth it. Regarded by many gardeners as the queen of flowering vines, the clematis likes to grow with its head in the sun and its feet in the shade. Plant this vine in as much sun as possible. Dig a very wide planting hole enriched with plenty of organic matter, and then mulch with large flat stones to keep root temperatures as cool as possible. There is one maintenance requirement that demands a little extra time and thought—when to prune. Prune early spring bloomers immediately after flowering if needed. Prune large-flowered hybrids that bloom before the first day of summer only immediately after flowering. Prune hybrids that bloom after the first day of summer on new wood, like sweet autumn clematis, any time needed and cut to the ground after the vine becomes unsightly in winter. See "Clematis" in Part Four.

Clematis maximowicziana (Sweet Autumn Clematis) A woody, tendril producing, rambling-twining, late summer/fall flowering vine. The fragrance of this vine's fleecy, pure white flowers is reason enough to have one in every garden. The absolute easiest of all clematis to grow, foolproof. Coming upon this vine covered with thousands of flowers is akin to discovering a hidden treasure.

Decumaria barbara (Decumaria) A woody, deciduous, aerial-root forming vine. This often overlooked Georgia native is a real Jekyll and Hyde. It is found in shady woods sometimes crawling along the forest floor and occasionally rather sparsely climbing a tree always rather benign in appearance. When given a site with a rich soil and full sun it really comes out with dense, shiny, dark green foliage and is covered in mid-spring with fragrant, creamy-white, hydrangea-like flowers. You can expect rich yellow color in fall and a sculpturesque character through the winter. A winning combination when allowed to climb on a rock wall surface or spread across the roof of a rustic structure.

Dolichos lablab (Hyacinth Bean) An annual, twining, flowering vine for full sun. This remarkable vine was a favorite of Thomas Jefferson's at Monticello and is easy to grow from seed. It begins to flower when only a few inches tall. The lavender flowers are complemented by the similar shades found in the leaves, stems, and pods. This vine will continue to bloom right up until a killing frost.

Euonymus fortunei (Climbing Euonymus) Actually a woody shrub behaving as a vine with aerial roots. Grown primarily for ornamental foliage, this plant sometimes rewards us with attractive red and orange fruit in the fall. Tolerating either full sun or light shade, it is **prone to scale**, although some cultivars seem to be somewhat resistant. Treat scale with Volck Oil in winter. Being evergreen is an advantage for screening purposes. Often overused as a groundcover, this plant has yet to be tapped for all of its uses as a vine.

Gelsemium sempervirens (Carolina Jessamine) A woody, rambling-twining, early spring flowering, semi-evergreen vine. This vine is for full sun only. In less light, it will be rather unattractive with few flowers. It is an aggressive plant that covers quickly with pure yellow flowers that have a fragrance not unlike baby powder. A good choice for screening chain link fences. Cut back severely to major canes every few years when it becomes twiggy.

Hedera helix (English Ivy) An immature vining form of a woody shrub with aerial rootlets for sun or shade. Considering the literally hundreds of ivy cultivars that go unnoticed, here is an unlimited new source of foliage vines to be used in the garden. Using them as you would an evergreen perennial, these plants can successfully brighten the darkest spots of your garden with their variegated, silver, and gold leaves. Oftentimes the cultivars are not as aggressive as the common English ivy, so you might even consider letting a few with unusually textured foliage climb on a wall or other garden structure. Investigate new dwarfs, too.

Lonicera x heckrottii (Goldflame Honeysuckle) A woody, twining, warm season, flowering vine. This vine is the vine you dream of; it flowers all season long, has few if any pests, requires no special pruning or soil preparation and does not escape cultivation or eat the landscape with excessive growth. The yellow and red flowers never cover the entire vine, but they are striking and are evenly spaced on the plant to make quite a show. Does best in full sun and a well-drained soil. Can be infected with spider mites and/or leaf miner. Spray as needed.

Parthenocissus quinquefolia (Virginia Creeper) A woody, deciduous, tendril forming vine for full sun or shade. Another often overlooked native vine. Should be used in the south instead of its Asian cousin, Boston Ivy *(Parthenocissus tricuspidata)*, because of better heat tolerance and outstanding fall color. The leaves turn shades of orange, red, and yellow near the end of October. Excellent for softening large barren walls whether brick, stone, or stucco. The use of this vine could easily make the south the new ivy league section of the country. Good for native gardens.

Rosa banksiae (Lady Banks Rose) A vine-like, thornless, spring-flowering rose. Rapid growing, this rose is ideal for training over arbors, doorways, and any garden structure that could support its weight. It is covered in spring with quarter-sized, double yellow blossoms. There is also a white variety. Constant pruning is required to keep this rose in bounds but since it is thornless, this is a relatively easy task. Full sun.

Trachelospermum jasminoides (Confederate Jasmine) An evergreen, twining, spring-flowering vine. Foliage is the asset of this plant, dark green and lustrous. The white, star-shaped flowers are heavily scented with a musky, sweet fragrance that perfumes the garden just as the nights are becoming warm. A star performer, this vine will tolerate quite a bit of shade and still reward with abundant foliage and flowers. Being a twiner, it often needs help in training upon a wall or otherwise flat surface. Although cold damage often occurs in 10 degrees F. or less, the variety 'Madison' from Cedar Lane Farm is said to be more hardy.

Vitis coignetiae (Crimson Vine) A woody, deciduous, tendril-forming vine. This grape is not grown for its fruit but for its fall color. Bright crimson is the fall color that gives this plant its common name. It also tolerates shade quite well. The rapid growth that can be expected from this vine can be accelerated with the light addition of fertilizer. The foliage of this plant gives a coarse scalloped appearance. There are several varieties of grapes that should be grown more for their ornamental character, such as one with purple foliage.

Wisteria floribunda (Wisteria) A woody, deciduous, spring-flowering, twining vine. Full sun is required among certain other less understood things to cause this plant to flower. The lacy foliage is reason enough to allow this species into any garden where space permits. The pendulous blossoms, in shades of pink, blue, purple, and white, perfume the air with a delicate sweet fragrance. Upon aging, a character-ridden trunk will develop on this plant. Of all the things mentioned to ensure success with blooms on this plant, those most often spoken of are application of superphosphate in late spring or early summer, heavy pruning in mid-spring, and root pruning in summer. The plant seems to have a mind all its own and will bloom when it's ready, indicating the possibility of a maturity factor. Being aggressive, this plant should not be allowed to climb trees. Quite happy in a container, this species can give a mass of foliage while being confined to a restricted root area. Plant in a 15-20 gallon pot in the soil to eliminate having to root prune. Don't plant in prepared garden soil.

G.R.A. ADDITIONAL RECOMMENDATIONS FOR VINES

Perennial vines

Botanical Name	Common Name	Decid./Evgr.	Height	Exposure	Description
Aristolochia macrophylla	Dutchman's Pipe	E		Part shade/sun	Curiously bent, tubular, yellow-green flowers mostly in spring; native to eastern North America; annual unless lifted
Bignonia anisostichus	Crossvine	E	50-60'	Sun/part shade	Burgundy leaves in winter; tube-shaped, orange-red flowers in late spring; rapid grower
Clematis armandii	Armand's Clematis	E	15-20'	Sun	Showy white flowers; March-blooming; rapid growth; froze spring '96
Clematis 'Dr. Ruppel'		D	6-8'	Sun	Large rose flowers marked with deep carmine bars; blooms May-June, occasionally thru summer
C. lanuginosa 'Candida'		D	20'	Sun/part shade	9" pure white blooms; June peak, smaller size in summer; spectacular
C. florida 'Sieboldii'		D	3-4'	Part shade, sheltered site	Creamy white with a cluster of rich, deep purple petals in the center and an electric green eye; not robust
C. x durandii		D	5'	Sun	Stunning; intense blue with a dazzling yellow eye (stamens); non-stop blooms July-September

G. R. A. ADDITIONAL RECOMMENDATIONS FOR VINES cont'd
Perennial vines

Botanical Name	Common Name	Decid./Evgr.	Height	Exposure	Description
C. jackmanii		D	10'	Sun	4-6" purple flowers; vigorous plant; June-October blooms
C. 'Montana Rubens'		D	over 25'	Sun	Small pink flowers; blooms May-June
C. 'Nellie Moser'		D	10'	Sun	White/hot pink flowers; blooms April-August
C. 'Comtesse de Bouchard'		D	8'	Sun	Free-flowering; 4" bright mauve pink flowers all summer; the best for Atlanta
Clematis integrifolia	Bush Solitary Clematis	D		Sun	Nodding 1" lavender-blue urns on 1-2' thin, wiry stems
Dicentra scandens	Yellow Bleeding Heart	D	20'	Part shade	Small yellow flowers July-October; survived freeze '96
Ficus pumila	Climbing Fig	E	30' rapidly	Part shade/ shade	Light green foliage; leaves flat against wall; prune young erect growth and old mainstem to prevent insect problems; frost damages fruiting branches; protective overhang needed
Hydrangea anomala var. petiolaris	Climbing Hydrangea	D		Sun/part shade	Slow growth first few years, then moderate grower; flat lace-cap white flowers in spring

Perennial vines

Botanical Name	Common Name	Decid./Evgr.	Height	Exposure	Description
Lonicera sempervirens 'Dropmore Scarlet'	Dropmore Scarlet Honeysuckle	Semi-evergreen	50'	Sun	Scarlet tubular flowers June-October; vigorous growth
Millettia reticulata	Evergreen Wisteria	Semi-evergreen	unlimited	Sun/part shade	Flowers pinkish blue in clusters 8" long; blooms late summer; leaves almost leathery; grows more slowly than other wisteria; the higher it grows, the more likely it is to lose leaves in winter
Polygonum aubertii	Silver Lace Vine	D	30'	Sun	White blooms June-October; vigorous to aggressive
Solanum jasminoides 'Album'	White Potato Vine	E	climbs 15'	Sun/part shade	Drooping clusters of small white stars; severe cold kills to ground, but resurrects in spring vigorously (except '96) flowers June-frost

G.R.A. ADDITIONAL RECOMMENDATIONS FOR VINES

Annual vines

Botanical Name	Common Name	Height	Exposure	Description
Allamanda cathartica	Allamanda		Sun	5" trumpet-shaped yellow blooms; continuous blooming during warm weather; weak climber, needs to be tied to support
Clitoria spp.	Butterfly Pea	8'	Sun	Large double sweet pea-like royal blue flowers
Ipomoea alba	Moon Vine	40' rapidly	Sun/part shade	Large fragrant white flowers open at dusk, lasting one night; mid-summer thru October; gather seeds to re-grow in spring
Ipomoea batata 'Blackie'	Sweet Potato Vine		Sun	Dark purple foliage
Ipomoea coccinea	Scarlet Morning Glory	15'	Sun	Dime-size orange morning glory; blooms early summer-October
Ipomoea multifidi	Cardinal Vine	10'	Sun	Red, rounded star flower; leaf highly dissected
Ipomoea purpurea 'Heavenly Blue'	Morning Glory		Sun	Summer/fall bloomer; new trumpet-shaped blooms open each morning and last until noon (late afternoon in cooler weather)
Ipomoea quamoclit	Cypress Vine	vigorous grower to 10'	Sun	Small red or white star-shaped flower; leaf looks like a fish skeleton
Mandevilla splendens	Mandevilla		Sun/part shade	Tropical, beautiful pink-red bloom; protect from midday sun; keep moist during growing season; over-winter in greenhouse;

G.R.A. ADDITIONAL RECOMMENDATIONS FOR VINES

Annual vines

Botanical Name	Common Name	Height	Exposure	Description
Mina lobata	Spanish Flag	15'	Sun	1" angular tube flowers are red-orange fading to yellow then white; deeply lobed leaf
Passiflora incarnata	Passion Flower or May Pop		Sun	Conspicuous, intricate flowers; edible ovoid green fruit; deeply three-lobed leaves; aggressive; reseeds
Thunbergia alata	Black-eyed Susan Vine		Sun	Golden orange, yellow or white flower with brown center; summer to frost; easy to grow from seed
Senecio confusus	Mexican Flame Vine	8'	Sun	Unrefined looking vine; bright orange double composite flower; poor soil; spreading; best growing over a shrub

Ferns

by

Lloyd H. Snyder, Jr.

Best Ferns for Atlanta

What is a Fern?*

Ferns and fern allies, or pteridophytes, are among the oldest of our land plants, having evolved some 400 million years ago. They reproduce by spores and have an organized vascular system to carry water and other necessary materials. They have neither flowers nor seeds. True ferns have large leaves with a branching vein system. The fern allies (horsetails, clubmosses, spike mosses, and quillworts) have small, scalelike leaves and only a midvein.

Fern spores are minute bodies, smaller than grains of pepper and usually black, brown, or yellow. They are contained in a case called a *sporangium*. Many (often about 50) sporangia are grouped together to form a *sorus*. Sori are usually located on the undersides of fertile leaves and novice growers often believe the sori to be some form of insect life or disease harmful to the plant. Sori may be arranged on or near the leaf margin, scattered over the surface, in rows along the midvein, or on the edges, of the leaves.

On many ferns the sorus is covered by a thin, membranous structure, or *indusium*. This structure varies with different species and may be circular, kidney-shaped, or elongated. It may be attached by a central stalk or along its side. In some ferns with the sori along the leaf edge, the leaf margin inrolls to form a false indusium. The location of the sori and the shape of the indusium are often excellent means for identifying a fern.

Sporangia are found on the fern's fertile leaves. Ferns may have both fertile and sterile leaves, which are often identical except for the presence of the sori on the fertile ones. In other cases the two kinds of leaves are either slightly or completely different, in which case the fern is said to be *dimorphic*.

The blade (the flat, green part of the frond or leaf) varies in size according to the species. It may be simple and undivided or cut into various degrees. The primary division of a compound leaf blade is the pinna.

---

*Adapted from Snyder, Lloyd H. and J. G. Bruce. *Field Guide to the Ferns and other Pteridophytes of Georgia.* University of Georgia Press, 1986.

The life cycle of pteridophytes is unusual. When spores mature, the sporangia burst open, scattering the spores. There are literally millions of spores on each fern plant but very few, if any, of them germinate. In fact, much fern reproduction is vegetative.

A distinctive feature of most ferns is the way in which the fern leaf grows. The immature fern frond is tightly coiled like a watch spring. The immature frond is called a crozier (from the head of a bishop's staff) or a fiddlehead (like the narrow end of a violin). The fern leaf matures from the base to the tip as the coil gradually unrolls. Fern fiddleheads are an attractive sight in swamps and woodlands in springtime, and some fern fiddleheads are edible. In fact, a company in New England cans fiddleheads for sale in grocery stores, and the American Fern Society publishes a recipe booklet, "Feasting on Fiddleheads."

Ferns in the Garden

Most ferns grow in cool, moist shady woodlands, conditions that should be approximated in the garden. However, few ferns need continual moisture or deep shade. Most thrive with some sun in semi-shade. Poor or clay soil should have leaf mold or compost added.

Ferns are ideal for woodland gardens and foundation plantings. Since they do not have flowers, and their primary provision is shape, they can be used either by themselves or mixed with flowering plants. Native wild plants that complement ferns include jack-in-the-pulpit, solomon's seal, foam flower, trillium, mayapple, Dutchman's breeches, wild ginger, bloodroot, and wild geranium. Ferns also fit well with such plants as azalea, hosta, astilbe, and cyclamen.

For rock gardens, the marginal wood and Christmas fern can be put in large openings; the ebony spleenwort and hairy lipfern in smaller ones. Common throughout Georgia, and especially prolific along the coast, is the resurrection fern, *Pleopeltis polypodioides* (L.) Watt. It grows primarily on trees, but also on rocks, and is difficult to transplant and grow.

Choosing Ferns

Most of the ferns listed on the chart that follows are native to Georgia and the Atlanta area and are found locally in the wild. A few are common in South Georgia, but are moving north and growing successfully in Atlanta gardens.

Three Japanese ferns (painted, holly, and climbing) have escaped from gardens and are growing in the wild (primarily in South Georgia), or are being successfully cultivated in Atlanta. Their distinctive features justify their serious consideration for use in the home garden.

Most of the ferns listed are of medium size. An exception is the osmundas (royal and cinnamon) which can grow rather large and are, therefore, suitable for background or foundation plantings.

The following list is not exhaustive, but suggests some of the basic ferns that might be used in the home garden in the Atlanta area. Hopefully most, if not all, are available from local nurseries.

Fern	Fronds	Sori	Soil	Light	Remarks
Marginal Wood *Dryopteris marginalis* (L.) A Gray	Circular cluster, dark blue-green above, lighter below; leathery, evergreen L: 18-24"; W: 6-10"	Marginal; large, prominent	Moist, but well-drained	Partial shade	Often grows on rock ledges and slopes; fronds appear in spring or summer, persist 'til next year.
Christmas *Polystichum acrostichoides* (Michx.) Schott	Circular, arching clumps; spreads slowly; dimorphic, shortest sterile; leathery, dark lustrous green, lighter below L: 24-36"; W: 3-5"	Round in rows; on upper 1/2 to 1/3 fertile frond	Moist; all sorts	Full to partial shade	Fronds green in winter; used by early settlers as Christmas decorations, hence name; very common, easily grown
Southern Lady *Athyrium filix-femina* (L.) Roth	Clustered, arching, deciduous; finely cut and delicate; yellow-green L: 18-24" ; W: 5-15"	Elongate; along midvein; herringbone pattern	Moderate to fairly acid; moist to wet	Partial shade	Easily grown; common in North Georgia
Northern Maidenhair *Adiantum pedatum* L.	Blade 6-10" long, 8-16" wide; flat, horizontal to ground, fan shape; stipe 8-16" long, light to medium green; delicate, dainty, deciduous	On underside of reflexed margin	Rich, moist; some lime; good drainage	Shade	Beautiful, mix crushed limestone or oyster shells in soil

BEST FERNS FOR ATLANTA GARDENS cont'd

Fern	Fronds	Sori	Soil	Light	Remarks
Japanese Painted *Athyrium japonicum* (Thunb.) cv Pictum.	Color unusual; wine-red blended with gray-green; lanceolate; delicate; deciduous. L: 24-30" W: 6-20"	Along midvein; herringbone pattern	Neutral to slightly acid	Medium shade	Appears early; will last to fall if kept watered
Japanese Climbing *Lygodium japonicum* (Thunb.) Sw.	Deciduous; vine-like, trailing, and twining; dimorphic; yellow-green L: 20 or more feet	On margin of finger-like segments	Neutral	Full or partial sun	Should be grown on fence or trellis
Holly *Cyrtomium falcatum* (L. f.) Presl	Leathery; veins netted, dark shinning green above, lighter beneath; leaf like holly	Large, round, scattered	Neutral; moist, well-drained	Open shade	Evergreen in Atlanta; often grown next to buildings
Sensitive (or Bead) *Onoclea sensibilis* L.	Strongly dimorphic; produced singly; sterile: coarse, dark green above, lighter below; deciduous L: 14-30"; W: 6-14"	In two rows of bead-like structures on erect stalk	Wet, slightly acidic, or neutral	Partial sun	Likely to spread rapidly
Bracken *Pteridium aquilinum* L. (Kuhn)	Triangular; coarse; deciduous; leathery; deep green L: 18-36"; W: 14-30"	Along margins of leaflets	Wet or dry; humus or sandy	Full or partial sun	Primarily of sunny areas; needs to be controlled

BEST FERNS FOR ATLANTA GARDENS

Fern	Fronds	Sori	Soil	Light	Remarks
Widespread Maiden *Thelypteris kunthii* (Desv.) Morton	Delicate; lanceolate with long tapering tip; deciduous; yellowish-green L: 20-45"; W: 6-16"	Medial; sorus covering kidney shape	Neutral to slightly acid; moist	Partial sun	Common in South Georgia; will grow in Atlanta
Mariana Maiden *Macrothelypteris torresiana* (Gaud.) Ching	Light green; clustered, spreading; delicate; broadly triangular L: 24-48"; W: 10-20"	Circular; in rows along midvein	Neutral to slightly acid; moist	Full shade	Common in South Georgia; spreading northward
Royal *Osmunda regalis* L.	Deciduous; clustered; resemble leaves of locust tree L: 24-60"; W: 10-20"	In clusters on stalk growing from frond tip	Wet, acidic	Open shade	Known as var. spectabilis
Cinnamon *Osmunda cinnamomea* L.	Strongly dimorphic; sterile, somewhat coarse, yellow-green; fertile - stalk with only brown naked sporangia; scaly L: 24-48"; W: 5-10"	Sporangia in opposite clusters along stalk of fertile frond	Wet, acidic	Partial to full shade	Because of large size, excellent or background planting
Broad Beech *Phegopteris hexagonoptera* (Michaux) Fee	Dull green; broadly triangular L: 14-28"; W: 6-14"	Small, round, marginal	Moist;. moderately acid	Shade	Spreads fairly rapidly

BEST FERNS FOR ATLANTA GARDENS cont'd

Fern	Fronds	Sori	Soil	Light	Remarks
New York *Thelypteris noveboracensis* (L.) Niewi.	Delicate; deciduous; tapers at both ends; light yellow-green L: 12-24"; W: 2-6"	Small, round	Moist.; slightly acid	Partial shade	Spreads rapidly; turns brown easily
Ebony Spleenwort *Asplenium platyneuron* (L.) BSP	Small tufts; fertile; 6-16" long, 1-2" wide; tardily deciduous; erect; sterile; evergreen; flat L: 2-4"; W: 1/2"	In rows along midvein; elongate	Well-drained; slightly acidic	Sun to shade	Common throughout nearly all of Georgia in all kinds of locations
Hairy Lipfern *Cheilanthes lanosa* (Michx.) D.C. Eaton	Loosely clumped; dark green; evergreen; hairy; sterile, shorter and broader L: 8-16"; W: 1/2-1"	Along reflexed margins	Non-calcium or lime, rocky	Sun to some shade	Fronds curl up when dry, but revive with rain

Native Plants

by

Sandra Sandefur

Southeastern Native Plants for Atlanta Gardens

To successfully utilize native plants in a cultivated setting, you need only common sense, a keen eye for observation, and a little research. Take a walk through a forest area or along a roadside or stream and observe the plants growing there.

Notice the microhabitat as well as the overall environment in which a plant is naturally found. Is the plant growing at the base of a slope or on the edge of a stream? The microhabitat at the base of the slope may be cooler than the top of the slope just 15' away because cold air is heavy and tends to fall into low areas. The stream plant probably thrives in an evenly moist area rather than in a wet situation like a bog, so growing a stream plant in a garden with regular watering should prove successful.

The microhabitat also is important for seed germination. When seeds mature and disperse, they fall on all types of sites, from damp to dry and sun to shade. Only those sites which offer just the right combination of factors will promote germination and successful growth. Some species have a very narrow range of environments which will promote germination and growth, while others will germinate in a wide range of environments.

Species which are most particular in germination requirements usually display wider adaptability as mature plants, and therefore can be grown over a wider range of habitats. For example, *Lobelia cardinalis* (cardinal flower) requires a constantly moist environment for the very fine seeds to germinate, so this flower is usually found in damp, boggy sites. The mature plant can perform just fine in a drier garden site, if regular watering is provided. However, in a drought period, these same cultivated plants will need monitoring for drought stress, so a site closer to the faucet is more desirable than one at the back of the garden.

C h o o s i n g   a   S i t e

With moderate soil preparation, one can grow native herbaceous perennials successfully in the landscape. Try to duplicate in the cultivated garden the same natural environment from which these plants spring, but do not be afraid to experiment with growing plants outside the parameters of their native habitats.

For those species which like a north facing, deciduous forest environment such as bloodroot, trilliums, and mayapple, a rich humus soil is ideal. Organic amendments of fine ground bark, leaves, or compost will help the clay soil present in most Atlanta gardens mimic the woodland forest setting. Top dressing with a mulch imitates the high leaf litter content found at soil level in a deciduous forest setting and helps to conserve moisture during drought times.

Keep in mind that nothing blooms profusely in dense shade, and most woodland shade plants give good results when taken into higher light situations. However, guard against placing plants where they will receive hot afternoon sun after 3 p.m.

Planting in Sunny Sites

If the garden site is sunny, try growing roadside species of Southeastern perennials, but beware of the trap of over-preparing the soil. So-called meadow species, such as lance-leaf coreopsis, black-eyed Susan, birdfoot violet, and oxeye daisy, are of hardy stock which struggle to grow in a harsh environment. If they are planted in soil that is too well-prepared and fertile, these species become thugs in the garden, falling over other plants, rotting out, or aggressively taking over the site.

Some soil amending is necessary to keep the clay particles from aggregating. Without any attention to the soil, plants languish above ground and spend all their energy struggling to become established. This is acceptable along a roadside where acres of goldenrod grow, but not in a garden where from a division you expect three plants to bloom the first year. In addition, be sparing with the fertilizer, or flowers will be forsaken for lush foliage.

Planting in Shady Sites

Flowers look picturesque when planted at the bases of trees, but good initial soil preparation and continued soil aeration will be needed. Tree roots tend to move into the well-prepared soil to gain moisture and nutrients, so perennials will do better if planted at least 6' from the trunk of a tree.

Shallow-rooted trees in particular are extremely difficult to underplant. Top offenders are two popular shade trees, red maple and river birch. Groundcovers like partridge berry, evergreen and deciduous native gingers, or green and gold give a nice show at the base of these troublesome trees.

If a densely shady site is your only option, consider removing some trees. If trees are spaced less than 8-10' apart on center, tree removal will improve the forest's health as well as the encompassed environment. Another plus for selective tree removal from a site is the elimination of tree roots that compete with other plants for water and nutrients.

An alternative to tree removal is canopy thinning—selectively removing limbs in the tree canopy and/or limbing up the canopy from the ground. This will give better air circulation as well as dappled light penetration. Thinning tends to be a temporary measure; over time, the remaining branches will grow to fill in the holes created by thinning.

Choosing Plants

The following charts list Southeastern native trees and native shrubs for use in the landscape.

NATIVE TREES FOR LANDSCAPE USE

Common Name	Botanical Name	Mature Size	Decid./Evgr.	Comments
Chalkbark Maple	Acer leucoderme	25' ht; 15' wd	D	Good fall color; drought tolerant
Fringe Tree	Chionanthus virginicus	25' ht; 25' wd	D	Fleecy fragrant flower display May-June; male showier, female has blue berries
Alternate-leaved Dogwood	Cornus alternifolia	20' ht; 30' wd	D	Branches strongly horizontal; fruits eaten by many bird species
American Smoketree	Cotinus obovatus	25' ht; 15' wd	D	Excellent fall color; male flowers showier than female
Parsley Hawthorn	Crataegus marshallii	20' ht; 20' wd	D	Attractive red berries persist all winter; thorny
Ben Franklin Tree	Franklinia alatamaha	15' ht; 10' wd	D	Needs well-drained, moist, organic soil; hard to establish but worth trying
Carolina Silverbell	Halesia carolina	35' ht; 25' wd	D	Needs well-drained, moist, organic soil; best in woodland borders; showy spring flowers
Two-winged Silverbell	Halesia diptera	25' ht; 15' wd	D	
Winterberry	Ilex verticillata	10' ht; 10 wd	D	Showy red berries in winter if both sexes present; tolerates wet conditions
Eastern Red Cedar	Juniperus virginiana	40' ht; 15' wd	E	Historically used for windbreaks; host for rusts, bag worms
Bigleaf Magnolia	Magnolia macrophylla	40' ht; 30' wd	D	Specimen tree; coarse texture; protect from wind
Umbrella Magnolia	Magnolia tripetala	25' ht; 15' wd	D	Huge leaves (24") at ends of branch; red 4" fall fruit

NATIVE TREES FOR LANDSCAPE USE   cont'd

Common Name	Botanical Name	Mature Size	Decid./Evgr.	Comments
Sweetbay Magnolia	*Magnolia virginiana*	20' ht; 20' wd	Semi-evergreen	Tolerates wet, swampy soils; white lemon-scented summer flowers
Ogeechee Lime	*Nyssa ogechee*	30' ht; 20' wd	D	3/4" red fruits used as lime substitute; occurs naturally on wet sites, but good drought tolerance
Black Gum	*Nyssa sylvatica*	60' ht; 40' wd	D	The best red fall color! Birds like small black fruit in fall
Sourwood	*Oxydendrum arboreum*	25' ht; 15' wd	D	Nice specimen tree; lacy flowers and dark green leaves in summer, crimson in fall
Sycamore	*Platanus occidentalis*	100' ht; 100' wd	D	Huge tree; good in natural setting; but messy on street or lawn; drops limbs and fruit
Cherry Laurel	*Prunus caroliniana*	30' ht; 20' wd	E	Cultivar 'Bright 'n Tight' good substitute for red-tip photinia; limbs broken by ice and snow
Sassafras	*Sassafras albidum*	50' ht; 25' wd	D	Roots historically used to make tea and flavoring; leaves have three distinct shapes; excellent fall color
Bald cypress	*Taxodium distichum*	60' ht; 20' wd	D	Conifer; good specimen tree; lacy leaf effect
Blackhaw Viburnum	*Viburnum prunifolium*	15' ht; 10' wd	D	Red fall color; edible fruit turns from white to light pink to rose, then navy blue

NATIVE SHRUBS FOR LANDSCAPE USE

Common Name	Botanical Name	Mature Size	Decid./Evgr.	Comments
Florida Leucothoe	*Agarista populifolia*	8' ht; 6' wd	E	Multi-stemmed, arching habit; good screen for shade; medium green color
Bottlebrush Buckeye	*Aesculus parviflora*	12' ht; 15' wd	D	Likes moist, well-drained, organic soil; full sun or shade; excellent massed under shade trees
Serviceberry	*Amelanchier arborea*	25' ht; 15' wd	D	Yellow, apricot, red fall color; edible fruits in June, but you have to beat the wildlife to them
Red Chokeberry	*Aronia arbutifolia*	8' ht; 5' wd	D	Colony forming; good display of red fall fruits when massed; cultivar 'Brilliantissima' displays excellent red fall leaf color
Sweet Pepper Bush	*Clethra alnifolia*	8' ht; 6' wd	D	Fragrant white flowers July-August; cultivar 'Hummingbird' good for smaller gardens
Fothergilla	*Fothergilla gardenii*	3' ht; 3' wd	D	Honey-scented, bottle-brush flowers in April-May; brilliant yellow, orange, scarlet fall leaf color
Florida Anise	*Illicium floridanum*	10' ht; 6' wd	E	Red spider-like flowers in mid-spring; pungent scented foliage; good evergreen screen even in heavy shade
Sweetspire	*Itea virginica*	5' ht; 8' wd	D	Lightly fragrant flowers in late spring; good naturalized in moist areas; 'Henry's Garnet' displays reddish purple fall color
Mountain Laurel	*Kalmia latifolia*	8' ht; 8' wd	E	Good shade garden addition; needs well-drained, moist soil
Drooping Leucothoe	*Leucothoe fontanesiana*	4' ht; 4' wd	E	Gracefully spreading; likes shade; foliage bronzes in winter; leaf spot can be a problem

NATIVE SHRUBS FOR LANDSCAPE USE cont'd

Common Name	Botanical Name	Mature Size	Decid./Evgr.	Comments
Devilwood	*Osmanthus americanus*	20' ht; 15' wd	E	Small fragrant flowers in leaf axils open in early spring; blue fruits mature in September; good for naturalizing in moist shade
Florida Azalea	*Rhododendron austrinum*	8' ht; 6' wd	D	Fragrant; flowers vary from yellow to orange to red; blooms April-May; one of the easiest to grow
Carolina Rhododendron	*R. carolinianum*	5' ht; 6' wd	E	Open habit; flowers white to pink
Winged Sumac	*Rhus copallina*	20' ht; 10' wd	D	Forms large, spreading colonies in dry, rocky sites; not for small garden; crimson fall color
Smooth Sumac	*Rhus glabra*	10' ht; 10' wd	D	Suckers colonize; good fall colors-orange, red, purple
Staghorn Sumac	*Rhus typhina*	20' ht; 20' wd	D	Spreading open habit; excellent choice to encourage wildlife
Silky Camellia	*Stewartia malacodendron*	15' ht; 10' wd	D	Showy white flowers in late summer; slow growth rate
Mountain Camellia	*S. ovata*	12' ht; 10' wd	D	Specimen plant; good fall color; slow growth rate
Spanish Bayonet	*Yucca aloifolia*	6' ht; 6' wd	E	Coarse, bold texture for hot, dry site

Getting More Information

When working with woodland plants, nothing is better than first-hand knowledge. You can research a new plant through symposia with expert speakers or the Master Gardener's Hotline sponsored by the Cooperative Extension Service. Books, pamphlets, and catalogs contain a wealth of information, and experienced gardeners are always willing to share what they have learned. Just ask.

Sources for Native Plant Material

See Appendix A for addresses and phone numbers.

In Georgia:

Chattahoochee Home and Garden, Inc.

Goodness Grows (250+ perennials)

Habersham Gardens

Lost Mountain Nursery

Melton's Nursery

Piccadilly Farm (hostas, helleborus, and perennials)

Wild Wood Farms

In surrounding states:

Gardens of the Blue Ridge

Native Gardens (native perennials)

Natural Gardens

Niche Gardens (native perennials)

Passiflora Wildflower Company (seeds and perennials)

Savage Wildflower Gardens

Sunlight Gardens (native perennials)

We-Du Nurseries (rare and unusual natives)

Woodlanders, Inc. (woody ornamentals)

Chapter Twenty-Five

Atlanta's Native Plant Treasures

by

Sandra Sandefur

Unclaimed and Unexpected Treasures

Wooded areas, fields, and roadsides in and around Atlanta abound with wildflowers, shrubs, and trees worthy of saving from bulldozers and backhoes. These native treasures, found in undisturbed areas within the city limits, immediate suburbs, and even your own backyard, may be encouraged and integrated into the home landscape.

Recognizing Native Treasures

It's necessary to learn to recognize native plants in order to save them. One way is to attend wildflower identification classes, such as those taught by George Sanko at DeKalb College. Sanko has installed a garden of native plants on the south campus of DeKalb College that is open to the public for viewing without charge. Twice a year he holds native plant sales to raise money to buy more plants for the garden. Buying plants at Sanko's plant sales and at the Chattahoochee Nature Center is a good way to add to your native plant collection and contribute to a public garden at the same time.

Visiting nurseries which carry native plants is another way to learn to identify native plants. (A list of such nurseries is at the end of Chapter 24, "Native Plants.") The recently established Georgia Native Plant Society is growing. Call the Atlanta Botanical Garden for information.

Plant Rescues

Participating in a plant rescue is another way to learn about native plants. Plant rescues, undertaken by knowledgeable people who have obtained written permission from a landowner, save plants from the onslaught of development. Obtaining permission is essential; without it, you are trespassing and stealing. Sometimes participants are asked to sign a waiver absolving the owner from responsibility if injury occurs on the premises. The Georgia Native Plant Society coordinates plant rescues locally. Call the Atlanta Botanical Garden for a contact.

Choosing Plants

The following charts list some of the wildflowers, shrubs, and trees found growing in the greater Atlanta area that are worth learning about, saving, and incorporating into your home landscape.

WILDFLOWERS WORTH RESCUING

Common Name	Botanical Name	Height	Bloom Color	Bloom Time	Comments
Wild Columbine	*Aquilegia canadensis*	30"	yellow/red	March-June	Light shade; large nodding flowers; 5 yellow petals, 5 red sepals
Jack-in-the-Pulpit	*Arisaema triphyllum*	1-3'	green or green and maroon	April-May	Great variability of maroon striping on spathe; red fruits in fall
Queen's Anne Lace	*Daucus carota*	4-5'	white	June-July	Good cut or dried; can be invasive
Tawny Daylily	*Hemerocallis fulva*	2-3'	orange	June	Wet-site adaptable; nice combined with Queen Anne's Lace
Dwarf Crested Iris	*Iris cristata*	3-6"	blue, violet occasionally	April	Will grow even in gravel; 1-2 week bloom period
Passion Vine	*Passiflora incarnata*	20'	pale blue and white	June-July	Interesting, complex flowers; good climber for trellis; egg-shaped fruits extend interest; butterfly larval food
Wild Blue Phlox	*Phlox divaricata*	8-12"	lavender blue	April	Nice evergreen groundcover; long blooming; fragrant
Solomon's Seal	*Polygonatum biflorum*	1-3'	white	April-June	Arching stems make good vertical accent; blue-black berries in fall
Mountain Mint	*Pycnanthemum spp.*	3-6'	white, lavender	July	In bloom appears splashed by white paint; bruised foliage has mint fragrance
Mountain Ruellia	*Ruellia caroliniensis*	1- 1 1/2'	lavender blue	June-August	2" tubular flowers attract hummingbirds

WILDFLOWERS WORTH RESCUING cont'd

Common Name	Botanical Name	Height	Bloom Color	Bloom Time	Comments
Lyre-Leafed Sage	*Salvia lyrata*	1-2'	lavender	May-June	Best feature is burgundy leaf basal rosette
Bloodroot	*Sanquinaria canadensis*	1'	white	March-April	Brief flowers and deeply lobed leaves; mass planting is fabulous shade attraction
Blue-eyed Grass	*Sisyrinchium angustifolium*	1-1 1/2'	blue	May	Short lived; grass-like leaf; clumps display vivid blue flowers in late spring
Indian Pink	*Spigelia marilandica*	1-1 1/2'	red and yellow	May-June	Striking red tubular flowers visited by hummingbirds; re-blooms if deadheaded
Catesby's Trillium	*Trillium catesbaei*	1-1 1/2'	pink or white	April	Flowers found below leaves; nice addition to shade garden
Bellwort	*Uvularia perfoliata*	6-18"	yellow	May-June	Single flower at end of nodding stem; stem appears to pierce leaf
Bird-foot Violet	*Viola pedata*	2-6"	violet, lavender	April	Prefers dry, poor soil

SHRUBS WORTH RESCUING

Common Name	Botanical Name	Mature Size	Decid./Evgr.	Comments
Red Buckeye	Aesculus pavia	15' ht 15' wd	D	Red tubular flowers in early spring welcome hummingbirds back to Atlanta area
Painted Buckeye	Aesculus sylvatica	10' ht 8' wd	D	Variable flower color, cream to red; good understory plant
American Beautyberry	Callicarpa americana	5' ht 5' wd	D	Brilliant purple and white fruits at leaf axils in fall; cut back periodically for good fruit production
Sweetshrub	Calycanthus floridus	6' ht 10' wd	D	Fruity fragrance on reddish brown flowers; stoloniferous; good yellow fall color
New Jersey Tea	Ceanothus americanus	3' ht 4' wd	D	White blooms in summer
Strawberry Bush or Hearts a Bustin'	Euonymus americanus	4' ht 3' wd	D	Gaudy scarlet/purple seed capsules produce orange seed in fall; kids love this plant
Smooth Hydrangea	Hydrangea arborescens	4' ht 4' wd	E	Flat white blooms in summer
Oakleaf Hydrangea	Hydrangea quercifolia	6' ht 8' wd	D	Four-season plant; white conical flowers in early summer; burgundy fall foliage; exfoliating bark
Possumhaw Holly	Ilex decidua	10' ht 10' wd	D	Showy red berries in winter if both sexes present; dry-site tolerant
Spicebush	Lindera benzoin	8' ht 8' wd	D	Yellow fall color; larval food for butterflies

S H R U B S W O R T H R E S C U I N G cont'd

Common Name	Botanical Name	Mature Size	Decid./Evgr.	Comments
Sweet Azalea	*Rhododendron arborescens*	8'-16'	D	Best mid-season white-flowered azalea; wonderful fragrance
Flame Azalea	*Rhododendron calendulaceum*	8' ht 10' wd	D	One of the showiest; colors vary, can be yellow, apricot, flesh, orange, scarlet; blooms May-June
Piedmont Azalea	*Rhododendron canescens*	12' ht 10' wd	D	Fragrant; blooms early March-April; stoloniferous
Oconee Azalea	*Rhododendron flammeum (speciosum)*	6' ht 6' wd	D	Scarlet blooms in mid-April
Carolinium series	*Rhododendron minus var. minus*	4-5'	D	Attractive pink flowers late May; 'Alba' form, too
Sparkleberry	*Vaccinium arboreum*	10' ht 8' wd	Semi-evergreen	Good for dry understory; black fruits inedible; bark exfoliates
Highbush Blueberry	*Vaccinium corymbosum*	8' ht 10' wd	D	Multi-stemmed; blue-gray foliage, scarlet in fall; summer fruits prized by humans and wildlife
Lowbush Blueberry	*Vaccinium pallidum*	2' ht 2' wd	D	Multi-branched clump former; medium green leaf edged with pink; good on dry, shaded slope

TREES WORTH RESCUING

Common Name	Botanical Name	Mature Size	Decid./Evgr.	Comments
Devil's Walking Stick	*Aralia spinosa*	15' ht 20' wd	D	Thicket forming; spiney; cloud-like summer blooms; purple fruits in fall prized by birds
Ironwood	*Carpinus caroliniana*	25' ht 20' wd	D	Smooth, sinewy gray bark; tolerant of wet sites
Eastern Redbud	*Cercis canadensis*	25' ht 25' wd	D	Nice as single specimen or in groups; 'Forest Pansy' has purple leaves
Common Dogwood	*Cornus florida*	25' ht 20' wd	D	Understory tree; white bracts in spring; crimson in fall; foliage outstanding; red fruit for fall wildlife
American Holly	*Ilex opaca*	40' ht 20' wd	E	Specimen or screen; need male and female for fruit
Southern Magnolia	*Magnolia grandiflora*	70' ht 40' wd	E	Coarse, dark green screen even in shade; lemon-scented white flowers in early summer
Hophornbeam	*Ostrya virginiana*	25' ht 20' wd	D	Nice small tree with interesting catkins

Part Three

Special Effects

Shade Gardens

by

Jackie Heyda

Shade Gardens

Shade in the garden is an asset. Exciting plants can be grown in the shade, and the cooling effect of a shade garden is one of life's refreshing pleasures.

Gardening in the shade is an exciting experience. Many plants are available that provide texture, height, and varying shades of color. Remember that *green* is a color. By trying various combinations, a wonderful, diverse garden can be planted and enjoyed. Because light affects the look and health of a garden plant as much as soil and water do, it is important for gardeners to identify the quality of light plants prefer and to identify it among the degrees of sun and shade.

With time and experimentation, you will discover more about the shade around your property. You'll also discover plants that can be nudged into or out of the darkness. Some sun lovers will thrive in the shade if given compensation in the form of excellent air circulation, more moisture, and more phosphorus from plant food. Flowers may be fewer, but at times they will be bigger and, with no sun to fade them, deeper in hue. Others, unfortunately, need sun to bring out color—you'll find out. Some sun-loving nursery stock may not transplant easily into the shade, but small seedlings or rooted cuttings of the same plant may adapt. Sowing seeds can be a way to get some of these plants to take hold.

Degrees of Shade

Light shade: This is shade from mature pine trees with only high branches and sparse foliage. This is a fairly bright situation and lightest shade category. Direct sun on particular areas is minimal and brief.

Medium shade: This is open shade, but light is further obscured by deciduous tree foliage. The area has either morning, afternoon, or intermittent sun. Shade created by trees can be modified by "limbing up"—removing the trees' lower branches. Some trees may have to be eliminated entirely. Because all trees are valuable to the landscape, removing them can prove difficult and may not be desirable. Tree removal is dangerous and should be done by competent professionals.

Deep shade: This is shade under trees which cast a deep shadow in the summer. The sky is largely blocked and plants get only indirect light.

Requirements of Shade Gardens

Soil: Since all soils benefit from regular additions of organic matter, I mix in compost, well-rotted manure, peat moss, chopped leaves, small amounts of grass clippings, sand, and Nature's Helper. Most shade plants are woodland flora by nature. This indicates to me a desire for a garden soil lighter than the loam that sunny garden plants prefer. The ideal shade garden soil is mildly acid; made rich, light and moisture-monitoring with humus; further lightened with sand; and fortified and made more nutritious by a minor amount of clay.

Drainage: Excellent drainage is imperative because shaded gardens tend to stay damp much longer. Adding organic materials to the soil and digging them in 12-18" is extremely important.

Fertilizer: Spread 10-10-10 with a small hand spreader in early spring. Spread a flower enhancing fertilizer about six weeks later.

Watering: Deep soakings help plants develop deep, strong root systems, allowing them to withstand drought and occasional neglect. Consider installing a drip system which loses little water to evaporation.

Spacing plants: In shade gardening, leave more space between plants than would be necessary in the sunny garden. To offset lack of sun, plants should have additional breathing space.

Choosing Plants

Shade plants are interesting in each season. Leaf texture, bud development, plant shape, and bloom provide beauty throughout the year. By combining various textures, heights, and colors, you can create a dynamic shade garden.

The following is a listing of shade plants that have been successfully grown in the Atlanta area. They are divided for Light Shade, Medium Shade, and Full Shade garden areas. Under each section, the plants are listed in alphabetical order by botanical name for easy reference.

Recommended Plants for Light Shade

Aster curtisii Tall aster, with 1" blue rayed flower heads.

Astilbe tacquetii '**Superba**' Vivid raspberry-pink flowers grow on strong, erect spikes. The coarse, rounded leaves are tinted with mahogany. It is one of the latest astilbes to flower. Spikes add a lot of texture to the winter landscape.

Calycanthus floridus (Carolina Allspice or Sweetshrub) This shrub has a wonderful fragrance when it is blooming. The fruits are food for chipmunks and other woodland creatures.

Calycanthus floridus '**Athens**' Unusual chartreuse yellow flowers, dark green foliage.

Carex morrowii '**Evergold**' (Striped Weeping Sedge) The white leaves with dark green edges have a weeping appearance. These plants do well in light shade to shade.

Carpinus caroliniana (American Hornbeam, also called Ironwood or Musclewood) This 20-30' tree has bark that develops a slate gray, smooth appearance on older branches.

Chelone lyonii (Pink Turtlehead) The flower heads look a bit like turtles' heads. Unusual.

Chrysogonum virginianum (Goldenstar, Green and Gold) The sunny yellow flower is a low-growing member of the composite family that does well in partial to heavy shade with rich, well-drained soil. This plant has bright golden flowers that bloom from May to October. Although evergreen, it does die back in most areas to leaf clusters in winter. Seedlings appear in spring and are easily transplanted. Dividing old plants in late spring is another easy way to get new plants. Although tolerant of drought, some may develop mildew in hot, dry conditions. For a dramatic planting, pair *C. virginianum* with lavender, purple, yellow or blue flowered perennials.

Claytonia virginica (Spring Beauty) This dainty plant, 3-6" tall, appears very early in the spring from small, tuber-like corms. Each slender stem bears a pair of opposite, narrow leaves and a loose cluster of five-petaled white to pale pink star-like flowers with deeper pink colored veins.

Clematis armandii The white star-like flowers enhance this evergreen vine that has leathery compound leaves. Since this vine blooms on old wood, it should be pruned after flowering.

Clematis 'Silver Moon' Some shade helps develop the unique mother-of-pearl color of this clematis.

Corydalis flavula This plant has finely divided blue-green foliage; small yellow flowers. It will self-sow.

Corydalis lutea This is a wonderful perky plant with bright yellow flowers with blue-green, fern-like foliage. This plant adds a nice touch of color and will self-sow.

Erigeron pulchellus (Robin's Plantain) Since this evergreen plant spreads rather rapidly from creeping stalks, it makes an attractive groundcover. In May and June, the plant is covered with numerous 1-2" pink ray flowers.

Iris cristata (Dwarf Crested Iris) The light blue flowers have white crests. The low arching foliage disappears in late summer. Spreads by rhizomes. The tip of the rhizome should be planted slightly above the soil line. Compost and bone meal are beneficial. It is an Eastern American native plant.

Itea virginica (Virginia Sweetspire) Sweetspire grows in wet soils and in partial shade. In full shade, it becomes leggy and produces fewer flowers. If grown in the shade, the fall color is bronze yellow; it is a garnet color when the plant is given more sun. Blooms appear in late April or early May .

Lamium maculatum 'White Nancy' This the most successful lamium because it stays green all year long.

Lobelia cardinalis (Cardinal Flower) This species is remarkable for its deep, richly colored flowers which contrast with the deep green coloring of the foliage and stems. The leafy, unbranched stems are 2-4' tall with a terminal cluster of vivid, scarlet flowers. Lobelias look beautiful planted among ferns in the shade garden or naturalized with other moisture lovers in wet areas. As long as they are never allowed to dry out, cardinal flowers will grow in exposures from full sun to shade. Their color looks richest in bright shade or where they receive only morning sun. A short-lived perennial, new seedlings and offshoots are needed to maintain it. The leafy offshoots at the bases of the plants' stems produce food all winter; if the shoots are smothered, the plants die. Because the petals are split, fragile, and cannot hold the weight of insects, flowers are pollinated by hummingbirds.

Lonicera pileata (Royal Carpet Honeysuckle) This evergreen ground-cover has very small white flowers and purple berries. Several plants make a great groundcover on a slope.

Lunaria annua (Money Plant or Honesty) This is a biennial plant with purple flowers. The seeds are located in discs which look like silver dollars.

Lycoris squamigera (Magic Lily) The blooms may appear after many years or not every year, but they are worth the wait.

Lysimachia clethroides (Gooseneck Loosestrife) Invasive. Curved, pure white flower spikes look like the necks of white geese. The medium-green 30" foliage adds texture to the shade garden.

Lysimachia congestiflora 'Eco Dark Satin' This plant has small yellow cup-shaped flowers with red throats that appear in clusters at the terminal ends of creeping stems. The plants form dense mats.

Lysimachia nummularia 'Aurea' (Creeping Jennie) Beautiful golden-yellow rounded leaves on creeping stems.

Mahonia bealei (Oregon Grape) This tall evergreen shrub has bright yellow flowers followed by many blue berries which the birds enjoy. It performs best in partial or filtered shade and spreads by rhizomes. Rooted side shoots can be detached and grown as new plants.

Mahonia repens (Creeping Mahonia) This low evergreen stoloniferous shrub has compact, holly-like shiny green foliage.

Mertensia virginica (Virginia Bluebells, Virginia Cowslip, and Roanoke Bells) It is a member of the borage family. In March, tight bunches of purple-pink buds expand into clusters of five-petaled nodding bells of purest sky blue. The foliage withers rapidly after bloom ends; usually by May the plant has vanished. Virginia bluebells are reliable and look best if they have ample water in the spring. Overplanted with ferns or a ground cover, their roots will be safe from the gardener's trowel during the long months of dormancy.

Mimulus ringens (Allegheny Monkey Flower) Native perennial. 1" pale blue-purple blooms midsummer.

Mitchella repens (Partridgeberry) This groundcover is also called twinberry because a pair of flowers that are united at their bases forms one berry.

Mitella diphylla (Bishop's Cap or Miterwort) This plant gets its name from the shape of the white flowers. The flowers grow on slender spikes 12" tall during May. There are two sessile leaves on the flowering stem which give rise to the species name.

Myrica cerifera **var.** *pumila* (Dwarf Waxmyrtle) This is a wispy, broad-leaf evergreen that can grow 10-15' high and wide.

Ophiopogon planiscapus '**Nigrescens**' This mondo grass with black foliage is a ground cover. It looks great with *Lysimachia nummularia* 'Aurea'.

Osmanthus fragrans (Fragrant Olive) This wonderful plant has a great fragrance and it starts blooming during the winter months. Plant this olive near a window or door.

Pachysandra terminalis 'Variegata' This variegated groundcover adds a colorful contrast.

Penstemon smallii (Small's Beard Tongue) This erect perennial herb rises from a rosette of basal leaves. The stem leaves are opposite and each flower cluster is purplish to pink. Add some sand to ensure good drainage. A short-lived perennial, it is worth the effort.

Phacelia bipinnatifida This biennial plant prospers in moist, shaded soil. Though not a perennial, it is easily naturalized in the woodland garden. The lavender-blue flowers, borne in masses, bloom in early spring and sporadically throughout the spring/early summer on 2' tall pinnately divided leaf clusters.

Phlox stolonifera '**Iridescens**,' '**Pink Ridge**,' '**Sherwood Purple**' Great groundcovers.

Podophyllum peltatum (Native Mayapple) Two light green, umbrella-shaped leaves are borne at the top of the flowering 12-18" stem. The single, white, very fragrant flower, sometimes 2" across formed at the junction of the two leaves, has its beauty concealed by the immense peltated leaf above it. The round fruit, an inch or more in diameter, ripen in late summer and are edible. The foliage and root are said to be poisonous. Mayapple, a vigorous colonizer, spreads from creeping root stalks and is easily divided and transplanted. The deeply lobed leaves disappear in summer. Label the area so other plants are not placed there.

Polemonium reptans (Jacob's Ladder) This American native is a short-rhizomatus species that soon forms a loose mat of foliage. Blue flowers bloom in April and May.

Porteranthus stipulata The 2-3' plants can be grown in sun or shade in ordinary loam. The fine textured foliage is brightened by terminal panicles of 1" wide, white star-like flowers in June.

Rhododendron calendulaceum (Flame Azalea) and *Rhododendron prunifolium* (Plumleaf Azalea) See Chapter 13, "Native Azaleas."

Rhododendron 'Royal Purple' Fish emulsion applied after bloom will keep plant healthy and vigorous.

Scilla bifolia 'Rosea' (also called *Scilla carnea*) This is a rare, 6" ivory-pink February-blooming form of *Scilla bifolia*.

Scilla hispanica 'Blue Queen' or *Hyacinthoides hispanicus* (Wood Hyacinth and Spanish Bluebell) Blue, dainty, bell-shaped flowers appear in clusters on stalks 10-15" in height. Plant in medium to heavy shade, feed liberally with bulb booster. These bulbs have a pretty flower but also lots of foliage that takes a long time to dry. I use *Phlox stolonifera* 'Bruce's White' and some ivies to cover.

Skimmia japonica The garden will need a female and male plant to produce flowers and berries.

Smilacina racemosa (Native False Solomon's Seal) This is a wonderful plant with a plume of cream-colored blossoms at the tip of the stems. The berries are bright red in the fall.

Thalictrum aquilegifolium (Meadow Rue) A great plant with a delicate range of colors. The plant appears to billow and produces a grayish cast in the shade. It looks great with hostas and epimediums.

Viburnum acerifolium (Possum Haw) Flat white flowers bloom in the spring. This deciduous viburnum, which can reach a height of 6', has 5" maple-shaped leaves that turn a brilliant red in the fall..

Viburnum setigerum (Tea Viburnum) In the spring, 2" white flowers cover this deciduous shrub that can grow to 12'. Abundant red fruit is enjoyed by birds in the fall.

Vinca minor 'Alba' This strong, vigorous ground cover has glossy, deep green foliage and white flowers.

Waldsteinia fragarioides (Barren Strawberry) This rhizomatous perennial somewhat resembles a strawberry plant. It has golden yellow strawberry-like blossoms on 6- 9" stems, with light green, shiny three-parted leaves. Plant in light-medium shade. Grow in moist acid soil. Use as a low maintenance groundcover, too.

Recommended Plants for Medium Shade

Acanthus mollis (Bear's Breeches) This plant has never bloomed for me, but the textured foliage is beautiful when planted with hostas, ferns, and hellebores.

Acanthus spinosus Leathery, heavily dissected toothed foliage with tall spikes of white-purple bract flowers.

Acer palmatum **var.** *atropurpureum* (Japanese Red Maple) This plant has reddish purple leaves in the spring and a wonderful red in the fall. The texture is great for the shade garden.

Acer palmatum 'Beni Schichihenge' A great variegated maple, blue green foliage with white margins, superior orange-red color in the fall

and bright crimson branches. This tree is a slowgrower in my yard. Variegated forms tolerate less sun.

Aesculus sylvatica **var.** *georgiana* (Georgia Buckeye) This buckeye has pinkish flowers.

Aesculus x mutabilis (Red Buckeye) This buckeye has five leaflets that are elliptic, pale, and hairy beneath and the panicles can reach a length of 4-6". The yellow-red flowers are unusual.

Aesculus parviflora (Bottlebrush Buckeye) This buckeye has opposite, palmately compound leaves, each with 5 to 7 leaflets. The white flowers with four petals produce long, pinkish-white threadlike stamens with red anthers. The pear-shaped fruit is a light brown smooth capsule.

Anemone x hybrida 'Margarette' 20" spires of double pink-rose flowers, which bloom in the fall, have 12" mounds of foliage at the base.

Anemonella thalictroides (Rue Anemone) Each plant produces two to three flowers emerging from a whorl of pale-green bracts at the stem top. Each flower consists of 5-10 sepals, centered with yellow stamens. This native plant's delicate white-pink flowers appear in early spring and last for 10 weeks or more. A diminutive plant, best grown in large colonies which it forms naturally. Dormant by midsummer.

Aquilegia canadensis (Eastern Wild Columbine) Flowers are composed of five long spurs that point upward and five petals that hang down. Stamens protrude from the center of the drooping, bell-like flowers. The foliage is light and graceful. The 3 lobed, 4-6" leaves are an attractive blue-green. Columbines tolerate full sun but prefer partial shade. They need well-drained soil, rich in organic matter. Columbines are susceptible to leaf miner, tiny insects that bore through the leaf tissue. Leaf miners rarely threaten the plants. If they do become a problem, cut off the damaged foliage and dispose of it. Columbines are one of the easiest native wildflowers to grow. Plants are short lived but do self sow. Nursery propagated, pot grown plants can also be added or seed may be scattered. Do not cover since light is needed for germination. This Columbine attracts early migrating hummingbirds.

Arisaema triphyllum (Jack-in-the-Pulpit) Plants emerge from well-drained soil rich in organic matter rapidly in late March-early April growing as much as 2-3" a day for several days. The palmately divided leaves with 3-5 segments unfurl, revealing the inflorescence that gives its common name.

Arum italicum (Italian Arum) The beautiful, arrow-shaped variegated leaves appear in the fall, winter, and spring but go dormant during the summer. This plant produces a large, balloon-like, chartreuse funnel-shaped flower (spathe) in the spring followed by spikes of orange-red berries.

Aruncus dioicus 'Zweiweltenkind' These Goat's Beard plants, with feathery plumes, are readily established in shaded borders and wild gardens in ordinary garden soil. Must be kept moist during drought periods.

Astilbe x arendsii 'Bridal Veil' has white feathery spikes. *A. x a.* 'Fanal' has red feathery spikes. Leave uncut for winter interest.

Astilbe biternata Only astilbe native to North America. Resembles *Aruncus dioicus* giving it the common name False Goat's Beard. A tall, 3-6' plant arising from a stout rhizome with a showy cluster of small, white flowers that bloom in May and June. The petals, almost white or yellowish, are borne in a large, pyramid-shaped panicle. This astilbe should be grown in moist, shady soil.

Begonia grandis The pink flowers of this beautiful woodland plant, one of the few hardy begonias, are an unusual addition to the shade garden. The many interesting seed pods will self-sow into many seedlings. A white blooming form is less vigorous.

Carex morrowii '**Aurea-variegata**' This carex has bright yellow leaves with narrow green margins. The spider-shaped clumps spiral from the center.

Carex morrowii aurea-variegata '**Old Gold**' The white leaves of this evergreen sedge have green margins.

Carex nigra Variegated form. Slender, slightly grayish leaves with narrow white edges. The arching leaves form a slow-spreading clump.

Chasmanthium latifolium (Northern Sea Oats) These 3' grasses form oat-like flowers. The grassy foliage adds texture to the fall and winter garden.

Cimicifuga japonica '**Acerina**' The maple-like leaves have long pointed lobes and the white flowers are densely packed in a long raceme in late summer.

Cimicifuga racemosa (Black Cohosh, Black Snakeroot, and Fairy Candles) This is the first Cimicifuga to bloom in June or early July. Dense spikes, 5-6' tall, float above attractive, divided foliage and are studded with numerous small white flowers that open from the bottom to the top over a period of about two weeks. A showy, long-lived perennial, it should be planted against a dark background where the white candles stand out.

Dicentra cucullaria (Dutchman's Breeches) The feathery fern-like foliage grows from a small white bulb less than an inch in diameter. It readily breaks into many small sections which may be planted to form new bulbs. The plants may also spread from seed. The blossoms, on 6" stalks, resembling inverted trousers with a golden waistline, are borne several to a stem. After blossoming in April, the leaves stay green until June when they die back. The bulb, however, continues growing throughout the summer.

Dicentra eximia (Wild Bleeding Heart) This Eastern North American wildflower has narrow, 12" tall clumps of lacy leaves with rosy, slender heart-shaped blooms. *D. x* 'Luxuriant' is more vigorous.

Dicentra spectabilis This dicentra forms a large ferny clump, 3' high and 4' across, with crimson-rose hearts hanging in neat rows on horizontal stems. This plant needs a sheltered, half-shady location. There is also a white-flowered form.

Disporum flavum (Fairy Bells) The lemon-yellow nodding bell-shaped flowers turn into small dark berries in the fall. The foliage remains attractive all season and changes into a light yellow color in fall.

Diuranthera major (*Chlorophytum major*) (Hardy Spider Plant) A rare Chinese native with small orchid-type flowers with yellow stamens, which bloom four to a stem, on stalks emerging from rosettes of grassy, strap-like foliage. Unusual.

Dodecatheon meadia (Shooting Star) This perennial grows from a short fragile root stock. The white or pink flowers are borne on a tall flower stalk. The petals are reflexed so that they resemble the tails of a shooting star. The leaves form a basal rosette and disappear after flowering.

Epimedium grandiflorum This large epimedium has long-spurred pink and white 8-10" tall flowers above its 1' long leaves. This Japanese species is clump forming.

Epimedium x versicolor '**Sulphurem**' Semi-evergreen foliage has rather large, glossy leaflets that grow from 6 -10" tall and 12-15" wide. The flowers are a delicate pale yellow with deeper yellow centers.

Erythronium americana (Trout Lily, Dogtooth Violet, Adder's Tongue, and Fawn Lily) The yellow flowers stay closed on cloudy days. They do well in light shade with moist, well-drained soil. Many species have been dug in the wild, diminishing the native populations. Be certain the plants you purchase have been propagated, not dug from the wild.

Erythronium albidum This early spring bloomer has white flowers tinged with yellow in the center and violet on the back. The 6" leaves are mottled.

Euonymus americanus (Strawberry Bush or Hearts-a-Bustin') In the spring, the plain dime-sized yellow green flowers are inconspicuous. This stoloniferous shrub has unusual and small rough green fruits that develop from the flowers. As fall approaches, the fruits mature strawberry red. Then each fruit opens and reddish orange seeds are suspended by a thin silver thread.

Geranium maculatum This geranium's new leaves appear in early March. By late March, the plant is almost a foot high. Its pale pink, deep magenta-pink, or light purple flowers are most attractive in a woodland garden. Basal leaves are hairy and deeply lobed. Divide as new leaves appear.

Goodyera pubescens (Rattlesnake Plantain or Rattlesnake Orchid) The native woodland orchid's gray-green evergreen foliage has white spots. In summer, compact spikes of small white flowers rise above the basal foliage.

Helleborus x hybridus 'Atrorubens' The saucer-shaped plum-purple flowers 1 1/2-2" across are tinged with violet and become more violet with age. Evergreen only in mild climates. The leaves are broadly lanceolate and sharply serrated. Fertilize liberally with well-rotted cow manure/leafmold dressing.

Helleborus foetidus Blooms from February to April. Evergreen leaves are palmately divided and flowers are drooping, bell-shaped, and pale green. Some foliage dies back after three years or so, but new plants emerge near the original planting.

Helleborus lividus subsp. ***corsicus*** The apple-green flowers bloom above the coarse-toothed segmented, prickly edged foliage. Bees dote on the flowers. Covering the foliage is suggested in hard freezes as is keeping the plant out of the wind. This hellebore lives three to five years and leaves a few seedlings.

Helleborus orientalis (Lenten Rose) Evergreen foliage and winter bloom add wonderful color to the winter landscape. Colors range from white to light and dark lavender. Epsom salts, which contain magnesium and lime, can be added to the soil around the base of hellebore foliage.

Hepatica acutiloba (Liverleaf or Liverwort) This is a low, herbaceous perennial with relatively thick, almost evergreen leaves with three sharp pointed lobes. These plants, with light purple flowers, are among the earliest spring wildflowers to bloom. Plants grown in acid soil often have blue flowers and seem to grow poorly. Addition of dolomitic limestone is essential.

Hermodactylus tuberosus (Snake's Head Iris) This bulb is a rare and diminutive member of the Iris family, recorded in botanical history as early as 1597. The striking blooms, with their delightful rose fragrance, appear singly in early spring on 6-12" stems. Long leaves appear in the fall. Newly emerging spring blooms surprise the unwary with the unfurling form that gives the common name.

Heuchera americana Leaves of this plant are green during the growing season and deep red or orange during the winter. Small, greenish flowers produce a billowing effect in the shade garden.

Heuchera micrantha '**Palace Purple**' The semi-evergreen leaves are deep bronze and form clumps. The small, almost white flowers are produced on airy stems in late summer.

Hosta spp. All varieties. Hostas are great foliage plants for the shade garden.

Hydrangea quercifolia (Oak Leaf Hydrangea) The blooms are wonderful long panicles that change from white to soft rose. Large ornamental leaves turn a rich tint in autumn.

Hydrastis canadensis (Golden Seal) Attractive, broadly lobed foliage carries small white flowers in spring, followed by a tight cluster of red raspberry-shaped fruit. Golden seal grows best in deep, humus soil. The thick yellow root stalk and sometimes the leaves are used for the drug Hydrastine. It is scarce in the wild and endangered in many states; buy only nursery propagated plants.

Medeola virginica (Indian Cucumber Root) The slender stem, 8-12" tall, has a whorl of five to nine leaves near the middle with three leaves at the stem tip. Small greenish-yellow flowers are followed by purple berries. In the fall, the leaves turn purple.

Oxalis corymbosa The hardy pink shamrock, a southeastern native, is fine in woodland or rock garden.

Phlox stolonifera '**Blue Ridge**' and *P. s.* '**Bruce's White**' are great groundcovers for bulbs and around hostas.

Pollia japonica Small white flowers appear in July on this unusual 3' plant. Flowers turn into green berries which become bluish fruit for birds. Plant spreads rapidly, but is worth it. When young, it's easily removed.

Pulmonaria saccharata 'Janet Fisk' Has beautiful variegated foliage, pink flowers that mature to blue.

Rhapidophyllum hystrix (Needle Palm) This hardy palm adds foliage interest.

Sanguinaria canadensis (Bloodroot) Palmately lobed leaves are basal; solitary, white flowers are star-like and fragile. Each flower has eight to twelve white petals with numerous yellow stamens. In about a week, petals fall, leaving torpedo-shaped fruit. Finger-size underground rhizomes ooze a red-orange fluid if broken.

Saxifraga stolonifera (Strawberry Geranium, Roving Sailor, Mother of Thousands) An evergreen perennial from woodlands in Japan, the plant forms a mat of round leaves, the size of silver dollars. The small white flowers are produced on 1-2' stems. Threadlike stolons resemble those of strawberry plants.

Sedum ternatum (Stonecrop) One of the few sedums partial to shade. A prostrate native found in shady woods and rocky ledges, its flowers, on horizontal branches, have five green sepals and five white petals.

Senecio aureus (Golden Ragwort or Butternut) A native, herbaceous perennial that varies from 1-3' tall, it bears small, yellow aster-like flowers. The plants have two distinct leaf types:heart-shape basal leaves and deeply toothed leaves on the flowering stalks.

Silphium dentatum (Starry Rosin Weed) The plant produces yellow daisy flowers and does best in dry shade.

Stylophorum diphyllum (Golden Poppy or Celandine Poppy) A must for the woodland garden, the dark bluish-green foliage resembling oak leaves adds texture from spring to frost. In early to mid spring, 2" yellow poppies appear in profusion on attractive 1' clumps. Hairy seed pods follow. This poppy should be grown in moist, fertile soil abounding with organic matter.

Symphytum grandiflorum This attractive pulmonaria and mertensia relative grows best in shade and ordinary loam. Clusters of drooping, pale yellow flowers appear in May. The somewhat coarse, rough haired, evergreen foliage forms a clump rapidly but not alarmingly so.

Tiarella cordifolia (Foam Flower) This semi-evergreen groundcover produces fluffy clusters of white flowers. Long stolons run along the ground sending up a leaf every few inches, forming new rosettes here and there. Tiarellas require moisture retentive, highly organic soils in medium to heavy shade.

Tiarella wherryi This plant produces creamy white flowers.

Tipularia discolor (Crane Fly Orchid) Decorative leaves, purple beneath and green above, appear in the fall and disappear in early summer. A small stalk (10-18") of brown and white flowers appears midsummer.

Tricyrtis hirta (Toad Lily) Fuzzy, lilac and white orchid flowers form along the tall arching stem. Stems have deep green pointed leaves. Blooming in October, it is an excellent choice for the fall garden.

***Tricyrtis hirta* 'White Towers'** An unusual white flowered form with some pink in the center of each blossom. Plants should be grown in light to medium shade.

Trillium catesbaei (Nodding Wake Robin) The nodding pink or white flowers are hidden beneath the large green leaves. *Wildflowers of the Southeastern United States* mentions that the petals are usually white at first and later turn pink. It is a common plant that blooms from March to June.

Trillium cuneatum (Toad Trillium) The 1 1/2" flower of this native trillium is brown-purple or maroon. The large green mottled leaves can be 1 foot across.

Trillium grandiflorum (Great White Trillium, White Wake Robin) This trillium, found in rich woodland coves and gentle slopes throughout the Eastern United States, can grow to 2' tall and has dark green 2-6" leaves and a beautiful single flower composed of three pure white petals nearly 3" long. As the flower ages, or after pollination, petals turn a dusty rose. **Note:** *Many trilliums commonly found in woodlands are difficult to grow in a wildflower garden. Trilliums have been difficult for nurseries to propagate economically. It takes three to five years to grow flowering plants from seed. Many of the plants offered have been collected from the wild. Not only are collected plants under stress from transplanting, but collection endangers wild populations. To protect natural areas, refrain from buying collected plants. To be sure that a nursery propagates rather than collects, read* *their catalog. It must say that the plants are nursery propagated. You will probably pay a little more, but you will have the satisfaction of knowing that your plants were not taken from the woods.*

Uvularia perfoliata (Strawbell or Woods Merrybells) This unusual, striking woodland plant has grayish, lance-shaped, opposite leaves united around the stem so the stem appears to pass through the leaves. The up to 1 1/4" straw-colored, solitary bloom is produced at the end of a 8-15" stem. The fruit is a three angled capsule.

Viburnum x bodnantense **'Dawn'** Pink fragrant flowers bloom in midwinter on this deciduous plant that can grow to 8'. Enrich soil with lots of humus and keep well watered.

Vinca minor (Periwinkle) This excellent groundcover has small bluish flowers in the spring.

Viola labradorica Small mauve flowers rise above small, dark green leaves that are heavily infused with purple.

Viola pennsylvanica Smooth yellow violet. This violet has 6" stems and most leaves are finely haired.

Viola philippies Small bluish flowers are produced above 2" long narrow leaves. This viola reseeds rapidly in the garden and is interesting because of the leaf shape.

Viola striata This is a cream colored violet that blooms on 12" leafy stems for many months.

Viola walteri Produces a low evergreen mat with violet blue flowers that eventually lies flat on the ground. It roots at the nodes which develop into new crowns.The leaves are roundish, mottled dark green.

Xanthorhiza simplicissima (Yellowroot) The lacy foliage can reach a height of 2'. Purple-brown drooping flowers are produced in the spring followed by seed pods. Yellowroot is a rapid spreader and prefers damp soil. It makes an excellent ground cover and has lovely yellow leaves in the fall.

Recommended Plants for Full Shade

Asarum arifolium (Little Brown Jugs) Native species has bold evergreen triangular green or bronzy leaves with varying degrees of mottling; jug-shaped flowers form at the plant base. Wonderful woodland plant.

Asarum canadense (Wild Ginger) Deciduous leaves 2-7" across; large 1" brownish jug flowers at base.

Asarum europaeum (European Ginger) Glossy, vivid green leaves are evergreen here. The greenish-purple or brown 1/2" flowers are produced at the base of the plant.

Asarum shuttleworthii '**Callaway**' (Callaway Wild Ginger) Small, mottled evergreen leaves 1-3" across with mottled flowers that appear in early spring provide a great groundcover for a small area.

Asarum virginicum (*Hexastylis virginica*) Evergreen, usually mottled, 3" leaves; purple 1" flowers.

Aspidistra elatior (Cast Iron Plant) Great texture. It adds a nice touch of height when placed with low plants.

Carex austrocaroliniana This is a 10-12" rare sedge with narrow, yellow-green semi-evergreen leaves which form a dense clump. The bloom is small but interesting. Found only in the Carolina mountains.

Carex pendula This 3-3 1/2' semi-evergreen carex has a graceful pendulous habit. It is a must for contrasting with rounded clumps of hostas. The plant does well in part to full shade and blooms in April.

Chamaelirium luteum (Devil's Bit) This interesting plant has innumerable tiny flowers in arching spikes in May. Male plants have showier flowers. The rosette at the base of the plant is semi-evergreen.

Cymophyllus fraseri (Flowering Sedge) This unusual 8-10" tall plant has tufts of bold, evergreen strap-shaped leaves, with conspicuous white flower heads in April. The bloom is a wonderful surprise in the garden. A lovely, unusual plant, it is effective on a shaded bank.

Fatsia japonica (Japanese Fatsia) Lustrous 6-10' evergreen has palmately-cut leaves up to 16" across with whitish, long-stalked flowers in panicles up to 18" long. Cover in extreme low temperatures.

Galium odoratum (Sweet Woodruff) The 6" plant, with whorls of narrow evergreen or semi-evergreen leaves, soon carpets a large area. White flowers, scented with honey and horehound, appear in May.

Jeffersonia diphylla (Twinleaf) This plant has distinctive foliage which is divided into two kidney leaves with white flowers like bloodroot in May. Although my plants have never bloomed, the foliage adds a great deal of interest in the rock garden.

Leucothoe axillaris (Coastal Leucothoe or Dog-Hobble) This evergreen shrub can grow up to 6'.

Mazus reptans (Creeping Mazus) The tiny foliage forms a dense mat. The curious miniature three-lobed lavender flowers have white centers speckled with burnt-yellow spots.

Pachysandra terminalis (Spurge) Extra-hardy evergreen with bright glossy 6-8" high foliage, white 4-5" flower spikes.

Pachysandra procumbens (Allegheny Spurge) This southern native looks its best only in moist, shady spots enriched with humus or leaf mold. It is slow to increase. The foliage has an emerald base overlaid with deeper green. Leaves are puckered along the veins, which are a paler shade. The leaves are alternate with nodes that become progressively shortened toward the tip of the stem. Since each pair of leaves is smaller than the one beneath, the leaves create the pattern of a wheel.

Polygonatum biflorum (Solomon's Seal) Delicate arching stems with green and white bell-shaped flowers hang from the leaf-axils. This 1-2' plant is the most common native species.

P. giganteum or *P. commutatum* (Giant Solomon's Seal) Flowers are greenish-white on arching 3- 4' stems.

P. humile (Japanese Solomon's Seal) This low-growing plant has erect rather than arching stems. Large flowers for size.

P. odoratum variegatum (Eurasian Solomon's Seal) White flowers bloom along the erect, tall arching stems. Turn into blue-black berries.The variegated green leaves edged in yellow are up to 6" in length. Tip: All polygonatums are wonderful for the shade garden when placed with hosta, fern, dicentra, poppy, and impatiens. They should be grown in rich, moist soil.

Rohdea japonica (Lily of China) Leaves 2' long and 3" across form in basal rosettes. Pale yellow flowers are concealed by the foliage. Conspicuous red fruit is a wonderful addition to the winter garden.

Sarcococca hookerana humilis (Sweet Box) This compact, stoloniferous, 12-15" high evergreen shrub with glossy leaves makes an excellent groundcover. Small, white very fragrant flowers that appear in winter are followed by blue-black fruit.

Stephanandra incisa '**Crispa**' This groundcover plant has fern-like leaves with small white flowers in the spring. The bare branches provide interest in the winter garden.

Ferns for the Shade Garden

Ferns add wonderful texture to the shade garden. These have been successful in my garden. For more information about ferns, see Chapter 23.

Adiantum pedatum (Maidenhair Fern) Its early rising little crosiers, of earth-matching color, later turn into dainty, fan-shaped arching branches. The wiry black branches and light green foliage attain a height of 2'. Foliage remains attractive from spring until fall. Plant in groups spaced 18" apart or tuck in here or there for its fine texture and softening effect.

Athyrium Filix-femina (Lady Fern) Moist, loamy, humus rich soil is a must for this bright yellow-green fern with deeply cut fronds. This deciduous fern, which grows to a height of 2-3', spreads easily by spores falling on moist earth.

Athyrium goeringianum '**Pictum**' (Japanese Painted Fern) The combination of silvery-gray and green fronds with red petioles (the supporting stalk) is striking in the shade garden. This fern, which looks wonderful with early spring bulbs, makes an excellent accent plant. Many can be used for a mass planting. New fronds of this 2' fern appear in mid-spring.

Athyrium otophorum (English Painted Fern) Deciduous oriental native. The erect growing fronds emerge and go through stages of gold and green to mature dark green with a burgundy red midrib.

Botrychium dissectum (Common Grape Fern) The single sterile frond is evergreen and turns reddish or bronzy in the winter. A separate fertile frond appears in the summer and withers away in late fall

Cyrtomium falcatum (Holly Fern) This evergreen fern, with bold, lustrous, leathery foliage resembling a holly leaf, is clump forming. In extremely cold temperatures, it must be covered.

Dryopteris erythrosora (Autumn Fern) Young fronds are a beautiful copper color which gives the common name. As the fronds grow and open, they turn into the green foliage. This fern produces scarlet spore capsules and is semi-evergreen.

Dryopteris goldiana (Goldie Fern or Giant Wood Fern) Tallest wood fern, the 36" golden-green lustrous oblong-triangular fronds narrow abruptly at the tip. The deciduous fronds turn yellow in fall.

Onoclea sensibilis (Sensitive Fern or Bead Fern) The fern is "sensitive" because the sterile fronds are easily frost killed. Narrow, fertile "bead stick" and broad yellow-green to green sterile leaves make an unusual combination. Beads first appear green, later change to deep brown. Spreading, it's easily controlled.

Osmunda cinnamomea (Cinnamon Fern) This fern is dimorphic (fronds of two types). Cinnamon stick appearing fertile fronds borne in early spring soon disappear. Sterile fronds are yellow-green and leafy with a dense tuft of rusty hairs beneath the base of each leaflet. The crowns should be set at or just below soil level. Cinnamon ferns grow in wet, acid soil in partial shade.

Polystichum acrostichoides (Native Christmas Fern) Most common fern in northern Georgia. In early March, new fronds, fiddleheads, appear and uncoil among the previous growing season's fronds. At this point, last year's foliage can be removed. The fern is 8-14" tall; about 2' across.

Polystichum polyblepharum (Tassel Fern) The very dark green, glossy leaves are elongated with sharp toothed margins. This fern grows well in moist, well-drained woodland soil.

Polystichum setiferum 'Angulare' (Alaskan Fern) This hardy, tropical-appearing fern appears from rosettes. Graceful, arching 2' fronds have narrow lance-shaped fronds and feathery leaflets. The fronds last two years before dormancy and are replaced by new growth.

Polystichum tsus-simense (Korean Rock Fern) A holly fern that grows from a partially underground tufted, dark scale-covered crown.

Thelypteris palustris (Marsh Fern) Dull green deciduous fern has creeping rhizomes and 2 1/2' long leaves 6" wide.

Woodsia obtusa (Blunt-lobed woodsia) Clustered, light-green, 8" fronds grow well in light shaded hillsides and woodlands.

Sources for Shade Plants

In Georgia

Eco Gardens

Goodness Grows

Outside Georgia

Niche Gardens

Plant Delights Nursery

Robyn's Nest Nursery

Shady Oaks Nursery

Sunlight Gardens

We-Du Nurseries

Woodlanders, Inc.

Chapter Twenty-Seven

Container Gardens

by

Mildred Pinnell

Container Gardens

If you have limited time and space, consider a container garden. Containers can bring greenery and color to a deck, porch, or patio, allowing you to have plants where you don't have soil. The container you choose should harmonize with its surroundings. A wide range of containers is available, from the original half-barrel to terra-cotta, cement, plastic, and even fiberglass. The size of the container should be in scale with the plants you want to grow. It must have proper drainage and provide adequate root space for the plants.

A soilless mix of ground pine bark, ground peat, and perlite provides an excellent growing medium for container culture. If you use a polymer or "water grabber" in a container, use it at one-fourth of the recommended strength. During periods of heat and drought it may be necessary to water a container in full sun once a day.

The key to successful container gardening is grooming. It is better to regularly deadhead and cut back plants than to wait until they become leggy and unkempt. Check regularly for pests and diseases and treat as needed.

Plant Combinations for Container Gardens

Don't feel like you have to put only one plant or one kind of plant in your containers—many annual plants can be combined successfully. When selecting plants, consider color and textural contrasts. Here are some suggestions for combinations:

Combinations for Sun

Snowbush (*Breynia nivosa* 'Rosea-pictus')
Petunia (*Petunia* 'Pink Pearl,' 'White Pearl')
Dwarf Gomphrena (*Gomphrena globosa* 'Little Cissy,' 'Little Buddy')
Trailing Verbena (*Verbena tenuisecta* 'Gandy')

Geraniums (*Pelargonium*)
Asparagus Fern or Sprenger Asparagus (*Asparagus sprengeri* or *A. densiflorus*)
Variegated Swedish Ivy (*Plectranthus coleoides* 'Variegatus')

Scaevola *(Scaevola aemula* 'Blue Wonder')
Trailing Petunia *(Petunia integrifolia)*
Licorice Plant *(Helichrysum petiolaris)*
Dusty Miller *(Senecio cineraria* or *Cineraria maritima)*
White Mandevilla *(Mandevilla laxa)*

Polka Dot Plant *(Hypoestes)*
Daisy Fleabane *(Erigeron karwinskianus)*
Geranium *(Pelargonium)*
Variegated Swedish Ivy *(Plectranthus coleoides* 'Variegatus')

Plumbago *(Plumbago auriculatus)*
Trailing Geraniums (Balcon Series)
Brazilian Verbena *(Verbena bonariensis)*

Glory Bower *(Tibouchina urvilleana)*
Geranium *(Pelargonium)*
Trailing Vinca *(Vinca rosea* or *Catharanthus roseus)*

Purple Fountain Grass *(Pennisetum setaceum* 'Rubrum')
Gomphrena *(Gomphrena globosa)*
Trailing Lantana *(Lantana montevidensis* 'Alba')

Lantana
Gomphrena *(Gomphrena globosa)*
'Victoria Blue' Salvia *(Salvia* 'Victoria Blue')

Scaevola *(Scaevola aemula* 'Blue Wonder')
Purple Heart *(Setcreasea pallida)*
Trailing Lantana *(Lantana montevidensis)*

Combinations for Shade

'Christmas Candy' Begonia
'Concorde Blue' Streptocarpella *(Streptocarpella* 'Concorde Blue')

Caladium
Asparagus Fern or Sprenger Asparagus *(Asparagus sprengeri* or *A. densiflorus)*
Purple Heart *(Setcreasea pallida)*
Variegated Swedish Ivy *(Plectranthus coleoides variegatus)*

And remember, have fun! If you make a mistake or don't like a combination, simply start over. That's the ease of container gardening.

Mail Order Sources for Container Gardening

See Appendix A for addresses.

Glasshouse Works

Sandy Mush Nursery

Logee's Greenhouses

Kinsman Company (Baskets)

Chapter Twenty-Eight

Water Gardens

by

Tara Dillard

Water Gardening

If you think, "I can't have a pond, they are too difficult," you are wrong. A pond does not have to be expensive. Maintenance requirements of ponds are comparable to those of a well-designed perennial garden of the same size.

A pond will reflect the plants growing in and around it and provide relaxation and tranquillity. Feeding the fish will become a high point of your day, especially when the fish trust you enough to swim between your fingers! If you opt for a pond with a pump, the sound of the water will be a special treat.

Installing a Pond

Select the site. Decide how big a pond you want and select a place to locate it. Ponds need sun—they perform best with at least six hours of sun each day—so choose your site with that requirement in mind. **CAUTION:** For safety's sake, ponds are best located within fenced areas. NEVER leave young children unattended near a pond.

Choose a pond liner and dig the hole. There are flexible and rigid pond liners, and each kind has different requirements. Rigid pond liners, available at most garden centers, are sturdy and long lasting, but you'll have less space on the bottom for potted plants due to the liner's rounded sides. You'll want the hole to fit the liner, so choose the liner before you dig the hole. Some rigid pond liners have a shelf at the edge. Beware! Raccoons appreciate that shelf because it helps them fish.

For a flexible pond liner, you can dig a hole of any shape, but a hole with straight sides is preferred so plants can be placed anywhere in the pond. Be aware that digging even a small pond will produce a pile of dirt that will seem much larger than the size of the hole!

To determine the flexible liner size to buy, dig a hole that is the size of the pond you want and at least 18" deep. Use a string to measure, securing the string at the edge of where you want the liner. Follow the contour of the hole along the maximum width and again along the maximum length. The flexible liner edges should overlap the pond edge by at least 1-1/2', so add that measurement (3' to each dimension). This will give you the dimensions of the liner to buy. Any excess can be trimmed.

Install the liner. Place the liner in the hole, following manufacturer's instructions.

Fill the pond and add chemicals. With the hole dug and the liner installed, the pond is ready for water. Before you start, check your water meter. Then check it again when the pond is full. This will tell you how many gallons of water your pond holds. The amount of chemicals you need for pond ecosystem treatments is measured in ounces per number of gallons. Follow package instructions for measuring and adding chemicals.

Finish the edges. An edging of stone will blend your new pond naturally with the garden surrounding it. Fieldstone is a good choice. The stones should hang over the water by 1-2" to conceal the pond liner.

Select plants. A newly filled pond will have cloudy water. This is normal. To ensure that the water clears, half of the surface of the pond needs to be covered with plant material. The plants prevent sunlight, which causes algae to grow, from entering the pond. It can take the water a few weeks to clear, so don't think you are doing something wrong if it stays cloudy that long.

Some good floating plants for Atlanta ponds are water hyacinths *(Eichhornia crassipes)*, water lettuce *(Pistia stratiotes),* and water lily *(Nymphaea).*

Pond water also requires the addition of oxygenating plants to keep it healthy and to support fish. Hornwort *(Ceratophyllum demersum)* and elodea *(Elodea canadensis)* are two good choices.

Add fish. Wait at least 24 hours to add fish. (The wait will give the chlorine from the tap water time to evaporate.) Goldfish are preferable; koi eat plants.

What About a Pump?

If three-quarters of the surface of the pond is covered with plant material that includes oxygenating plants such as elodea and includes fish, a pump is not always needed. When fish are not present, a pump will keep the water moving enough to prevent mosquitoes.

Local Sources for Pond Liners, Plants, and Fish

See Appendix A for addresses and phone numbers.

All South Stone and Water Garden Center

Coastal Pond Supply

Eco-Gardens (Don Jacobs)

Garden South

Hall's Greenhouses

Hastings Nature and Garden Center

Home Depot

Intown Hardware

Pike Family Nurseries

Pond Bloomers

Randy's Nursery & Greenhouse

Chapter Twenty-Nine

Walkways in the Garden

by

Brencie Werner

Walkways in the Garden

The walkway through a garden is like an open door. It invites you into the garden to examine and admire, to touch and smell, to linger and enjoy. A walkway shows you how to proceed through the garden, to get from one point of interest to another. It also gives the gardener access to plants for cultivating and grooming without compacting the soil. A walkway can establish the desired feeling for the garden. Straight walks built of materials with straight edges give a formal feeling, while curved walks built of irregular materials give an informal feeling. Walks disappearing around a bend lend an air of mystery and anticipation to the garden, beckoning you to explore.

Materials for Walks

Materials used for walks can include poured concrete, stone or bricks laid in mortar or sand, crushed or pea gravel, wood chips, turf, and even wood planks. Each material has advantages and disadvantages. Poured concrete is smooth, good for wheelchairs, and long lasting—but not very aesthetic or natural looking. Stone or brick set in concrete is more aesthetic, is long lasting, and requires little upkeep. Stone or brick set in sand will allow small plants and moss to grow between the stones or bricks, giving an even more natural look to the walk. Edging is necessary to hold the sand in place, however. Crushed or pea gravel also requires an edging, or the gravel spills over the ground and looks unkempt. Pine bark and wood chips are inexpensive and look natural in the garden, but they decompose quickly and have to be replaced. Wood planks walks are usually built over boggy areas, installed so that they are raised above the water table.

For a unified appearance, it is best to use a material that is already in use in the home construction, such as bricks with a brick home or stones if the home is of stone. Since stones are so prevalent in our Atlanta soil, they are a natural material for walk construction. Crab Orchard stone from Tennessee, with natural beige coloration, is also popular. Slate is not mined in this area and tends to be very slippery when wet, making it a less popular choice.

Installation

To install a walk in your garden, first determine where you want the walk to be. Lay it out and walk over the route for several days to make sure that it goes where it is needed. The walk can be delineated with garden hoses, landscaping flags, stakes and string, or whatever you have. Determine whether you need steps. In Atlanta, you probably do. Your walk should slope at least 1% for adequate drainage, but no more than 8% for comfort in walking. This translates to a minimum of 1/2" in 4' to a maximum of 4" in 4'.

Steps can be made from railroad ties cut in thirds for a 34"-wide walk, or in halves for a 51" walk. Steps can also be made with large slabs of a single stone or several stones or bricks mortared together, or forms can be built and concrete poured to face with stone or brick. Steps should follow the rule 2R + T = 27", where R = riser and T = tread. The most comfortable tread is at least 9" wide, and the most comfortable riser is no more than 9" high.

Building a Stone Walk Set in Mortar

For a stone walk set in mortar, install temporary edge strips about 3" high to contain the mortar until it dries. These can be made of plywood for curves or 1 x 4s for straight paths. The top of the edge strips will be the finished top of the walk. Secure edge strips on both sides with stakes. Rake out all pebbles, sticks, roots, and dirt to the bottom of the edge strips. Cut galvanized wire fencing to fit between the edge strips. Galvanized wire gives strength to the mortar, allowing a shallower base than would otherwise be required, and helps prevent cracking. Fit stones loosely into a 3' square section of the walk to determine the pattern. Start with the edges and work to the center of the walk, as with a jigsaw puzzle. Stones on the edge should go against the edge strip. Mortar on the edge of the walk will get damaged.

Mix mortar in a wheelbarrow for ease in moving it to the walk site. Use three parts sand to one part mortar mix, type N. One (five gallon) bucket filled to the brim of coarse river sand and two (one gallon) milk jugs (with spout cut off, but not handle) of mortar mix can be mixed in a normal-size wheelbarrow. Mix dry sand and mortar mix together thoroughly with a hoe. Then add enough water to mix to the consistency of cottage cheese. Use within a couple of hours, and keep mixing with a trowel to prevent drying around the edges.

Move a few stones at a time away from the walk and trowel mortar onto the galvanized wire. Pull wire up into the mortar with a cotter key extractor or claw hammer. Lay stones on top of mortar and push into the mortar with a twisting motion to seat. Fill in around edges of stone with more mortar. Use a straight edge (either a level or a board) to make sure that all stones are the same height, flush with the top of the edge strips. Thicker stones have to be tamped down further into mortar with the butt of the trowel or a hammer.

Cut off all excess mortar that is higher than the stones with a small trowel. Cover all exposed mortar larger than a fist with stones and make sure no excess mortar covers exposed wire mesh, so that you can begin again later where you left off. Use all mortar that has been mixed. Clean trowels by stabbing them into dry sand until all mortar is rubbed off. This will prevent rusting. Clean the wheelbarrow by hosing with a strong stream of water.

Let mortar set until firm, but not completely dry. This usually takes two to four hours depending on the humidity and temperature. Brush mortar and stone surfaces with a whisk broom or house broom to roughen mortar surfaces and clean stone of mortar. Remove edge strips after mortar is completely dry. (This is usually the next day.) If stone surfaces have residual mortar on them, clean them with a solution of one part (25%) muriatic acid and three parts (75%) water with a wire brush after mortar is completely set. This usually takes a few days.

This same method could be used to install a brick walk in mortar.

Sources of Supplies

Tools such as trowel, level, brickset, hammer, etc.	Maxwell and Hitchcock
Galvanized fencing	Home Depot
Mortar mix	Home Depot
Sand	Ace Sand Co. (truckload) Home Depot (bags)
Muriatic acid	Pool supply or hardware store
Stones	Jimco Stone

Chapter Thirty

Herbs

by
Jean Johnson Givens

Best Herbs for Atlanta Gardens

Herbs have been grown throughout history because they are useful in many different ways. Because of the oils they produce, herbs can be used for medicines, teas, dyes, culinary seasonings, and fragrances. Many contain insect-repelling substances; others can be dried for winter bouquets. Some herbs are listed as woodland or meadow wildflowers, favorite garden perennials, long-blooming annuals, and even as shrubs and trees.

Herbs fit happily into many garden situations. A garden devoted strictly to herbs is a pure delight, but herbs may be tucked in wherever space and conditions are adequate. They are excellent companions for vegetables, and herbs make vegetable plots look more attractive.

Soil

Since herbs originated mainly in alkaline Mediterranean soils which are pebbly and well drained, amending our Georgia clay with granite sand and enough dolomitic lime to bring the pH up to about 6.8 helps to create the ideal medium for growing herbs. Adding organic matter in the form of composted animal manures, leaves, grass clippings, and vegetable trimmings from the kitchen should be done every year because these materials break down in the soil and are used by the plants. Remember also that raised beds and the organic mulches improve drainage and help prevent soil crusting after heavy rains.

Planting Considerations

Morning and mid-day exposure, with some protection from the blistering afternoon sun, will benefit most herbs. Some herbs are more shade tolerant, and a few such as sweet woodruff survive heavy shade. Just as with vegetables, plants grown for foliage require less sun than those grown for flowers, seeds, or roots. In well prepared soil, herbs grow vigorously. Be sure to give them adequate space, because air circulation is so important. Mulching will help keep soil from splashing up on the leaves of herbs. Most perennial herbs should be divided every two to four years to retain vigor. Plants with flowers in umbels, such as parsley, dill, fennel, and coriander, tend to have tap roots and should be seeded where they are to grow. For practical reasons, keep perennial herbs out of areas which must be frequently tilled. Herbs can be excellent container plants too.

Problems

Difficulties with herbs are associated with our climatic conditions. Our hot, wet, muggy climate makes tarragon and certain gray-leaved plants, such as lavender, difficult to grow. Atlanta's sudden wild swings in temperature may prevent plants from becoming properly acclimated to cold weather. Our night temperatures during the growing season are not different enough from day temperatures to promote optimal growth of many herbs.

Tips from the Experts

For an outdoor herb garden, start seeds of basil, parsley, chives, sage, and sweet marjoram indoors about four to six weeks before planting outside. Herbs such as dill, caraway, fennel, and sorrel can be sown directly into the garden after the danger of frost has past.

To grow herbs all year long, Pete Pike suggests planting herbs in a window box that can be brought indoors during the winter months.

To propagate from herb plants, root cuttings in sand or a mixture of peat and perlite. Use recycled orange juice cartons—slice off the slanted top and snip holes in the corners for drainage. This allows for 6" of rooting media so that the longer stems may be inserted to facilitate rooting. The added volume of the medium also helps retain moisture. Cuttings may be crowded into the container. Keep moist and somewhat shaded. When a slight tug on a cutting shows some resistance, roots have probably formed. The cutting may then be potted up individually.

It is good practice to immediately propagate each new plant that you buy. Often your own cutting or division will outgrow its parent.

When sage stems get woody, the old plant may be declining. To rejuvenate, root cuttings from fresh growth.

Garlic chives produce abundant seed. Remove the flower heads before seeds mature, unless you wish abundant seedlings! The flowers may be used in salads, vinegars, or dried for winter bouquets.

Never work around rue *(Ruta graveolens)* when you are perspiring, especially when it is in flower. It can cause blisters and long lasting brown spots on the skin. This beautiful plant is well worth growing, but do take precautions.

Lavender is difficult to grow in our hot, muggy climate and heavy clay soils. Good circulation of air and excellent drainage are essential. Some gardeners place a stone in the hole below the plant and add sand and pebbles to the soil. Lavender likes lime and will grow happily by a curbstone. The most successful lavender grower I know dusts her plants weekly with sulfur to prevent fungal growth.

Hose down plants the night before harvesting herbs for drying. (This may eliminate the need for washing them after they are gathered.)

When drying bunches of herbs with seed heads, hang them upside down in brown paper bags with holes punched in the sides for circulation. The bag will catch seeds as they shed.

Attend Herb Education Day at the Atlanta Botanical Garden on the last Saturday in April. It is sponsored by the Chattahoochee Unit, Herb Society of America. Experts offer demonstrations and answer questions on growing herbs, cooking with them, and using them in arts and crafts. This is the largest sale of fresh herbs in Atlanta.

Some Local Sources for Herbs

ABG Spring Plant Sale

GardenSmith Greenhouse and Nursery

Hastings Nature and Garden Center

Flowery Branch (Mostly seeds, some plants)

Intown Hardware (Particularly fine selection of herb plants in spring)

BEST HERBS FOR ATLANTA GARDENS

Common Name	Botanical Name	Varieties	Use	Height	Type	Propagation	Expos.	Comments
Basil	Ocimum basilicum	Sweet Basil Spicy Globe Cinnamon	C	1 1/2'	A	seeds	FS	Pinch flowers for maximum foliage production
Bay	Laurus nobilis		C, I	3-6'	TS	stem cuttings, buy plants	FS, PtSh	Grow in double pot, well-drained, inside in winter
Bee-balm	Monarda didyma	'Cambridge Scarlet,' 'Violet Queen'	B, D	2-3'	P	stem cuttings, division	FS, PtSh	Use in teas and potpourri; attracts hummingbirds
Borage	Borago officinalis		C, D	2-3'	A	seeds	FS, PtSh	Cucumber flavored leaves-salad, sky-blue flowers-garnish
Chervil	Anthriscus cerifolium		C, D	1 1/2'	A	seeds in cool weather	PtSh	Lacy leaves; anise flavor. French cuisine

Abbreviations Used on Charts

Use	Type Plant	Exposure
B-Beverage	A-Annual	FS-Full sun
C-Culinary	B-Biennial	PtSh-Part shade
D-Decorative	P-Perennial	Sh-Shade
F-Fragrance	T-Tender	
I-Insect repellent	S-Shrub	

BEST HERBS FOR ATLANTA GARDENS cont'd

Common Name	Botanical Name	Varieties	Use	Height	Type	Propagation	Expos.	Comments
Chives	Allium tuberosum A. schoenoprasum	easiest best	C, D	15"	P	bulbs, seeds	FS	Mulch in winter, divide every 3 years, cut back after bloom
Cilantro (leaves) Coriander (seeds)	Coriandrum sativum		C	2-3'	A	seeds in cool weather	FS	Keep flowers cut for leaf production
Dill	Anethum graveolens		C	2-3'	A	seeds, repeated plantings	FS	For dill weed, promote active growth; freeze seed stalks for pickles
Fennel	Foeniculum vulgare	Green, bronze	C, D	3-4'	P	seeds, division	FS	Airy, fern-like leaves; copper fennel especially nice
Germander	Teucrium chamaedrys	Gray forms less hardy	D	1-2'	P	stem cuttings	FS	Good edging, knot gardens
Hyssop	Hyssopus officinalis		D	1 1/2-2'	P	stem cuttings	PtSh	Low hedge
Lamb's ears	Stachys byzantina		D	12"	P	division	FS	Silver fuzzy foliage; flower stalks dried for arranging

Common Name	Botanical Name	Varieties	Use	Height	Type	Propagation	Expos.	Comments
Lavender, Spanish	*Lavendula stoechas*	Try other lavenders too	C, F, I	3'	P	stem cuttings, division	FS	Air and soil drainage critical; moth repellent
Lemon balm	*Melissa officinalis*	Variegated one available	C	1 1/2-2'	P	stem cuttings	FS, PtSh	Clump forming; less invasive than other mints
Lemon thyme	*Thymus x citriodorus*	Caraway thyme nice in bloom	C	4-6"	P	stem cuttings	FS	Needs ventilation, drainage, pruning
Lemon verbena	*Aloysia triphylla*	Vigorous grower, tender	C, D	4'	TP	stem cuttings, division	FS	Pot plant, winter indoors; retains fragrance when dried
Marjoram	*Origanum majorana*		C	8-12"	TP	seeds, stem cuttings	PtSh	Take cuttings to over-winter indoors
Mint marigold	*Tagetes lucida*	Substitute for more difficult French tarragon	C, D	2'	P	seeds	FS	Blooms late; dries well for bouquets
Mints	*Mentha spp.*	*M. spicata* (mint juleps) *M. pulegium* (pennyroyal)	C D	2-3'	P	division, root cuttings	PtSh	Rampant spreaders; keep contained; groundcovers

BEST HERBS FOR ATLANTA GARDENS cont'd

Common Name	Botanical Name	Varieties	Use	Height	Type	Propagation	Expos.	Comments
Oregano	*Origanum heracleoticum*	*O. onitum* and *O. vulgare* have less flavor	C	2-3'	P	division, stem cuttings	FS, PtSh	Rich, moist soil; keep blooms pinched back
Parsley	*Petroselinum crispum*	Flat leaf Italian also good	C	1 1/2'	B	seeds, plant every year	PtSh	Soak seeds 24 hours; excellent edging
Pinks	*Dianthus spp.*	Petals edible if white heel removed	C, D	6-12"	P	seeds, division, stem cuttings	FS	Fragrant blooms; evergreen foliage
Pot marigold	*Calendula officinalis*	Yellow, orange, apricot	C, D	1-2'	A	seeds	FS	Dried ray flowers substitute for saffron
Rosemary	*Rosmarinus officinalis*	'Arp'-upright varieties more winter hardy	C, D	2-4'	P	stem cuttings, buy plants	FS, PtSh	Protected site, mulch
Sage	*Salvia officinalis*	Species 'Tricolor,' 'Aureus,' 'Purpurescens'	C D	2-4'	P	seeds, stem cuttings, or layering	FS	Trim to prevent woody stems; dry leaves for culinary purposes
Salad burnet	*Poterium sanguisorba*		C, D	3'	B	seeds, plant every year	FS	Cucumber flavor; good border plant; unattractive after rosette stage

Common Name	Botanical Name	Varieties	Use	Height	Type	Propagation	Expos.	Comments
Santolina (Lavender cotton)	*Santolina chamaecyparissus*		D	6-12"	P	stem cuttings	FS	Withstands dry, hot sites when established
Scented geranium	*Pelargonium spp.*	Many scents and leaf forms	C, D	2-3'	TP	leaf and stem cuttings	FS, PtSh	Take cuttings or over-winter indoors; dry for potpourri
Sweet Woodruff	*Galium odoratum*		D	6"	P	stem cuttings, buy plants	PtS, Sh	Shade groundcover
Tansy	*Tanacetum vulgare*	A fern-leaf type is available	D, I	3-4'	P	division	FS, PtSh	Lacy foliage; yellow, late summer flowers
Yarrow (golden)	*Achillea filipendulina*	'Coronation Gold'-yellow	D	2'	P	seeds, division	FS	Flower heads good for drying
Yarrow	*Achillea millefolium*	Pastel shades	D	2'	P	seeds	FS	Good cut flowers

Part Four

Cultivation Guides for Special Plants

Daylilies (*Hemerocallis*)

General Information

This plant could have been invented for Atlanta gardens. Daylilies are trouble-free. If you don't care about blue ribbons, simply plant them shallowly in friable soil in sun, and water them adequately before blooming. If you are eager for top-quality blooms and lots of them, then you will have to work a little harder. First, select varieties when in bloom. Choose from the new tetraploids for larger flowers with heavy substance and more intense color. These plants tend to have a high bud counts, and scapes or stems are sturdier.

Daylily Forms

The very popular, old-fashioned species types are still available. There are also dwarfs and small-flowered daylilies particularly useful for planting in fronts of flower beds. Daylilies vary greatly in flower color, texture, and pattern. Blooms have a number of different forms—recurved, spiders, flaring, doubles, and more. Daylily foliage habit can be evergreen, semi-evergreen, or dormant.

Planting

Daylilies prefer a slightly acid soil. Site your plant in **full sun** for heaviest flowering. However, hot afternoon sun fades blossom colors. Plant in early spring or late fall ideally. Daylilies planted here when temperatures and humidity are extremely high face a greater probability of rotting.

Plants purchased through mail order should be soaked a few hours in a weak fertilizer or humus solution and planted immediately. Freshly dug plants purchased from local gardens can be planted any time—immediately into the ground. Dig a hole larger than the root mass and work soil to a depth of 1'. Additives to our red clay can be planting soil, compost, granite sand, or well-rotted manure to give a friable soil that provides roots with the enhancement to grow rapidly and become established. When planting, make a mound in the center of the hole. Place the plant on the mound and spread the roots on each side of the ridge.

New plants should be planted as deep as they grew originally. However, never place more than 1" of soil above the crown (the point where roots and foliage join). A band of white indicates the part of the plant that was underground. The American Hemerocallis Society recommends that you work soil around and between roots as you cover the plant. Firm the soil and water well. Make certain there are no air pockets to interfere with good plant growth. When the water has soaked in, fill in with more soil, leaving a slight depression. Remember to leave plenty of space for your daylily to multiply, 18-24" on each side. Mulch with pine straw to control weeds and retain moisture during summer.

Fertilizing

Avoid all high nitrogen fertilizers—they will make plants grow too tall, decrease the number of flowers, and possibly cause bloom wilt in heat. For plants planted in good soil, probably one light application of a complete fertilizer, 4-12-12, 6-12-12, or 5-10-10, in granular form in early spring is adequate. Be careful to keep the fertilizer off the daylily foliage. Water in the fertilizer. Another fertilizer application can be made about the time the first sign of flower buds is noticed.

Outstanding local daylily gardeners Bob George and Owen Shores recommend applying 20-20-20 every 10 days from the first of April through the blooming season. Before blooming, they add Seaborn (seaweed) at the time of each application. They also use drip irrigation to keep their plants evenly watered before and during bloom season to increase flower size and substance.

Spraying

Thrips sometimes disfigure daylily flowers; spider mites cause discoloration of the foliage. A spray with 50% Malathion at two teaspoons per gallon of water is both safe and effective. Apply as soon as growth starts in spring in such a way that the solution runs down into the tight places between the leaves at the plant base. A second spraying six weeks later and a third six weeks after that assures complete coverage for the year. The insecticide Cygon is also effective against thrips. A specific miticide like 35% Kelthane can be used on spider mites, too.

Local Sources for Daylilies

Call for an appointment. See Appendix A for names of contacts, addresses, and phone numbers.

Alcovey Nursery (Mail order, too. Excellent selection.)

Damascus Gardens

LeGro Gardens

Erling and Lilian Grovenstein (Also seedlings and hostas. Mail order catalog, too.)

Mary Howard

Tucker Top Cat Gardens

Mickey Harp

Atlanta Botanical Garden Fall Festival (Daylilies can be purchased very inexpensively. Information sheet also available.)

Tips from Ray Stevens

The local Daylily Society's Ray Stevens has these tips for growing daylilies.

Soak newly purchased daylilies bought locally overnight in a solution of B-1 (Upstart) to overcome transplant shock.

Dayliles ordered from Florida should be planted here with sand in the bed to help them acclimate.

If you cannot plant daylilies immediately, plant them temporarily in play sand and wet them down. This will hold them until you are ready to plant.

Remove seed pods from daylily stems (unless, of course, you are trying your hand at hybridizing). Fruiting pods sap the plant's strength, making it more vulnerable to insects and disease.

Apply dehydrated cow manure around each plant in the fall for increased numbers of flowers on each stem and larger flowers. Cover with pine straw to hold the manure in place.

Fertilize in late February or early March, using granular 6-8-6 dug in close to roots. Follow in April with 10-10-10 liquid (Peters) sprayed on foliage.

For a new plant, take the older (darker) part of a daylily clump, slice it off, and barely cover with soil. New growth will come to form a new plant. Always put rootone on the new, sliced section to help new growth develop and prevent insect invasion.

Trim daylily foliage to 6" after flowering to stimulate a weak root system to grow. (**Note:** Some growers disagree with this practice.)

Iris

Bearded Iris (German Iris)

General Information

Keep iris beds free of leaves, debris, and weeds. Do not mulch. Mulch draws snails, insects, and fungus. Do not trim iris leaves except to remove dead or infected foliage. Cut or break off flower stalks at the base (rhizome) when blooms fade. This eliminates the plant's expending energy on seed production and discourages insects and disease. Divide every two to four years in mid-July to early September when clumps become crowded. Trim foliage then to reduce top heaviness.

Soil Preparation

Bearded iris need neutral soil (pH 6.5 to 7); add lime to reduce acidity. Site in an area that receives full sun to a half-day of sun in a slightly elevated spot that sheds water quickly. Prepare soil 1' deep by adding sand, humus, compost, gypsum, etc. to make friable. Dig that $10 hole for your $2 plant.

Planting

Plant in late winter, summer, or fall with rhizome "toes" pointed toward each other to form a triangle. The rhizome should peek out of the soil when the soil settles after thorough watering in. (The rhizomes will look like ducks on a lake.) Nothing should shade the top half of the rhizome.

Make a map and label named varieties. Iris are drought tolerant, needing water only at planting and during active growth in spring.

Fertilizing

Add 6-12-12 or 5-10-10 at time of soil preparation, mixing well. For established plants, fertilize in early spring (when daffodils are blooming) and again two to three weeks after flowering.

Pests and Diseases

Use Malathion on **aphids** and Cygon 2E on **borers** in early spring when leaves are 6" tall. Treat at least two times two weeks apart. (These problems are not common in Atlanta.)

For **leaf spot**, which is initiated by rain, use fungicides Funginex and Maneb. Cut off all infected leaves and destroy them. Spray continuously until rains subside.

For **snails**, try Deadline. (The English scatter dried holly leaves around plants to discourage snails.)

To treat **rot**, dig rhizome, cut off rot, soak remaining healthy rhizome in a solution of 1 part chlorine bleach to 10 parts water for 20 minutes. Let dry in sun for two weeks. Replant rhizome in fresh soil. (Rhizomes are smelly and mushy when affected with rot.)

When spraying iris, mix fungicide with insecticide and add a little Ivory liquid as a "sticker." Remember to read directions on containers carefully for amounts and method to use.

10 Bearded Irises for Atlanta

Arctic Fury - white

Mary Frances - light orchid blue

Beverly Sills - coral pink

Stepping Out - purple and white

Blue Sapphire - light blue

Vanity - pink

Carolina Gold - gold

Victoria Falls - powder blue

Debbie Rairdon - white and creamy

Winter Olympics - white

Mail Order Sources for Iris

Schreiners (catalog $4)

Cooley's (catalog $4)

Quail Hill Gardens

Cal-Dixie Iris Gardens

Tips from the Experts

Local Iris Society member Carolyn Hawkins has these recommendations:

To improve drainage (a serious problem for tall bearded iris), place the iris rhizome on a hill of pea gravel and cover the rhizome with some soil to hold the plant in place. The soil will work its way into the gravel, keeping the iris roots growing in a healthy, normal manner.

Fertilize bearded iris with granular 5-10-10 or 6-12-12 when the early daffodils bloom and repeat in June. "Others who have superior memories and disciplined behavior patterns apply liquid 15-30-15 every 10 days from the end of February through April," she says. Hawkins combines both fertilizing schedules, following the granular feeding with liquid fertilizer, beginning in mid-March.

Control aphids effectively on iris by simply washing them off with a hose.

Japanese, Louisiana, and Siberian Iris

General Information

Divide **Japanese iris** and **Louisiana iris** in fall every two to four years when clumps become crowded. **Siberian iris** should be divided every six to seven years.

Keep beds clear of leaves, debris, and weeds. Mulch with pine straw or oak leaves for winter protection and to add acidity. Clear away mulch in early spring, because mulch attracts snails and insects and encourages fungus. Do not trim leaves except to remove dead or infected foliage. Cut or break off flower stalks at base when blooms are gone.

Planting

Plant Japanese, Louisiana, and Siberian iris in acid soil (pH 5.5-6.9) **Don't apply lime.** Louisiana and Japanese irises can stand wet feet—they are happiest with damp feet and dry ankles. Light shade can be tolerated by Siberians. Plant in a depression in the soil and **do not allow the roots to dry out**.

Follow all other directions given for bearded iris.

Lilies (*Lilium*)

General Information

True lilies are fragrant, bulbous perennials 1-6' tall. In Atlanta, we easily can have different lilies blooming mid-May through early September. Lilies require perfect drainage such as a gentle slope can provide. They prefer a deep, rich soil with plenty of organic matter. Good air circulation is important, too, in order to keep insects and diseases away. Lilies need to sited to receive sun at least until early afternoon. Filtered sunlight or semi-shade may result in more delicate colors, but the stems will be weaker and the flower substance poorer. Do not plant lilies near walls, walks, or driveways that reflect sunlight and heat. Cutting spent flowers to prevent seed set is beneficial. Cutting the foliage is harmful in direct proportion to the amount taken. Cutting stems and foliage year after year can kill the plant.

Planting

Lilies like a very slightly acid soil (pH 6.0-6.5). If your site is level and your soil is clay, dig a round hole 18" deep and 12" wide. Place 6" of gravel on the bottom. Fill hole with a mixture of two parts sandy planting soil, one part compost, and one part river sand. Place some extra sand under and around the bulb, taking care not to damage roots. Try actually placing the bulb on a small mound of sand. Alternatively, you may also want to prepare raised beds for your lilies.

Some lilies, like Madonna Lily, *L. candidum* 'Cascade Strain' and 'White Elf,' should not have more than 1" of settled soil over the bulb. All others need no more than 4" cover. For best effect, lilies should be planted in groups of three or more, spaced 8-12" apart.

Lilies are heavy feeders and root deeply. Apply a rich compost mulch several times during the growing season to keep the soil cool, discourage weak growth, and eliminate the need for surface cultivation which might hurt the stem roots. (Planting a shallow-rooted ground cover around lilies will also keep the ground cool.) Do not expect your lilies to compete with other plants and win. Lilies more than 3' tall should be staked.

Fertilizing

A handful of 5-10-10 scattered around your lilies in early spring and repeated two or three times during the growing season will keep lilies strong and healthy.

Pot Culture

Lilies do well in containers if the soil mixture is loose and porous and there is at least 1" of gravel. Cover bulbs with at least 3" of soil. Water and label at planting.

Pests and Disease

Control **aphids** by spraying with nicotine sulfate, Black Leaf 40, and Malathion. Any all-purpose garden dust will control most diseases and insect pests.

Common Garden Peony
(*Paeonia lactiflora*)

General Information

Peonies are challenging perennials in Atlanta gardens. They require a cold weather winter with a certain number of hours below 40 degrees F. to grow and flower the following spring. Allan Armitage urges you to select only early to mid-season bloomers. He also suggests you choose only single or Japanese forms.

If you hold cherished childhood memories of the marvelous intoxicating peony fragrance as I do, early-blooming (mid-April) double peonies are the only choice for your Atlanta garden. The perfume seems to come only with some of the fully doubles. Later flowering varieties face higher temperatures and humidity which can bring about weak stems, more disease, and unopened double flowers. Listed below are some excellent fragrant doubles. You must be ready to accept that more petals trap more water, and this encourages disease development such as the disfiguring botrytis.

Peonies are sturdy and are more reliable when left undisturbed. They definitely resent transplanting.

Planting

Plant in fall. The red buds on the rootstock crown should be just beneath the soil surface—if they are more than 2" deep, the plant will not flower. Peonies prefer a sunny, well-drained location and abundant water, particularly in spring. They prefer friable, well-drained, neutral to slightly alkaline soil, but are tolerant of a wide range of pH conditions. If your soil is acid, add a little lime at planting and again each spring. A light application of compost worked gently around the plant every other year is sometimes advised.

Fertilizing

Fertilize peonies with a low nitrogen/high phosphorus fertilizer (5-10-5, 5-10-10, or even 12-55-6 or 8-24-10 or 0-50-0) about March 15. Overfertilizing will reduce flowering.

Maintenance

In late fall, cut back all foliage to the ground and dispose of it to prevent disease spread. Do not toss into compost pile. As a preventative, spray plants with a fungicide such as Sevin or Captan starting with the first early spring soft growth; repeat several times until foliage is mature.

Recommended Peonies (Fragrant Double Flower Forms)

'Festiva Maxima' is old reliable type with strong stems. Very fragrant, fully double, white flowers flecked with dark red. Early and heavy blooming.

'Monsieur Jules Elie' has double flowers of silvery rose-pink. It is fragrant, early flowering, and good for cutting.

'**Pink Hawaiian Coral**' has coral blooms that fade to delicate pink at the edges, forming a rose shape. Cream carpels and compact foliage. Lovely fragrance, early flowering.

'**Heritage**' is a magnificent, scarlet-crimson double. Large outer petals frame lemon fringe center. Lightly scented.

Tips from the Experts

From perennial authority Barbara Allen: On February 1, when peony shoots have emerged from the ground and are still red and about 4" tall, sprinkle about 1 tablespoon crushed copper sulfate granules around the outside of each peony plant to encourage flowering. Testing her practice, one year Allen treated only half her peonies with copper sulfate. The treated peonies' flowering far surpassed that of the untreated plants. Caution: Copper sulfate is a caustic chemical; be careful. Allen also fertilizes March 15 with 0-50-0.

Other gardeners who boast heavy flowering of peonies recommend sprinkling the soil around the plants with Milorganite several times during the year.

Tree peonies are challenging to grow here, but some gardeners have success. See Chapter 15, "Perennials."

Blueberries

General Information

Blueberry bushes yield delicious fruit and display fiery red foliage in December, when the garden is usually drab. Rabbiteye is the group of blueberries to plant here. Plant more than one variety of Rabbiteye blueberries to ensure the cross pollination necessary for fruit production. It is recommended that half your plants be Tifblue and half Climax or a combination Climax, Delite, or Bluebelle. (Tifblue, Climax, Delite, and Bluebelle are all Rabbiteye blueberries.)

Planting

Plant blueberries 6-8' apart in a light, well-drained soil in full sun. (They will tolerate partial shade, but the harvest will be less.) Dig a hole at least 18" deep. Work in Nature's Helper. Set the plants at least 1" deeper than they grew in the container or set them so the top roots are slightly above ground, mound soil to cover, and tamp the soil so the plants are held firmly in place. Mulch with 2-3" pine straw to help keep the fibrous root system moist. Water during dry weather year-round.

Fertilizing

About six weeks after planting, fertilize with 1 tablespoon 10-10-10 or azalea fertilizer around roots. Water well to avoid burning. It is best to cut off blossoms the first year after planting to strengthen the plant. You will be rewarded with increased berry yields in years to come.

After new growth begins in March or April, fertilize with 1/2 cup of either 10-10-10 or azalea special. Repeat a month later. Use a product that contains iron and other trace elements to keep the foliage a healthy, deep green. In June, apply 1 oz. ammonium sulfate to each plant to maintain acidity. **Do not apply any fertilizer within 6" of the trunk.**

Pruning

Prune blueberries only if you care to shape the bush. After four or five years, you may choose to prune out older canes more than 1" in diameter to encourage new growth.

Pests and Diseases

You won't need to spray. Blueberries are rarely attacked by insects or infected by diseases. When berries begin to ripen, you need to cover them with netting to protect them from hungry birds. A net structure can be easily constructed using PVC pipe.

Clematis

General Information

Because clematis perform weakly the first year planted, it's advisable to place bare-rooted plants (the way you usually receive them from mail order sources) in a 1 gal. pot containing a mixture of equal parts ground pine bark (humus), peat moss, and vermiculite and a *tablespoon of lime*. Add 1 tablespoon of slow-release fertilizer. The soil should be so loose and well-aerated that you can move it with your hand. Warning: An additive like manure causes the soil to pack and thwarts oxygen from reaching the roots. Top dress with Nursery Special any time from March 15 to April 1. No further fertilizing is needed. This promotes root growth but not extensive top growth which can get out of control in a container. Clematis planted in a container, heavily mulched, will over-winter outside here in a protected area.

Planting

The following year—or immediately, if the vine is growing or flow-ering vigorously—plant in full or partial sun. Blooms will fade in afternoon sun. Clematis such as *Clematis florida* 'Sieboldii' and *C.* 'Royal Velvet' do better than other varieties in slightly shaded areas.

Clematis vary on how vigorously they grow and their potential height under optimal growing conditions. Research the variety you've purchased before planting. Then dig a hole 1' wide by 1' deep. Plant the clematis in well-prepared, well-aerated soil. Use sand, Nature's Helper, planting soil, and compost and remember to keep the soil friable. Add a generous handful of lime. To ensure survival in case of accident or clematis wilt, plant the vine with at least two dormant nodes under the soil level. Set a stake next to plant for support. Water in with Peters 20-20-20.

Top dress with granular 10-10-10. Because clematis roots insist on a cool run, mulch with a large stone or pine straw. Clematis need a verti-cal place to run. Even those draped on shrubs require something to twist around. Fence wire (available in 10" x 3" sections) can be used to train clematis to cement, a brick wall, a mailbox, or up on a shrub. As the vine grows, add more wire sections.

Fertilizing

Clematis like to eat and drink water. Feed with 20-20-20 every time you water, about every five days but never more often. In wet seasons, fertilize on that five day schedule anyway. Continue to top dress every three to four weeks with granular 10-10-10. On established plants, be-gin granular feeds (10-10-10) mid-March and liquid applications of 20-20-20 on about April 1. If you maintain the vine well, you should not have to administer a high phosphorus fertilizer such as Super Bloom to produce strong flowering.

Pests and Diseases

To control insects that suck juices from the plant leaves, spray with Malathion. Clematis wilt, a fungus disease, is best treated by removing and destroying all affected vines. Hard pruning at the proper time seems to prevent this disease.

Pruning

Without pruning, clematis develop larger and larger gaps between the ground and the first blooms. For pruning purposes, all clematis vines are placed in one of three groups. The first group blooms in spring on last year's vine. Prune after blooming to control size. The second group blooms in early summer. To groom, remove dead wood. If desired, cut back 6-8" to a pair of strong buds in March. The third group blooms during summer and fall and requires pruning yearly in March to 12" from the ground for best performance. Most catalogs and clematis books list each variety with its group number along with a description.

Recommended Sources for Clematis

Local Sources

Goodness Grows

Henderson Plants

Hastings Nature and Garden Center

Pike Family Nurseries

Mail Order Sources

Wayside Gardens

Park Seed

White Flower Farm

Part Five

My Atlanta Garden

by

Avis Aronovitz

Illustrations by

Linda Fraser

My Atlanta Garden

When I write about Atlanta gardens—what they look like and what's blooming at a particular time—I am really writing about my own garden because I know it best. However, in this chapter, I have included the observations and experiences of other local gardeners, particularly Georgia Perennial Plant Association members, in their own gardens as well. I also have included some blooming times at the Atlanta Botanical Garden, even when dates conflict with those of my own garden eight miles north of ABG. Blooming times and noteworthy plants, good ones and not so good ones, are derived from sporadic recordkeeping and memory from 1989 through 1996.

My garden is a writer's garden. I select plants with the intention of studying and writing about them. I have a general design for my beds, but serendipity too often decides which plants become neighbors. (However, I never ignore exposure and cultural requirements.) I like to say that I have rarely written about a plant that I, myself, don't grow. If there is a plant reputed to be impossible here, I cannot resist trying to make it live and bloom in my garden. And if that plant's flower is blue (my favorite color), then I must have it in my garden. Plants that don't make it are missed and those that survive, sometimes against odds, are all the more loved.

A garden should bring pleasure to the gardener. When gardening is just another chore, the design and plants are wrong for that gardener. My garden is right for me because it gives me immense joy.

My Atlanta Garden in Spring

Traditionally, the garden year begins in spring. I will not break with that convention, but I recognize that in Atlanta the year's first bulbs and flowers appear much before the calendar proclaims the arrival of spring. In fact, some years we don't have a true winter. Other times it seems as if Atlanta passes from winter to summer without pausing, even briefly, for spring. The spring flowering season begins in early or mid-February and lasts through late May with a progression of bulbs, flowering shrubs, perennials, and cool weather annuals that are occasionally drizzled with ice or wilted by 80 degree temperatures.

Cold snaps, however, remind me true spring isn't until late March. It is then that I use any excuse to come out to my flower beds to observe what's blooming. March to me is the most exciting month. I experience the thrill of discovery again and again, year after year. Unlike later spring months when so much blooms at once, in early spring each flower appears on stage solo, a little starlet to be applauded alone.

Early March drifts of my favorite wildflower, Virginia bluebells, cover the mud in the upper front bed with a reversible quilt of pink tinted flowers that changes quickly to sapphire blue. This playful, often overlooked perennial disappears before early summer leaving no evidence of itself. Nearby, 'King Alfred' daffodils in peak bloom ring a sculpture in the upper front straw area. They return year after year, blooming robustly. Bulb experts say the true 'King Alfred' would not do that in Atlanta. I suspect the impostor 'Carlton' has assumed a royal name.

Along the backyard Woods Walk path, where they narrowly miss being trampled, I pass the delicate yellow flowers of *Epimedium* 'Sulphureum,' their thin stems holding them high above their winter bronze leaves. Soon, nearby are native columbines, *Aquilegia canadensis*. Before mid-March, I uncover from beneath my red hot poker plant's messy stragglers the first bloodroot, *Sanguinaria canadensis*. I catch that flower gently between two fingers and try to imagine walking through tidal waves of these "clean white flowers," an experience that Allan Armitage wrote "reaffirms one's faith in this crazy world." I would like to duplicate a tiny piece of his ethereal scene. So far, I haven't even come close.

Sanguinaria canadensis

Linda Fraser

In my faux rock garden, masses of pale trout lilies spring from mottled foliage to join *Narcissus* "Ice Follies" and a relative, miniature *N. campernelli*. When they combine with fragrant hyacinths and the blues of grape hyacinths and *Iris reticulata*, I, too, am renewed. Spring confirms for me a covenant of continuation made to earth's inhabitants. When I see the sock-it-to-you red bloom of *Anemone coronaria* 'Hollandia' with its wide white band circling a black center, I am validated. It's a treasure even if the bulb is short-lived.

Although it's not supposed to even grow here, for more than 10 years where my driveway twists to enter my carport, I have had two winter heaths, *Erica carnea* 'Winter Beauty' and *E. c.* 'Springwood Pink,' growing in ordinary builder's fill. In each winter warm spell, the heaths throw pink, urn-shaped blossoms; peak bloom is definitely now. Under my kitchen windows, old camellias reblooming after the zapping early flowers received from a mid-February 20 degrees, seem a fitting backdrop for those heaths and the cold and heat tolerant, heavily-flowering 'Crystal Bowl Yellow' and 'Universal Blue' pansies sharing that narrow triangular plot. Pushing through the pansies 'Delft Blue' and yellow 'City of Harlem' hyacinths complete the small landscape painting.

In 1993, spring came in winter after several warm, wet months without freezing temperatures. There was not even a hint of the mischief the capricious jet stream would bring before mid-month. Then on March 13, all this came to an end.

The onslaught was silent and sudden. No warning, except some dire snow predictions in the previous days' weather reports. But who believes weather forecasters? At 5:00 a.m., I had gone to my bedroom window, and peering out and seeing nothing amiss, returned to sleep. At 6:30, I arose to an entirely different landscape. Later that day, standing close to the window to catch the light reflected off piling snow, I recorded the scene in my garden diary and with my camera.

By then, the power had been out for several hours. Drifting, blowing snow, fed by high winds, blurred any view of houses across the road. By midday, at least 15" of snow lay on my back deck. This snow protected plants by covering them before temperatures plummeted and saved some of them. Rhododendrons were covered in snow, shrunken, and folded into themselves as if accepting the need to survive, but not resist.

With no radio or TV, the activity of the day became watching the birds at the feeders. We saw bright-colored male cardinals and females in red-trimmed brown feather coats, lots of reddish house finches, rufus-sided towhees, tufted titmouses, black-capped chickadees, sparrows, and wrens all sparring for a position at the feeder. The next day, following freezing night temperatures, two brown thrashers dug shelters in adjoining hanging baskets above the snowy deck.

A week later, I tallied plant survivors. Some, like the winter heaths and hyacinths, seemed exhilarated by the freak storm, but most forsythia blooms were "wasted." The pansies remained vibrant, undamaged. The foliage was badly injured on another cool weather annual, the pot marigold, calendula. Daffodil blooms were intact but their stems, severely weakened due to cell wall freeze damage, were bent over, sprawling the flowers on the ground. The storm had destroyed open buds and blooms on cherry and pear trees.

In the early period after nature's havoc, star magnolia and flowering almond blooms were a terrible shade of brown, but within 10 days new flowers emerged on both. These shrubs adapt to spring freezes through an unusual survival mechanism, reserve buds. However, nature is not easily beaten, and by summer, the two dwarf almonds succumbed to bark freeze damage. Michael Dirr calls them the "bargain basement of shrubs," but they had been with me 20 years, faithfully pretty in pink. They supplied needed height to the low-flowering bulbs and perennials on the driveway embankment. I will replace them.

In the same garden area, a 7' pieris's delicate white vase-shaped flowers, attached like grapes to threads cascading down the lustrous bronze foliage, had turned an unpleasant rust color in the cold. However, the bush lived to bloom the following year.

There was hidden damage, too. This would have been a spring without one deciduous magnolia bloom, except for my wonderful Brooklyn-bred M. 'Elizabeth.' Her large, soft yellow blooms were not affected. I recognized another casualty in early summer—the lack of spring purple sprays on my *Buddleia alternifolia*, the fountain butterfly bush.

Snow and strong winds caused serious damage. Huge broken limbs were everywhere and shrubs torn from their moorings lay with roots exposed on the ground. In a shady, moist corner, my beloved Florida anise-tree, a special *Illicium floridanum* many years before obtained from Don Jacobs at Eco-Gardens, lay on its side. When its leaves are crushed, an intoxicating aroma of green apples escapes. Jim Harrington, who helps me turn my flower beds into a garden, staked and cabled the shrub upright. Midsummer, I was saddened that only the center stem foliage remained alive. Then, suddenly, new growth began emerging everywhere alongside the main root system. This special shrub recovered completely.

By month's end, nature was back on course. Crabapples were in flower and, in the understory, a *Fritillaria imperialis* 'Aurora' displayed a bundle of orange bell-like flowers. This bulb in bloom is a rare sight in Atlanta. Success came from following the suggestions of Dr. George Motchan, a Marietta gardener specializing in challenging plants. He says to plant the bulb immediately on arrival, almost on its side. Perfect drainage, absolutely necessary, can be had with a 2' deep, carefully prepared bed with 6" of fine gravel on the bottom, topped by 6" of sand into which the bulb is planted. My own excellent drainage was achieved when a section in my front garden collapsed under me and I fell down a hole up to my hips, a la Alice in Wonderland. The materials used to fill this treacherous cave-in, where an old tree stump had decayed, provided the fastidious crown imperial's drainage.

Early Glenn Dale azalea 'Festive' and its red sport 'Mike Bullard,' my first azaleas to bloom, were splashed with color. Later-blooming *Pulmonaria saccharata* 'Mrs. Moon,' whose pink flowers turn blue, had joined the continuing show of large-flowered *P.* 'Sissinghurst White,' in the midst of a drift of star-shaped 3" blooms of *Crocus fleischeri*. By then, there were only faded pink blossoms on the Darley heath. *Tulipa clusiana's* cherry-red peppermint sticks that open snow white and the spidery, fire-flamed *T. acuminata* were vibrant.

Tall purplish *Hyacinthoides hispanicus* and miniature bluebell-like *Scilla bifolia* 'Bright Pink' are in flower a week by March 15. Early white flowers on *Helleborus niger*, the Christmas rose, have faded. Across the path, still in good bloom, both white and blue hepaticas play with common blue *Scilla siberica*. In a sunny spot a rather ordinary quince is enveloped in scarlet flowers, while under a canopy of bare tree branches, a large *Helleborus orientalis* clump seemed fatigued by the weight of its greenish purple flowers.

In years with no spring chills, the clipped 'paper streamer' flowers of *Magnolia stellata* appear to be decorations for a party about to begin. This star magnolia leads my backyard parade of flowering small trees—tulip magnolias, redbuds, crabapples, and April native dogwoods. March 20, celandine poppies, foam flowers, native violets, fire pinks (*Silene virginica*), shooting stars (*Dodecatheon*), and *Trillium grandiflorum* bloom on my woodland floor. Pretty, pale blue *Anemone nemerosa* 'Robinsoniana' colors a narrow path, my shortcut to the back rhododendron thicket. Biennial lavender money plant (*Lunaria annua*) begins to bloom. A long flowering period keeps it a smart contrast through the season with the yellow-flowering bulbs.

In several garden sunny areas, no matter the weather conditions, my pink perennial tulips bloom this third week in March. Southern Indica azaleas, in sharp contrast, flower only when buds have not been killed by cold, perhaps one year in every five. Then my 10' 'George L. Tabor,' hardiest of the group, blooms so magnificently that I never regret growing it. The Kurume azaleas, 'Hino Crimson' and 'Snow,' and more Glenn Dale azaleas are right on schedule. So are the green blossoms of *Rhododendron* 'Shamrock' that open for St.

Patrick's Day. A daffodil named for this Irish holiday blooms at its feet. Also this week, *R. pseudochrysanthum*, near my living room window, wraps itself in soft pink gauze. The first large pink bleeding hearts appear. These *Dicentra spectabilis*—both pink and white forms—and their flowers are more vigorous and beautiful than I had ever seen them in Atlanta. The frigid January was a tonic for this perennial.

There are interesting additions in my March 1994 garden. *Chinodoxa* 'Pink Giant' in full bloom is reaching for the sun from beneath the treacherous Chinese hollies in the entrance plantings. On March 5 I find three garden gems—pale blue striped *Puschkinia libanotica*, squirrel resistant *Crocus tomasinianus*, and new clumps of nymph-like *Cyclamen coum*. The main attraction now for me is *Magnolia loebneri* 'Ballerina' with its inviting perfume drifting from blush pink cups. Across the lawn, fuchsia flowers further enhance *Loropetalum chinense* 'Mansaku,' a dark purple foliage beauty. This

Magnolia 'Elizabeth', yellow perennial tulips beneath.

Chinese fringe shrub, purchased at the 1993 ABG plant sale, lives in the shadows of my large black maple, a particularly attractive sugar maple form.

Peonies have been up 6" for a few days, and I remember it is time to review their fertilizing schedule. In the shrub border, *R.* 'Mary Fleming' covers herself in a charming manner with small yellow and pink blooms and *R.* 'April Rose' shows off her own deep violet clusters. The smallest tulip, 3" *T. bifolia*, lends needed white to the rock garden. Then a surprise! This year for the first time, I have the wildflower spring beauty *(Claytonia virginica)* flowering a second year. Neighboring plump, opening pussy willow buds look down to admire with me a study in white: violas, snowflakes, *Pulmonaria* 'Sissinghurst White,' a host of pansies, and English daisies—all romping merrily together. The nearby *Pieris japonica* is overlaid with dangling white pearl necklaces. For the first time, the pinkish-red necklaces of *Pieris* 'Valley Valentine' join in the celebration of spring.

On March 20 there is a moment when the garden appears ethereal as the low-angled morning sun, traveling through translucent petals on cream-yellow *Magnolia* 'Elizabeth,' combines with the moist atmosphere to produce a dazzling, transient effect that makes my yellow perennial tulips beneath shimmer as the light reaches them. Later, the dew on the flowers dries and the magic is gone. The strong pink tint of the daffodils down by the mailbox may have been influenced by an addition of recommended epsom salts. Apple-scented daffodil 'Mondragon,' from three bulbs purchased from Wayside Gardens in 1992, blooms seven stalks of golden orange. *Clematis armandii* threads its way through a dogwood, stopping to lower white blossoms from the tree's branches. I lost this vine in the cold spring of 1996, but Carolina jessamine's golden flowers still decorate the tree limbs.

From the third week in March through mid-April, gardeners come to admire huge, long-lasting perennial tulips from White Flower Farm. The exhibit is a combination of recent purchases and bulbs that have been blooming in my garden for 12 years. These tulips welcomed the cold January temperatures, but their success may be due to the Milorganite (sludge) incorporated at planting time along with deep planting and heavy bulb food feedings. (I fertilize in spring as foliage appears, and again in the fall.)

The third week in March 1995 following the warm winter, April flowers arrive in my garden. Perhaps this is the most glorious week this spring. The spectacular flower combinations overwhelm me: *Narcissus* 'Jenny' with the previous year's *Primula vulgaris* is an exquisite study in yellow and white. There are blues that seek out each other, *Ipheion uniflorum* (starflowers 'Wisley Blue' and 'Rolf Fiedler') and a white tulip with a steel blue base named *T. puchella alba caerulea.*

The real show is the pink-flushed saucer magnolia blooming late this year, looming over the rooftop of my house. R. 'Mary Fleming,' demure in delicate pink and yellow ruffles, bends low over a row of pink perennial tulips. The last days of the month, this pair is joined by a lovely blue form of western camassia, *C. leichtlini* 'Blue Danube.' Beyond the snow white *Iberis* border, the cutleaf lilac blooming since early March overpowers visitors with its beauty and perfume. Sadly, in spring 1996, all its flower buds were killed.

The new arbor, a contemporary gothic-styled sculpture created by local artist Clark Ashton to mark the entrance to my backyard Wood's Walk, is crowned now with a dogwood branch poised to open its blossoms by week's end. Beneath is a second strong blooming of *Helleborus niger*, its golden anthers a perfect pairing with the yellow epimediums surrounding it. I planted some white and several yellow Iceland poppies to draw the eye back through the arbor.

The week's special treat is the Wayside Gardens spring 1994 offering, *Daphne genkwa*, growing successfully in woodland soil laced with mini pine bark nuggets. The rose lilac flower clusters pair well with the translucent, sulfur-yellow florets of fragrant *Iris bucharica*. Competing for acclaim are the corydalis. Golden *C. lutea* blooms in early March and continues until frost. Subtle yellow-tipped *C. ochraleuca* and purplish pink *C. solida* flower this week too. On the scene also is the difficult-to-grow blue-flowered Jacob's-ladder. Golden celandines (wood poppies) romp at the feet of winter's *Helleborus orientalis* providing a collision of seasons. A blizzard of small white flowers hovering within the wild thyme azalea (*R. serpyllifolium*) enlivens my front garden bed.

In open woods, both purple and white wisteria tangle with frilly redbuds and glistening dogwoods in an incredible show. In gardens, crabapples have replaced cherry blooms while the sweet honey aroma of *Fothergilla gardenii* drifts from beneath emerging pink dogwood blooms. After heavy March flowering, the garden glides with a gentle transition into April.

April flowering varies due to freezes and other factors. However, an early April bloom inventory is likely to include James Harris's lilac-colored azalea 'Rivermist.' When it is in bloom, people always ask its name. The robust foam flower, *Tiarella cordifolia* 'Oakleaf,' prospers beneath a front yard native dogwood. This plant deserves its fine reputation. Large, deep purple tulip 'Negrita' from the previous ABG fall plant sale is exquisite beneath pale pink R. *pseudochrysanthum* blooms. Overhead, the majestic crabapple in full bloom acts as a sentinel, guarding plants below.

Rhododendron 'Manitau,' outstanding in a recent Homeplace Garden's Southeastern Flower Show exhibit, demonstrates garden hardiness by covering itself in pink cotton balls just before mid-month. Native Catesby's trillium are blooming already a week. Wake-robin trilliums, the great white *T. grandiflorum*, appear among native violets.

Mid-April, jewel-like blue *Iris cristata* drips down the rock garden ledges. By the back fence, Jack-in-the-pulpits play under bull magnolias and native evergreen rhododendrons, *R. maximum*. Here also is tall *Trillium erectum*, sporting a maroon bowtie. Yellow bellworts (uvularias) join the wildflower lineup. Yellow buttercups, *Ranuculus repens* 'Flore Pleno,' creep everywhere through the garden. Solomon's seal with tiny white bells clinging to vaulting wands add elevation, if not wisdom, to the flowery landscape. This non-varie-gated type was transplanted from my father's New York State garden following his death 12 years ago.

Dianthus plumarius 'Sonata' with silver streaked foliage forms a color and foliage composition when it combines with the woolly spikes, tacked with tiny hot pink flowers, of adjacent lamb's ear (*Stachys byzantina*). Shasta daisies have hopped about the garden, anchoring themselves in places I probably would have chosen to plant them. *Hesperis matronalis*, a wonderful 3-1/2' tall, deep lavender-flowered plant, starts to bloom now and serves as a strong accent. Its twin in white by the driveway is also a star summer performer.

With an eye to the upcoming Azalea and Rhododendron Tour, pink azalea 'Easter Parade' is on schedule. Three other popular azaleas, fragrant, pink, ca-mellia-flowered 'Mary Lou Kehr,' James Harris's outstanding, red flowered 'Miss Susie,' and tall, deciduous, yellow-flowered 'Hazel Hamilton' are each blue ribbon worthy.

One spring, it was apparent that the plants were performing strangely. Al-though early blooming hybrid rhododendrons flowered heavily and well, the late varieties followed them too closely. Some buds never opened. That year's cold damage was far greater than had been immediately evident. Likewise the earliest evergreen azaleas flowered well, but subsequent blooms were disfig-ured with a petal spot caused by warmth and rain. Even *Calycanthus* 'Athens,' whose early April flowers were quite normal, produced scarred, distorted blooms by late month. By May all new flowers appeared normal. Moreover, it was a good year for lilacs. The pale lavender cutleaf *Syringa laciniata* was in full bloom in late March, and Korean *S.* 'Palibin' opened by April's second week to replace aromatic *Viburnum juddii*. Each shrub has its own seductive fragrance.

In April red buckeye (*Aesculus pavia*), a dramatic, small tree with bright fluorescence, captures attention from across the way where it grows on the strip of the neighbor's yard that I have usurped. Other shrubs in flower are pink-flowered rhododendrons 'Wheatley' and 'Trude Webster.' In the lower garden, R. 'Bashful,' a variety bearing rose-colored flowers that are proportioned perfectly to the plant's diminutive size, is performing alongside early perennials. Simultaneously, along the mid-driveway the white wild indigo (*Baptisia alba*) rules.

Across the lawn, dwarfish azalea 'Elsie Lee' blooms reddish purple, semi-double fistfuls of color—my favorites because they nicely fill the gap between early and late blooming azaleas and distract the eye from ugly faded Kurume flowers. Within days, 'Elsie Lee' is joined by matching lavender tulips, lavender and white hybrid columbines, English iris, and yellow bearded iris.

Red orange gerbera daisies bloom nearby nearly hidden from view by *Amsonia* 'Blue Star.' You need good fortune to have gerberas return year after year, particularly after severe temperatures. These gerberas are from an original planting in this protected spot nine years ago. Earlier in April they made an attractive pairing with an orange native azalea, *Rhododendron austrinum*. That native soon will be surrounded by 'Snow' azaleas and spicy-scented, white-flowered *R. alabamense*.

One more rhododendron for April is *R.* 'Markeeta's Prize' with large scarlet flower clusters that look striking in my shrub border beneath the neighbor's oak trees. Right on cue, heavy flowering a true blue, *Clematis* 'Will Goodwin' scampered over the adjoining carport bricks. Close by, an excellent spring groundcover *Ajuga repens* grows, its foliage almost hidden by its blue-flowering stalks. Under the black maple, a native trillium and the cream flowers of false Solomon's seal are clearly visible.

In the white garden, ground-hugging well-flowered *Deutzia gracilis* 'Nikko' merges with the pale yellow flowers on the low-hanging branches of exbury azalea, *R.* 'Primrose.' *Viola* 'White Queen' carpets the garden floor. The star-of-Bethlehem (*Ornithogalum umbellatum*) has flower stalks, each crowned with 20 white, star-like flowers striped with green. After many years, it has yet to show any evil inclination to overrun its neighbors.

This white garden in late April features a Goodness Grows catalogue selection *Clematis lanuginosa* 'Candida' so spectacular that friends come to photograph its 9" white flowers. These giant, glistening blooms continue into May. Summer flowers are somewhat smaller. Another clematis that is a survivor of the extreme weather is the Wayside 1993 cover girl *C. florida* 'Sieboldii.' It is now draped dramatically through a tall white pine's naked lower limbs. Its presentation of creamy white flowers, each with a large purple central boss of petal-like stamens, puzzles the eye. At first guess, the blooms appear to be passion flowers.

Every year about now, I am roused by the beauty of the red spring foliage on a Japanese maple, *Acer palmatum* 'Crimson Queen.' I remember a walk through Ireland's Anne's Grove Gardens along a path that borders a sea of similar dwarf Japanese maples, all the identical variety. They looked like thousands of flame-painted umbrellas left open to dry.

Late in April the purple red florets of Mediterranean native, hardy gladiolus (*G. byzantinus*), planted in my garden for the first time in the fall of 1993, are a smashing accent in the small garden patch below my bedroom windows. Felder Rushing writes, "Some folks have an innate need to be gaudy." I guess I am one. Although I have enjoyed it in many gardens in the British Isles, I've never before seen it growing in our area. It did not return in my garden in 1996.

Butterfly Weed
Asclepias tuberosa

Linda Fraser

In both April 1995 and 1996, something wonderful happened. Long rose pink rabbits' ears protruded from curious knobs on *Lavandula stoechas pedunculata*. Rarely seen in our area, but growing at my mid-driveway lamppost since 1994, this novel lavender holds up to our summer heat if planted in very well-drained soil. In the shrub border, loose white clusters on *Rhododendron* 'Dora Amateis' join *R.* 'Mary Fleming,' now emphasized by yellow perennial tulips below. Spanish and English bluebells in peak bloom aid the display. Without even seeing its flowers, I know *Viburnum juddii* is in bloom from the intoxicating perfume drifting through the garden. (It is flowering weeks later than in previous years!)

Between mid-month and April 25, alliums such as lilac pink *A. schubertii*, which resembles a birthday sparkler, demure white *A. neopolitanum*, and rosy *A. unifolium* from the northwest coast grab the limelight. Weird, tall *Nectaroscordum siculum* with its large, nodding bell-shaped flowers blooms, and everyone asks, "What is it?" Across the garden, early peony 'Pink Hawaiian Coral' opens its sweetly fragrant, coral-tinted flowers. Nearby there is a generous drift of *Dianthus* 'Bath's Pink.' Every year Jane Bath's found treasure becomes more beautiful.

Blue in the garden now is provided by *Corydalis* 'Blue Panda,' which is still experimental in Atlanta gardens, and the blooms on early-flowering clematis in prussian blue to cerulean shades that are splashed over the carport ivy. Clematis 'H. F. Young,' 'William Kinnett,' and 'Multi-Blue' journeying together up that wall is just the effect that I admired in England on Sissinghurst's "Purple Wall."

Off the back deck, 8" rose-red blooms with a carmine bar from Clematis 'Dr. Ruppel' drape themselves dramatically on the purplish pink blooms of Rhododendron 'Madrid.' At this moment in the garden, when clematis reign supreme, accolades still go to polished white C. candida slithering up the dogwood and out over scarlet azalea 'Miss Susie.' In a change of mood, high in a 10' photinia shrub, discreetly displayed are the deep pink flowers of C. montana rubens. Native cross vine threading a nearby arbor ends its season's persimmon colored trumpets.

As the days pass, azalea and rhododendron displays grow more beautiful. 'Anna Kehr' and Kehr's 'White Rosebud' are followed quickly by fragrant pink camellia-type blooms of 'Mary Lou Kehr' and finally by Dr. Kehr's red 'Great Expectations.' 'Helen Curtis,' blanketed in semi-double, frilly white blooms provides competition. To be admired now also is a deciduous azalea, Lewis Shortt's discovery, lovely 'Chattahoochee Dawn.' Rising temperatures put a quick end to other native azalea blooms. Mayapples bloom briefly the second week of April.

To my delight, rhododendrons planted long ago that hadn't flowered at all or in recent years are blooming. There are crimson clusters adorning 'Halfden Lem' and yellowish flowers decorating 'Champagne.' Flowers on 'Elizabeth Poore' remind me of a lavender pink souffle dribbled with mint sauce. Faithfully, every year when deep purple clusters enhance 'Anah Kruschke' and 'A. Bedford,' rose pink ones embellish 'Normandy' nearby. Making their debut in my garden, blooms looking like scoops of strawberry ice cream festooned with butterscotch sauce dollops open on 'Bass River.' Under my workroom windows, deep pink buds expand to apricot yellow bundles on twin bushes of 3' R. 'Percy Wiseman.' Suddenly, all the tall rhododendrons (R. 'Catawbiense Boursault') dispersed around my rear garden are shrouded in lavender spheres. The springs of 1995 and 1996 will be remembered for their outstanding rhododendrons.

Late April 1996, my camera records that day's best in blooms: fragrant 'Angel' roses behind the mailbox and deep crimson Knautia macedonica that is obviously content in slightly limed soil in the front garden. The bletilla orchids, purple ones in the blue garden and white ones in the white garden, bloom well again. There is a wonderful exhibit of evergreen azaleas. 'Maria Derby,' in spite of blooming heavily in fall, is covered with scarlet red hose-in-hose flowers. Nearby Robin Hill 'Betty Ann Voss' reveals lovely double pink flowers. Too late for the holiday this year the azalea 'Easter Parade' is nonetheless breathtaking. The year's unusually warm temperatures and drought, followed by monsoons and blackberry winter, did not undermine a strong and beautiful flowering for April.

The month of May can arrive in my garden like a plunge off a diving board directly into summer weather, or it can drop in gingerly, tiptoeing slowly into rising temperatures and humidity. Early May, however, always launches late-spring flowering. Even better than promised is the little golden reblooming *Hemerocallis* 'Stella de Oro,' which in early May begins displays in local gardens. Located on my property on the north slope of a steep hill, scattered clumps in my sunny areas do not bloom until mid-month. Supplemented with water during dry periods, 'Stella' performs sporadically until heavy frost.

Early May is the usual blooming time for late-flowering rhodies. I am fond of the pale purple blooms of 'Madrid,' but the rhododendron that dominates the entire garden from 10' in the sky is 'Caroline.' Its abundant flowers have thrown a pale, lavender pink haze over the area every spring at this time for 20 years. Not until May 15 do I notice the firehouse red blooms on R. 'Wild Affair' have ignited. A season extender, plain pink 'Maxecat' blooms in latest May.

Between May 15 and 20, herbaceous perennials, annuals, and bulbs make real impact. Underneath the clematis-covered carport wall, the violet biennial dame's rocket *(Hesperis matronalis)* continues to sparkle in the late afternoon sun, while the blue fan-shaped flowers of *Scaevola* 'Blue Wonder' scramble about at its feet. Both will be as strong here in hot, humid summer temperatures as they are now in May. The new *Allium* 'Globemaster' has an enormous blue ball on a tall sturdy stem. Now in full bloom, it's astonishing. 'Globemaster,' an expensive bulb, is a garden focal point for over a month! Also in the corner is tender, newly installed Mexican bush sage *(Salvia leucantha)* greenhouse-forced into premature flowering. It will rebloom at its normal time, late fall.

Each year, the rim of the mailbox garden is planted with pink and blue petunias segregated by Swan River daisies. In 1996, I discovered the veined, cascading, heat-resistant *Petunia* 'Surfinia.' This South American native traveled a serpentine route to England, then to California, and at last it arrived here. It is great combined with the 'Purple Wave' petunias. Across the driveway, where sun touches its branches, lightly fragrant, white fuzzy blooms decorate Virginia sweetspire *(Itea)*. Pumpkin gerberas and gazanias skirt the orange butterfly weed. Red gerberas here accentuate the crimson color in the nearby snapdragons, while yellow gazanias and wallflowers emphasize the saffron hue in the same snapdragon flowers. At this time in May, forced blue delphiniums, planted in early spring for background contrast, begin to perform. Although a dainty flower, blue knautia buttons reinforce the delphiniums' color. The large, violet blue spheres of *Allium* 'Giganteum,' now over 2' high, provide their own spectacular backdrop for hot pink *Salvia greggii* and *Penstemon* 'Garnet.'

Sprawling on the ground are splendid evergreen, low-growing campanulas, *C. poscharskyana* with pale blue stars and later-blooming *C. portenschlagiana* 'Resholt' with violet bells. These are the only campanulas that consistently return each spring in my garden. *Iris* 'Blue Skies' blooms reliably with them as do two kalmias, 'Elf,' a compact plant that envelops itself in light pink buds that open to transform the bush into a white cloud, and 'Nipmuck' with intense crimson buds exploding into soft pink blooms. Both these hybrid mountain laurels proved their value by surviving the summer heat and drought of 1993 that killed most kalmias in Atlanta gardens.

An early May feature in the white garden is a special vine, *Solanum jasminoides*, that overlays many of the shrubs. This white potato vine blooms by May 1 (much earlier in 1995) and does not cease bearing pendant clusters of white, star-shaped flowers until severe frost. Following January 1994 freezing temperatures, it died back to the ground for the first time. I was about to count it out when it revived in mid-May, furiously growing and flowering. Spring of 1996 was more cruel—no resurrection that time.

On May 15, Confederate jasmine decorates the side fence's wooden slats with scattered 1", five- petaled, fragrant white blooms. Most Mays, the vine's flowers engulf me in their perfume as I pass. (Blooms continue sporadically through the summer.) I missed that pleasure in 1996, when its flowers froze. In 1993, in front of a fence post, I would have found *Kalmia* 'Ostbo Red' peppered with deep red buds, fully living up to its reputation as a great beauty. That mountain laurel was the undisputed star of the May garden tour. Unfortunately, this was its last hurrah! It succumbed that autumn, a victim of disease abetted by high summer temperatures and drought. No one can predict the consequences of Atlanta's weather. That is why I grow a variety of plants. Only then will something always be blooming in the garden.

My *Ornithogalum thyrsoides* (chincherinchee in the florist industry) are in flower. Their legendary shelf life makes them much prized as cut flowers. Allan Armitage writes that chincherinchee is an onomatopoeic word that describes the sound of south winds as they blow through these flowers in Cape Province, South Africa hedgerows. In my Atlanta garden, I hear only airplanes, but these pure white flowers with brown centers are delightful.

As I stroll through my garden after mid-May, I stoop to study the dramatic orange Asiatic lilies on 3' stems. Yellow versions follow quickly. In late May, along the side fence a charming wildflower, transplanted years ago from the open woods behind my property line, begins to bloom. These Indian pinks (*Spigelia marilandica*), with flowers looking like yellow stars pasted atop red tubes, have recently been discovered by Wayside Gardens. Fortunately, they multiplied everywhere in my garden.

An onion made its debut in my 1994 May garden. Imported from an English bulb specialist (though it is listed in U.S. mail-order catalogs now) amethyst-colored *Allium albopilosum* (*A. christophii*) has huge heads of star-shaped flowers. This bulb was selected for my shrub border after my husband saw it in an Irish garden that we visited and declared it to be his favorite. Across the lawn, dwarf *Lavandula angustifolia* 'Martha Roderick,' the second lavender variety I find that will persist through summer heat and humidity if planted with excellent drainage, blooms beautifully in May. The cool wet spring seems to have encouraged as well a neighboring coral bells, *Heuchera* 'Bressingham Hybrids,' to produce masses of slender panicles of red flowers. How can I explain the copper red blooms that suddenly, after so many years, appeared on my *Iris fulva*? This iris, a Georgia swamp native, may have found something familiar about Atlanta's recent weather.

Suddenly, in the final days of May, spring gives way to summer.

My Atlanta Garden in Summer

In earliest June the summer sun and humidity have not yet seared the garden's riches. The daylilies are in full bloom, colors vibrant. These new, large-flowered, tetraploid (extra chromosomes) hemerocallis with their heavier substance, more intense colors, and sturdier stems dominate. June is also the month that the silver lace vine blooms and begins its quest to conquer every shrub near the backyard arbor. Its aggression persists unchecked until frost.

Along the path to the backyard, my stokesia's first blooms are showing. Nearby pink callas, many seasons in this garden, unfurl their lovely pink waxen spathes from arrow-shaped foliage to bloom with purple pink and white echinaceas. (There were no pink spathes in 1996.) Traffic-light yellow shines from the cushion mums 'Yellow Grandchild,' which if unpinched bloom all summer by the mid-driveway. Several *Hydrangea macrophylla* in distinct hues of blue to deepest purple begin their display now, lasting through July. Their color comes from the amount of aluminum ions the plant absorbs from the soil, determined by the soil acidity. I can turn the flowers pink for the following seasons by adding lime, but I prefer blue shades.

The overpowering perfume in the garden now originates with blooms on the tall, hardy gardenia bushes beneath the bedroom windows. Along paths in partial shade are the giant stalks of Turk's cap lily (*Lilium superbum*). These are super-sensitive bulbs, prone to rot. Success comes only with perfect drainage. Dutch iris planted in pansy beds are now in bloom, but I know I cannot count on them for more than two or three years.

Late May flowers continue blooming, including white *Phlox* 'Miss Lingard,' and some lavender blue plants: *Adenophora* (ladybells), larkspur, annual lobelia, cleome, Chinese foxglove, forget-me-not, both bearded and Japanese iris, and the mysterious purple hyacinth bean vine. I find more blooms on 'Stella de Oro,' red gerbera daisies, *Lythrum* 'Morden's Pink,' and *Coreopsis* 'Sunray.' 'Lady Bountiful,' an old hybrid, spider-form daylily, has already completed this season's blooming. Between June 6 and 8, the butterfly weed (*Asclepias tuberosa*) introduces more orange flower heads high above a peacock blue *Ceratostigma plumbaginoides* carpet. This delightful summer groundcover blooms into autumn when its foliage is transformed by brilliant color. It's an outstanding perennial and deserves more attention.

At the edge of my wooded area, *Hosta* 'Golden Tiara,' which is low-growing with small, light green, heart-shaped leaves edged in gold, sends up attractive lavender flowers. Small white flowers in arched clusters sit on tall, swaying stems above gooseneck loosestrife (*Lysimachia clethroides*). Although attractive in bloom, this plant clones itself aggressively through the white garden. It definitely belongs in an undeveloped area.

Before mid-June, five 7' tall yellow *Lilium* 'Golden Splendour' assume the role of sentinels over remaining daylilies and everything else. Far below, native cerise-flowered *Callirhoe involucrata* shocks the eye. Friends who grow the ornamental grass *Miscanthus sinensis* report reddish tinged flower plumes then, too. The beautiful villain in my garden border, the sprawling shrub *Lavatera* 'Barnsley,' has overpowered its neighbors. With pink and white flowers on separate branches, it is certainly every bit as pretty as the one I fell in love with one summer in the garden of a B & B attached to a 16th century oasthouse (hops drying silo) in Kent, England.

About June 23, along the driveway *Rudbeckia fulgida* 'Goldsturm' begins its long season of razzle-dazzle. Now also is the time for annuals like golden yellow melampodium and golden orange *Zinnia linearis* to come on stage. Out in the front garden, *Sisyrinchium* 'Quaint and Queer' has 3/4" tan flowers escaping from iris-like stalks that protrude from a small, gray green foliage clump. An adjacent daylily 'Moon Traveler,' Saul Nursery's new introduction, also flowers. This plant has the good points of 'Stella de Oro,' but its true yellow color makes its easier to use in most gardens.

The jewel-like, summer- flowering *Tricyrtis formosana* var. *amethystina* is exquisite; the blue shines like a sapphire. However, it cannot tolerate winter wetness and must be moved into the designated dry area of my greenhouse. In the rock garden, I discover that 'Baby Moon,' the last daffodil on my property to perform, is now in flower. Blooming since June 10, red and green spotted alstroemerias (the Peruvian lily, a popular cut flower) are now commanding clumps of brilliant parrot feathers in front of the Japanese snowbell (*Styrax japonicus*). Blue knautia now looks so pretty with dwarf yellow perennial wallflower. In recent years, crimson *K. macedonica* has performed even better. It's not widely known that penstemons and knautias do well in Atlanta gardens. These plants need better press. Tall, rose violet *Verbena bonariensis*, beneath the snowbell tree, is imposing. Nearby Satsuki azaleas are still flowering. If the previous winter was not too severe and the heavy pine straw cover adequate, the month closes with *Crinum* 'Milk and Wine' flowers.

July in an Atlanta garden is hot and gets hotter. Local gardeners usually find the first pink, angel-wing blossoms on hardy *Begonia grandis* by July 1. Also in flower then are golden *Patrinia* and purple coneflowers. My records begin July 4 with the woody vine, *Campsis* 'Madame Galen,' blooming since late June, looking radiant displayed up against the front deck walls beneath the unfurled American flag. Sheltered now from hot sun by maple leaves, fibrous begonias, some red and others white, prosper in pots that earlier held pansies. Replacing pansies, blue ageratum and yellow marigolds interplay to mark the straw island's limits. July 4's spectacular sight is always my thicket of firecracker red *Crocosmia* 'Lucifer.'

Verbena bonariensis
Linda Fraser

On the back deck I reflect upon the shading tulip poplar that has watched for easily 100 years over all my land. A red-headed woodpecker flies to its limbs and the sound of rat-tat-tat breaks the delicious silence. Encouraged, wind chimes stir. A late daylily, *Hemerocallis* 'Chicago Ruby Red' seems abandoned in the front garden. On July 5, I document sideyard daylilies that have bloomed well since June 15: 'Golden Prize,' 'Art Exhibit,' 'Joan Senior,' 'Chicago Candy Cane,' and 'Chicago Firecracker.'

The fragrant, pink spires of clethra will soon be visible to me and the bees, with whom I care not to tangle. *Phlox* 'Miss Lingard' naps now, but secondary blooming will resume soon. Many of the flowers of June have become the flowers of July. Pink boltonia, *Lythrum* 'Morden's Pink,' and Tennessee coneflower are prevalent. 'Hello Yellow,' a dwarf *Belamcanda flabellata*, can be seen from across the garden. By early July in years past, the garden phloxes in the front bed that should dominate this month's garden were already diseased. A good spraying program under Jim Harrington's control has achieved this outstanding parade of garden phloxes in shades and hues of pink to purple.

The double balloon flower (*Platycodon grandiflorus* 'Double Blue') takes center stage in my front sun gardens after mid-June and through July. Some replace the spring daffodils guarding the cement sculpture. Lavender blooms surround the stems of weedy, wild petunias (*Ruellia carolinensis*), a found treasure abundant naturally in my front garden. Old-fashioned, orange double daylilies are in bloom as well as LeGro Gardens' *Hemerocallis* 'Sonata Pink,' and Ray Stevens's scrumptious 'Sex Symbol.' Six garden phlox plants are flowering heavily and present a progression of deeper colors from right to left across the front garden. The deepest purple one at the far end collides with the foliage of the Japanese maple (*Acer palmatum* 'Crimson Queen') and the combination is stunning. 'Harrington's Pink,' a terrific aster that blooms now until late autumn, is sensational. Along the fence, dwarf *Spirea* 'Little Princess' appears to have pink cobwebs enmeshed in its thin branches. The narrow bed's mood changes as I move on to where a series of *Heliopsis* 'Orange Sunflower' bloom. Beneath, splashes of bright yellow *Lysimachia* 'Eco Dark Satin' lap at their feet like waves washing a beach.

In front of the house, *Buddleia* 'Black Knight' with darkest purple flower racemes lounges against the carport bricks. Fuchsia-tinted gladiolus blend with this purple wall. Nearby, eerie pineapple lilies (*Eucomis comosa*) flower in the front straw area. Once too bizarre for my taste, I have developed a liking for them. After mid-month, exotic looking hardy hibiscus—hybrids in all possible versions of 'Disco Belle' and 'Southern Belle'—bloom, each with dinner-plate-sized flowers that last but a day. Yellow foxgloves hide behind gossamer fashioned by gaura's wiry wands of pink and white butterflies. The incomplete veiling adds an ethereal quality to the entire planting. In wetter areas, a multi-hued collection of impatiens have volunteered each of the last 10 years to either complement or contrast with every flower color in that garden bed.

As July closes out, pink rain lilies flower and the lovely pink magic lilies (*Lycoris squamigera*) emerge to bloom after being "no shows" for several years. (I read that these bulbs need a longer dormancy period than our winters provide so I now follow a Houston grower's suggestion to plant them deeper.) *Caryopteris* 'Blue Mist' adds a pleasant shade of powder blue. The numerous graceful, rose crimson blooms on *Lilium* 'Uchida' are spectacular when the sunlight settles on them late in the afternoon. Alongside, black-eyed Susan (*Rudbeckia fulgida* 'Goldsturm') is in peak bloom now, dazzling me with deep yellow explosions from black centers.

The attractive foliage of the Brazilian plume (*Justicia carnea*) is giving just a hint of hot pink bracts to come. In damp areas along the property line, red cardinal flowers bloom over orange red impatiens. I know these lobelias are in bloom before I even see blossoms because always, almost out of nowhere, hummingbirds congregate over them. Offbeat, but gorgeous, dense heads of red violet flowers on 3' stalks hover over the weird biennial *Angelica gigas* by the fence. (Its foliage died back later, and it did not self-sow as I had hoped.) The last stars in my July stage show are lavender blue shoo-fly plant (*Nicandra*, a Peruvian annual that reliably reseeds), midnight blue *Salvia x* 'Indigo Spires,' *Phygelius aequalis* (a cape fuchsia with golden yellow tubular flowers on 3' stems), and in filtered sun, Japanese *Kirengeshoma* with yellow 1-1/2" bells. Buds on the *Kirengeshoma* plant, described in catalogs as a "rarity with wonderful palm-like foliage geared for the connoisseur," aborted in 1993 because of serious drought. This plant must have moisture.

In the white garden, 'Casa Blanca' lilies have been blooming since July 20. They are large and lovely, with as many as eight blooms on 3' stalks even in partial sun. In front sun areas in 1996, just before mid-month, White Flower Farm's outstandingly fragrant *Lilium auratum* 'Gold Band' took command of the garden. Juxtapositioned with 'Casa Blanca' in an area where the sun shines briefly each day, *Hosta* 'Royal Standard,' with large, fragrant white flowers above the foliage, enhances this garden. There is a pleasant combination of contrasting flower forms and foliage—lacy *Calamintha neptoides*, a variegated *Tulbaghia violacea*, and newly acquired *Chrysanthemum* 'Becky,' the best, long blooming daisy I've seen here. As a counterpoint in color, a steely blue globe thistle (*Echinops*) lends strength to the white garden for weeks.

By the middle weeks in a dry July like 1993, I sense the damage of heat and drought. On the mailbox, blue morning glory blooms no longer open fully and the vine is woody and parched. The blue native passion flowers cease. *Rudbeckia* 'Goldsturm' blooms seem always thirsty. Colorless borders outline the glorious summer leaves of the Japanese maple 'Crimson Queen.' Only the hibiscus, planted last summer, are inspired to skirmish with each other for room to stretch in the blazing sun.

About this time I realize what a remarkable find my *Cypella plumbea* is. Ignoring the drought, a succession of box-shaped flowers on abbreviated stems, very much like those of *Tigridia*, bloom in sequence with only brief intermissions until early October. Their unusual flowers remind me of square teacups in ultra-contemporary Rosenthal china patterns. This summer iris should be more popular.

Through the month, scruffy white powder puffs grace hollyhocks high over the silver leafed groundcover *Lamium* 'White Nancy' in the white garden. Jet black cups stand out from another hollyhock, 'Nigra,' in a front yard sunny spot. Dwarf spiraea and 'Red Heart' rose-of-Sharon meet to romp together by the fence. In very wet and cool summers, after mid-month, the exceptional, long-blooming native azalea *R. prunifolium x R. arborescens* is cloaked in immense pink coral blossoms that demand an audience. So do the large yellow blooms of *Crocosmia* 'Jenny Bloom' below.

Climbing the fences in semi-shaded north facing areas, I have *Dicentra scandens*. I first saw this bright yellow bleeding heart vine in Ireland decorating the back wall in the garden of designer Helen Dillon. I recreated that scene with those yellow bleeding hearts in my own garden.

In August, the sunlight filtering through dogwood branches reaches the sweet autumn clematis which forms a white shroud over shrubs and bricks as well as fence. A generous clump of hardy, rose pink *Cyclamen hederifolium* flowers suddenly stand up naked from an oval, brown rock-like bed below. Since late July, lavender buddleia, tangled silver lace vine (*Polygonum aubertii*), and gold flame honeysuckle (*Lonicera x heckrottii*) vie for space on an arbor and surrounding plants. *Zinnia linearis* and yellow Dahlberg daisies are happy

companions beneath azaleas and rhododendrons where the rays from the summer sun, now low in the sky, just reach their hiding places. The fragrance of lightly perfumed soap coming from the Dahlberg daisies is carried in the wind.

August brings the continuation or secondary blooming of earlier summer flowers. Tall garden *Phlox paniculata* persists. New pink varieties of cardinal flowers are the month's offering. *Begonia grandis* is almost smothered now with small translucent pink purses. It underscores *Gaura lindheimeri's* swarming butterflies, a colony moved now only by a warm wind.

Azaleas this late in the summer? Yes, definitely! Blooming nonchalantly, the offspring of *R. prunifolium* and *R. arborescens* refuses to cease flaunting its beauty in my lower front garden. Later, beneath the suspended bamboo screen, orangey red *R. prunifolium* blossoms loom from behind low hydrangea bushes on the shaded side of the back deck. Often by August 7, I find the tall, fragrant *Lilium philippinense* with funnel-form, horizontal flowers in bloom in my white garden. This bulb is not tolerant of drought and in dry times the flowers are of poor quality and open incompletely. The next week, I find the delicate pink flower heads of lovely *Thalictrum actaefolium* mixing with blue *Lobelia siphilitica* in the wildflower woodland setting.

Summer in my garden traditionally ends with the close of August. *Physostegia virginiana*, the knave of the late summer garden is in peak pink bloom. This obedient plant's spike-like flower heads—white or lavender pink—are visible in too many places, mostly where I do not want them. 'Autumn Joy' sedums dressed in plum pink are a perfect match with the pink turtleheads (*Chelone lyonii*) in the ravine across the driveway. At the rim above, *Phlox* 'Miss Lingard' and the blue mist shrub behind are blooming again. Patrinia's wispy clusters cover the green pieris with thin gold foil. *Anemone* 'Pamina,' named for the opera heroine, opens pink flowers. Yellow *Rudbeckia* 'Goldsturm' is still the August garden's glowing beacon above blue *Ceratostigma plumbaginoides*. Above them all, my crape myrtle reigns as undisputed August monarch.

In the blue garden, *Cypella plumbea*, like the magician who produces an endless number of handkerchiefs from his sleeve, fashions an incessant string of blue flowers. In 1996, newly planted in the back garden, *C. herbertii* opened golden orange copies of *C. plumbea*. Revived by cooler nights, snapdragons reblooom. Hot pink *Salvia greggii* growing in sandy soil flowers furiously.

In the shrub border, I note the serendipity of the variegated leaves of shrub dogwood (*Cornus serica* 'Silver & Gold') with that of the *Buddleia* 'Harlequin,' still heavy with midnight blue flowers. *Arum italicum's* torch of orange berries continues to light up the woodland below the back deck. In the lower yard in a usually moist area, striking red blooms appear on my tall, hardy swamp hibiscus (*H. coccineus*). Even drought never dampens its performance.

In 1994, also in late August, there were magnificent reddish, spidery flowers of *Lycoris radiata*, arising suddenly and naked from the ground. In spite of a January freeze, this bulb has never bloomed so well. As if it could read the calendar, the trumpet vine that ensnared the front deck ceases blooming. The focus shifts to the black-eyed Susan vine (*Thunbergia alata*) now hidden by orange blossoms that will continue until frost. The elegant loblolly bay (*Gordonia lasianthus*) reveals 2" white cups with yellow stamens between its shiny evergreen leaves. By this point in the season, the hyacinth bean vine (*Dolichos lablab*) has deeply penetrated *Magnolia* 'Elizabeth,' leaving it enmeshed in purple mist.

Salvia 'Van Houttii'
Linda Fraser '96

In 1993, two obscure bulbs that I planted that spring back by the rock garden in light shade suddenly surprised me with blooms in August. *Scilla scilloides*, supposedly an autumn bloomer produced a showy spike of bluish pink flowers mid-month on the last 6" of a 20" stem. *Scilla autumnalis* bloomed later that month, opening lilac flowers in interrupted bands along 8" thin stalks. (In wet 1996, both bloomed in mid-July.) The bottle-shaped flowers on the closed gentians (*G. andrewsii*) now turn vivid blue purple. During the final days of August, my garden's treasures include a sprawling lavender pink *Sedum* 'Brilliant,' more colorful at this moment than *Sedum* 'Autumn Joy.' I discover annuals at their best now—yellow four o'clocks and knockout red *Salvia* 'Van Houttii.' I am still not sold on this salvia; it requires a lot of foliage to support its flowers.

Dry, hot Augusts result in plants blooming later, for shorter periods, and the flowers are often not at their best. Whether there is drought or monsoon, summer comes to a close; however, there is no lull in the garden.

My Atlanta Garden in Autumn

My garden in autumn has hues of blue and purple pinks with only an occasional yellow-flowered plant serving as a foil. There are also white flowers to referee infrequent chromatic conflicts. September days introduce more tall

spikes of *Physostegia virginiana* to areas where purple coneflowers and rud-
beckias have been blooming through hot, humid summer days. A Tennessee
coneflower clump of pretty, pink purple wildflowers outlasts its cousin coneflowers that continuously bloom through October. This nursery propagated
plant on the endangered species list differs from other echinacea. Its flower is
held horizontal and has a greenish pink disc. Unusually early blooms on the
pink sasanquas, double-flowered 'Cotton Candy' and single-flowered
'Cleopatra,' launch a sensational season of heavy flowering. Close by, late-last-
ing *Sedum* 'Indian Chief,' with its giant carmine pink flowers, and autumn
aster, salvia, and anemone introduce a smoky hue to the scene and make the
yellows of the rudbeckia and helianthus all the brighter. Early autumn pro-
longs late summer in an Atlanta garden.

On a quick turn through my early September garden, I find much activity
in the narrow strip lining the redwood fence that separates a neighbor's terri-
tory from the cement stepping stones leading to my backyard. The 4'
Rudbeckia triloba remains the undisputed star performer here every year. This
biennial reseeds to produce magnificent clumps like lanterns that mark the
passageway from the front to back yards. Early helianthus (perhaps *H.
augustifolius*, but classification of this group is confusing) with its own yellow
daisy flowers is blooming well here also. In 1992 I added to the fence area several clusters of long-blooming, heat tolerant *Heliopsis scabra* 'Summer Sun.' In
1996, these splendid 2-3' tall plants sport large bright yellow flowers still. The
adjacent butterfly bush adds blue violet pigment to the picture. A periwinkle
blue, tender plumbago that is used for mild vertical emphasis leans back on a
fence post. It is surrounded by a thicket of near-matching annual browallia.
The different blue hues give the illusion of space and distance, an advantage in
this narrow garden.

In a bed that I recently cut from a weak spot in the back lawn the Peruvian shoo-fly plant continues to challenge *Hemerocallis* 'Stella de Oro.' Nearby
I plant each year either *Salvia* 'Indigo Spires' or *S. guaranitica*. Their autumn

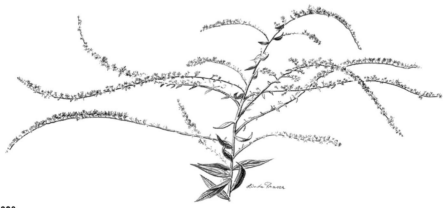

intense blues make them invaluable, even if they are not often hardy in my garden. Sadly, unlike *Nicandra*, they never reseed.

Alongside the lean-to greenhouse, old-fashioned, too-tall yellow goldenrod tumbles over giant bamboo supports. This creates a dramatic color contrast to the phlox remaining in bloom. In 1994, I pulled it all out and replaced it with a new dwarf variety that branches like a child's sparkler. Goldenrod has been exonerated as the allergy attack provoker, but unfortunately the prejudice remains.

Returning to the front yard, I notice the cool lavender flowers of *Verbena x hybrida* 'Abbeville,' a Goodness Grows introduction still serving as an attractive groundcover below the changing foliage of a small 'Crimson Queen' Japanese maple growing by the driveway. In the front straw area, my crape myrtle remains in full bloom, later than early bloomers in the neighborhood.

The first week in September 1993, unusual flowers appeared in the small garden fronting the azalea circle. I planted just one bulb of *Lycoris albiflora* in 1992, but no flowers appeared that autumn. Now on nine naked stalks that rose from the ground quite suddenly, there are a multitude of thin, white-smudged-with-red flowers. (Apparently, this bulb was particularly pleased with the hot, dry summer; it has not returned in the wet years since.) About mid-month, they were joined by a lone *Lycoris radiata*. (Lycoris with evergreen foliage may be inhibited by severe cold temperatures from producing blooms the following autumn.)

In the wild area of the ravine below the driveway, where less refined plants are banished to be almost ignored until bloom time, are the blue-violet puffs of perennial ageratum *(Eupatorium coelestinum)* and the bright purple *Aster* 'Hella Lacy' that lasts to frost. They are a perfect backdrop for *Aster* 'Harrington's Pink' which has bloomed uninterrupted since midsummer. Chelone's short, rose purple flowers that somewhat resemble a turtle's head continue to play below the golden smoke enveloping the patrinia blooming here. They pinch hit for the buff pink plumes of another exile, the vigorously spreading macleaya that is at its best in midsummer.

During the second week of September, I notice that with cooler night temperatures in the upper 50s plants look fresher, even without recent rain. The moonflower vine *(Ipomoea alba)* which has been in bloom since August is now completely enveloped in large, fragrant white flowers that open in late afternoon, fresh each day. All morning glory vines in the garden have suddenly become alive with flowers. The 'Heavenly Blue' morning glory that I plant each year near the now invigorated sky blue bog salvia (*S. uliginosa*) is particularly stunning. The morning glory will be replaced in October by pink daisy mums in bloom, creating another pleasing combination. The tall summer

Ornithogalum saundersiae (star of good hope) is topped by continuous new clusters of creamy white flowers, each with its own dark green, pincushion eye. Pineapple lilies that remind me of corn cobs remain as if suspended in time. That same week in September 1994 marks the emergence of an early colchicum on a leafless stem, returning from the previous autumn. C. 'Violet Queen' with large, chalice-shaped, checkered fuchsia and white flowers is unexpected. Unlike the fall crocuses, colchicums are wrongly considered a one season bulb here.

In the shrub border, the semi-double pink blooms of the fall flowering cherry *(Prunus subhirtella* var. *autumnalis)* are following the calendar closely. Holdovers from the summer, annual *Salvia* 'Purple Fountain' and *Buddleia* 'Pink Charm' intensify the small tree's impact through early autumn. Three other plants continue to please. The white *Echinacea purpurea* is taller, sturdier-stemmed, and carries larger flowers than ever before. By the street, the coarse-looking Mexican flame vine's orange flowers blanket the prickly Chinese hollies. The bright color is reinforced by a small, orange red reseeded morning glory vine *(Ipomoea coccinea)* that climbs the nearby telephone pole.

Activity has not slowed in the garden plot I reserve specifically for blue/purple pink flowers. The Brazilian plume *(Justicia carnea)* appears to be decorated by lots of hot pink, thick glowing candles. Adjacent to it is a generous plant of Mexican bush sage *(Salvia leucantha)* whose long stems now for the second time this season hold tight, velvety violet purple fleece that is dabbed with white. In 1996, this plant was outstanding through November. *Salvia* 'Purple Majesty' blooms are more intense now and an adjacent lobelia is adorned in jolting dark lavender. Nearby is graceful, floriferous *Lespedeza thunbergii*, whose purple pink flowers cascading over azaleas give an outrageous splash of late color. There is also some sudden, strong reblooming of my favorite balloon flowers, *Platycodon grandiflorus* 'Double Blue.' *Caryopteris* 'Dark Knight' that was extraordinarily beautiful in 1996 completes this tiny garden now.

Several plants attract my attention as I walk through the garden. The white form of *Tricyrtis hirta* is in peak flowering. A compact *Aster* 'Raspink,' bought in flower as an annual filler, surprisingly returns pretty in bright pink every year. That 'sleeper' plant purchased locally, the charming mauve purple toad lily *(Tricyrtis formosana* var. *amethystina)*, expected to bloom only from May to July, is still going strong in mid-September. Its flowers look like designer-created jeweled pins.

Plants like the salvias, petunias, astermoea, and *Penstemon smallii* withstand autumn's light frosts and just keep performing. Atlanta's summer is delightfully long, yet the progression of autumn flowers continues. Ten days later my garden is different. Now after a mild, rainy summer, the fall anemones—clear pink *A.* 'September Charm' and rosy red double *A.* 'Bressingham Glow'—are the early autumn performers in part shade along the far side of a narrow footpath bordering the white garden. In that garden, *A.* 'Whirlwind' will wait until October to perform. These Japanese anemones ask little yet deliver selflessly.

In 1993, I noticed the first *Cyclamen hederifolium* on September 17. On September 23, in a shady corner of my rock garden, early autumn snowflake (*Leucojum autumnale*) developed tiny pink-tinged white pendant bells. That same day a variegated version of *Tricyrtis hirta* opened its first purple-spotted flowers. In 1994 a seedling from this plant unlocked a sunny yellow lightly spotted and upward facing bloom.

In many years, true autumn arrives suddenly like a recoil of a gun on a chilly morning early in October. The October form of tall-stemmed *Helianthus angustifolius* or *H. simulans* (from Niche Gardens), which are our native swamp sunflowers with 3" yellow daisy flowers, joins the now 7' stately blue flowered *Aster tataricus* from Siberia to oversee autumn in the garden. Yellow dwarf dahlias worship at the asters' feet. Reliably every year, there are never-fail cushion chrysanthemums in all the shades of autumn. Next to sprawling clumps of indestructible pink daisy mums, short red 'Rosevere' cannas bloom. Together they replicate Monet's favorite monochromatic color scheme.

At the other side of my driveway, the sasanquas are solid pink from flowers that will be carried through to November. To emphasize these shades, I have planted near them the pink sedums 'Vera Jameson,' 'Brilliant,' and 'Indian Chief,' but only 'Autumn Joy' maintains good posture. Below, repeating the colors of the carport wall, the ajuga's rich purple pigments are rejuvenated by cooler temperatures. In the same area fall blooming, floppy *Crocus speciosus* forms small pools of blue, which is even bluer at a distance due to deeper veining in the flower. Its bright orange stigmas are a smashing contrast. As a color companion for these orange stigmas, chrysogonum's small golden flowers reappear for the year's final blooming.

Back under the Southern magnolia and almost to the fence, I discover orchid-like flowers liberally speckled with dark purple against a lighter background. They are growing at the terminal end of a stem of *Tricyrtis formosana* var. *stolonifera*. It is a late, long-lasting little gem for shady, cool spots with moisture retentive soils. Another unusual tricyrtis, *T. macranthopsis*, flowers huge, drooping yellow bells this month beneath my workroom window. It will not tolerate sun.

The beauty of the composition that certain flowers form when grown together in early October bears telling. In the back garden that swamp sunflower slowly opens its golden daisies that, because the plant was not cut back by 1/3 in early summer, now reach roof-top level. This plant could easily be the model for Jack's beanstalk. Covering its shins is 'Ryan's Pink' chrysanthemum, while huge, ruffled white double angel trumpets hang down behind the sunflower's knees. On the back deck, the potted mandevilla vine has scampered midway up the tall hemlock devouring the shrub's branches with its huge pink flowers. An annual red passionflower vine chooses to hang its vividly colored, exotic blooms above the front garden. To calm the scene, the final shasta-like daisy, my Nippon daisy by the carport wall, exposes 3" flowers to sunlight.

Always at the carport during October, the display of large violet chalices on leafless stems that were planted in late summer is singular. There is *Colchicum* 'The Giant' (aptly named), free flowering rosy purple *C. cilicicum purpureum*, and my favorite *C.* 'Waterlily,' which looks like it belongs floating in a pond. To enhance the picture, a huge clump of *Cyclamen hederifolium* is a sea of reddish pink under nearby *Rhododendron* 'Van Nes Sensation.' Adding the proper ambience, the 'Angel' rose by the street continues to permeate the air with its own sweet fragrance. On October's first weekend in 1994, I saw the first blooms on my yellow crocus, *Sternbergia lutea*. Ten days later there were blooms on those planted in the driveway entrance planting. This was my first success with this bulb, but it has rebloomed in my garden every year since just as it does in my friend Lewis Shortt's garden. In 1996, thoroughly off course, these bulbs bloomed on August 31.

Mid-October, fragrant *Crocus goulomyi*, which is not as top-heavy as the earlier *C. speciosus* and has shorter, sturdier stems, begins its peak blooming. This crocus will continue into November, creating in several areas of the garden, a show of intense blue star shapes against the ground. (In 1996 the show of fall crocus, including diminutive, pale lilac *Crocus zonatus*, in my garden was sensational!) On October 23 I find the first bluish blooms of the winter iris (*Iris unguicularis*) tucked into the plant's foliage. Afterwards, every few days, there would be a fresh flower to enjoy. It is said that if the flowers are cut while still in bud and brought into a warm room wafts of a fabulous perfume fill the air. (Severe temperatures in recent years have destroyed this iris.)

Sasanqua 'Yuletide' is in full bloom just before Halloween and continues until New Year's. This had been true every year, but in 1993, *C. s.* 'Yuletide' did not open its first bloom until mid-November. However, in 1994, closer to schedule, this sasanqua began flowering early in October, continued blooming heavily late that month and on into November, but passed its peak before Christmas. This shrub typifies the variability of plant blooming times in Atlanta.

In Octobers and Novembers, I record outstanding fall foliage and berry exhibits. These include the bright yellow foliage on the coral bark Japanese

Aster carolinianus
Linda Fraser '96

maple and the balloon flowers, plus the Chinese eggplant-violet berries outlining *Callicarpa dichotoma* stems. Across the garden two Japanese maples, both *Acer palmatum dissectum* 'Crimson Queen,' are electrifying in their scarlet garb. The combination of the smaller one and the 'Yellow Grandchild' mums is breathtaking. Off the back deck, another Japanese maple, an unnamed seedling, has donned a firehouse red cloak now, making it look as if the setting sun is resting just there in my garden. Dogwood leaves are also brilliant red in early November. From my bedroom window, I enjoy the bronze orange needles of my dawn redwood spilling over the glossy, dark green leaves of the adjacent Southern magnolia. Some years, climatic conditions can predispose muted autumn colors, almost an absence of the usual show.

Those pansy displays planted in late October to outline the resting flower beds now add needed color. In November 1996, Mexican sage flowers, ladybells, *Penstemon smallii*, Daffodil Mart's creamy white late fall crocus (*C. ochroleucus*), and We-Du's rare native clambering *Aster carolinianus* with flowers that twist like pinwheels continue to brighten dark corners through December. My heather (*Calluna vulgaris* 'Robert Chapman') is wearing its rich, bronze winter outerwear. Throughout the garden, almost as pleasing to me as the flowers to come, are the fat, pregnant buds in hues of straw, beechnut, and red on my rhododendrons. Walking to the rock garden I am wowed by the brilliant blue *Crocus goulimyi* colony. It is resolute in a setting now devoid of any flowering plant.

Late November is the time to winterize my garden displays. Jim and I put in the winter arrangement of pink purple flowering cabbages, more pansies in imperial pink shades, and red mustard. All of these plants are color coordinated with the still-blooming purple wallflower there in the left driveway entrance. We place red mustards and pansies near the mailbox. The final autumn demonstration staged is in late November when the sugar maple's leaves complete their kaleidoscope of color changes to arrive at a warm, golden yellow. It is as if the tree has captured the sun within its branches. Then, all at once, every leaf falls to the ground and the earth is golden. Gusts of wind soon blow them away.

At Thanksgiving, after the feast is prepared and eaten and the washing up complete, I plant the last pansies, Dutch iris, and hyacinths. In late October, Jim and I had planted the bulk of the bulbs, some perennials, and shrubs to assure the following spring's beauty. I had clipped back the trumpet vine, (*Campsis* 'Mme. Galen') before the guests arrived. To encourage heavy flowering next summer, in late winter I must prune this campsis so severely that it looks mutilated.

After the holiday, there are always important tasks to complete. The first is the great fall cleanup. To prevent plant disease spread and to satisfy aesthetic requirements, all dead foliage and flowers must be cut, collected, and carried to the compost bin. I don't subscribe to dead foliage and stems as winter beauty. That is for Northern gardeners who delude themselves because they can't have the winter gardens that we enjoy. Next comes the raking of the leaves. Since our neighbors wait until all the leaves are off the trees before they begin raking, anything we do before then is wasted energy. Their leaves fill our clearings. We long ago substituted a leaf vacuum/mulcher, always just recently retrieved from the repair shop, for manual rakes. Ground-up leaves are excellent mulch or additions to the compost bin.

In late November and early December, Jim and I planted two new winter gardens that I had wanted for years. The first is a garden of containers on the small deck outside our informal dining area. It can be clearly seen from within the house. Covered by a roof overhang, most of the deck is in shade, limiting our plant choices for the pots. We arranged the containers, some ordinary, others distinctively odd-shaped--low and high ones, most round, but a few oblong--as one would organize cut flowers in a large vessel. Some entertaining sculpture is integrated, but the most important elements, of course, are the plants—red mustard, yellow pansy, and viola—where the sunlight comes. Elsewhere we place a giant aspidistra, a short, spreading cephalotaxus, several rohdea, *Ajugas* 'Burgundy Glow' and 'Bronze Beauty,' some pachysandra, liriope, parsley, golden sweet flag (*Acorus gramineus* 'Ogon'), and mondo grass (dwarf and black varieties), evergreen hardy ferns, helleborus, mahonia, and foam flowers. Some are dug from my few remaining untamed garden areas; others are purchased. The result brings me much pleasure. So does the garden that we shaped outside my writing room windows. There we used some of the same hardy plant varieties adding only a straight up, slightly taller version of *Cephalotaxus harringtonia*, the common lungwort *(Pulmonaria spp.)*, and smiling-faced blue pansies. These garden spaces provoke a relaxed but upbeat mood.

My Atlanta Garden in Winter

The chill of the Atlanta winter clears away embellishments and indelicately exposes the bones of my garden for examination. As I gather remaining leaves and dried perennial stems, I realize that these bones hold promises of rebirth. Swollen buds and the green foliage of early bulbs and perennials are previews of spring that waits impatiently.

Even before the solstice, winter comes with brief stretches of cold. Temperatures in the low 30s, occasionally the 20s, are paired with rapid returns to moderate 40s and 50s. That's why on one December 20, my yard is a mixed bag. The final autumn blooms stubbornly hang on through the cold that intrudes upon scenes of a Southern winter's own subtle beauty. There are red fibrous begonias in the hanging baskets above the back deck and some forlorn sweet alyssum in last spring's clay pottery. They remind me that in the right spot with the right cultural conditions plants are amazingly resilient.

Late one afternoon from my bedroom window, I watch the dark, lustrous green branches of an immense bull magnolia embrace the cinnamon colored trunk of my dawn redwood *(Metasequoia glyptostroboides)* above an understory of stilted, coarse *Mahonia bealei*. Those grape hollies' tousled golden tresses glisten in the fog. In my imagination the scene becomes a giant Rorschach ink blot. The wind reveals the tan velvet undersides of the glossy, green magnolia leaves that perfectly match the redwood bark. There is harmony as well as contrast within this view.

Most deciduous trees and bushes are bare now, naked limbs against the gray sky like driftwood on sand. I find the exception in the small fruit garden tucked deep into my backyard. Fiery orange-red blueberry leaves are reluctant to release their grip on the mother bushes. Color coordinated with this foliage is the season's attention grabber in my shrub border, the coral bark maple. This Japanese maple is valued for the striking red of its young twigs in winter.

As I stroll down the driveway, I see my December garden's brightest accent, the paper-flat scarlet blooms on the sasanqua 'Yuletide' espaliered to the brick below the kitchen windows. The yellow stamens stand out from the flowers and add a startling dimension to the shrub. However, in 1994, it is the adjoining camellias 'Professor C. S. Sargent'—undaunted by a few chilly nights—that now are at peak bloom. They are covered in red flowers like polka dots of bright crimson.

As if to compensate for a lack of winter flowers, colorful foliage on certain evergreen azaleas and small-leafed rhododendrons now pleases the eye. Across the lawn, 'Elsie Lee' is vivid orange red and *Rhododendron* 'Olga Mezitt' has turned a rosy mahogany. In the left front area, my giant 30-year-old Savannah holly is heavy with red berries that the birds have temporarily spared, reserved perhaps for harder winter days. A companion 7' Japanese pieris's rosette foliage is almost hidden by woven scarlet threads holding clusters of immature flower buds. The effect of the two plants side by side is striking.

Each time I walk to the street to check the mailbox during the colder months, I dawdle over the ornamental kales' intense colors in my entrance planting. Colors grow stronger with the cold. Because they are severely damaged by freezing, they are my cold temperature gauge.

It is a warm late autumn and early winter in 1994, but on Christmas Day I am amazed to see three small, fragrant blooms together on one stem of a miniature *Narcissus canaliculatus*. Each dainty flower of this tazetta daffodil has rounded white petals and a yellow cup. Across the driveway, there are yellow blooms on primulas. *Crocus sieberi* 'Firefly,' whose buds were lifeless gray, open to unexpected color. Their flowers are painted with rich lilac on a yellow base. In the shrub border, the buds on the winter-blooming Japanese apricot tree (*Prunus mume* 'Peggy Clark') have exploded into rose pink clouds. These replace the autumn-flowering cherry that has suspended its own show. Quaint French hollyhock *Alcea zebrinus* continues as a companion here. In the shade gardens, 'Wester Fliske' and other *Helleborus foetidus* have hung out awesome clusters of green bells rimmed in maroon that match the color of the French hollyhock.

On a warm late December morning after Christmas, the fragrance of winter honeysuckle invades the air as I pass this unruly shrub. They are insignificant cream blooms on an inelegant bush, but oh the perfume! I prune it harshly, but I can never bring myself to do away with it. There's a meager showing of early yellow blooms on nearby forsythia. The "advance team," I call them, indicating hopefully the eagerness of spring. *Arum italicum's* arrow-shaped leaves, darkest green with lighter mottling, continue to brighten the dark corners of my shade garden. Repeated freezing and thawing through the winter leaves this foliage unscathed. I was disappointed that I had never seen the guaranteed late summer show of spikes of bright orange red berries from these plants. In recent summers, there have been such glorious stalks.

The pansies, yellow ones paired with those in three tints of blue that were planted that autumn to edge some of the flower beds, will guide the garden from winter through spring into early summer. The varieties that I use bounce back after a freeze "meltdown" and stand up to June heat waves, too. Several *Crepis rubra* (cool weather annuals purchased at the Atlanta Botanical Garden Fall Sale) also color my winter garden. Winter honeysuckle perfume continues to follow me as I walk.

January is usually the true wintry month in my outdoor areas, though in recent years March competes dramatically. I am surprised by the behavior of the mauve-colored wallflower, *Erysimum* 'Bowles Mauve' that was planted early in the summer of 1993. It blooms through the worst of January's freezing temperatures and shows a further explosion of color as the cold months progress. When I choose a rare January sunny day to tour my garden, I discover the enchanting, carmine pink flowers of *Cyclamen coum* snug under rhododendron eaves and beneath naked dwarf Japanese maples. The cyclamen, performing from within their small wire cages just beneath the soil's surface, are secure at last from marauding critters.

In wooded areas, I spot the first flowers rising from the rough foliage of *Helleborus orientalis*. Their lavish flowers bloom during Atlanta's dreariest months. These nodding, open, cup-shaped flowers are painted intriguing hues of dappled palest pink, dusky purple, even emerald. One year, as spring was turning into summer, Pike's Nursery had a great sale on these plants. Their colors, after many months of splendid bloom, had faded. I watched as a customer refused the clerk's recommendation and backed away from a real bargain on winter's premier flowering plant for shade. (As gardeners learn, ignorance is never bliss.)

There is something spectacular in a neighbor's yard! *Jasminum nudiflorum* is making a bold display. Its trailing branches arise from a central crown like a fountain spraying waxy, bright yellow flowers. I am glad to have the view because this shrub is much too large for my small garden. In scale are my heaths, poised to burst into color.

Heaths and heathers are not supposed to do well here. I have found that although heathers are tricky, heaths are easy. They are worth trying several places in the garden, until just the right conditions, exposure and drainage in particular, are found. Then they become a no-care plant. *Erica carnea* 'Winter Beauty' and *E. c.* 'Springwood Pink' are two that have performed more than satisfactorily in my garden for over 10 years. *Erica x darleyensis* and *E. c.* 'Springwood White' are newer, but they also seem destined for a successful stay.

The first week in January 1994, temperatures fell to single digits without protective snow. Plant cell walls collapsed and the picture-postcard-perfect pansies, red mustard, and frilly flowering kales turned to brown muck. Only the wallflowers shivered against the cold and continued to bear half-closed blooms that cowered in the freezing wind. On January 12 *Amaryllis* 'Pasadena,' comfortable under layers of plastic covering in the greenhouse, opened huge double-red and white textured flowers atop a thick stalk. I grabbed the plant and ran with it into our house. I desperately needed it at my side.

Spring flowering can be affected by winter's unusual climatic events, but the impact is not always as anticipated and there are definite surprises. All of my earliest spring bulbs—the winter aconite, crocus, snowdrop, and iris—choose to stay under wraps until February. They are finally brought to life by temperatures of 70+ degrees on February 8 and 9.

Plants tend to play catch up. By mid-February the flowering shrubs *Hamamelis* 'Arnold Promise,' the winter honeysuckle, old favorite *Camellia japonica* 'Professor C. S. Sargent,' and all of my heaths are back on schedule and unusually floriferous. A mid-season camellia, 'Professor C. S. Sargent' is often zapped by cold weather. When that happens, its buds and flowers turn an awful brown. Since the frigid temperatures came early in the year when the buds were still tightly closed, this spring is outstanding for this camellia. Unusually warm climatic conditions late in 1994 will bring it to peak bloom again in December, providing holiday decorations for some Atlanta homes.

Whether through a mantle of snow or the more likely red brown background of muddy clay, the first cheerful yellow buttercup-like flowers on stiff green rosettes appear suddenly to announce spring. These winter aconites (*Eranthis hyemalis*) bloom in my sunny front beds and shady back garden nooks, and they breed like rabbits so that a few bulbs cover a bank quickly. Said to be difficult, they simply require soaking before planting and some lime. In 1993, a January 11 stroll leads me to the first winter aconite, flowers on heaths, and bulging purple *Daphne odora* buds. Those sparse early blooms on *Eranthis* look every bit like scouts sent by the spring blooming bulbs to test the climatic conditions. On that same day in another northeast Atlanta neighborhood, a bush of pink, old-fashioned roses was in full bloom. *Iris danfordiae* were flowering cheerfully at ABG. However, mine that are planted in a container were only green foliage with a hint of yellow showing and would not come into bloom until month's end.

Most years, mid-January is the usual time to hunt for early bulbs. From a pile of leaves I can uncover the yellow blooms of dwarf *Iris danfordiae*. I must replant new bulbs every year, but it is a small price to pay for even a brief sighting of this golden jewel. Along another backyard garden path I find a few single flowered white snowdrops. The earliest daffodils, 'February Gold' and 'Early Sensation,' are in bud in the front border. Along my woodland path, I discover intriguing flat, lime green flowers, each with a large core of golden stamens on *Helleborus sternii*. Nearby, a refreshing sight is that of the fragrant, pink flowers on *Viburnum x bodnantense* 'Dawn.' (There were no flowers on it in 1996.) I photograph my tall green frogmore sculpture holding its lantern and rising through a jumble of paperbush (*Edgeworthia papyrifera*) and oakleaf hydrangea (*Hydrangea quercifolia*) that are growing in heavy shade. The native hydrangea holds a few scraps of deep burgundy winter foliage, while the paperbush from China carries plump buds that appear momentarily ready to open to silky yellow flowers. The paperbush is splendid in dark corners and should be more popular in Atlanta.

By January 28 in every year but 1995 and 1996, there is a yellow shawl of winter aconite covering the brown mud in the lower southwest-facing flower bed. During these years, I find only a few aconites and snowdrops. In 1995, across the driveway, clumps of early lavender crocus with their very prominent orange stamens are scattered beneath the azaleas. Edging a small portion of the driveway, heads of 30-year-old creamy hyacinths are emerging from their stiff green shells. The fragrant deep magenta flowers of *Cyclamen coum* appear beneath *Rhododendron* 'Dexter's Cream'. My flowering quince can be in full bloom any time from November (1990) or December (1994) to after January (1993). This shrub is scorned for the harsh color that its flowers sometimes have. It is seen as an irritation in winter's decorating scheme. For me it is a beacon to light a bleak morning.

Every year, early February visits to the garden are loaded with the joy of discovery. They make me more aware of the beauty of the early-flowering, bare-limbed shrub *Hamamelis* 'Arnold Promise.' It is now overlaid with spidery, yellow inflorescences. Next, suddenly the understory of my garden is turned yellow by the blooming of 'February Gold' daffodils. On February 16, while walking back from the mailbox, I discover some 5" high, tiny, individual flowers of the palest blue, distinguishable only on close inspection. They are *Scilla tubergeniana* that are blooming two weeks later than they did in 1993. Flowers open just as they emerge from the ground. This bulb, with blooms larger than *S. sibirica*, had been in this garden nook since 1990, but it had never bloomed as strongly or for so long a period as during the springs from 1994 onward. On a February 23, my earliest-blooming species rhododendron (*R. mucronulatum* 'Mahogany Red') flowers. Rhododendrons prefer the protection of a snow blanket during frigid temperatures, so these blooms are a welcome sight.

Each day something new seems to come into bloom. The first hepaticas greet me February 3. (It was January 29 in 1995.) These flowers are white, but they are soon joined by pink, then blue ones on adjacent plants. Winter aconites reaching their peak bloom have become wide stretches of gold in the flower bed, creating a winning combination with the nearby purple-veined blue bunch crocuses. I see early greigii hybrid tulips in a neighbor's front yard. A warm day transforms my heaths into a mass of rosy urn-shaped blossoms.

As the month progresses, the various narcissus bulbs bloom in order. Fifteen days after 'February Gold,' my most reliable daffodil, 'Ice Follies,' flowers. After months of teasing, appearing poised each day to open momentarily, the pregnant, rosy buds of winter *Daphne odora* at last unveil perfect white stars. This plant does not deserve the reputation of being difficult to grow. Of all daphnes, 'Aureomarginata' is the easiest. The fragrance is said to carry 20' even when the wind is still, but I find I must kneel alongside to breathe in whiffs of its perfume. Another escaping scent that is propelled by the breeze leads me back to the garden's shadier recesses where the bright yellow flowers of *Mahonia bealei* still enliven the landscape.

On February 16 white pinwheels appear on the naked twigs of my *Magnolia stellata*. My pink-budded tree blooms weeks after one that's fully exposed at curbside near the top of our hill. That tree has stark white blooms, but my flowers have a lovely pinkish cast. On the nearby streets, the Bradford pears are glorious with this year's crop of white blossoms. Soft pink blooms decorate flowering cherry trees. Defying the probability of cold temperatures and imminent disaster, the purplish pink flowers of *Magnolia x soulangiana* are stunning this year. In 1995, all this occurs a month later.

From my kitchen window, I see in peak bloom what Shakespeare called snake's-head iris in his plays. Sometimes called widow's iris, they are more often known as *Iris tuberosa*. Their correct name is *Hermodactylus tuberosa*. This exotic iris's tall-stemmed plum purple and lime green velvet flowers rise from foliage present since the previous September. I usually plant white with a darkest-purple blotch pansies as companions to these striking bulbs. In recent years, I have used violas, which seem to last longer because they withstand our weather conditions better.

Since February 7, edging the embankment that plunges from mid-driveway, deep purple, jewel-like blooms sparkling from within *Iris reticulata* foliage have been a delight. All the colors on this iris, even the blues splashed with yellow, are intense. One year, I fed them too heavily and the blooms were overwhelmed by foliage. Later pretty grape hyacinths, along with the large purple ones, join the bulb display. In the sheltered rear area of the front straw island, the first fragrant white flowers on the Korean forsythia (*Abeliophyllum distichum*) have arrived,. These blooms precede by a week the prime blooming of my deep yellow forsythia. The flowers on the white forsythia had always been sparse. This was due possibly, I thought, to some precocious fall blooming. However, Mildred Pinnell told me to prune the shrub severely after blooming and then to feed it. It seems to work, and now I have much heavier spring flowering.

The year's first color show in my white garden, as always, is *Pulmonaria* 'Sissinghurst White.' It blooms earlier and more vigorously (early February continuously through mid-April) than the more familiar 'Mrs. Moon.' It never disappoints me if I conscientiously give it breathing room and thin out dogwood branches overhead that can obstruct sunlight. By late February this year, my foundation planting of those 32-year-old camellias has sidestepped cold damage and the shrubs are still peppered with red blooms. During too many years, the buds and flowers are so badly injured that the shrubs appear splattered with soggy brown mush. Also unharmed, dangling red ropes on *Pieris japonica* are now stretched tight with the weight of white urn-shaped flowers.

For many years, sometime in late February or early March—weather permitting—John Schulte has pruned my shrubbery. This includes what he calls the "killer Burford holly hedge" and the crape myrtle. Schulte's huge frame makes the work look like child's play. Jim Harrington hacks back the trumpet vine and cuts back all the tattered liriope. I am now ready for spring to begin.

One early spring years ago, I planted tall pink, rose, and blue plants of tender *Primula obconica* from Pike's in pots. This was to replace bulbs rotted from the cold. Except for napping midsummer, these primula have bloomed through mild, rainy seasons until November frost every year since. I bring them into the greenhouse where they flower extravagantly through the winter. A few plants left outdoors in the ground during the mild winter of 1995 bloomed again in late March. Nearby a white *Crocus biflorus* clump is splendid alongside my driveway lamp. Other crocus are evident everywhere. Blankets of soft cobalt violet *C. tomasinianus* and yellow combinations of *C. chrysanthus* cover bare ground in the upper front bed. 'Baby Lucia,' a tiny pansy purchased at the ABG Fall Sale, has bloomed all winter and lays an oriental rug over the mud. By late January 1995, *Helleborus orientalis* has its own first purple-spotted flowers. White forms were already in flower. *H. niger* buds, however, are still shielded by pink coverings that are not quite ready to release the flowers.

In 1996, before the spring equinox, I was drawn to the giant Savannah holly in the lower front garden. Flocks of cedar waxwings were flying erratically through its branches, intoxicated by its holly berry fruit liquor. I had discovered the feathered connoisseurs for whom the berries had been saved through the long winter months. This day the winter ended and spring claimed the garden.

Those few days that cold temperatures and severe weather keep the Atlanta gardener a prisoner within the house lend time for contemplation. Seeking explanation to mysteries locked within my own plants keeps gardening fresh and exciting for me. As the years pass, my garden matures and evolves and, hopefully, so do I as a gardener. Fortunately, the cycle of the seasons brings the incomparable beauty of an Atlanta spring to motivate us out of our own dormancy.

Sources for Plants

Sources for Plants

Alcovey Nursery
Mary Lois and Jesse Burgess
775 Cochran Road
Covington, GA 30209
770-787-7177

Jacques Amand
P. O. Box 59001
Potomac, MD 20859
800-452-5414

All South Stone & Water Garden Center
Box 979
2142 Stone Mountain-Lithonia Rd.
Lithonia, GA 30058
770-482-6052

Antique Rose Emporium
5565 Cavender Creek Rd.
Dahlonega, GA 30533
706-864-5884

Arrowhead Alpines
P. O. Box 857
Fowlerville, MI 48836
517-223-3581

Autumn Hill Nursery
4256 Earney Rd.
Woodstock, GA 30188
770-442-3901

Azaleas-To-Go
Earl Hester
1370 Redwine Rd.
Fayetteville, GA 30215
770-461-9786

Karl Bluemel, Inc.
2740 Green Lane
Baldwin, MD 21013

Boothe Hill Company
23-B Boothe Hill
Chapel Hill, NC 27514

Bridges Roses
2734 Toney Rd.
Lawndale, NC 28090

W. Atlee Burpee Seed Co.
Warminster, PA 18974
orders: 880-888-1447
fax: 800-487-5330

Cal-Dixie Iris Gardens
14116 Pear Street
Riverside, CA 92508
909-780-0335

Camellia Forest Nursery
125 Carolina Forest Rd.
Chapel Hill, NC 27516
919-967-5529

Cardinal Nursery
Route 1, Box 316
State Road, NC 28676

Carter's Nursery
3526 Thompson Bridge Rd.
Gainesville, GA 30506
770-536-3626

Chattahoochee Home and Garden, Inc.
Hardy Kaplan
4773 Lower Roswell Rd.
Marietta, GA 30068
770-977-0981

Melissa and Barry Claus
1050 Little River La.
Alpharetta, GA 30201
770-740-1371

Coastal Pond Supply
2605-2 Mountain Industrial Blvd.
Tucker, GA 30084
770-496-5740

Collector's Nursery
16804 N.E. 102nd Ave.
Battle Ground, WA 98604
360-574-3832

Cooley's
P.O. Box 126
Silverton, OR 97381
800-225-5391

The Cummins Garden
22 Robertsville Road
Marboro, NJ 07746

Daffodil Mart
7463 Heath Trail
Gloucester, VA 23061
800-255-2852
fax 800-420-2852

Damascus Gardens
Bob Belcher
4454 Francis Court
Lilburn, GA 30247
770-921-3670.

Dean's Nursery
Roscoe Dean
Route 1, Box 491
Lucedale, MS 39452
601-947-2280

Dutch Gardens
P. O. Box 200
Adelphia, NJ 07710
908-780-2713
fax 908-780-7720

Eco Gardens
Don Jacobs
P.O. Box 1227
Decatur, GA 30031
404-294-6468

Edmunds' Roses
6235 S.W. Kehle Road,
Wilsonville, OR 97070

Farmers and Consumers Market Bulletin
Ga. Dept of Agriculture
19 Martin Luther King, Jr. Dr.
Atlanta, GA 30334
404-656-3722

Flora Farm
Hwy. 141
Cumming, GA 30061
770-889-3559

Flowery Branch
Dean Pailler
P. O. Box 1330
Flowery Branch, GA 30542
770-536-8380

Forest Farm
990 Tetherow Rd.
Williams, OR 97544

Forget-Me-Not Flowers
22R East Andrews Dr.
Atlanta, GA 30305
404-233-4412

Forrester's Flowers
2070 Cheshire Bridge Rd., N.E.
Atlanta, GA 30324
404-325-0333

Garden Party
488 Kennesaw Ave.
Marietta, GA 30060
770-421-0245

Gardens of the Blue Ridge
P. O. Box 10
Pineola, NC 28662

GardenSmith Greenhouse & Nursery
231 Hogans Mill Rd.
Jefferson, GA 30549
706-367-9094

GardenSouth (Gold Kist, Inc.)
950 Hwy. 20 South
Lawrenceville, GA 30245
770-963-2406

Gerbing's Camellia Growers
George C. Gerbing
7098 Old Nicholls Hwy.
Millwood, GA 31552
912-283-1590

Glasshouse Works
P. O. Box 97
10 Church St.
Stewart, OH 45778

Goodness Grows
Highway 77 North
P. O. Box 311
Lexington, GA 30648
706-743-5055
fax: 706-743-5112

Gossler Farms Nursery
1200 Weaver Rd.
Springfield, OR 97478
503-746-3922
fax: 503-744-7924

Goza Nursery
100 Harmony Grove Rd.
Lilburn, GA 30247
770-923-1194

Greenhouse Nursery
5907 Covington Hwy.
Decatur, GA 30035
770-987-4066

Greer Gardens
1280 Goodpasture Island Rd.
Eugene, OR 97401
orders 800-548-0111
customer service: 541-686-8266
fax: 541-686-0910

Habersham Gardens
Brian Morris
2067 Manchester St., N.E.
Atlanta, GA 30324
404-873-4702

Hall's Greenhouses
5706 Memorial Drive
Stone Mountain, GA 30083
404-292-8446

Heronswood Nursery, Ltd.
7530 N.E. 288th St.
Kingston, WA 98346
360-297-4172
fax: 360-297-8321

Mickey Harp
1692 Hwy. 92 South
Fayetteville, GA 30215
770-461-1821

James Harris
538 Swanson Drive
Lawrenceville, GA 30245
770-963-7463

Robert Harris
2158 Tucker Industrial Rd.
Tucker, GA 30084
770-493-8336

Hastings Nature and Garden Center
3920 Peachtree Road, N.E.
Atlanta, GA 30319
404-869-7448

Heirloom Old Garden Roses
24062 Northeast Riverside Dr.
St. Paul, OR 97137

Heistaway Gardens
1220 McDaniel Mill Rd.
Conyers, GA 30207
770-483-7808

Henderson Plants
171 Marietta Street
Alpharetta, GA 30201
770-475-6503

Highland Hardware
1045 Highland Ave., N.E.
Atlanta, GA 30306
404-872-4466

Hills Nursery
Route 3, Box 62
Pavo, GA 31778

Home Depot
Many Metro Atlanta locations

Homeplace Garden
P. O. Box 300
Harden Bridge Rd.
Commerce, GA 30529
706-335-2892

Hortico Roses
723 Robson Road
Waterdown, Ontario, Canada LOR 2H1

Hosta for Sale
JoAnn Newberry
6835 Hembree Dr.
Austell, GA 30001
770-739-2152

Mary Howard
590 South Indian Creek Dr.
Stone Mountain, GA 30063
404-292-2350

Intown Hardware
854 North Highland Avenue, N.E.
Atlanta, GA 30306
404-874-5619

Intown Hardware
1404 Scott Blvd.
Decatur, GA 30030
404-378-6006

Jackson-Perkins
Medford, OR 97501
800-292-4769

Arthur A. "Buck" Jones & Assoc.
P. O. Box 339
Grayson, GA 30221
770-963-8227

Arthur A. "Buck" Jones & Assoc.
7470 Hickory Flat Hwy.
Woodstock, GA 30188
770-345-5506

Kinsman Company
River Road
Point Pleasant, PA 18950

Klehm Nursery
Route 5
197 Penny Rd.
South Barrington, IL 60010
312-551-3715

Ladyslipper
7418 Hickory Flat Hwy.
Woodstock, GA 30188
770-345-2998

Land Arts, Inc.
809 Broad St.
Monroe, GA 30656
770-267-4500

Lazy K Nursery
Ernest Koone
705 Wright Road
Pine Mountain, GA 31822
706-663-4991

LeGro Gardens
Erling and Lilian Grovenstein
2424 Briarmoor Rd, N.E.
Atlanta, GA 30345
404-938-3229

Limerock Ornamental Grasses
Rt. 1, Box 111-C
Port Matilda, PA 16870

Living Colors Unlimited, Inc.
2925 Browns Bridge Rd.
Gainesville, GA 30504
770-536-8346

Loft Seeds, Inc.
Chimney Rock Rd.
P. O. Box 146
Bound Brook, NJ 08805

Logee's Greenhouses
55 North St.
Danielson, CT 06239

Lost Mountain Nursery
Teena and Ron Barnes
824 Poplar Springs Rd.
Dallas, GA 30132
770-427-5583

LushLife
146 E. Andrews Dr.
Atlanta, GA 30305
404-841-9661

McClure and Zimmerman
108 West Winnebago
P. O. Box 368
Friesland, WI 53935
414-326-4220
fax: 800-692-5864

McGinnis Farm
5610 McGinnis Ferry Rd.
Alpharetta, GA 30202
770-740-2820

Melton's Nursery
Jack and Winona Melton
1810-B Old Hwy. 41
Kennesaw, GA 30152
770-499-9406

Mini Roses
Box 4255A
Dallas, TX 75208

Grant Mitch Novelty Daffodils
P. O. Box 218
Hubbard, OR 97032

Moore's Miniature Roses
2519 E. Noble Avenue
Visalia, CA 93277

Morrison Farms
3086 Osborne Rd., N.E.
Atlanta, GA 30319
404-261-3502

Mountain View Gardens
(Formerly Funkhauser's)
Hwy. 115
P. O. Box 280
Dahlonega, GA 30533
706-864-5157

Native Gardens
5737 Fisher La.
Greenback, TN 37742
615-856-0220

Natural Gardens
113 Jasper Lane
Oak Ridge, TN 37830

Niche Gardens
1111 Dawson Rd.
Chapel Hill, NC 27516
919-967-0078

Nor'East Miniature Roses
Box A
Rowley, MA 01969

Nuccio's Nursery
3555 Chaney Trail
P. O. Box 6160
Altadena, CA 91003
818-794-3383

Oregon Miniature Roses
8285 SW 185th Avenue
Beaverton, OR 97007

Outdoor Environments, Inc.
2265 Hwy. 20
Grayson, GA 30221
770-962-0606

Park Seed Co.
Cokesbury Rd.
Greenwood, SC 29647
800-845-3369
fax: 800-275-9941

Passiflora Wildflower Co.
Route 1, Box 190-A
Germanton, NC 27019
919-591-5816

Piccadilly Farms
Sam and Carleen Jones
1971 Whippoorwill Rd.
Bishop, GA 30621
706-769-6516

Pickering Nurseries
670 Kingston Road
Pickering, Ontario, Canada LlV lA6

Pike Family Nurseries
More than 20 Metro Atlanta locations

Plant Delights Nursery, Inc.
9241 Sauls Rd.
Raleigh, NC 27603
919-772-4794

Planters
3144 E. Shawdowlawn Ave., N.E.
Atlanta, GA 30305
404-261-6002

Plumeria People
910 Leander Dr.
Leander, TX 78641
512-259-0807

Pond Bloomers
5748 GA Hwy. 20
Covington, GA
770-786-7599

The Potted Plant
3165 Shadowlawn Ave., N.E.
Atlanta, GA 30305
404-233-7800

Providence Garden Mart
825 Beaver Run Rd., N.W.
Lilburn, GA
770-279-8333

Quail Hill Gardens
2460 Complin Bridge Rd.
Inman, SC 29349
803-472-3339

Randy's Nursery & Greenhouse
523 W. Crogan Street (Hwy. 29)
Lawrenceville, GA 30245
770-822-0676

Reflective Gardens Nursery
24329 N.E. Snow Hill La.
Poulsbo, WA 98370
360-598-4619

Reids Azaleas
4414 Highway 138 SW
Stockbridge, GA 30281

Robyn's Nest Nursery
7802 N.E. 63rd St.
Vancouver, WA 98662

Rolling Oaks Farm (Hanson Farms)
4701 Piney Grove Dr.
Cumming, GA 30130
770-844-1462

Franz Roozen
Vogelenzangseweg 49
2114 BB Vogelenzan
Holland

Roses of Yesterday and Today
802 Brown's Valley Road
Watsonville, CA 95076

Roses Unlimited
Rt. 1, Box 587
Laurens, SC 29360

Roslyn Nursery
211 Burrs La., Dept. CM
Dix Hills, NY 11746
516-643-9347

Sandy Mush Nursery
Route 2, Surrett Cove Rd.
Leicester, NC 28748

Savage Wildflower Gardens
Box 163
McMinnville, TN 37110

Schreiners
3629 Quinaby Road, N.E.
Salem, OR 97303
800-525-2367

Schild Azalea Gardens and Nursery
1705 Longview Street
Hixson, TN 37343

Siskiyou Rare Plant Nursery
2825 Cummings Rd.
Medford, OR 97501
541-772-6846
fax: 541-772-4917

Shady Oaks Nursery
700 19th Ave.
Waseca, MN 56093

Shooting Star Nursery
444 Bates Rd.
Frankfurt, KY 40601

Smith Ace Hardware
601 E. College Ave.
Decatur, GA 30030
404-373-3301

Ed Stephens
Cobb, GA
See *Farmers and Consumers Market Bulletin.*

Stubbs Shrubs
23225 S.W. Bosky Dell La.
West Linn, OR 97068

Sunlight Gardens
174 Golden La.
Andersonville, TN 37705
orders: 800-272-7396
information: 423-494-8237
fax: 423-494-7086

Tammia Nursery
Rt. 3, Box 238
La. Hwy. 1091
Pearl River, LA 70452
504-643-3636

Tiny Petals Nursery
489 Minot Avenue
Chula Vista, CA 92010

Transplant Nursery
1586 Parkertown Rd.
Lavonia, GA 30553
706-356-8947
fax: 706-356-8842

Thompson and Morgan
P. O. Box 1308
Jackson, NJ 08527
908-363-2225
fax: 908-363-9356

Tucker Top Cat Gardens
Ray Stevens
2446 Cofer Circle
Tucker, GA 30084
770-938-9633

Van Bourgondien Brothers
P. O. Box 1000
245 Route 109
Babylon, NY 11702
orders: 800-622-9997
customer service: 800-622-9959
fax: 516-669-1228

Varnadoe Nursery
Colquitt, GA
See *Farmers and Consumers Market Bulletin.*

Andre Viette Farm-Nursery
Route 1, Box 16
Fisherville, VA 22939
703-943-2315

Walker Nursery
2024 Walt Stephens Rd.
Jonesboro, GA 30236
770-471-6011

Ward's Nursery, Inc.
4961 Peachtree Industrial Blvd.
Chamblee, GA 30341
770-493-8336

Wayside Gardens
1 Garden Lane
Hodges, SC 29695-0001
orders and customer service: 880-845-1124
fax: 800-817-1124

We-Du Nurseries
Route 5, Box 724
Marion, NC 28752
704-738-8300
*Note: Under new ownership as of
1/1/97.*

White Flower Farm
Litchfield, CT 06759
800-503-9624

Wild Wood Farms
Terry Tatum
5231 Seven Island Rd.
Madison, GA 30650
706-342-4912

The Wildwood Flower
Thurman Mannes
Route 3, Box 165
5233 U.S. 64 West
Pittsboro, NC 27312
919-542-4344 (7:30-9 p.m.)

Wilkerson Mill Gardens
9595 Wilkerson Mill Rd.
Palmetto, GA 30268
770-463-9717

Wilson Bros. Nursery
1759 McGarity Rd.
McDonough, GA 30253
770-954-9862

Winterthur
Winterthur, DE 19735
orders: 880-448-3883
customer service: 800-767-0500

Woodlanders, Inc.
1128 Colleton Ave.
Aiken, SC 29801
803-648-7522

Yucca Do Nursery
Peckerwood Gardens
P. O. Box 450
Waller, TX 77484
409-826-4580

Recommended Reading and References

Recommended Reading and References

Chapter 1, "Getting Your Garden Started"

Creative Home Landscaping (Ortho Books)

The Home Landscaper by Ann Reilly and Susan A. Roth (Home Planners Co., Tucson, Ariz.)

Chapter 2, "An Atlanta Landscape"

The Southern Gardeners' Book of Lists by Lois Trigg Chaplin (Taylor Publishing Co. - 1994)

Gardens Are For People by Thomas Church (McGraw Hill - 1983)

Manual of Woody Landscape Plants by Michael Dirr (Stipes Publishing Co. - 1990)

Bold, Romantic Gardens by Wolfwang Oehme and James van Sweden (Acropolis Books Ltd. - 1990)

The Garden Design Book by Anthony Paul and Yvonne Rees (Salem House Publishers, Topsfield, Mass. - 1988)

Private Landscapes by Caroline Seebohm and Christopher Simon Sykes (Clarkson Potter, Inc. - 1989)

Creating Small Gardens by Roy Strong (Villard Books - 1987)

How to Plan You Own Home Landscape by Nelva M. Webber (Bobbs-Merrill - 1976)

Home Landscape Companion by Edith Henderson (Peachtree Publishers, Ltd. - 1993)

Chapter 3, "Color in the Garden"

Color in Your Garden by Penelope Hobhouse (Frances Lincoln, Ltd. - 1985)

Colour Schemes for the Flower Garden by Gertrude Jekyll (Antique Collectors Club Ltd., Woodbridge, Sussex - 1982)

Chapter 10, "Flowering Shrubs"

Ortho Shrubs and Hedges by Cedric Crocker (Sinnes and McKinley - 1990)

Random House Book of Shrubs by Roger Phillips and Martyn (Random House - 1989)

Taylor's Guide to Shrubs (Houghton-Mifflin - 1987)

Chapter 11, "Camellias"

The American Camellia Yearbook Annual Journals by the American Camellia Society

The Camellia, Its History, Culture, Genetics, and a Look into Its Future Development by the American Camellia Society, edited by David L. Feathers and Milton H. Brown (R. L. Bryan Co. - printers)

Color Dictionary of Camellias by Sterling Macaboy (Landsdown Press)

You Can Grow Camellias by Mary Nobel and Blanche Graham (Dower Publications, Inc.)

Chapter 12, "Evergreen Azaleas" and Chapter 13, "Native Azaleas"

Great American Azaleas, A Guide to the Finest Azalea Varieties by Jim Darden (Greenhouse Press) Good color photos, good information, evergreen azaleas only. Also available as a VHS video from Greer Gardens.

Southern Living Azaleas by Fred Galle (Oxmoor House) Informative, black and white photos only, evergreen and native azaleas.

Azaleas by Fred Galle (Timber Press) This is the definitive book on all azaleas.

Chapter 14, "Rhododendrons"

Greer's Guidebook to Available Rhododendrons by Harold Greer (Available from Greer Gardens) color photos, excellent information; both hard and soft cover.

Rhododendrons of the World by Dr. David Leach. Definitive book on rhododendrons.

Catalog of Roslyn Nursery, Dept. A, P.O. Box 69, Roslyn, NY 11576 ($3)

Chapter 15, "Perennials"

Herbaceous Perennial Plants by Allan M. Armitage (Varsity Press) Best discussion of perennials; Southern viewpoint.

Allan Armitage on Perennials Burpee Expert Gardener Series (Prentice Hall Gardening) Not as comprehensive as *Herbaceous Perennial Plants*; excellent color photos.

Perennials for American Gardens by Ruth Rogers Claussen and Nicolas H. Ekstrom (Random House) Comprehensive descriptions; excellent color photos.

Successful Southern Gardening by Sandra F. Landendorf (Univ. of North Carolina Press) Southern view of gardening, but from North Carolina, which has different climatic conditions from Atlanta.

HP Perennials by Pamela Harper and Frederick McGourty (HP Books) Inexpensive book with excellent photos, good general information.

Gardening Southern Style by Felder Rushing (Univ. Press of Mississippi)

Passalong Plants by Steve Bender and Felder Rushing (Univ. of North Carolina Press) Delightful; sets the stage for Southern gardening.

The Gardens of Two Sisters by Barrie Crawford and Kay Reeves (Buckeye Press, Hamilton, Ga.) Contrasts Georgia and New Jersey gardening; good insights on Georgia gardening.

The Hosta Book by Paul Aden (Timber Press)

The Genus Hosta by George Schmidt

Hemerocallis, The Daylily by R. W. Munson, Jr.

Daylillies, Beginner's Handbook by The American Hemerocallis Society (Sold at the local hemerocallis show.)

The World of Iris by The American Iris Society (Charles Lack, 718 West 67th Street, Tulsa, OK 74132)

Growing Iris by G. E. Cassidy and S. Linnegar (Timber Press) English viewpoint on iris.

A Southern Garden, A Handbook for the Middle South by Elizabeth Lawrence (Univ. of North Carolina Press) Also recommended: Other books by Lawrence on Southern gardening.

Southern Gardens, Southern Gardening by William Lanier Hunt (Duke Univ. Press - 1982) If you like Elizabeth Lawrence, you will enjoy this.

Chapter 16, "Annuals"

Annuals (HP Books)

Color with Annuals (Ortho Books)

Park's Success with Seeds (Park Seed Co., Cokesbury Road, Greenwood, SC 29647-0001)

Successful Seed Raising (Thompson and Morgan, Inc., P.O. Box 1308, Jackson, NJ 08527)

Chapter 17, "Bulbs"

Bulbs by Phillips and Marty Rix (The Pan Garden Series from England, available in U.S. bookstores) This paperback contains 1,000 color photos of bulbs in flower and extensive information on bulb origin and all phases of growing, roughly listing bulbs in flowering order.

Garden Bulbs for the South by Scott Ogden (Taylor Publishing Co. - 1994) Excellent information on bulbs specific to the south; remember Atlanta is not Texas.

The American Gardener's World of Bulbs by Judy Glattstein. Good general information on spring bulbs, but northern viewpoint. Fine suggestions for bulb combinations with bulbs and other plants.

The Complete Guide to Growing Bulbs in Houston by Sally McQueen (order from The Plumeria People catalog, Leander, Tex.) Atlanta isn't Houston, but growing conditions are similar. Much information on unusual bulbs (spring, summer, and autumn blooming) not easily available elsewhere.

The Little Bulbs, A Tale of Two Gardens by Elizabeth Lawrence with introduction by Allen Lacy. Classic book for southeastern bulb lovers.

Chapter 18, "Roses"

All About Roses by Ortho An excellent basic reference, inexpensive and widely available.

The Old Shrub Roses by Graham Thomas

Landscaping with Antique Roses by Liz Druitt and G. Michael Shoup

Climbing Roses by Stephen Scaniello and Tania Bayard

Chapter 19, "Lawn Grasses"

Lawns in Georgia by Gilbert Landry, Jr., Extension Agronomist for Turf (Cooperative Extension Service of the Univ. of Georgia)

Chapter 21, "Ornamental Grasses"

The New American Garden by Carole Ottesen

Ornamental Grasses, The Amber Wave by Carole Ottesen

Ornamental Grasses Idea Garden (Published by Longwood Gardens, P. O. Box

501, Kennett Square, PA 19348) At $4, it's an excellent buy.

Ornamental Grass Gardening by Thomas A. Reinhardt, Martina Reinhardt, and Mark Moskowitz

Chapter 22, "Vines"

A Harrowsmith Gardener's Guide edited by Karan Davis (Camden Publishing, Inc. - 1992)

A Southern Garden by Elizabeth Lawrence (Claitor's Publishing Co.)

Clematis for Color and Versatility by Keith and Carol Fair (Crowood Press Ltd., England - 1990)

Climbers and Wall Plants for Year-round Colour by Jane Taylor (Ward Loch Ltd., London)

Creative Planting with Climbers by Jane Taylor (Ward Loch Ltd., London - 1991)

Gardening with Groundcovers and Vines by Allen Lacy (Harper-Collins)

Making the Most of Clematis by Ramond J. Evison (Floraprint Ltd., Nottingham - 1985)

Vines by Richard H. Cravens (Time-Life Books)

Chapter 24, "Native Plants"

Gardening with Native Wildflowers by Samuel B. Jones Jr., and Leonard E. Foote (Timber Press - 1990)

Wildflowers of the Southeastern United States by Wilbur H. Duncan and Leonard E. Foote (Univ. of Georgia Press - 1975)

Nature's Melody, A Guide to Georgia's Wildflowers by Betty L. Benson for The Garden Club of Georgia, Inc. (1994)

Gardening with Native Plants in the South by Sally Wasowski (Taylor - 1994)

Chapter 26, "Shade Gardens"

Herbaceous Perennial Plants by Allan M. Armitage (Varsity Press, Inc. - 1989)

The Wildlife Gardener by John V. Dennis (Alfred A. Knopf - 1985)

Manual of Woody Landscape Plants: Their Identification, Ornamental Characteristics, Culture, Propagation and Uses, 4th Ed. by Michael A. Dirr (Stipes Publishing Co. - 1990)

Trees of the Southeastern United States by Wilbur H. Duncan and Marion B. Duncan (Univ. of Georgia Press - 1988)

Wildflowers of the Southeastern United States by Wilbur H. Duncan and Leonard E. Foote (Univ. of Georgia Press - 1975)

The Natural Shade Garden by Ken Druse (Clarkson Potter - 1992)

The Naturalist's Garden by Ruth Shaw Ernst (Rodale Press - 1987)

Native Shrubs and Woody Vines of the Southeast by Leonard E. Foote and Samuel B. Jones, Jr. (Timber Press - 1989)

Ferns to Know and Grow by F. Gordon Foster (Timber Press - 1984)

Gardening with Native Wildflowers by Samuel B. Jones Jr., and Leonard E. Foote (Timber Press - 1990)

The Garden in Autumn by Allen Lacy (Atlantic Monthly Press - 1990)

Gardening in the Shade by Harriet K. Morse (Timber Press - 1982)

The Complete Shade Gardener by George Schenk (Houghton-Mifflin Co. - 1984)

Field Guide of the Ferns and other Pteridophytes of Georgia by Lloyd H. Snyder, Jr. and James G. Bruce (Univ. of Georgia Press - 1986)

Chapter 28, "Water Gardens"

Garden Pools and Fountains by Edward B. Claflin (Ortho Books - 1988)

Pools and Waterside Gardening by Peter Robinson (Royal Botanical Gardens, Kew - 1987)

Water Gardens for Plants and Fish by Charles B. Thomas (T.F.H. Publications, Neptune City, N.J. - 1988)

Chapter 29, "Walkways in the Garden"

Landscape Design by Leroy Hannebaum (Reston Publishing Co. - 1981)

Chapter 30, "Herbs"

An Atlanta Sampler by the Chattahoochee Unit, Herb Society of America (1984)

Southern Herb Growing by Madeline Hill and Gwen Barclay (Shearer Publishing, Fredericksburg, Tex. - 1987)

A Complete Book of Herbs by Lesley Bremness (Viking Studio Books - 1988)

Landscaping with Herbs by Jim Wilson (Houghton-Mifflin - 1994)

The Complete Book of Herbs and Spices by Sarah Garland (Viking Press - 1979)

Rodale's Illustrated Encyclopedia of Herbs (Rodale Press - 1987)

Rodale's Successful Organic Gardening Herbs edited by Patricia F. Michalak (Rodale Press - 1993)

Avis's List for Research and Pleasure

Annuals for Connoisseurs by Wayne Winterowd (Prentice-Hall - 1992)

Daffodils for American Gardens by Brent and Becky Heath (Elliott & Clark - 1995)

Bulbs for Temperate Climates by Jack Hobbs and Terry Hatch (Timber Press - 1994)

National Arboretum Book of Outstanding Garden Plants by Jacqueline Heriteau with Dr. H. Marc Cathey (Simon & Schuster - 1990)

Designing with Perennials by Pamela Harper (MacMillan - 1991)

The Impressionist's Garden by Derek Fell (Random House - 1994)

American Horticultural Society Encyclopedia of Garden Plants edited by Christopher Brickell (MacMIllan - 1989)

The Sissinghurst White Portrait of a Garden by Jane Brown (George Wiedenfeld and Nicholson - 1990)

The Green Tapestry by Beth Chatto (Simon & Schuster - 1989)

Resources for Special Help

Resources for Special Help

This appendix contains information about public gardens to visit, retail nurseries that have display gardens, and annual public tours, flower shows, symposia, and classes. We also listed information about plant sales, TV and radio gardening shows, local newspapers and regional magazines, and plant societies in the greater Atlanta area.

Public Gardens

Atlanta Botanical Garden
Piedmont Park at the Prado
Box 77246
Atlanta, GA 30357
404-876-5859
(Landscaped Gardens, Dorothy Chapman Fuqua Conservatory, Storza Woods)

Atlanta History Center
130 West Paces Ferry Road, N.W.
Atlanta, GA 30305
404-814-4000
(Frank A. Smith Rhododendron Garden, Swan Woods Trail, Mary Howard Gilbert Memorial Quarry Garden, Cherry-Sims Asian American Garden, Tullie Smith Farm)

Barnsley Gardens
597 Barnsley Gardens Road
Adairsville, GA 30103
770-773-7480

Callaway Gardens
U.S. Hwy. 27
Pine Mountain, GA 31822
404-663-2281
1-800-282-8181
(John A. Sibley Horticultural Center, Cecil B. Day Butterfly Center, Ida Cason Callaway Memorial Chapel, Mr. Cason's Vegetable Garden, and Azalea, Rhododendron, Holly, and Wildflower Trails)

Carter Center Library Gardens
1 Copenhill Ave., N.E.
Atlanta, GA 30308
404-331-0296

Cator Woolford Memorial Gardens
1815 Ponce de Leon Ave., N.E.
Atlanta, GA 30307

Chattahoochee Nature Center
9135 Willeo Road
Roswell, GA 30075
770-992-2055

DeKalb Botanical Garden
3251 Panthersville Road
Decatur, GA 30034-3897
404-244-5077

Fernbank Science Center
156 Heaton Park Drive, N.E.
Atlanta, GA 30307
404-378-4311
(Fernbank Forest and Staton Rose Garden, an All American Rose Selection Test Garden)

Founders Memorial Garden
State Headquarters
The Garden Club of Georgia, Inc.
325 South Lumpkin Street
Athens, GA
706-542-3631

Georgia Governor's Mansion
and Gardens
391 West Paces Ferry Road
Atlanta, GA 30305
404-261-1776
*(Open to the public on Tuesdays,
Wednesdays, and Thursdays,
10 -11:30 a.m.)*

Hamilton Rhododendron Garden
Georgia Mountain Fair Grounds
Hwy. 76
Hiawassee, GA 30546
706-896-4191

Lockerly Arboretum
1534 Irwinton Road
Milledgeville, GA 31061
912-452-2112

Massee Lane Gardens
American Camellia Society
Headquarters
One Massee Lane
Fort Valley, GA 31030
912-967-2358

Oak Hill (Martha Berry Home and
Gardens)
189 Mount Berry Station
Rome, GA 30149
706-291-1883

State Botanical Garden of Georgia
2450 South Milledge Ave.
Athens, GA 30605
706-542-1244

Vines Botanical Gardens
3500 Oak Grove Road
Loganville, GA 30249
770-466-7532

Retail Nurseries with Display Gardens

Antique Rose Emporium
Rural Route 1, Box 630
Dahlonega, GA 30533
706-864-5884

Goodness Grows
P.O. Box 311, Hwy. 77 North
Lexington, GA 30648
706-743-5055

Hastings Nature & Garden Center
3920 Peachtree Road, N.E.
Atlanta, GA 30319
404-869-7448

Penny's Garden
Black's Creek Road
Mountain City, GA 30562
706-746-6918

Piccadilly Farm
1971 Whippoorwill Road
Bishop, GA 30621
706-769-6516

Mountain View Gardens
P.O. Box 280, Hwy. 115
Dahlonega, GA 30533
706-864-5157

Transplant Nursery
Parkertown Road
Lavonia, GA 30553
706-356-8947

Wild Wood Farms
5231 Seven Islands Road
Madison, GA 30650
706-342-4912

Wilkerson Mill Gardens
9595 Wilkerson Mill Road
Palmetto, GA 30268
770-463-9717

Annual Public Tours of Private Gardens

Check local papers for dates and details.

Gardens for Connoisseurs Tour
Atlanta Botanical Garden
Mother's Day Weekend

Druid Hills Home and Garden Tour (usually last weekend in April)

Hosta Society Tour

Pond Society Tour

Azalea Chapter - American Rhododendron Society

Decatur Arts Festival Garden Tour
Memorial Day Weekend

Georgia Historic House and Gardens Tour (second Saturday in April)

Gardens for Peace Tour

Annual Flower Shows

Southeastern Flower Show - February

Camellia Show - February

Daffodil Show - March

Iris Show - April

Azalea and Rhododendron Show - April

Rose Show - May

Bonsai - May

Hemerocallis (Daylily) - June

Yellow Daisy Festival - September

State Flower Show - October

Chrysanthemum - November

Annual Educational Events at the Atlanta Botanical Garden

Fall Festival (October)

Rose Pruning Day - last Sunday in February

Herb Education Day - last Saturday in April

Annual Two- or Three-Day Symposia

Callaway Gardens Southern Gardens Symposium - January

Atlanta Botanical Garden Spring Perennial Symposium (Co-sponsored with Georgia Perennial Plant Association)

Refining the Garden, Fall Perennial Symposium at the Atlanta History Center (Collaboration with Georgia Perennial Plant Association)

Gwinnett Technical School

Adult Education Classes in Gardening-Related Subjects

Agnes Scott College

Atlanta Area Tech

Atlanta Botanical Garden

DeKalb College

Emory University

Georgia State University

Kennesaw College

Oglethorpe University

Spruill Center for the Arts

Certificate and Degree Programs in Landscape Technology

Gwinnett Technical School

North Metro Tech

Annual Non-Commercial Plant Sales

Atlanta Botanical Garden - Spring and Fall

Chattahoochee Nature Center (Native plants)

DeKalb College Botanical Garden (Native plants)

Orchid Society

Bonsai Society

Azalea Chapter - American Rhododendron Society (Native and evergreen azaleas, hybrid rhododendrons)

Vines Botanical Gardens

Free Telephone Hotlines for Gardening Advice

Atlanta Botanical Garden 404-888-GROW (404-888-4769)

DeKalb County Extension Service Tele-tips (24 hours) 404-370-8198

TV and Radio Gardening Shows

The Victory Garden on public TV stations

For answers to gardening questions on the **radio**:

Walter Reeves' Gardening Show, WSB AM (750) 6-10 a.m. Saturdays 404-872-0750

Local Newspapers and Regional Magazines

The Home and Garden section appears every Saturday in *The Atlanta Journal/ Constitution*. Calendar gives the area's weekly gardening events. Articles by local columnists and reporters are informative. Wire service reports from other areas of the country are usually not applicable to our area.

Pete Pike's "Down to Earth Garden Tips" in Neighbor Newspapers has good seasonal information.

Roy Wyatt's column in *Dekalb News/Era* - excellent information!

Atlanta Homes & Lifestyles magazine

Southern Accents magazine

Southern Living magazine has excellent articles, garden tips, and a question/answer column. Beware of gardening instruction not applicable to our area; most information is very specifically noted.

Publications of General Gardening Interest

Horticulture magazine

Fine Gardening magazine

BBC Gardeners' World (on newsstands or by subscription)

The American Gardener (American Horticulture Society magazine)

The Garden (Journal of the Royal Horticultural Society)

The Avant Gardener
P.O. Box 489
New York, NY 10028

Plant Societies in the Greater Atlanta Area

Call the Atlanta Botanical Garden (404-876-5859) to find out the current contact person for each organization.

African Violet Club of Greater Atlanta

American Bamboo Society

American Hydrangea Society

American Ivy Society

American Rhododendron Society, Azalea Chapter

Atlanta Bonsai Society

Atlanta Branch - The American Begonia Society

Atlanta Cactus and Succulents Society

Atlanta Camellia Society

Atlanta Orchid Society

Dahlia Society of Georgia

Georgia Botanical Society

Georgia Chrysanthemum Society

Georgia Daffodil Society

Georgia Hosta Society

Georgia Iris Society

Georgia Native Plant Society

Georgia Organic Growers Association

Georgia Perennial Plant Association

Greater Atlanta Bromeliad Society

Greater Atlanta Hemerocallis Society

Greater Atlanta Rose Society

Herb Society of America, Chattahoochee Unit

North Georgia Camellia Society

The Pond Society

South Metro Orchid Society

South Metro Rose Society

Southeastern Palm and Exotic Plant Society

Water Lily Society, Georgia Chapter

Terms & Nomenclature

The Atlanta Gardener's Glossary

Gardens and gardeners have a language all their own. Here are some terms defined:

Annual: A plant that completes its entire life cycle in one blooming season. Whether you grow it from seed it or buy it, it will not live to bloom again next year, no matter how great a gardener you are. Most bedding plants are annuals--they are only meant to last one season.

Bed: A planting area where plants (hopefully) don't sleep, but bloom. It is open on all sides.

Biennial: A type of plant that flowers and forms seeds in its second year. (When a biennial plant doesn't bloom the first year, it's not your fault.) After it forms seeds, the plant usually dies. If you are lucky, the seeds will germinate and you will have new plants that will bloom their second year.

Border: A planting area that backs up to shrubs or a fence. (We don't have many old brick or stone walls in Atlanta, or it could back up to those also.) You can walk around a bed, but you would be hard pressed to circle a border.

Bract: The modified part of foliage, usually colored, that is often mistaken for a flower, but is not a true flower. Example: Dogwood–the white or pink "petals" are actually bracts.

Conifer: An evergreen with needle-like leaves; usually the fruit is a cone.

Cultivar: Short for "cultivated variety," a selected plant that was developed under cultivation, with unique characteristics not usually found in the wild. It can be cloned for exact duplication. The name of the cultivar follows the plant's botanical name, but is not latinized or italicized. The cultivar name takes initial capitalization and is set apart by apostrophes. Example: *Miscanthus sinensis* 'Silver Feather.'

Culture: It doesn't mean refinement, but simply the cultural requirements of a plant such as sun/shade, wet/dry, acid/alkaline soil, or anything else it needs.

Deadheading: The removal of spent flowers to prevent seed formation, so the plant can direct its efforts into forming more flower buds for the next year, as in the case of rhododendrons and bulbs, or even more flower buds for this season, in the case of crape myrtles and many perennials. Deadheading is a way to conserve the plant's energy. Your plants will look neater, too.

Deciduous: A woody plant that drops its leaves in autumn.

Dormant: At rest, no longer growing or carrying out normal functions. Dormancy is usually a plant's adaptation to escape and survive unfavorable conditions. Often the best time to prune and transplant trees and shrubs is when they are dormant.

Drainage: The soil's ability to absorb water and allow the water to flow through it and not be trapped. Generally, the larger the particles that comprise the soil, the better its drainage.

Evergreen: A plant that retains its leaves through the year. Broadleaf evergreens include azaleas and southern magnolias; needle-leaf evergreens include pines and hemlocks.

Exotic: A plant from a faraway place that usually has something very unusual about its foliage or flowers.

Exposure: Indicates a plant's requirement for or toleration of an amount of sunlight, such as:
>**Full sun**: A minimum of six hours direct sunlight per day. (Caution! Atlanta's western afternoon sun is too intense for some plants labeled "full sun.")
>**Full shade**: Mostly shaded site with two hours or less of direct sun. (No green plant blooms profusely in full shade.)
>**Part shade**: Periods of direct sun, but protection from midday and western sun in late afternoon. No more than three to four hours of sun; afternoon shade is preferable.
>**Part sun**: Just a little more sun than part shade.
>**Dappled shade**: The amount of sunlight that shines through deciduous trees.

Floriferous: A word used to describe a plant's flowering. It can mean many flowers in proportion to foliage, continually flowering, or reliably flowering.

Friable: Word used to describe the texture of good garden soil. See "tilth."

Genus and species: The plant's botanical name, which begins with the generic name capitalized and ends with the specific epithet which is not capitalized. It is in Latin and, therefore, is underlined or italicized.

Habit: Growth pattern of a plant such as upright, sprawling, compact, open, etc.

Habitat: A place where a plant naturally lives and grows in the wild.

Humus: End product of decomposition of vegetative matter or compost, which increases the friability of soil.

Hardy: Able to survive our Atlanta area winter, no matter the weather.

Herbaceous perennial (often shortened to simply "perennial"): A plant in which the top dies down for the winter, but the roots live on and push up new growth in spring or summer. The plant will return every year (at least for a few years).

Hybrid: The offspring of a cross between two separate plant species that breeds true. This can be accomplished by human hand or by nature. Many native azaleas are nature's hybrids.

Mulch: A soil covering around plants to conserve moisture and prevent weeds, such as shredded pine bark or pine straw. Mulch gives the garden a more attractive, professional finish.

Native (plant): A plant that occurs naturally in our area. Many exotics, however, have escaped into the wild and become naturalized. Some were introduced from other areas long ago.

Naturalize: Adaptation of a plant to a non-native environment.

Perennial: See "herbaceous perennial."

pH: An indication of the amount of hydrogen ions in a substance. It is actually the negative log of the hydrogen ion concentration, so the lower the number, the more hydrogen ions there are, and the more acidic the substance is. You may not care, but plants do. Some need a more acid soil, others a more basic soil to be able to access vital nutrients. The pH affects the availability of nutrients in the soil. The pH range is 1 to 14, with 7 being neutral. Between 1 and 7 is acidic, between 7 and 14 is basic or alkaline.

Pinch (back): To remove terminal (end) growth on branches of a plant, such as a mum, to encourage branching and consequently more flowers on a shorter, more compact plant.

Self-seeding: The ability of a plant to reproduce itself by dispersing its seeds, which have a high percentage of germination. There is a fine line between this as a good characteristic and the point where the plant becomes a weed.

Sessile: Stemless; attached directly at the base.

Sport: A mutation or offshoot of a plant, occurring suddenly, that can be propagated; a new plant capable of being duplicated. Example: 'Mike Bullard' is a red sport of the Glenn Dale azalea, 'Festive.'

Stolon: A horizontal stem, rooting at the nodes. Some plants spread in this manner, including certain grasses, azaleas, and tricyrtis. Those plants are referred to as **stoloniferous**.

Tender: Not able to live through our Atlanta winters. The list is constantly revised.

Texture: Visual or tactile surface characteristic of a plant.

Tilth: Soil's workability, described as "friable," "crumbled," or "pulverized" for good drainage.

Variety (var.): Plants within a species that have naturally occurring characteristics that set them apart from the species' mainstream. Varietal designations are usually latinized and not capitalized. Example: *Miscanthus sinesis* var. *purpurascens*.

Weed: Plant growing where you don't want it. One gardener's weed is another gardener's treasure.

Zone: Climatic areas, which have been numbered on a United States Department of Agriculture map. The higher the number, the warmer the climate. Used to express the northern climatic limits for a plant. (Zones are discussed in Chapter 4, "Climate and Hardiness.")

Latin Lingo Guide

When you know how to translate the latin lingo in botanical names, you will immediately know a lot about a particular plant.

alba, album, albus (form matches genus gender): white

alpina: growing above the timber line

aureus: golden yellow

aureo-marginata, -us: edged in yellow

canadensis: native to Canada

chinensis: native to China

elatia, -us: taller

gigantea, -us, -um: large, immense

grandiflora, -us, -um: large flowers

grandis: large, showy

japonica, -us, -um: native of Japan

humilie, -s: low-growing or dwarf

macrophylla, -us, -um: large leaves

maculata, -us, -um: spotted

major: greater or larger

maxima, -us, -um: largest

microphylla, -us, -um: small leaves

nana, -us, -um: small or dwarf

niger: black

officianalis: medicinal

orientalis: old world, orient, eastern

odorata, -us, -um: fragrant

palustris: growing in a marsh

pendulous: drooping, hanging down

pubescens: covered with down or soft hairs

procumbens: trailing

quercifolia, -us, -um: oak-leaf shaped

racemosa, -us, -um: growing along a central stalk from the bottom up

repen, repens, reptans: low, creeping along the ground

rubens, ruber, rubra: red

semperflorens: continuing to bloom

sempervirons: evergreen

sexatalis: growing in rocks

tomentosa, -us, -um: felt-like or rigid hairs

vulgaris: common

For additional information, see:

Gardener's Latin: A Lexicon by Bill Neal (Algonquin Books)

New Pronouncing Dictionary of Plant Names (Florists' Publishing Company, 111 North Canal Street, Chicago, IL 60606)

Common Names & Scientific Names

Index to Common Names

A

B

Baby blue eyes, 164
Baby's breath, 164
Bachelor's buttons, 164
Bald cypress, 284
Balloon flower, 143, 375, 382, 385
Balsam, 169
Barberry
   Japanese, 66
Basil, 335, 337
Bay, 337
   loblolly, 112, 379
Bearberry, 68
Beard tongue
   Small's, 305
Bear's breeches, 307
Beautyberry
   American, 293
Bee-balm, 143, 337
Begonia
   Christmas candy, 323
   fibrous rooted, 175, 374
   hardy, 149, 309
   strawberry, 247
   wax, 175
Bellflower
   Dalmatian,146
   Serbian, 146, 243
Bellwort, 292, 366
Ben Franklin tree, 283
Birch
   river, 282
Bishop's cap, 305
Bishop's hat, 245
Bishop's weed, 244
Blackberry, 253
Black-eyed Susan, 43, 55, 137, 161, 253
Black-eyed-Susan vine, 269, 379
Black gum, 284
Blanket flower, 169
Blazing star, 143
Bleeding heart, 149, 363
   fringed, 149
   yellow, 266
   wild, 245, 309
Bleeding heart vine, 377
Bloodroot, 273, 292, 313, 359
Bluebell
   California, 171
   English, 192, 368
   Spanish, 192, 306, 368
   Virginia, 152, 304, 359
Blueberry, 49, 79, 353-354, 388
   highbush, 294
   lowbush, 294
Blue Daze, 169
Blue-eyed grass, 292
Blue mist shrub, 83, 378
Blue star creeper, 244
Blue star flower, 143
Bluestem
   little, 256
   splitbeard, 256
Boltonia, 58, 374
Borage, 337
Brazilian plume, 170, 376, 382
Brodiaea, 210
Broomsedge, 256
Browallia, 175, 380
Brunnera
   heartleaf, 155
Buckeye
   bottlebrush, 81, 285, 307
   Georgia, 307
   painted, 293
   red, 83, 293, 307, 366
Buddleia, 377
Busy Lizzie, 176
Buttercup, 366
Butterfly bush, 58, 79, 380
Butterfly pea, 268
Butterfly weed, 144, 370, 373
Butternut, 313

C

Cabbage
   flowering (ornamental), 386
Caladium, 323
Calla, 184, 205, 372
Calliopsis, 164
Camassia, 202, 365
Camellia, 56, 57, 85-92, 360, 388, 390, 393
   Japanese, 74
   mountain, 286
   sasanqua, 25, 56, 57, 383, 384, 388
   silky, 286
   Yuletide, 25
Campanula, 49
Candytuft, 142, 160, 161, 164
   perennial, 248
Canna, 205
Cape fuchsia, 376
Cardinal flower, 303, 376, 378
Cardinal vine, 268
Carolina allspice, 302
Carolina jessamine, 262, 364
Caraway, 335
Cast iron plant, 154, 316

Y

Z

Index to Scientific Names

A

C

W

X

Y

Z

About the Author, Avis Aronovitz

The U.S. Public Health Service brought our family to Atlanta in 1960, just in time to witness the city's metamorphosis from southern small town to American big city. We were the forerunners of the second great wave of Yankee carpetbaggers. Atlanta's transformation in those next few years—the result of two seemingly unrelated events, the civil rights movement and the advent of central air-conditioning—brought more people, more development, and eventually even a new gardening style beyond azaleas and dogwood in April and clipped boxwood borders.

My first Atlanta garden, planted immediately, was a 3' x 8' plot beneath the kitchen window. Facing Lullwater Road in the Emory area, the apartment, the city's first to offer central air-conditioning, was beautiful; my garden was not. Flowers were scant and plants sputtered and died. I began to imagine small voices pleading for help—help I did not know how to give.

It occurred to me that my M.S. in plant science from Syracuse University and my several years' experience establishing my father's backyard flower beds in New York State, weren't useful here. Gardening in Atlanta was considerably different from gardening somewhere else.

The nicest memory of that first garden was the view through a fence to a colorful field of chrysanthemums grown by local garden columnist Roy Wyatt. Wyatt was leasing the carriage house of the adjacent Druid Hills home. We were immediate allies through our shared determination to plant a garden, even if it were on someone else's land.

I recall the day that Roy peering over from his side of the fence at my struggling garden patch, called to me and thrust several of his prized cushion mum plants into my eager upraised hands. With the plants passed over the fence came Roy's advice on their planting and care here in Atlanta.

Sharing knowledge and experience is the most valuable gift one Atlanta gardener can give another. That is what this small book is about. I want to share the knowledge and experience of many veteran Atlanta gardeners with you. This book answers the novice gardener's three most often-asked questions: "What should I plant? Where can I get it? How can I make it grow?"

I have been gardening in Atlanta for 37 years. During that time, I have written about Atlanta gardens and plants for local and national publications. This is the book I wish I had when I began both gardening and writing in Atlanta.

About the Co-author, Brencie Werner

Gardening is reported to be the favorite pastime of most Americans. Unlike most sports, gardening is an activity that we can enjoy throughout our lives. It's a consuming passion, but one that has brought me many friends and untold hours of pleasure.

My formal education, both undergraduate and graduate degrees, is in biology, but I concentrated on medicine, not plants, with a career at the Centers for Disease Control as a research microbiologist. When the necessity of caring for an invalid parent required an early retirement, I began to consider how I would focus my interest for the rest of my life. Gardening had always been a love that lack of time had repressed. Living all my life in the South and having a Georgia grandmother who was an avid and accomplished gardener made me no stranger to Georgia's particular growing conditions. Watching my father gently prod new potatoes out of the soil of his World War II Victory Garden has always been a very pleasant childhood memory.

With great anticipation, I applied for the 1984 Master Gardener class at the North Fulton annex. My service hours were spent giving programs to garden clubs and coordinating the Fulton County Master Gardener speakers' bureau. This led to wanting to learn more and wanting to garden more seriously. The possibility of building a greenhouse consumed my thoughts. While searching for a class in greenhouse management, I discovered the landscape technology program at DeKalb College (now at Gwinnett Tech and North Metro Tech), and within a few years I had another degree!

Shortly thereafter, I built my greenhouse. Searching for places in the yard for its products has led to designing gardens and building walks to connect them. Membership in numerous plant societies and garden clubs was a natural consequence, and now, almost every waking hour involves some aspect of gardening or gardening organization related activity.

To newcomers to Atlanta, and to longtime residents with a little spare time, I extend an invitation to try gardening. It draws friends and fills hours with discovery, learning, and sharing. Whether you prefer to pursue it alone, with friends, as a lecturer, or a writer, the subject of gardening provides an unlimited format, just waiting for your discovery.

About the Contributors

Both an artist and a gardener, **Barbara Allen** expresses her creativity in the garden and on the canvas. Her own garden has been the subject of numerous newspaper and magazine articles as well as the subject of many oil paintings. The owner of Exquisite Gardens Landscape firm, Allen teaches gardening at Spruill Center for the Arts in Dunwoody, Ga. and is a past president of the Georgia Perennial Plant Association.

A registered landscape architect, **Nancy Beckemeyer** is president of Autumn Ridge, Inc., an Atlanta landscape architecture firm. She teaches landscape design at three area colleges and lectures at garden clubs, the Georgia Perennial Plant Association, the Southern Gardening Symposium at Gwinnett Tech, and Master Gardener classes. Beckemeyer holds a bachelor's degree in Landscape Architecture from the University of Georgia.

Eve Davis grew up gardening in Charleston, S.C. With Ryan Gainey and Tom Woodham, she started The Potted Plant and later on her own opened Eve's Garden, a nursery, cutting garden, and floral design business. She now runs a bed and breakfast called the Hawk and Ivy in the mountains outside Asheville, N.C. Her gardens and floral designs have been featured in national and regional magazines, in books, and on television.

Tara Dillard, who holds a B.S. degree with a double major in industrial engineering and horticulture, is a residential garden designer, lecturer, and writer. Dillard has appeared on local television and radio. She believes a good garden requires depth, dimension, and dementia.

Cathy Farmer has been growing roses for 24 years. She has served as president of the Greater Atlanta Rose Society and is an Accredited Rose Judge and Consulting Rosarian for the American Rose Society. Farmer is also a member of the Heritage Rose Foundation, the Heritage Roses Group, and the Georgia Perennial Plant Association.

Artist **Linda Fraser** is working on a chronological series of botanically accurate paintings of Georgia's native plants. As Bird Chairman for The Garden Club of Georgia, she edited and illustrated "Bird Watch in Georgia," which was used in public schools. She also has painted a mural and banners for the Southeastern Flower Show. Linda designed the logo for the Georgia Native Plant Society and is the society's Hospitality Chairman. Her yard has been designated a Backyard Wildlife Habitat by the National Wildlife Federation. Linda is also known as the pianist for the Atlanta Steeplechase, California Cafe, and other parties and luncheons.

Photographer, lecturer, and writer **Jean Johnson Givens** was a Charter Member of The Chattahoochee Unit of the Herb Society of America, the Atlanta Botanical Garden, the Georgia Perennial Plant Association, and the Georgia Master Gardeners Association. She serves on the Board of Directors of the Lullwater Garden Club, DeKalb Federation, The Garden Club of Georgia, Inc. (as Horticulture Chair), Deep South Region of NCSGC, and the North Georgia Judges Council.

Raymond Goza owns Goza Nursery in Lilburn. He is a member of the American Rhododendron Society, the Azalea Society of America, and the International Plant Propagators Society.

Jim Harrington has developed Hort Info, a perennial garden design, installation, and maintenance company in the North Atlanta area. A former Cooperative Extension Service Agent, Harrington has served as Charter President of the Georgia Native Plant Society and President of the Georgia Perennial Plant Association. He enjoys writing about perennial maintenance and insects for *Perennial Notes* and other gardening publications.

Jackie Heyda's interest in shade gardening started in 1986 as a pursuit for unusual plants that can be found in small nurseries. By using leaf and tree textures, subtle colors, and native and other plants, she developed a natural look for native habitat gardens. Her knowledge about shade gardening comes from reading, hands on gardening, and sharing ideas with others.

Dottie Myers is an award-winning landscape architect who has been practicing since 1981 with an emphasis on residential landscapes and garden design. She also has taught landscape design-related classes at the University of Georgia and Gwinnett Tech.

Mildred Pinnell is Horticulturist at the Atlanta Botanical Garden, a position she has held since 1986. She is responsible for the development and maintenance of the outdoor plant collections. Pinnell is a member of Georgia Green Industry, Metro Atlanta Landscape and Turf Associates, the Georgia Perennial Plant Association, and the American Rock Garden Society. She holds a master's degree in Horticulture from the University of Georgia.

Jeff Potter built his first greenhouse at age 12 and graduated from the University of Georgia in 1992 with a B.S.A. in Horticulture. He has worked as a horticulturist for the State of Georgia on the grounds of the State Capitol and the Governor's Mansion. He also has maintained a plant nursery for a landscape company and the grounds and gardens of Fernbank Science Center. Potter is a charter member of many local plant societies and remains active in these groups.

Paula Refi is a landscape designer with experience in both residential and commercial landscape design. She holds a master's degree in biology from Georgetown University, studied landscape horticulture at DeKalb College, and has gardened in Atlanta for 25 years, specializing in perennials and native plants. Refi writes the "Perennial Search" column in *Perennial Notes*, the newsletter of the Georgia Perennial Plant Association.

Since 1985, **Sandra Sandefur** has practiced residential landscape design under the name Dogwood Knoll Design, specializing in perennials and native plants. An instructor and lecturer in landscape design and plant identification, Sandefur is a longtime member of the Georgia Perennial Plant Association, where she was president in 1995-96 and is future director of the Cullowhee Conference on landscaping with native plants.

A retired architect, freelance garden designer, consultant, and lecturer, **Lewis Shortt** has collected and grown native plants and exotics in the Atlanta area for 35 years, specializing in rhododendrons and azaleas with an emphasis on southeastern natives. Shortt is the Azalea Chapter of the American Rhododendron Society's Garden Chairman for the Frank Smith Rhododendron Garden at the Atlanta History Center.

R. Allen Sistrunk, Executive Director of Vines Botanical Garden in Loganville, Ga., has worked with Post Landscape Services to create a master site plan that will guide the development of the gardens over the next decade. For 14 years, Sistrunk was Director of Gardens at the Atlanta History Center where he developed 32 acres of gardens telling the landscape history of the Atlanta region. He is a sought-after speaker and has been an Adjunct Faculty member in the landscape management programs at DeKalb College and Gwinnett Tech.

Lloyd Snyder's hobbies are gardening and botany, especially ferns. A member of the Georgia Botanical Society, he has taught courses at Life Enrichment, several Elderhostels, and Senior University of Greater Atlanta. He leads nature walks and collected ferns from all 159 Georgia counties for the University of Georgia herbarium. Snyder is the co-author of *Field Guide to the Ferns and Other Pteridophytes of Georgia*.

Gardening has been **Gary Spikula**'s passion since childhood. He received a B.S. degree in Botany and much horticultural training at North Carolina State University, and he worked for the Atlanta Botanical Garden during its early years of development. A frequent lecturer at meetings and symposia, Spikula is owner of Gary Spikula Landscape Design, emphasizing year-round color and fragrance in a wide range of styles.

Sue Vrooman has worked as a horticulturist in the 32 acres of gardens at the Atlanta History Center for six years, where her primary responsibility is the care of native plants in the Quarry Garden. She is a member of numerous plant societies, including the American Horticultural Society, the Georgia Native Plant Society, and the Georgia Perennial Plant Association, where she has served as a board member. She has spoken to numerous groups on plant-related topics. Vrooman has a degree in biology from Mercer University.